W9-CRK-631

PHILOSOPHY & HISTORY

PHILOSOPHY
&
HISTORY

edited by

RAYMOND KLIBANSKY

and

H. J. PATON

HARPER TORCHBOOKS / THE ACADEMY LIBRARY
HARPER & ROW, PUBLISHERS
New York, Evanston, and London

HARPER TORCHBOOKS / THE ACADEMY LIBRARY
Advisory Editor in the Humanities and the Social Sciences: Benjamin Nelson

PHILOSOPHY AND HISTORY

Printed in the United States of America.

This book was originally published in 1936 by The Clarendon Press, Oxford, England, and is here reprinted by arrangement.

First HARPER TORCHBOOK edition published 1963 by
Harper & Row, Publishers, Incorporated
49 East 33rd Street
New York 16, New York

NOTE TO THE TORCHBOOK EDITION

It is now more than a quarter of a century since *Philosophy and History* was published in honour of Ernst Cassirer as a thinker and as a man. Unhappily he is no longer with us, although his influence remains; and many of the original contributors have also passed away. Among those who survive some may have modified their views during the long interval—this is so in the case of the joint-editor who was also a contributor—but we have thought it best to reprint the book in its original form without any change (other than that of bringing the bibliography up to date). As it stands, it represents the thought of a period when the topics treated were less widely studied than they are today. Because of this growing interest the issues raised are still very much alive.

We have to add a further reason for our gratitude to the officers of the Clarendon Press as we expressed it so many years ago. They have freely relinquished all their rights in order to facilitate the issue of the new edition. For this generosity we express our warmest thanks.

R.K.
H.J.P.

June, 1963

Ὄλβιος ὅστις τῆς ἱστορίας
ἔσχε μάθησιν,
μήτε πολιτῶν ἐπὶ πημοσύνην
μήτ' εἰς ἀδίκους πράξεις ὁρμῶν,
ἀλλ' ἀθανάτου καθορῶν φύσεως
κόσμον ἀγήρων, πῇ τε συνέστη
καὶ ὅθεν καὶ ὅπως.
τοῖς δὲ τοιούτοις οὐδέποτ' αἰσχρῶν
ἔργων μελέδημα προσίζει.

PREFACE

TO Professor Ernst Cassirer, on the occasion of his sixtieth birthday, this book is presented by the contributors and editors as a token of their respect and admiration. It reflects in itself the various interests and pursuits of the scholar to whom it is dedicated; but it seeks also, in his spirit, to rise above the merely personal and to concentrate on one particular, yet central, problem.

Philosophy and history are the two main activities to which Professor Cassirer has devoted his life. In his works the union of these activities is achieved, not merely postulated as an ideal; and this union is to be found alike when, as a historian of philosophy, he is retracing the development of the theory of knowledge and when, as a creative and systematic thinker, he offers us his doctrine of civilization in *The Philosophy of the Symbolic Forms*. The relation between philosophy and history is thus naturally chosen as the theme of the present volume. It gives rise to a series of problems, the solution of which is necessary for a full understanding of the nature of philosophy and history themselves.

The variety of approaches to this subject may at first sight seem rather disconnected; but perhaps we may plead that they at least reflect the complexity of the subject itself. If the main problem is seen from very different angles and attacked in the most disparate ways, this very fact may serve to illustrate the maxim proclaimed by Nicholas of Cusa in his struggle against the fanatical imposition of uniformity: *Una veritas in variis signis varie resplendet.*

It is our hope that this book may bear witness to that enduring spiritual bond which unites scholars of different countries and different traditions; that it may introduce to English readers lines of speculation comparatively unfamiliar in this country; and above all that it may further the discussion of a basic problem which in the past has been subject to undue neglect.

As joint editors we owe a debt of gratitude for the help received from so many sources. We must express our warmest thanks to the Warburg Institute (whose activities are so intimately connected with the subject of this book) for the never-failing support without which the present publication would have been impossible; to its Director, Dr. Saxl, to its staff, and to those of its collaborators, especially Dr. H. Buchthal and Dr. O. Kurz, who have helped to procure the illustrations; to Dr. L. Labowsky and Miss M. A. Cox, who have so freely given us their time and their help; to Mrs. E. Gundolf for permission to include a chapter from one of the still unpublished works of the late Professor Friedrich Gundolf; to the scholars who undertook the arduous task of translating the foreign contributions into idiomatic English; and finally to the officers of the Clarendon Press for their constant advice and assiduous care in an undertaking of no little difficulty.

R. K.
H. J. P.

OXFORD, *February 1936*

CONTENTS

LIST OF ILLUSTRATIONS

A DEFINITION OF THE CONCEPT OF HISTORY

By JOHAN HUIZINGA

A GOOD definition must be succinct, i.e. it must with the greatest possible conciseness of expression accurately and completely establish the concept. A definition delimits the meaning of a particular word which serves to indicate a particular phenomenon. In the definition the phenomenon as a whole must be included and comprehended. Should any essential parts fall outside of the definition, there is something wrong with it. On the other hand, a definition need give no account of details.

Let us bring to the test of these requirements some of the current definitions of the concept of history. Most works on the epistemology of history refrain from an explicit determination of the fundamental concept. They take the phenomenon itself as a known quantity. Definitions are most readily found in manuals or text-books of historical method. Let us single out two of these: E. Bernheim's well-known *Lehrbuch der historischen Methode und der Geschichtsphilosophie*, and the more recent and concise work of W. Bauer, *Einführung in das Studium der Geschichte*.[1]

Bernheim's definition in the first edition of his book (1889) reads as follows: 'History is the science of the development of mankind in their activity as social beings.' Shortly afterwards there began the lively controversy, stirred up by Lamprecht, about the nature of historical knowledge. This led Bernheim in the third edition of his work (the second dates from 1894) to express in the definition his attitude towards the questions which were in the air. Accordingly, in the edition numbered 3/4, of the year 1903, this reads as follows: 'The science of history is the science which investigates and narrates in causal connexion the facts of the development of mankind in their activities (individual as well as typical and collective) as social beings.' In the edition numbered 5/6, of 1908, 'the facts' are further particularized as 'the facts in their temporal and spatial

[1] Second, improved, edition, Tübingen, 1928. The first appeared in 1921.

determinations', while instead of 'in causal connexion' we now read 'in relations of psycho-physical causality'.

Bauer's definition[1] is as follows: 'History is the science which seeks to describe and with sympathetic insight (*nachfühlend*) to explain the phenomena of life, so far as concerns changes brought about by the relation of men to society,[2] selecting them with an eye to their effect on subsequent epochs or with regard to their typical qualities, and concentrating chiefly on those changes which are temporally and spatially irreproducible.'[3]

In spite of the abbreviation to which it has been subjected since its first formulation, the succinctness of Bauer's definition is not striking; and it may be doubted whether the solicitude with which a short account of methodology is interpolated into the definition makes up for this defect. A more serious objection, which tells against both authors, lies in the fact that Bauer as well as Bernheim restricts in advance the range of the word 'history'. Bernheim, in defining the concept, expressly concerns himself solely with 'the science of history', with history as a science. This agrees with his doctrine that history passes successively through the phases of the narrative (descriptive) and the pragmatic or didactic form, before attaining in the third phase, which he calls the genetic or evolutionary, its genuine character as a science. Whether the tripartite division outlined by this high authority is in all respects satisfactory is not here in question. Indeed, for Bernheim, because of this division of his, the question whether the products of early and outgrown phases of historical study answer to his definition may be a matter of less significance.

Bauer starts out from the word 'history', but immediately lays it down that it is a 'science'. The account which he goes on to give of its function and essence concerns, in fact, just as much as that of Bernheim, the function and essence of modern historical science. Bauer himself, however, recognizes this restriction of the validity of his definition, and closes with the remark: 'Every epoch, in fact, has its peculiar conception of the essence and

[1] Loc. cit., p. 17. With the qualifying clause, 'without laying undue stress on the value of a definition of the concept of "history" '. See there also for some other examples of definitions.

[2] In the first edition of 1921: 'to human society'.

[3] First edition: 'the irreproducible singularity of which is given in the fact that they are distinguished by correlation with a particular time and a particular place'.

function of history.' But if the word 'history' possesses nevertheless a more general sense, it must still be possible so to define it as to make it express the conception of every epoch.

In respect to the use of the word, English occupies a quite peculiar position compared with German and Dutch and also French. To the word *Geschichte*, *Geschiedenis*, in the two former languages, the following may be said to apply: it suggests (1) something that has happened; (2) the narration of something that has happened; (3) the science which endeavours to be able to give this narrative. In common usage the second sense may fairly be said to predominate. The first has nowadays all but disappeared; *Geschichte* or *Geschiedenis*, in the sense of 'something that has happened', has been replaced by the equivalent *Geschehnis* or *Gebeurtenis*. A trace of it survives in such phrases as *das ist mir eine schöne Geschichte*. Moreover, in both languages the word *Historie* occupies a secondary place, with nearly the same double or even threefold meaning. The French *histoire*, too, coincides almost completely with it. In English, on the other hand, the Romance *historia* has become *story*, which, however, occupies only the sphere of meaning (2): 'the narration of something that has happened'. Moreover, it was only later on that technical terminology, borrowing afresh from the language of the learned, introduced the word *history*. In its predominantly technical application, the word stands closer to the original Greek, which meant precisely 'that which we come to know as a result of inquiry'. In another respect too English is different, inasmuch as *history* has retained more definitely and for longer the more general meaning, in which the relation to the past is not essential. French has it still in *histoire naturelle*; English works about 1800 still constantly have *history* in the title in a much wider sense.

Now, whether we use one name for history or another, as soon as we lay the emphasis on its character as a science,[1] it follows at once that most of the great historiographers of former times can only constrainedly be brought under the given definitions. If the definition of Bernheim or Bauer is applied to

[1] In the old system of the sciences history never occupied an independent place. There was, however, by way of compensation, a Muse of history. Schopenhauer still contested her competency as a science. In England even to-day a defence of the scientific value of history, if not necessary, is nevertheless appropriate; see R. Seton Watson, *A Plea for the Study of Contemporary History*, in the periodical *History*, XIV. i, 1929.

Herodotus, Gregory of Tours, Joinville, Villani, Michelet, or Macaulay, it is difficult to suppress a feeling of uneasiness. It seems impossible, without a more or less violent anachronism, to find the definition verified in all these historians; and it does not help us that certain other personalities, like Thucydides and Machiavelli, can rather more readily be brought into accord with it. In order to be able to sustain the definition, we find ourselves constrained first of all to draw a fatal and impossible distinction between historiography, historical research, and historical reflection, and then to banish the great historiography of the past, like Hagar, from the house of science. Finally, if any one draws the conclusion that this *must* be done, because historiography is properly speaking an art, then the confusion of ideas is complete.

Even if it happened that every historical fact, no matter how or by whom described, could with a little good will be brought into accord with the categories set up by Bernheim and Bauer, the aspiration by which human nature is driven to history is in no way comprehended in their definition. *What* does Herodotus relate, and *why* does he relate it? To this neither definition gives any answer. A grasp of historical facts, be they great events or small details, is aspired to neither *in* the connexion nor *for the sake of* the connexion which the definitions presuppose as essential to history.

Would it not be worth while to seek for a delimitation of the concept of history which does without the distinction between historical science and historiography, and is able to comprehend also the earlier phases of history and recognize them in their full value? It is, of course, questionable whether such a definition will have any practical utility for our science; but that is not the chief point; the main thing is to get the concept clear.

The starting-point of both the definitions to which we have referred is history as a *modern science*, and they determine the essence of this concept in accordance with the requirements imposed by this restricted connotation. Let us take up the problem from quite a different side and begin with history as a phenomenon of civilization; let us ask what is the constant form and function of this phenomenon. Whether the definition so reached applies to our modern science will then only come into consideration as a final test.

In order to understand correctly the form and function of the phenomenon of history, it is necessary first of all to free ourselves from the naïve historical realism which represents the initial attitude of educated men in general and no less of a great many historians. As a rule it is supposed that history strives to relate *the* story of *the* past, even if it is in the restricted sense of Bernheim and Bauer. In reality history gives no more than a particular representation of a particular past, an intelligible picture of a portion of the past. It is never the reconstruction or reproduction of a given past. No past is ever given. Tradition alone is given. If tradition were at any point to make the total reality of the past accessible to us, still no history would result; or rather, then least of all. The idea of history only emerges with the search for certain connexions, the essence of which is determined by the value which we attach to them. It makes no difference whether we think of a history which is the result of researches strictly critical in method, or of sagas and epics belonging to former phases of civilization.

History is always an imposition of form upon the past, and cannot claim to be more. It is always the comprehension and interpretation of a meaning which we look for in the past. Even mere narration is already the communication of a meaning, and the assimilation of this meaning may be of a semi-aesthetic nature.

It would be a misunderstanding to believe that the recognition of these facts opens the door to historical scepticism. All historical scepticism, which thinks little of knowledge thus acquired, must end in a general philosophical scepticism, from which neither life itself, nor any science, even the most exact, would be exempt.

If history as an intellectual activity is an imposition of form, then we may say that as a product it is a form—an intellectual form for understanding the world, just as philosophy, literature, jurisprudence, physical science, are forms for understanding the world. History is distinguished from these other intellectual forms in that it is related to the past and nothing but the past.[1] Its purpose is to understand the world *in* and *through* the past. The intellectual fascination which underlies the form of history is the desire to understand the meaning of that which has happened in former times. The mind is attracted, engrossed by the

[1] Needless to say, many of the natural sciences contain also an important historical element, for instance, geology.

past. The impetus and value of this mental tension and of its product, history, lie in the complete earnestness which distinguishes it. There is an absolute craving to penetrate to the genuine knowledge of that which truly happened, even when we are aware of the inadequacy of the means to the end. The sharp distinction between history and literature lies in the fact that the former is almost entirely lacking in that element of play which underlies literature from beginning to end.

In such terms as these we can speak in the same breath of historiography and historical research, of the writers of their own memoirs and of students of the most remote past, of the local annalist and of the designer of an historical cosmology, of the most primitive and the most modern historical efforts.

The attitude taken up by history in respect to the past may be most appropriately called 'a rendering account to oneself'. This expression conveys the complete earnestness just mentioned, the need for authenticity and reliability in knowledge. Besides, it is adapted to eliminate the apparent contrast between a narrative, a didactic, and a scientific treatment of history, which Bernheim postulates as being essential. 'To render account to oneself of' includes all three of these endeavours. Finally, the term 'to render account to oneself' implies that this must be carried out under the headings which are decisive, *massgebend*, for the historical worker himself. The events which we wish to explain in their connexion may be conceived under the antitheses of virtue and vice, wisdom and folly, friend and foe, might and right, order and freedom, interests and ideals, will and limitation, the individual and the mass, and in each case a difference of structure in the history which is described will be the result. Every man renders account to himself of the past in accordance with the standards which his education and *Weltanschauung* lead him to adopt. This, of course, does not mean that every one of these antitheses is capable of producing an equally trustworthy historical result.

It remains for us to establish *who* renders account to himself, and *of what*. To the question about the subject which concerns itself with history, the answer is implicit in what has just been said. It can only be a civilization, inasmuch as that word is best adapted to indicate the ideal totalities of social life and creative activity realized in a definite time and place which for our thinking constitute the units in the historical life of mankind. We are entitled to speak of a civilization, no less than of a people, a society, as a thinking subject, without falling by the use of this metaphor into the gross anthropomorphism which constitutes one of the chief dangers to historical thought. Moreover, it is hardly necessary to define the concept of civilization more precisely than has just been done, until we employ the word as a term in a definition. Every civilization creates its own form of history, and must do so. The character of the civilization determines what history shall mean to it, and of what kind it shall be. If a civilization coincides with a people, a state, a tribe, its history will be correspondingly simple. If a general civilization is differentiated into distinct nations, and these again into groups, classes, parties, the corresponding differentiation in the historical form follows of itself.[1] The historical interests of every sectional civilization are determined by the question: what are the things which 'matter' to it? Civilization has meaning only as a process of adaptation to an end; it is a teleological concept, as history is an explicitly purposive knowing.

But this differentiation of historical insight can only be scientific, and consequently the corresponding historical product can only be convincing to the critical modern mind, in so far as the craving for historical truth is inspired by the highest aim which the carrier of the civilization, in virtue of its moral and intellectual faculties, is able to conceive. The power of a people or of a state is too limited and too obscure an aim. That it could be necessary to point this out in so many words had not yet occurred to me six years ago when the first version of this essay was written.

In this way the object of history also can be more precisely indicated. We have already said: the past, without further particularization, means merely chaos. The subject-matter of history too requires further explanation. *The* past is limited always in accordance with the kind of subject which seeks to understand it. Every civilization has a past *of its own*. This does not, however, hold in the sense that this past is bounded by the destiny of the group which is the carrier of the civilization, but

[1] On this consequence for the humane sciences in general, see the paper by Eduard Spranger, *Der Sinn der Voraussetzungslosigkeit in den Geisteswissenschaften*, read at the meeting of the philosophical and historical section of the Prussian Academy of Sciences, 10 January, 1929.

in the sense that the past can only become history for this group in so far as it is intelligible to it. Civilizations whose outlook is limited or narrow produce a history which is likewise limited and narrow, and contrariwise those whose horizon is wide give rise to a history able to understand a wide range of diversity and even contrast. It is the essence of a civilization that whatever its intellect conceives becomes a part of it. This retains its validity even if the extraneous material comprehended attracts the mind, and is understood, just as being strange, different, antithetic. The Merovingian civilization still saw a small part of antiquity at the closest range, but in a dim light. This was the best part of its own civilization. Each subsequent epoch conceived antiquity ever anew with wider and deeper insight: the ninth century, the twelfth, the fourteenth; and in each case antiquity became in a more essential sense a part of its own growing civilization. For us, both classical antiquity—deciphered ever anew—and the ancient and the more recent East, the primitive civilizations of the whole world, have become constituent parts of our own civilization, in a much more profound and essential sense than for the most part we are aware, through the knowledge of them which we possess, and through the understanding of their meaning which we bring to their study. This point of view has been criticized as an overstraining of the concept of civilization. Still, after thinking it over again, I must hold to it as expressing a fundamental truth which all our thinking leads up to. Any one who is shocked by the boldness of the statement may interpret it so as to fit into the system of his own convictions.

Our civilization is the first to have for its past the past of the world, our history is the first to be world-history. Even the most minute research into local antiquities partakes in the whole and gets its meaning by this participation.

But besides that it is something more. A history adequate to our civilization can only be scientific history. The instrument of modern Western civilization for the intellectual understanding of the world is critical science. We cannot sacrifice the demand for scientific certainty without injury to the conscience of our civilization. Mythical and fictitious representations of the past may have literary value for us even now as forms of play, but for us they are not history.[1]

[1] Compare Th. Litt, *Wissenschaft, Bildung, Weltanschauung*, pp. 97 ff.

The succinct definition at which we have thus arrived would read as follows:

History is the intellectual form in which a civilization renders account to itself of its past.

It seems perhaps so simple, so self-evident, that one is reminded of the Dutch proverb: 'The soup is not worth the cabbage.' Simplicity, however, cannot be called a defect in a definition, provided that everything essential to the phenomenon is expressed. We have still to examine our definition, analysed into its separate terms, somewhat more closely, in order to see whether it satisfies the last-named requirement.

History is here qualified as 'an intellectual form'. This designation is both wider than 'a science', which it includes, and more precise, inasmuch as it formulates the essence of the phenomenon itself. If we call history an intellectual form, we are relieved of the forced and disturbing distinction between historical research and historiography, and we likewise escape the irrelevant question how far history has anything in common with art.

As the subject in which this form becomes conscious, we have named 'a civilization'. Every civilization creates this form anew, according to its own peculiar style. By using the term 'a civilization' we admit all the unavoidable subjectivity implied in every history. Further, inasmuch as within the same civilization every group which is united by a particular *Weltanschauung* represents a sectional civilization of its own, it is admitted at the same time that a Catholic history must look different from a Socialist one, &c. Every civilization and every sectional civilization must hold *its own* history to be the true one, and is entitled to do so, provided that it constructs this history in accordance with the critical requirements imposed by its conscience as a civilization, and not according to the cravings for power in the interests of which it imposes silence upon this conscience. It is the doubtful privilege of our scientific civilization of to-day to be for the first time able consciously to survey the possible plurality of the forms of history. If it has sufficient self-knowledge, it can unhesitatingly assert the relative value of its own intellectual product.

The kind of intellectual activity from which history takes its rise is described as a 'rendering account to oneself'. This expression bridges once again the gulf between research and composition. It eliminates likewise, as has been remarked above, the apparent opposition between the narrative, the pragmatic, and the genetic treatment of history. It comprises every form of historical record; that of the annalist, the writer of memoirs, the historical philosopher, and the scholarly researcher. It comprehends the smallest antiquarian monograph in the same sense as the vastest conception of world history. It expresses the constant presence of the pragmatic element. We always have to do with understanding the world, gathering wisdom of higher importance than the knowledge of mere facts. The expression 'account' expresses at the same time the inexorable earnestness on which all historical activity is based. *Ne quid falsi audeat.*

The definition restricts the subject-matter of history to the past of the civilization in which it is rooted. (It must be understood that a civilization which embraces the whole world in its desire for knowledge sees in the whole world the reflection of its own restricted past.) The definition hints that all knowledge of historical truth is limited by a capacity for assimilation which in its turn arises out of the study of history. History itself, and the historical consciousness, becomes an integral constituent of the civilization; subject and object are recognized in their mutual interdependence.

Taken as a whole, this definition offers the further advantage that its wide formulation—which is not, as I believe, a sign of vagueness—leaves room for all sorts of controversial systems and conceptions. It pronounces no judgement as between the idea of a cyclic structure for the world-process and that of continuity. It opens a way of escape from the dilemma about the character of historical knowledge as inclining rather to the abstract or to the concrete; it does not force upon us the determination of the indeterminable, viz. of historical importance, nor a choice between the particular and the general as the object of the historical interest. Negative merits, if you like, but advantages none the less.

Translated by D. R. Cousin, University of Glasgow.

THE HISTORICITY OF THINGS

By S. ALEXANDER

IT has become a commonplace to say that the world and everything in it is historical, that the world is a world of events. Instead of space *and* time, a world laid out in space and moving forwards in time, we have space-time, time entering into the very constitution of things: a four-dimensional and no longer a three-dimensional world. Objection to this statement might come from two quarters. It might be urged that though all things are in time, the universe itself is not. As a whole it is timeless; time is in it, and not it in time. I have not succeeded in understanding this plea. It implies a completed or bounded universe. If the universe is timeful, how should it not always be occurring? True, time may have neither beginning nor end, may be an endless string, but the string goes on in endless motion, like a revolving band or an escalator. The other objection is much more serious. Space and time, to say nothing of space-time, are applicable to the familiar or macroscopic world. Do they apply to the microscopic world of sub-matter, below the atoms? Yet even here the elements have behaviour which occurs, and some even think it not only occurs, but occurs wilfully. Something will be said of this hereafter.

It is interesting to compare this new dignity of history, which is now a commonplace (not a commonplace, be it observed, of philosophy, but of familiar, ordinary, everyday thinking) with the attitude of half-contempt for history entertained in the earlier part of the nineteenth century, before Darwin. It was a sign of the weakness of nature (Hegel speaks of the *Ohnmacht der Natur*) that Nature cannot maintain the calm of the conceptual realm but falls apart into particulars and their history. This statement of mine sounds like sheer and splenetic injustice. No thanks can measure our debt to Hegel in particular for the historical turn he gave to thought. But, after all, his history was not so much true history as the marshalling of types in Aristotelian fashion in their order: and the value of the work was immense. The thoroughgoing conception of history in its application, not only to the affairs of man but to nature itself, is due, as I suppose, chiefly to Darwin.

I am proposing in this paper to draw out some of the consequences for philosophy of this commonplace. I am not going to ask what history may learn from philosophy. I have no doubt it may learn a great deal. Just as the men of science are returning to the good old days when philosophy and science went hand in hand, and are ready to acknowledge that the interests of the two meet at many points, and that each may learn from the other, so it may be that historians may listen with profit to philosophers. But that is the business of the historians, and the task is beyond my powers. I am proposing to sit at the feet of history and ask how philosophy is affected if it keeps constantly in mind the timefulness of things.

I

1. For the moment I confine myself to the familiar macroscopic world, reserving certain problems presented by recent speculations on the sub-material world. The historical view means in philosophy first that the real world is made of particulars, and that universals are but the patterns of their behaviour. The historian recognizes such patterns of behaviour, some of them common to human nature, as that power without control ends in the abuse of it; some of them patterns characteristic of special epochs, like the Greek view of politics or the *laissez-faire* spirit of English political life in the Victorian age. But these patterns belong to the events themselves in their grouping.

Universals, then, are nothing but arrangements in their particulars, arrangements of events. To speak more strictly we should say a universal is an arrangeability in events, for an actual arrangement is our creation, the work of the observer; yet there is something in the events which gives the excuse for such arrangement, and this something is the universal. So, to borrow an illustration from Sir Arthur Eddington, the stars in Orion's belt have certain relations of position towards each other which justifies that metaphorical description. The universals may properly be regarded as a higher order of existence than the historical events themselves, because they connect them together. But the patterns come into existence with the examples; the examples are not moulded, as it were, upon a given pattern. The universals are habits which are realized only in their exercise, and the exercise of them varies with the circumstances. The variation may be so slight that the habit repeats itself, or it may be so great that the habit is no more than a statistical uniformity. It is such statistical uniformities that we call laws of nature, the averaging out of particular groups of events which all differ from one another more or less. Unalterable laws are but a limit of real laws, which limit exists only in our desire. The propositions of mathematics may seem to offer an exception, but do not. For numbers are themselves singular and are not repeated. Two and two are universally four. But there are only one two and one four.

It follows that the conceptions we use in correlating things (if the conceptions are well founded) are features of the things themselves, and are not invented by the mind but discovered by it, though much invention may be needed for the discovery. Many notions begin as conveniences of description but they become valid only through application to facts. They are more than conveniences, or merely compendious descriptions as it was once the fashion to say, and less than independent realities. This is true not only of the special notions used of things, but also of those alleged supreme notions called categories. Now it may or may not be true that, as some think, the so-called categories, or some of them, have broken down in the microscopic world. My concern is rather to say that, where they obtain, they are features of things themselves and are not creations of the mind. The Kantian idea of categories as contributed to knowledge by the mind is no longer available for use under the historical view, if only because ostensibly they are not themselves empirical. For, to speak historically, nothing is real but what is given somehow in experience. How did the mind light upon these notions, and then introduce them into experience? Their only validity comes from their being indispensable for the constitution of experience itself. They are fictions introduced in order to account for the experience we actually have by introducing them into another fiction of an experience which awaits ordering by them—one fiction helping out another. The experience we have is already ordered, or it is nothing. Apart from it, the categories are taken from a nowhere which is for shortness called mind. They are not otherwise verifiable than by the real experience itself, are names for certain elements verifiable within that experience. Outside experience, non-empirical, no one can tell what induced mind to invent them. Within experience they have a real and definable meaning, given in experience. Kant himself indeed builded better than he knew, as is the way of the greatest men. For when he comes to 'prove' the principles which embody the categories, he shows what real experience is, and at the same time what the categorial elements in it are. Take substance, which for some reason that I do not understand is treated as an outworn notion. It means that in the spatio-temporal world of things there are groupings of characters which retain their pattern in the shifts and changes of process. We cannot do with less, and we do not want more. Such a category is historical, both because it is verifiable in fact, and because it is itself, as all categories must be, a moving pattern of things, caught up itself in the eternal unrest. Assigned to the mind, it is turned into a mystery. Individual minds, being one kind of things, are substances in the strictly limited and comprehensive sense that substance bears. (Kant himself was perverse upon this topic.) And as for the mind which is not an individual mind or a group of minds, where is it, and what is it? If we do not want it, why not leave it in limbo till we do?

Substance, then, and the other categories are moving patterns, not of eternity, if I may desecrate a glorious phrase by misuse, but patterns found in things. Their credentials are experience itself. The revolt against substance is led by a misapprehension. If substance meant some basis of the coherency of things, expel it with all my heart, for there is none such discoverable in experience. If it means the actual coherency among events which we know as a thing, you may expel it if you choose, *tamen usque recurret*. And like substance, even so wide a category as relation is empirical like the rest. I have never rid myself of the uneasy feeling that, like mind in other days, it is used to conjure with, even by the thinkers I most respect. It, too, if it is used intelligibly, must be experienced; we cannot, for instance, in philosophy say that space and time are relations between things, till we can say what relation is in experience. Useless to say that before and after are relations of events. Of course they are if you are already familiar with historical events. But the time itself is not a relation between the events; the relation of events is itself experienced as time slipping over from before to after. Relation is the verifiable experience that events in experience are, in experience, linked up with one another, and experienced so.

2. There are certain corollaries from this general statement

which I will touch upon briefly. If everything is historical, including the world itself as a whole, it follows that we can no longer interpret eternity as timelessness. To be out of relation to time can belong to no character of things, nor as we have noted, even to the whole universe. To pass to the eternal must, it would seem, be a change of quality, as is maintained by those who contrast the life eternal with the mundane life, and refuse to identify it with the everlasting or sempiternal. It would be better to avoid altogether the word eternal, which raises notions of time; but regarded as a name for that element which is distinct from lapse of time, eternal may be applied to the qualities, colour or taste or life or consciousness, which are the surd or irreducible or unexplainable characters of things. We cannot ask why things have their qualities, why, for instance, a certain complexity of chemical and physical process possesses life. We accept these qualities. In this sense we may accept Mr. Whitehead's designation of them as eternal objects.[1]

The historical conception of things rejects of necessity a creator of the world, while accepting creators and creation within the world. The world as a whole when viewed historically is self-creative. If, indeed, we take God to mean no more than the creative impulse by which the world goes its restless way in time, in this sense there is indeed a Creator God. This is not, however, the sense which commonly attaches to the notion of a Creator God, if only because it implies that the creator is himself created along with his world. We are involved otherwise in all the mystery of a God who can foresee the history of the world, and this, if history is history, is self-contradictory.

Which leads to the observation, too tempting to be discussed or more than briefly mentioned, that whatever God may be, he, too, is subject to the time-process and must change with the change of things, though it is not possible here to define what amount of change carries with it a change in the character of the divine. It is enough to remark that whether God be viewed theistically or pantheistically (and the conception of him must do justice to both these views), he suffers, or has the privilege of, the timeful passage of things. Pantheistic, he is at no stage of a growing universe complete; theistic, he is a projection into

[1] I make no attempt to indicate how far my statements about universals and qualities fall short of Mr. Whitehead's doctrines; with which every other doctrine must undergo comparison. And so I leave my own statements with all their defects.

a single individual of the universe with its as yet unsatisfied tendency or desire.

That there are no eternal values except in the sense of eternity before described is another instance of the general principle. Value being a certain quality is as eternal as colour but no more so; and it is doubtful if such a statement would satisfy those who uphold the creed of eternal values. The subject of value will be discussed more conveniently under a later head.

II

So far I have been dealing with what follows from recognizing that time enters into the constitution of things. I proceed now to a less artificial sense of history, as the record of the changes that take place in the growth of events. What matters for philosophy is that permanent features of things may appear at different epochs under different forms, and that it is important to make allowance for such differences. We inevitably think of the earlier in the familiar terms of the later; and this is legitimate provided the later is understood not in its surface character but in its essentials. I propose with this proviso in mind to approach some of the problems raised recently by microscopic physics, though it will be only in gingerly fashion.

Novelty is of the essence of history and so it is of the world of things. Every event is, considered strictly, new; and there is in particular an 'emergence' of novel characters in things. It is not novelty that calls for explanation so much as repetition, regularity, uniformity. The apparently wilful behaviour of the electron is not so surprising as the limits to its wilfulness. Yet these phenomena have cast doubts upon the usefulness of the conception of causality, and have inclined some to proclaim indeterminism or free will as the rule of nature and determinism as a now deposed idol of the nineteenth century.

Ordinary physics had already shattered the notion that a causal law was fixed and universal in its nature. It was recognized to be an average of many particular instances in the behaviour of events, a generality rather than a law in the strict sense. And, taken to mean that there was some necessary connexion between cause and effect, something in the cause which compelled the effect, that notion had gone the way of force, or rather force had followed its example, and the misconception had received its *coup de grâce* from Hume. Yet it may be suspected that the pre-Humian ideas are being attached to it, in the minds of those who now propose to dispense with causality in order to justify their case. It is therefore not so inopportune to ask just how much and how little causality implies. For Hume went too far, and left the world an atomic chaos. Atomism is no reproach; is it not the postulate of a great English philosophy of these years? But an atomism which permits a world, or even requires it. Atomism is one thing and disconnexion and chaos another. Absolute atomism and absolute unity are equally unacceptable. Hume himself betrayed his own excess of zeal in his break-down over volition. He urged that there was nothing in the passage from a purpose to its execution by the bodily limbs to indicate compulsion. Nor is there; but he forgot that we have direct experience of the passage and it is this transition which is all that causality in this case means. The lesson to be learnt from mental causality, the simplest and most obvious opportunity to become acquainted with it, is that between certain events there is an intimacy of connexion; and that what the inquirer into causal connexion does is to establish this intimacy of connexion, by excluding the less intimate connexions. Perhaps the relation, so understood, is poor and thin and abstract. But what matters so long as it is real? There is a great partnership in which events and groups of them exist; but only certain of the partners deal directly with each other, and the one is called cause and the other effect. Can we dispense with such a reality even in the sub-material world?

The same method may be applied to freedom and determinism. Before we expel determinism from the elements of the sub-atomic life and exalt their freedom, let us first be sure what they mean where we know them most easily. They do not mean much, but the little they mean is important. We humans are plainly free. Every one accepts the first part of Johnson's saying, 'Sir, we know we are free and there's an end on't,' without necessarily accepting the second part. What does our freedom mean? It means that when we act voluntarily we choose and know that we choose and what we are choosing; and it means that it is *we* who choose, being the kind of man we are (whence we accept responsibility for what we do). It does not mean that we have freedom *to* choose. The freedom lies in the choice and not in any capacity behind the choice to choose differently. We do indeed sometimes say we were free to have chosen otherwise, but we do not really know any such thing. All that we know is that if we had been different we should have chosen otherwise, and we add that we ought to have been different; and the language which remorse employs is open to fallacy. We wish we had been better men, for then we should have chosen better, and probably that is all that in our remorse we mean as to our knowledge of ourselves.

So much for our freedom. As for our determinism, it means only that the action, the choice, is determined by all the ingredients, of which the principal and decisive one is our own selves, our character. It does not mean that in our choice we know ourselves to be determined or fettered by our characters or our antecedents or the circumstances under which we act, in the same sense as we feel that it is we who choose. We do not think about the matter at all, at least in general we do not. We do not even in feeling that it is we who choose feel that we are the slaves of our characters. All that is the language not of action but of reflection upon it. No man, unless action is corrupted by morbid reflection, feels himself a jot less free even though he has convinced himself, as some persons mistakenly have, that the course of things is fixed once and for all. Freedom is an experience; determinism and indeterminism are theories, of which the first is verified, and the second not, by experience.

Next, determinism does not mean predictability. In a world of novel creation where new characters emerge, complete knowledge of the present and the past could not predict the shape of the future, though possibly it might predict the future in its measurable characters. I understand that the present state of an electron cannot be completely known because our observation interferes with the object observed, and so prediction is out of the question; but as determinism does not imply prediction, the matter is irrelevant. The issue is only probable because the data are insufficient for knowledge, but prediction, if it were possible, is at most a consequence and not the essence of determination.

Determinism in ourselves means therefore that the data being what they are (and our own selves the principal among them), whatever happens happens definitely and could not be different. To hold that it could, means only that it would if the data were different.

The electron for aught that I can see is as much free and as much determined as a man or a tree or a rock. Its freedom differs from ours only in that presumably it is not 'aware' of its action and has not the experience of choice. I am not equal to the question how much of the action is due to the acting thing itself and how much to its partners and dependencies, in the various cases. In other words, the electron may be a more (or a less) independent person than we, less of a social being. To treat its action as undetermined because it is erratic is as inexact as to deny that an eccentric man behaves for reasons, however he behaves. Are we prepared to say that the electron has no character at all? Indeed, to bring the behaviour of the electron within the region of probability is to admit, since probability is always relative to grounds, that grounds are not wanting even here.

Determinism does not or ought not to mean a pre-arranged necessity. Things do not admit necessity but only actual occurrence. And pre-arrangement implies a world given at a moment as a whole (a *tout donné* in Mr. Bergson's phrase), instead of a world engaged in its own process. It omits time from the world. Purged of those errors, determinism, or determinateness, is a universal feature of things. Similarly, indeterminism does not or ought not to mean caprice, enjoying the privilege of occasional exception. It means only that things move towards their future, and flowing from the past and present may exhibit new and unexpected features. So understood everything is also free.

Though I have alluded to it in passing, I have not thought it necessary to touch on the theological confusion between determinism and predestination. The problem is not acute if the Deity is regarded as evolving along with his world.

III

In the above I have tried to indicate under what proviso the categories of ordinary experience may be found applicable in the newly discovered world below the senses. The corresponding principle is that we may not extend characters of higher experience in the form in which we know them to a lower order of existence, except upon sufficient evidence. This is the obvious conclusion from the spirit of history which warns us to consider each stage of history for itself: not for instance, in spite of the same name, to identify the democracy of Athens founded upon slave labour with the democracy of free men established in 1789, or, in the interpretation of the history of philosophy itself, to understand the materialism of early Greek philosophy as if it were materialism in our modern sense. I shall take two illustrations of possible error in philosophy from disregarding this limitation.

It is common to attribute mind to all existences, and in some sense, I believe, the hypothesis is well founded. But in what sense? One form of it which finds much favour at present is that we must seek the reality of things in something akin to our own minds, what we are conscious of in our own direct experience, not of external things which we are supposed to know indirectly only, but of ourselves, our consciousness, and our sensible experience, and in the experience we have of value, beauty in particular. I do not propose to examine the theory of knowledge, which I believe to be mistaken, from which these conclusions or conjectures are drawn, but only to point out that, before we suppose things to be of the nature of mind-stuff, we must first find out how much of our human experience is fit for transference to other things. Just as the categories, so considered, shrink to very attenuated though exceedingly important structures, so with the transferable features of the human mind. Consciousness, for instance, is for all we can see distinctive of higher things. Does it exist even in plants? To endow stones or atoms with it would be a violent measure, and I think not contemplated by the sectaries of mind-stuff.

Two features of our minds we find transferable. The first is its organic character, which it shares with all life and with molecules for certain, and, it would seem, with atoms. There is the tendency to enter into wholes, 'holism' as Mr. Smuts calls it, even if the being in question is not already a whole or society, and, when it is, it too seeks to include within the compass and very essence of its life things outside itself. I may not speak of matters I do not understand (I remember Sir A. Eddington's warning to philosophers), and content myself with asking whether even the electron, whatever it is, even if it is elementary and is not a society, does not attach itself to other such elementaries in what may be called metaphorically a social relation. In this sense, at any rate, of organism, we may find throughout things the organic character familiar to us from life and mind, but only in this sense of the bare, if most potent, appetition towards wholeness, in obedience to the old adjuration of Goethe, *Immer strebe zum Ganzen, und kannst du selber kein Ganzes werden, als dienendes Glied schliess an ein Ganzes dich an.*

The other transferable feature of our mind is that our every experience, besides having an object or 'content' (for I will not boggle over words) or matter, has what Mr. Whitehead calls a subjective pole. Mr. Lloyd Morgan calls it the -ing as completed by the -ed (experienc-ing and experienc-ed), and I have spoken of it myself as 'enjoyment'. When I said the electron was as much free as we ourselves I was thinking of it as having this subjective pole, as being itself. We cannot tell perhaps what the electron feels like to itself. For that we should have to be an electron, and we cannot remember our babyhood. Still, if the electron is in some sense a mind, it is only in this reduced sense of having its own subjective or personal side (metaphors we can hardly avoid), and this is far enough from mind-stuff, and we need not ask whether there is anything comparable to our sensations in this highly simplified existence. Leibniz was the great exemplar to philosophers and to science of caution in discriminating the kind of life the separate ranks of his monads underwent.

The second example I take of the need for the caution proper to the historical method is that of value. Here, again, I feel no doubt that value is an integral element in the world, a fundamental feature, of things. But, once more, before we transfer it from the world of human values to the world in general, we must first find out what value means even for ourselves and consider how much of it is transferable. There is a marked inclination at the present day to leave the idea unexamined, and, because beauty and goodness and truth are so precious in our lives, to think that the conception admits no analysis, that value is something to adore, and that being so precious it cannot be lost for the universe itself, and is perhaps the most important element there. And so perhaps it is. But in transferable form it turns out to be something very simple and surrounded by no halo of sentiment.

For when we ask what constitutes the value of the great values, we find that it lies in their satisfaction of certain desires on our part, which, if this were a treatise on value, it would be necessary to describe and put one's finger on. Here perhaps it is enough to urge that goodness (to take one value only) is valuable because it satisfies the social craving of man, not of this, that, or the other man, but of man in the type and conformable to other men. Thus goodness and beauty and truth have indeed their peculiar flavour from satisfying man, but what makes their value is their fulfilment of our nature.

That conception is transferable to all things, and reveals itself as another side of the holizing character we have already recognized. Everything finds itself fulfilled in relation to other things, and the things which more immediately fulfil a thing's existence or life or nature are valuable and a value to it. There is accordingly, on the historical view, less affinity between value as a fundamental feature of things and the human values we treat as sacred than with the elementary idea of valency as used by the chemists, where atoms of different character enter into combination because each 'satisfies' the other. The satisfaction is, as this example shows, selective. Not everything completes the nature of everything else, but only certain things. In beauty this appears as the selection by the artist amongst his materials so as to satisfy the impulse which, because I am not describing its nature, I can only describe by the anticipatory epithet of his need for satisfying himself by the beautiful.

Value is therefore ubiquitous. It has forfeited the glamour which surrounds its unexamined idea and acquired a significance beyond human value, more extensive if less emotional.

IV

History demands of us that in using our experience of ourselves to help us in interpreting the world we should not take ourselves for more than we are; and up to this point I have been engaged in illustrating this principle. But history demands also that we should not take ourselves for less than we are. Of all things in the world ourselves are nearest to us, and if we take due care the easiest to understand; for we 'sit in the centre'. The central experience we have may enlighten us about the peripheral experience of what is not ourselves. I take for illustration the time-honoured contrast of monism and monadism, for each of which the arguments are so persuasive that neither is likely to be completely adequate, and probably no one has ever thought them so. At present the cry is discontinuity, and the physicists teach us that physical nature acts in packets of energy between which there are no gradations but sharp numerical differences. Where is there room for the continuity which in some way we demand, and without which for at least an ideal background discontinuity itself would be hardly intelligible? In this quandary can we find help, as history bids us try to do, from our own experience of our own continuity?

We must be careful of saying Yes. In the sense in which we speak of physical things down even to atoms and quanta we also are discontinuous. 'Every drowsy nod', we know, 'shakes their doctrine who teach that the soul is always thinking.' And yet, after intervals of sleep or insanity, the edges, as William James said, unite over the gap, and we feel ourselves one and the same. Further, we separate our thoughts from one another, and an emotion of anxiety may be followed by a separate and distinguishable emotion of joy. And yet our thoughts fall into wholes and our feeling is not anxiety and then joy, but of joy succeeding upon anxiety. (Again William James.) The answer is not to maintain that mind is continuous, in the face of the evidence that it is not, but that a certain experience we have of ourselves is what is meant by continuity. The same kind of answer was made before to Hume, when it was said that our experience of transition from purpose to execution was itself causality as we live through it. The same thing is true of, say, substance. We do not feel our mind to be a substance, but our experience of our own coherence of various processes is how we know substance in a glaring instance.

Substance and causality and continuity are not notions drawn from the void of our invention and found to be applicable or not to the world of things, but got from the world of things and most easily from ourselves. What we experience in ourselves as an element in the unity of our minds—that is continuity as revealed in this situation. Afterwards, when we are most familiar with separated things, we construct from them, and in terms of them, a notion of continuity such as the Cantorian and triumphant effort to squeeze numbers of a series so close to one another that no chink is left. But the original experience of continuity remains (and we may add of discontinuity) for what it is worth. It may be worth little or much to be told that a certain experience of ours *is* continuity. It remains for the philosophers and physicists together to translate the fact of discontinuity within continuity into satisfactory terms of our common thinking. Mr. Bergson and Mr. Whitehead in our day have made such attempts. All that I am concerned with here is that history forbids us to neglect what our own minds teach us. We are not to say merely that our minds like other things occur in time, but also that time is what we experience in our mental history.

V

I conclude with a brief notice of a quite different aspect of our subject, which has, however, already been alluded to. The sciences begin with history but they also end with it, and, at any rate, never forget their connexion with it. Now science, it is almost a platitude to say, is a highly artificial thing. Though not fine art it is a form of art, and at least is full of artifice. It deals with selected characters of things. Physics, for instance, with the measurable characters of things. Possibly it is the selectiveness of science which distinguishes it in the end from philosophy, which we may be content, after Plato and the common nineteenth-century view, to consider as the synoptic science, not as a science which summarizes the other sciences but as taking in the whole into one view, so far as such vision is possible. In pursuit of its purpose, science, and in particular physical science, moves far away from its historical foundation. So much so that many physicists hold that their science has nothing to do but to construct a coherent system of symbols which stand for sensible experience and through it for the real things of the world of which we can know nothing directly. I have avoided questions of theory of knowledge in this paper, and so I do not ask whether the supposed difference between direct knowledge of ourselves and merely indirect knowledge of the external world upon which the notion is based can be maintained. I do not think it can, but rather suppose that what happens in science is comparable to what happens when we go up into the air and see the landscape below us, not in all its detail but in certain determining outlines. These are still the outlines of the same landscape out of which we rose. Only so can we maintain continuity between thinking and sensible experience. Accordingly I plead, and I can do no more than plead, that in a science the data remain still in view though reduced to a compendious form, and represented not by symbols but, as it were, by delegates or plenipotentiaries. We seem to be here in agreement with the common notion of truth that it is in accordance with fact. At the same time we are in agreement with the more subtle description of truth by certain philosophers that it is coherence of science within itself. For the data even if in a delegated form are still a part of the science. History can claim to be mistress of science, as much as mathematics, though in a different sense. They stand for the two vital elements in every science which cannot be separated, if they can be considered separately: the constructive process by which we discover by our thought the order inherent in things, and the raw material itself, the brute givenness, the 'wandering cause' which Plato the mathematician, unlike some of his contemporary disciples, never forgot. We proceed out of history into history again. It must be remembered, however, of course, that historical *science* is but one of the sciences which arise from the facts and happenings of the world.

HISTORY AND PHILOSOPHY

By LÉON BRUNSCHVICG

THE problem of the relations between history and philosophy has a history of its own, and one which deserves to be written out in detail, for presumably it will be found to be both unexpected and instructive. But I will confine myself, in this short study, to enumerating some points which appear to me characteristic.

I

The first fact to be noticed is this. In the guise in which history first appears to the philosopher there is nothing properly historical about itself: *Primitive people, like children, retain in their memory what has taken place before their eyes far less than what has been transmitted to their ears.* This is why all sacred books, and even those which inspire most reverence among civilized peoples, begin with legendary stories in which animals, demons, and gods mix with men, speak their language, and govern their actions. Revelation, in the guise of history, is current even at a time when history, properly speaking, did not exist.

It was left to Greece to bring clearly into consciousness this *fabulatory function* (to use the expression of Henri Bergson which has since become classical) from which the theogonies and cosmogonies proceed; and to set in opposition to it the *verificatory function* of reason which aims at establishing relations which are removed from all temporal determination by the intrinsic virtue of demonstration—relations which consequently have an eternal value. The opposition between these two functions, which was already so clear in the fragments of Xenophanes of Colophon, is fully established with Platonism. The rigour and probity of the use of dialectical method, based on the positivity of mathematical methodology, put in their proper place the 'impure' histories which had been given credit by the genius of a Homer or a Hesiod.

Yet in the course of antiquity the victory of truth over fable, which is also the victory of philosophy over history, was precarious and ephemeral. Plato himself first set an example in betraying Platonism. In his literary work he multiplied mythical tales intended to palliate the rational insufficiency of his physics and enhance the political efficacy of his moral theory. In this he used and abused the fabulatory function with such perfect art that he succeeded in getting his mythological fantasies taken seriously by the most learned and sometimes by the most subtle of his commentators, particularly in regard to the fall of the soul in the *Phaedrus* and its immortality in the *Phaedo*.

II

The struggle between fabulatory history and verifying reason was not resumed till the beginning of the seventeenth century. Just at that time, thanks to the labours of Galileo, the experimental certainty of the Copernican astronomy was finally brought to light; while on the other hand it was proved that physics only exists as a science in so far as it appeals to the instrument of mathematics and is in a condition to submit the results of its calculations to the control of the facts. Immediately the perspective in which the universe appeared to human intelligence was fundamentally modified.

The Middle Ages had lived on a vision which was itself inherited from the most ancient times. This vision consists in distinguishing in space two regions which form as it were two worlds apart, different not only in format but in nature: the *terrestrial region* and the *celestial region*. The heavens are the seat of those necessary and perfect movements of which we have a direct intuition in the case of circular motion, and in comparison with which the changes which we observe on earth seem corruptions and degradations. The passing from the celestial plane to the terrestrial plane was accomplished in time, or more precisely at the beginning of time, by an intervention from above which is at once mysterious and explanatory, and which the religious traditions of the various peoples all aim at revealing.

Now that which put an end to this more than millennial conception of things and constituted the spiritual basis of our civilization was the recognition of the fact, already half-seen by the physiologers of ancient Greece, that the method of the intellect and of truth is the same, whether it is applied to the phenomena of heaven or to the phenomena of the earth. Going back from condition to condition in accordance with the rules which bind that which results to its components, rational mechanics will never find itself faced with a break, a hiatus to render plausible the intervention of an extra-temporal processus and to make the invention of a fable about it pardonable. The science of Pythagoras and of Plato, being restricted to the domain of mathematics, was still helpless in the face of physical reality, and obliged to seek the help of, or to resign itself to being replaced by, a mythical tale. The science of Descartes and Newton subjects the cosmic infinite to the combined government of calculation and of experience; it is therefore sufficient unto itself without appeal to the transcendence of an external cause.

III

The capital fact is this: *the reversal of the perspective in which the spatial world appears brings with it a revolution in the very manner in which the problem of time is presented to us.*

The full bearing of this revolution was immediately grasped by Blaise Pascal. No one has brought out more clearly to what an extent the human mind, which in the Middle Ages had been absurdly subjected to the authority of the Ancients, was set on its feet again, face to the truth, by the mathematico-experimental method. Nor has any one recognized so profoundly how this spiritual order, based upon a continual accumulation of positive discoveries and consequently turned towards the future, was orientated in the opposite direction from the supernatural order which Christianity had proclaimed when it commanded us not to stop looking towards the past in which we find the double revelation of the Bible and the Gospel. The word of God, set down in the books of olden times, provides the believer with the secret of events which are explained, even before they are accomplished, by the decree of an all-powerful will. Profane history for Pascal, as later for Bossuet and Joseph de Maistre, is dependent, in its unfolding, upon sacred history. 'How beautiful it is' (we find written in the manuscript of the *Pensées*) 'to see with the eyes of faith Darius and Cyrus, the Romans, Alexander, Pompey and Herod unwittingly acting for the glory of the Gospel.'

IV

The unequalled clarity with which Pascal defined, doing justice to each of them, the nature of the two antagonistic forces—*the progress of positive science in the domain of reason which is properly spiritual, the primacy of faith in the domain of religion which is properly supernatural*—endows his work with that perennial interest and dramatic actuality with which it is generally credited. For the purposes of our study it seems proper to explain a misunderstanding which acted as a dead weight on the philosophical speculations of the succeeding centuries, and which has only been cleared up of recent years. We have just emphasized the fact that modern civilization, constituted as it is on the basis of an authentically rational knowledge, became conscious of its own character by setting itself in opposition to the historical, or more accurately, the trans-historical, conception of the world—a conception which is obviously imaginative and legendary. Now it so happened that this fact brought discredit on the development of specifically historical knowledge, as regards human affairs no less than as regards physics. Eighteenth-century psychology and sociology aim at discovering *laws*, that is to say, according to Montesquieu's famous definition, *necessary relations which derive from the nature of things.* Whether it was a question of the physical universe or of the moral universe, the purpose of research was always to arrive at general expressions applicable at all times and in all places, as appeared to be the case with the formula for Newtonian gravitation—the value of these expressions was bound up with the extent of their generality, and it was hoped to reduce them to the deductive form, under which geometry was seen to fall (in spite of the difficulty raised by Euclid's postulates), and which served as the model for classical mechanics.

The prejudice was so strong that when, in spite of everything, the development of historical studies might have called attention to the sinuous course of events, to the disproportion between the littleness of causes and the importance of effects (it will be remembered how brilliantly Voltaire forced this point upon the interest of his contemporaries), the only result of the observation was to provoke a fresh attempt to bring the singular realities which form the very thread of history within the framework of a general order including indifferently the past and the future, the beginning and the end of time. History, understood in this sense, is interpreted in the light of the *philosophy of history*, which was the darling vice of the nineteenth century. In this respect, the France of Auguste Comte has no ground either for envying or for condemning anything in either the Germany of Hegel or the England of Herbert Spencer.

We should, I am afraid, come very late indeed in attempting to pass a judgement on this philosophy of history. Happily, it is to-day out of date. We need only point out that if it went wrong this was due to two different and, in a sense, contradictory causes. On the one hand it was the legatee of the old apologetic, that of St. Augustine and of Bossuet, which after Herder had been brought into the province of immanence. On the other hand, by its claim to follow a positive and rational method, it suffered from an implicit reference to a conception of the science of nature which was itself artificial and deceptive. That in it which was called history was not history; that in it which was called science was not science. In the same way Karl Marx called his socialism *scientific* (as opposed to a socialism of ideas which he treated as *utopian*); but it is well known that it is Hegel's dialectical fantasy, completely theological as it was in its origin and in its teleology, which provided him with a means of covering with a façade, at once forbidding and impressive, the prediction of the providential catastrophe which will emancipate the proletariat by suppressing class. And, from a quite opposite point of view, the immediate and unimpeachable intuition on which Nietzsche rests the prophecy of the everlasting recurrence is to all appearance a transfiguration of a pure recollection, quite natural on the part of a scholar devoted to the study of the Greek thinkers. Moreover, from Karl Marx and Nietzsche was to come the thinker in whom the fabulatory function assumed, it might be said, the clearest self-consciousness. The exaltation of the myth for its own sake in the author of the *Réflexions sur la violence*, Georges Sorel, provided a metaphysic for the dictatorships of the extreme left and of the extreme right which have established themselves in post-war Europe.

VI

We now come to something still more important. When the philosophy of history in the nineteenth century was schematizing the past and anticipating the future in accordance with the necessary unfolding of a uniform process, it was under the impression that it was putting itself on a level with the scientific conception of the inanimate or animate universe. Now it is established to-day that this impression is an illusion. Twentieth-century science has liberated history, which was enslaved by the philosophy of history to an illusory imitation of the philosophy of nature—an imitation which we know to be illusory *because twentieth-century science itself has taken the form of a history.* Thanks to the intervention of the calculation of probabilities, irreversibility (which seemed a logical scandal to the first interpreters of the principle of Sadi-Carnot) has taken on a form which men are to-day agreed in recognizing as entirely satisfactory to reason. And the primary role attributed by Einstein to the velocity of light, treated as constant, established the solidarity of the configuration of cosmic space with the measure of time, itself conceived as a physical operation. In this respect the general appearance of contemporary science is clearly expressed by Eddington in these words from *The Expanding Universe*: 'Thus we can scarcely isolate the thought of vast extension from the thought of time and change; and the problem of form and organization becomes merged in the problem of origin and development.' And this movement is going so far, the brilliant advances which are brought to our attention by the correlation of the growing wealth of theories and the extraordinary precision of observation are extending our spatial horizons and our temporal perspectives to such an extent, that in the same work we find a formula which a few years ago would have seemed the height of paradox: 'The original radius of the universe has been given, but we are unable to calculate the present radius.'

From this there issues a decisive result. The rule of law has come to an end in speculative philosophy in so far as law was sufficient unto itself in its abstract expression independently of the determinate conditions of time and space. On the contrary these conditions, given in experience and connected with one another by means of mathematical analysis, now seem indispensable to the rational co-ordination of phenomena which results in the concrete constitution of the whole of the universe. Instead, then, of forcibly adjusting our philosophy of history to a utopian ideal of it as philosophy of nature, we are re-establishing philosophical unity in the domain of physics and in the domain of morals on the basis of a conception which is properly historical and which restores to duration the irreducible reality of an irreversible sequence. Whether we consider the expanding universe, or humanity divided at any moment between the weight of primitive traditions and the need for spiritual progress, we find that both, and each after its own fashion, are proceeding towards a destiny where the issue is not a mere function of the origin, where even the immediate future cannot necessarily be defined by simply continuing the curve which has already been described. Hence the systems which have procured so much honour for the genius of their authors, but which have discredited philosophy by their contradictory multiplicity as well as by their intrinsic weakness, have faded away to make room for a critical reflection which is freed from that superstition of the *a priori* which for too long has threatened to reduce to impotence the admirable work of the Kantian philosophy.

VII

If this is the conclusion to which we are firmly led by the scientific revolution which has been achieved in our times, it would nevertheless be an exaggeration to say that the way had not been prepared even as early as the nineteenth century.

As regards France, in particular, this attitude of attention to history for its own sake, with an exclusive attachment to the truth implied in it without any sacrifice of exactness and honesty of research in the pursuit of general principles, characterizes the works of such men as Augustin Cournot and Émile Boutroux. It is true that they are well known. Yet even in their own country it cannot be said that they have been studied deeply enough. Precisely because the philosophical spirit is in these works in constant opposition to the systematic spirit, they do not admit of being compressed into one of those magic formulae, at once simple and universal, which, following the example of the romantics and the dialecticians, the so-called positivists of the nineteenth century—biologists or sociologists—have so abundantly elaborated, and which nowadays interest nobody except the authors of school text-books. And yet it is of vital importance that we should reflect upon the teaching of such works as Cournot's *Considérations sur la marche des idées et des événements dans les temps modernes* (which has been opportunely republished by the Librairie Boivin), or Boutroux's thesis: *De la contingence des lois de la nature.* The definitive ruin of the systems which were at once pretentious and fragile, far from injuring the cause of rational speculation, serves to introduce us to a philosophy of the human mind in which history, taken by itself, is not only an instrument of knowledge but the very thing which must be grasped in the continuity of its development, in the fertility of the resources which it has prepared for a free working out of the future.

Translated by Mary Morris, Oxford.

ON THE SO-CALLED IDENTITY OF HISTORY AND PHILOSOPHY

By GUIDO CALOGERO

ONE of the most notable theories of contemporary Italian idealism is that of the identity of history and philosophy. This might indeed be called the essential mark of that school, the mark which distinguishes it from other philosophical and idealistic tendencies of our time. The systems of the two chief exponents of modern Italian thought, Benedetto Croce and Giovanni Gentile, in spite of all other differences, agree in the assertion of this identity. And this assertion, better than any other doctrine, expresses the rejection of all transcendence by this philosophy, which denies any existence, truth, or value except what belongs to the present process or history of the spirit. History, which Vico already held to be the true and peculiar realm of man, furnishes the basis and the quality of everything that happens in the universe. This it is which philosophy sets itself to understand, but from which it can never separate itself so as to view it from some higher level. For even philosophy can only live in the bosom of history. Without philosophy history cannot be understood, but without history philosophy cannot be born. Above and beyond this human realm of history there is no divine realm of nature, as Vico thought; for divinity and nature are themselves only products of the historical activity of the spirit. Spirit unifies and simplifies the manifold objects of its experience into types and laws, and forms its religious ideals in its own image and likeness.

This general idea of the identity of history and philosophy presents, however, certain difficulties, which arise in different shapes according to the different forms which the idea itself takes on in the systems of these two thinkers. In Croce the general identification is accompanied by a number of distinctions which modify the identity to a somewhat dubious extent. Philosophy, he admits, is history, since history is the reality or consciousness of all that happens, and this reality does not achieve its full consciousness apart from the category of philosophy which always accompanies it. At the same time, he distinguishes philosophy from history. For the latter always implies the element of individuality, whereby every event, whatever form of the spirit it realizes, is just the event it is, absolutely distinct from any other, real or possible, even within the same spiritual category.

In their universal character, on the other hand, which is the realm of philosophy, all the historical events exemplifying any one form of the spirit are intrinsically, and of equal right, that one form. The distinction becomes still clearer when we pass from the general consideration of history, as at once objective fact and subjective construction, *res gestae* and *historia rerum gestarum*, to the particular consideration of this second or subjective aspect. The intrinsic unity and inseparableness of the two sides, fact and construction, is, of course, another of the fundamental doctrines common to the theories of Croce and Gentile. From the time of Vico onward, in history *verum et factum convertuntur*; to know history is to re-create it, to recall to life dead experience, and so to make it occur anew. But in Croce's formulation of the theory the aspect of history as simply historical narrative is made far more conspicuous. From his point of view philosophy is seen as merely the methodological element in the historian's activity. The historian's task is to present the concrete individual of historical fact in its particular individuality as well as in its universal quality. Philosophy is only concerned with the clear distinction of the categories or forms of spirit, by means of which the historian can discern the character of all that spirit experiences. The work of philosophy is to make definitions which determine these categories universally. The work of the historian is to make singular judgements which apply the categories to particular realities. So the identity of philosophy and history is denied by the sharp distinction between the universalizing thought of the methodologist and the individualizing thought of the historian. Nor can we consider the denial cancelled by the admission that singular judgements and definitions imply one another; as indeed they must do, since every philosophy presupposes a historical setting and arises in a certain culture, and every definition of the pure forms of spiritual history rests on a given individual experience of events in that history. Such mutual implication does not really amount to identity, it is merely a circular process; we shall see later what new difficulties this same conception of identity as circularity reveals.

These are the questionable modifications introduced into the identification of history and philosophy by the very thinker who found in it his most fruitful stimulus both for the treatment of special philosophical questions and for his actual historical writing. But, besides these modifications, there are other difficulties arising, in his general theory, from the part assigned to philosophy in the system of spiritual forms.

On the one hand, as is well known, philosophy is only one of four such forms: art, philosophy, 'economic' or non-moral action, and moral action. It is the theoretic or contemplative activity at its universal stage, which arises out of the same activity's individual or aesthetic stage. Both these stages coalesce in the historical consciousness, which is at once individual and universal, and is therefore the culmination of theoretic consciousness. This, in turn, serves as the basis of practical activity, which is destined once more, in the eternal circle of the spirit, to furnish material for new aesthetic, philosophical, and historical experiences.

But, on the other hand, since philosophy surveys the whole system of spirit, it cannot itself be any particular activity, but must be a consciousness immanent in all; it can neither be born out of a contradiction in the activity which logically precedes it, nor by its own contradiction beget that which follows it, for it must assist at every contradiction and at every birth. Rather, as Hegel would have said, it is the rising and the setting which itself neither rises nor sets. This double role philosophy, of course, must share with the history which is more or less identified with it. For history, too, is, from one point of view, pure knowledge, and indeed the supreme form of knowledge, but, from the other, the consciousness of all forms of spiritual experience. Indeed, it is more than the consciousness of them; it must be their sole and sufficient reality, if it be granted that historical knowledge and historical facts are identical. The most obvious result of assigning this double role to philosophy and to history is the corresponding duality which Croce involuntarily ascribes to that element of individuality which combines with the element of universality in the cognitive synthesis of historical judgement. On the one hand, when we are thinking of history as purely theoretical, its individuality has the same necessary connexion with universality as art has with philosophy. Aesthetic intuition is simply the linguistic expression, the vesture of words, in which the historical judgement must realize itself if it is to express its conceptual truth. On the other hand, so far as history is the consciousness and reality immanent in every form and every manifestation of spirit, its individuality is simply the definite self-hood of each manifestation, and is thereby contrasted with the universal validity of its form. It is no longer the linguistic or aesthetic clothing of the historic judgement, but the only subject of such a judgement, and a subject not expressed in words, or in new words, that is to say, taken up into a subsequent spiritual experience, but directly existing in its own nature, whatever form of spiritual activity may have produced it.

The difficulties in Croce's account of the identity of history and philosophy are somewhat complicated by the wealth of detail in which his doctrine is worked out. But no less obvious is the difficulty resulting from the same doctrine as presented in the system of Gentile. For him the problem is simplified by the fact that, as is well known, he allows no plurality of distinct spiritual forms, but only the all-embracing, present activity of thought in the act of thinking.[1] This activity is constituted by, or may be abstractly analysed into, the eternal antithesis and synthesis by which the conscious subject produces over against himself the independent object. Only in the unity of these abstract terms he is, or becomes, a concrete subject. The subjective term of the relation answers to the artistic experience, the objective term to that of religion; their synthesis constitutes, as it already did in Hegel's philosophy of the absolute spirit, philosophy. Thus outside philosophy there is no genuine activity of the spirit; the whole history of the world is exhausted in the history of philosophy. This history is the history of human thought, expressing itself in the most varied forms and realizing itself in the most diverse actions, but always focused in a consciousness and a conviction. Gentile, then, can state the identity of philosophy and history more simply as the identity of philosophy with its own history. Doubtless the history of philosophy presupposes philosophy, since the latter alone can supply the ground and the criterion for its reconstruction, and thereby bring its history into being. But at the same time philosophy presupposes its own history, because it is the offspring of that history. What was called an identity

[1] *pensiero pensante.*

of philosophy with history of philosophy is therefore understood not really to be an actual equation or identity, but merely the mutual necessitation of the two terms. This reciprocal or circular relation has been held by others to be the inevitable fallacy of every philosophy and history of philosophy, a fallacy by which each is made dependent on the other and can never attain the independence of absolute reality. Gentile, however, recognizes in this circular relation an essential characteristic of spirit, since spirit is an organism in which all the parts are reciprocally cause and effect. But we need not now discuss whether such a circle need be vicious, because the circle in question does not really occur. For there to be such a circle at all, the two terms, between which the reciprocal necessitation is alleged, must remain the same from whichever end the relation is regarded. Here, however, 'history of philosophy' means one thing when it is said to *presuppose philosophy as its condition* on the ground that it is constructed according to a philosophical criterion; it means something quite different when it is said to be *the condition which philosophy presupposes* on the ground that philosophy can only arise out of historical conditions. In the first sense 'history of philosophy' means the thinking about past philosophies which is actually going on at a given moment in the mind. It is only in this sense that history can fulfil Vico's demand for the identity of *verum* and *factum*, of historical fact and historical thinking; only in this sense could we say with Croce that all history is contemporary history. In the second sense, on the contrary, 'history of philosophy' means philosophical development supposed to exist as an independent object preceding and determining our actually present thought about it. This second sense bears the same relation to the first as the independent reality of realism bears to the subject-object reality of idealism. Once the 'identity' has been thus explained as mere circularity or reciprocal conditioning, we see that it has been explained away, since there is no reciprocal conditioning at all.

If, then, of these two 'histories of philosophy' one is, without qualification, real and the other unreal, our problem has solved itself. For we are not bound to explain a relation which could only be supposed while we took that unreality for real. It is *not* true that present philosophizing is conditioned by the past 'history' or development of philosophy; for that 'history' would precede and condition it only on the assumption of abstract realism. But the converse *is* true: that the 'history' or development of past thought is conditioned by present thinking, which includes it and gives it life by thinking of it and constructing it. Whether the alleged 'identity' of history and philosophy had been understood as a simple equation or as mutual implication, it must in either case have involved the equal validity of the two terms. But we now see that this 'identity' really means that the first term (past development or history) is explained away as being nothing but the second (present thought of it or philosophy), which is therefore left in occupation of the whole field.

This explaining away of history (or development) into philosophy (or the thought of it) is inevitable. That is especially clear when the 'history' in question is the history of philosophy itself; and it is convenient to consider this case first, in order to see in what sense we can and must subsequently distinguish other cases where the 'history' concerned is that of other spiritual activities. Such an explaining away of 'history' is involved for Gentile by the fundamental principle of his system, by which the 'history' of philosophy is the only 'history' possible. But it is no less forced upon Croce by the difficulties arising from his explicit denial of this pre-eminence of philosophy. Indeed, it is to the exigencies of Croce's teaching on the connexion of philosophy with its history and with the universal history of the spirit that we must ascribe his theory that no philosophy is ultimate.[1] This theory has, no doubt, an extremely modern sound, and, moreover, serves the important purpose of getting rid of the abstract idea of philosophy as something that has only to solve its single ultimate problem and can then rest from its labours. But here it is the word 'philosophy' which is used ambiguously. In one sense it means the 'philosophy' which is never final because it has never finished its task. It has continually to solve the problems offered to it by the history of other spiritual activities, and, by its very solutions, it offers material for new actions generating, in their turn, new problems. This is the sense of 'philosophy' in which Croce sets it as one form among others in the system of spirit, a stage of development which recurs alternately with other stages. But he has a different sense of the word, in which 'philosophy' discovers and contemplates the whole of this system of forms; so that it must be omnipresent

[1] *non definitività.*

and eternal, if the reality of that historical development of spirit is to be assured. The very relativity of 'philosophy', in the sense of a particular stage in the development of spirit, necessitates that there should be a final 'philosophy' in the sense of that which asserts this development. In vain Croce replies, to such objections, that the historical relativity of every philosophical statement does not prevent its being felt as 'absolute' in its context, though not final. Certainly one may reply to a question with an 'absolute' negative, though that 'absolute' negative is 'relative' to the question inasmuch as to a different question one might answer yes.[1] That is true enough and, as we shall see later, has good reasons, but it is not to the point. For we are not now talking about the 'philosophy' which is asserted by the theory to be a stage of development, and which, for all its relativity to the historical context, has the absolute character proper to every spiritual event when it is actively manifesting itself. We are talking of the 'philosophy' which asserts this very theory, and which is not the offspring of historical development, but the very condition of the intelligibility, and therefore of the reality, of that development. Here we meet again the same ambiguity of the word philosophy, which, as we saw previously, caused a 'philosophy', asserted to be a single form of spirit, to be set alongside another 'philosophy', which, in virtue of its apprehension of all the forms, asserts the first. We now find that this same ambiguity leads to a final philosophy being required as the guarantee for the existence of a provisional philosophy. Now if we consider, with reference to this question of the relation between philosophy and history, the philosophy which Croce himself offers us, it evidently is of the nature of philosophy and not history, final philosophy and not relative. For it is not a philosophy possible in future history but a present philosophical conception of the possibility of future philosophies. Thus, a final philosophy is not only forced upon Croce to guarantee the existence of relative philosophy but actually absorbs and replaces it.

It is an ironical fate by which the philosophy about which we philosophize, when we make assertions about its possibilities and characteristics, is never the only philosophy. Behind it must lie the more fundamental philosophy which makes these assertions. But this ironical situation is only the most striking

[1] B. Croce, *Eternità e storicità della filosofia*, Rieti, 1930, p. 10 n.

instance of the self-contradiction essential to all epistemology from the point of view of a strictly subjective interpretation of idealism. The fundamental idealist doctrine, which absorbs all reality into thought, can never be really established so long as we consider thought itself as a reality which can be discovered and defined like an object. Thought so conceived would itself come under that law of the understanding by which an object is known only so far as it is limited and distinguished from others and can never therefore be the absolute whole in which all things have their being. The only absolutely unconditioned whole is the living, present, subjective activity of thought, which lies behind every definition of thought or of any object. This unconditioned is not the thought defined as an object but the thought which is defining it, to borrow the formula which most characteristically expresses the 'actualism' of Gentile. But from his theory follows the conclusion, not clearly drawn by orthodox actualists, that any theory of knowledge must be self-contradictory. For in epistemology thought sets out to define itself, or to establish the forms and conditions of its possible activities, not noticing that it could never define these limits without, in the very act, transcending them. In so doing, it must effectually know the very spheres of reality which it judges to be unknowable, and realize in thought the very kinds of knowledge which it pronounces impossible; in general, it must, in thinking, transcend the bounds which it imposes on thought in defining it and distinguishing it from what is not thought. No theory of knowledge is ever universal and necessary, since it has always to admit one exception, namely, the thought it is now thinking. And on the theory that this thought includes all reality, so that the thought it is now thinking is the only one which deserves the name of thought at all, the exception proves to be so considerable as to deprive the rule of any philosophical application. Whoever then produces a theory or logic of philosophy, defining its place in the spirit, the laws of its manifestation, and, in a word, the possibilities of its present and future life, has forgotten that the real philosophy is not the one whose conditions he is describing but the one which claims to describe them.

After all that has been said, we cannot deny the primacy of philosophy over history, in virtue of which present thought rejects any universal and necessary laws that would determine the forms of its historical development. How then can present thought escape the absurd presumption of being the sole depository of the one absolute truth and of having gained the summit of philosophy's historical ascent, with no possibility of further development?

As regards the past, thought so conceived may indeed escape the difficulties of the strictly Hegelian philosophy of history; for, since it has concentrated in itself every possible object of thought, including all past realities, it is no longer obliged to project the logical conditions and stages of its knowledge into its own past evolution. It is no longer called upon to solve the insoluble antinomy of a first beginning, nor to hypostatize its own historical experiences into dialectical stages. Thus it escapes the risk that new evidences may appear, adding to our ideas of these experiences, and so proving the inadequacy of our dialectical construction. In short, thought so conceived finds in the past, that is to say, in the so-called sensible world to which, after all, the evidences belong, only mnemonic signs enabling it to revive in its present thinking something already thought. And what has to be so revived may differ indefinitely from present thinking, even if the customary reference of consequent to antecedent gives the succession of thoughts the general appearance of an evolving organism.

But, as regards the future, this philosophy is no less hampered than the Hegelian, which was constrained to make the history of thought, and therefore of the universe, culminate with itself. Indeed, a theory which identifies thought with its own present thought seems even more arrogantly paradoxical. In the older theory, the culminating philosophy, though it precluded any future, yet did homage to the past. But this one, in freeing itself from the past, subjects it to itself, and sits alone and infallible upon the throne of truth.

This difficulty is overcome when we examine more closely the relations of the present with the past and the future severally. Naïve realism pictures past, present, and future as the successive parts of a single dimension. The present then evaporates into past and future, since it has no extension of its own but is simply the line dividing the others. Speculative idealism, as is well known, draws an exactly opposite picture. For it the present, in which our consciousness is alive, is the real and eternal time, which hypostatizes its own abstract elements as past and future.

Since the thought which has reality for its object is always actual or present thought, there can be no reality outside the present. We must then admit that past and future have no reality, except as abstractions, save in the present and as ideas[1] of something which 'has happened' or 'will happen'; and that these ideas are not things which have happened or will happen. On these lines Croce can say that all history is contemporary history and Gentile can regard the eternal present as the absolute form of all reality. But we are then forced to the conclusion, however repugnant it may be to obvious and essential doctrines of these thinkers, that the present has the despotic ordering of all time, and present philosophy that of all others, both those which have developed in the past and those which may appear in the future.

The fact is that this impossible conclusion is drawn from its self-evident premiss owing to a certain incompleteness[2] of the premiss itself. There is undeniable truth in the assertions that past and future can only be thought in the eternal present; that both, considered in themselves, exhibit the same degree of abstraction and unreality; and that the past, however solid and permanent its written letters seem beside the blank pages of the future, is no less unreal, until it is born again in the present of the spirit. But such assertions attack the problem only from an epistemological point of view. And when we have granted, for the reasons just allowed, that every theory of knowledge, in the more modern and consistent form of idealism, must be essentially self-contradictory, we cannot be satisfied with any philosophical doctrine which, under the guise of a theory of knowledge, yet claims validity as a law of spiritual activity. The only truth which modern idealism can allow in the epistemological field is the mere doctrine of the complete immanence of all reality in consciousness, and in a consciousness which recognizes that it is and must be absolutely subjective and monochronous.[3] And this doctrine is not strictly a theory of knowledge, since a theory of knowledge is the recognition of the laws and limits of knowledge, the distinction of thinking from what is not thinking, and of the thinkable from the unthinkable. But this doctrine confines itself to the assertion that thought *cannot* be submitted to *any* law or limit. For whatever laws the epistemologist may establish, as belonging to the thought he is

[1] *coscienza.* [2] *aspetto inadeguato.* [3] *attuale.*

thinking about, are *ipso facto* transcended by the thought he is now subjectively initiating, which alone deserves the name.

All this only means that the ego cannot, without self-contradiction, undertake the task of defining its sphere of consciousness. Such a task would be as impossible as useless; for nothing can be so immediately known to us as the knowing in which we are now active; and the demand to know knowledge in any other way leads to an infinite regress by its requirement of knowing the knowledge which knows that knowledge. Consequently the philosophical activity of the ego is merely the consciousness and definition of the absolute laws of its own *practical* activity; for that practical activity must be understood as being the concrete manifestation of all its real forms of activity. Since then philosophy, which on the idealist theory is entirely philosophy of spirit, cannot be a philosophy of the theoretic spirit, because all epistemology is essentially self-contradictory, and since there must be some philosophy or absolute knowledge, because even the denial of philosophy is philosophy, we must conclude that the only philosophy is a philosophy of action. It is the absolute knowledge of the spirit's forms of action which must include and comprehend everything that the spirit really accomplishes. Even that seed of solid truth, which had formed on the stem of the logical and epistemological analysis of the spirit, but had remained stunted and self-contradictory while considered as the criterion of a merely theoretical activity, acquires organic coherence when transferred to the concrete level of the philosophy of action. This is so with the principle which, as can be shown in detail from an adequate historical interpretation, underlies and includes all logic and dialectic, whether ancient or modern. I mean the principle which demands that any concrete object of thought must always be determinate, definite, and limited, but must, by that very fact, have something other than itself and external, only in antithesis to which can it be determinate and definite. This principle is simply the transcendental condition of all practical activity, which could never take place in a consciousness whose object was something hard and fast or ultimate, which did not admit the possibility of going beyond it. Such a consciousness would be like Aristotle's God, who knows all that he can know, and therefore does not act but rests in contemplation of himself. A consciousness which is to be no unchanging mirror but a living, acting self, must, in spite of its infinity or rather because thereof, remain always unexhausted by its whole object at any one time. It is therefore a concrete act of consciousness in virtue of having a definite object, beyond which, and equally essential to it, must remain the possibility of something different, and so of eternal change.

We must now leave these general considerations on the internal contradiction of all theories of knowledge and on the necessity of their element of truth being restated in terms of a philosophy of action; we must turn to the problem of the relations between the three parts of time. The deficiencies and difficulties of the theory which explains past and future alike as merely modes of present consciousness, obviously arise from the merely epistemological nature of that explanation. That the past as much as the future has concrete existence only in the present is in fact unquestioned by any one who has satisfied himself that present thought includes, epistemologically speaking, all reality. But precisely because this latter doctrine covers and exhausts everything knowable about the nature of spirit as pure knower, any further belief logically founded upon it, while confining itself to the sphere of abstract epistemology, cannot be, at best, more than a well-founded empirical application of that doctrine (that present thought includes all reality) to a particular case. Consequently the first belief, that past and future are only real in the present, is, in this epistemological application, not a philosophical but an empirical truth, formally indistinguishable from any other by which we might exemplify the immanence of all things in thought from some other pair of empirical objects. This is confirmed by the fact that, notwithstanding the typically dialectic generation of the present out of the eternal negation of past by future, yet the relation and process between these two abstract parts of time is not identified or interwoven with the peculiar dialectics characteristic of the two systems whose resolution of past and future into present we have been discussing. With the dialectic of Croce, whether applied to the relation of contrary or of distinct conceptions, this resolution has nothing to do. In Gentile's dialectic, the object is projected by the subject, to be reabsorbed by it and so to form the concrete subject. And this may, in some aspects and with some modifications, look very like the process by which the present sets over against itself the past, and then resolves it in itself. But if we take this view, the future is either left out of the story or it simply replaces the past in its opposition to the subject, as any other particular object of experience might. No distinctive function or transcendental dialectic would then be attributed to these two parts of time or to their opposition. In both these systems past and future are reduced to the present in a way which would serve to reduce any other abstract part of time which might exist alongside these two. And that is quite consistent with the epistemological nature of the reduction in which they share.

The significant fact has been overlooked that time cannot possess any other parts than these two; indeed it is unthinkable that it should. In no possible world and for no possible thought can time be anything but a present arising from the generative clash of past and future. This trinity of time united from the duality of its dialectical moments is, then, apprehended not by empirical induction but by transcendental reflection. It is not the contingent outcome of experience, but a universal, necessary truth, imposing itself upon thought by that unique hall-mark of philosophic truth, the inconceivability of the contradictory. It ought then to be duly established in the system of the spirit as a necessary condition of spiritual activity. And it can be so established as soon as it is transferred from the abstract sphere of knowledge to the concrete sphere of action.

We have said that an active self is only conceivable if the infinite capacity of its consciousness is thought of as constantly achieving concrete reality in the consciousness of a definite object, beyond which we can still think of something else. And this involves the possibility of change. But there would be no change if this object and the other which is beyond it were thought of as having the same kind of reality. The one is indeed what it is; the other is what it may and must come to be, but, for that very reason, certainly is not yet. The former is the starting-point of action, the given situation, the fulcrum necessary if any action is to be achieved. For all action is change and innovation, and, if new is to be born, old must first be there, if it is only the empty void, which was before the *creatio ex nihilo* and is itself an effective historical situation of the mind of God. The latter, on the other hand, the 'other than what yet is', is a programme to be carried out, the picture of possible reality to be translated into actual reality. It is no less necessary to the life of action than the first. For a mind which, in its concrete acts of consciousness, was confined to the reality immediately perceived as existing, and had not therewith the idea of a reality not yet realized but realizable, could not will or act, and would remain unmoved like Aristotle's God.

All this, of course, agrees with any conception of practical activity which does not overlook the fact that will and action must always presuppose a situation historically conditioned, whence they can start. It will only be questioned by those who think that such a condition would destroy free will, since they suppose that freedom must mean absolute, unconditioned freedom. On their view this starting-point, too, must really be an arrival; a result, not an antecedent, of action. But it is easy to see that such an infinite freedom would only be freedom in the abstract, which could never generate any will or action. There is no deed of omnipotence, however creative and spontaneous we may conceive it, which does not presuppose, as its historical condition, at least the fact that what is to be done has not yet been done. The demand for an unconditioned freedom is a consequence of the problem, posed by epistemology, about the infinity of the spirit; it is an attempt, however unsuccessful, to satisfy the resulting need of translating that problem into terms of practical philosophy. From the purely epistemological point of view, the spirit, as actualized, is indeed unlimited, since there is nothing for it to be aware of but what is within it. It does not follow that this property, which is the self-evident possession of consciousness abstractly considered, should be realized in the concrete field of action. The realistic philosophy which flourished in classical times still influences modern idealism. According to it, in the relation of knowledge, the subject is affected by the object, while, in the practical relation, the object is affected by the subject. To reform this doctrine by simply identifying the two relations, with the intention of making knowledge an activity, merely whittles away activity into knowledge. What we must do is to transpose the two relations. The self, considered in its aspect of pure consciousness, presupposes no conditions, it includes everything in itself; the self, considered as realizing that capacity for consciousness in concrete life and activity, always implies such a condition in itself, which is the eternal starting-point of its eternal activity.

Only when the spirit's activity is so conceived is it possible to give an account of that distinction between reality perceived as existing and reality merely imagined or thought of, which could never be epistemologically justified from a strictly idealist point of view. On the level of pure thinking, everything is a mere idea, as Berkeley held, and there is no more to be said. Existence, as Kant knew, is not implied by a conception, and there is no distinguishing in thought between a hundred real dollars and a hundred imagined. The difference, in fact, is that the first are already coined and the second not yet. The first are a historical situation from which action can take off, the others are a programme which it can try to fulfil. This difference, between perceived reality and possibilities conceived, forces itself upon us with irresistible self-evidence, and is usually urged by realists against idealist theories of knowledge, which, when consistently formulated, are bound to deny any objective ground for the distinction. The true explanation of the difference is not in a theory of knowledge but in a theory of action. It is simply a transcendental condition of action that our consciousness of the world must be divided into the perception of reality and the idea of possibility.

But just as we have explained the two metaphysical or epistemological realms of reality and possibility, or the perceived and the imagined, as the two dialectical elements[1] of living spiritual reality, so we must explain the two abstract dialectical elements[1] of time as being identified in that same unity. The simplest definition we can give of these is that the past is what has been done and the future is what is to do. All the dialectical triads are here identified. To say that the subject is the eternal synthesis of past and future history, that the necessity of consciousness is the common basis of reality and of possibility, that the present is incessantly fashioned by the passage of the future into the past: all these are only different ways of defining the self, that is to say, the conscious will.

If then the dialectic of time is also the dialectic of the spirit, what conclusions can we draw for that problem of history, for whose solution we thought it necessary to define more exactly the meaning of 'past' and 'future'? First of all, we must remember that historical thinking is the present reconstruction of a spiritual experience from the traces of mnemonic signs preserved in the sensible reality transcendentally identified with the past. From this we can understand how the common-sense belief,

[1] *momenti.*

that history is always of the past, is philosophically consistent with the irrefutable doctrine that all history is contemporary. Historical knowledge is always the thinking of the past in the present, not of the future. It is simply impossible in the present to think of the future as an existing reality endowed with the immutable character known to belong to that past reality which even divine omnipotence cannot undo. We can only think of it as a possible reality capable of being realized by action. To try to think of it as existing is not only not 'history', in the sense of historical knowledge, but is the denial of the possibility of 'history' in the sense of real development and action. As we are aware, the certain knowledge that an event must happen excludes the event from the sphere of historical development, that is to say, of free activity. What can be certainly foreseen happens mechanically; freedom and history are only realized in the sphere of the unforeseen. The future can be defined as the home of freedom, just because we are ignorant of what it holds. This abstract freedom of the future must, of course, be distinguished from the concrete freedom of the will, as the *libertas indifferentiae* is distinguished from the synthesis of freedom and necessity which is effected in willing; but this distinction does not prevent the first freedom from providing the infinite possibility of the second, for the future *is* the realm of possibility.

This essential obscurity of the future, which is conceived as free just because it is conceived as unknown, might seem to limit the infinite capacity of knowing proper to the mind, in whose dialectic the future is a term. But no contradiction would arise so long as the infinity is conceived, as we have said, as a potential infinity, always concrete and finite in its actualization; but only if it were absurdly conceived as an actual infinity. The contradiction does indeed arise in the God of medieval theology, who, by the heritage of Greece, had to realize infinite knowledge, and, by the heritage of Christianity, to have infinite capacity of action; whereas the two characters are incompatible, and indeed even severally inconceivable owing to the undialectical absolutism in which they are founded. If this God were the realization of infinite knowledge, and therefore knew all the past, present, and future on one level of eternity, he could do absolutely nothing. If, on the other hand, he were absolutely omnipotent, unlimited by any condition, his consciousness would be completely empty of any true knowledge. The consciousness of the self does not answer to these inconceivable attributes of the medieval God, because though capable of infinity it is not infinite. It is infinite δυνάμει, not ἐνεργείᾳ. To say that it knows the future as unknown is only to say that it knows the future as knowable; and the fact that it does not actually know all that is thus knowable cannot be distinguished, in the sphere of knowledge, from the fact that it is not presently aware of all thinkable reality, though no reality can be thinkable of which it is not aware.

Here we find the solution of the greatest difficulty about the relation of philosophy to its history. The former must be given absolute primacy over the latter when the history in question is past history, but not when it is future; for the future has been defined as the realm of the unknown and the possible, of that which is still to be done, but as yet rests on the knees of the Gods. It is possible and empirically probable that, in the future, infinite new events may find place, and therefore infinite new philosophies, which, if we may judge by analogy from what has happened in the past, will recognize and avoid continuously better and better the limitations and defects of present philosophy. But the latter cannot foretell absolutely these unborn philosophies. To do so would be to theorize about the spiritual form which is philosophical activity, and so to construct a final philosophy of the philosophy which is never final. But this is impossible. Not only would a philosophy which attempted it fall into the most characteristic self-contradiction of epistemology, but it would incur the guilt of ridiculous arrogance, by flattering itself that it can impose on all future thought its formal standard of what philosophy ought to be. After all, then, the most modest attitude which present philosophy can assume is to take up all the past into itself and to leave the future alone.

All this, of course, is only true when the history in question is history of philosophy. For then the thought of the historian is bound to see itself, not only as the end and summit of the evolution, but as the universal system which includes and takes up into itself all the truth of previous philosophy. It is the little room into which all history is summed. The situation is very different when we turn to the history, not of philosophy, but of the concrete activity of the spirit, whose transcendental forms philosophy considers. Regarding the individual actions that have exemplified these forms in the past, the present philosophical consciousness, which knows them historically, has a very different task. Whilst it was considering past philosophies, just because it could not, without self-contradiction, discuss the epistemological possibility and formal conditions of philosophy, it was bound to take up and include all past philosophy into its own. The truths of Plato or Kant or any other philosopher belong to the history of philosophy, not because they can all be subsumed under a single concept of philosophizing, but because they still play their part in the system of present philosophy. In the other situation, on the contrary, when our history is not of philosophy, philosophical consciousness is the theory of the eternal forms of history, and the individual historical facts do not face it, like past philosophies, on equal terms as rivals it must absorb if it is not to be absorbed. When an artistic experience or a moral action is recalled, the philosophical criterion by which we understand and distinguish them is valid for all time, and does not treat them as past stages in its own evolution, since it is bound to stand above them all as the universal above the individuals. In the history of philosophy the present is ignorant of the future, but takes the past up into itself. In the history of the concrete activity of the spirit it does not take even the past up into itself; it only illumines it. To be conscious of the truths of past philosophy satisfies the supra-temporal interest of the spirit as pure knower. To revive the practical experiences of the past, on the other hand, satisfies the ever-changing interest of the spirit as the concrete whole, whose knowledge is the consciousness of desire and action. When some political or moral action is given a new life in history, the historian's interest is not that of the agent, who effectively translated his programme from the sphere of ideas to that of reality. The historian can only repeat the process in the world of his ideas. His interest is one for future action only, to which history is the *magister vitae*. When art is born again in history and, either by the emotional associations of the work or by help of so-called critical interpretation, we are put back into the moment at which the artist was tortured by his passionate ideal and, as he gazed on it, was freed from the craving for its existence and feasted on its pure semblance, then the interest of the historical experience coincides, for once, with that of the aesthetic experience it is reproducing. Time is conquered, and the joy we feel now is the same that was felt then.

Translated by E. F. Carritt, University College, Oxford.

RELIGION, PHILOSOPHY, AND HISTORY

By CLEMENT C. J. WEBB

IT has been an error characteristic of the last hundred years—a period which witnessed, in almost all spheres of thought and inquiry, so remarkable a progress in our knowledge and understanding of the antecedents of the present state of the world, material and spiritual, wherein our lot is cast—to assume too readily that we have explained a feature of this world, when we have but given a description of its antecedents. But the fear of committing this mistake must not lead us into the opposite fault of unwillingness to learn what is to be learned about a present fact from a study of its origins. Thus, in the case of the three forms of activity which go by the names of Religion, Philosophy, and History, it will be, I think, convenient to begin our discussion of their mutual relations by observing that it would seem to be as offshoots of Religion that both History, in the sense, which it commonly bears, of the investigation of human life in the past, and also Philosophy, in the sense of an inquiry into the ultimate nature of the world wherein we find ourselves and whereof we are ourselves a part, first came into existence.

Moreover, at that stage of its development at which the germs of Philosophy and History first become distinguishable, Religion itself is still (if, indeed, it ever ceases to be) *practical*, in the sense that it is envisaged as in the main a means to the general welfare of those who carry it on. It is because these seek to secure for themselves a position in which the potent and mysterious forces which haunt their life without and within, 'about their path and about their bed and spying out all their ways', may be counted upon to promote, or at the least, not to hinder the satisfaction of their appetites and desires that they endeavour to enter into relations with these forces by what becomes in the end cult or worship. Out of this endeavour comes the attempt to form (at first, no doubt, in pictorial or imaginative shape) a conception of their life with its environment as a whole or universe of reality, which is the beginning of Philosophy; while, because it is as one of a definite group of human beings, into which he has been born, that a primitive man confronts that universe and, through learning the group's ways of dealing with it, hopes to come to terms with it, there arises in him a curiosity about the past relations between it and the group, whereof these ways are a result; a curiosity which is the beginning of History.

Yet we have here to note in passing, as a precaution against falling into the error mentioned in the first sentence of my paper, that this account of the primitive man's essays in Religion, Philosophy, and History does not *explain*, but *presupposes* in him that capacity for 'large discourse', for 'looking before and after', which distinguishes him as the 'rational animal' from the other beasts with whom he had to fight for his place in the sun.

It is a long way from such essays to the Religion of the saint who aspires after the vision of God that is promised to the pure in heart; to the Philosophy of the thinker who would be, in Plato's phrase, 'the spectator of all time and of all existence'; to the History of the scholar whose ideal it is to survey the human past as a single and unique process, without prejudice or partisanship, confessional, national, or racial. And yet these things could never have emerged from those primitive crudities, had not there been already immanent therein that which the philosophers call 'reason' and the theologians 'the image of God'.

The problem, however, with which the present paper is concerned is that of the mutual relations of the three activities of which I have been speaking. One of the most distinguished of contemporary thinkers sees in Religion only an immature form of Philosophy, which to all outside its 'magic circle' must appear as mere mythology, and to the gradual supersession of which by genuine Philosophy we must look forward as the inevitable result of the spread of enlightenment, except so far as there may always be some souls which fall below what may be expected to become the average level of intellectual cultivation. This view is one which is not to be wondered at in a philosopher who can see, with Benedetto Croce, nothing in Religion but a purely cognitive kind of spiritual activity. For it cannot, I think, be denied that, as I have already intimated, when pointing out the religious beginnings of Philosophy, it is in connexion with Religion that men first philosophize, that is, frame a conception of the world as a whole. And, as there can be no doubt that, with the progress of civilization, this function tends to be more and more devolved upon Philosophy, it would seem to follow that, if this be the sole function of Religion, its whole field of operation must be eventually usurped by Philosophy. But I do not believe that this is the sole function of Religion. In Religion man seeks contact with what he divines to be at once at the back of all that he experiences and also of his own experiencing self. He wants not only to apprehend it as containing the ultimate truth about life, the secret of existence; but to enter into an intimacy with it, wherein it will be not only an object of knowledge but a partner in such an intercourse as he has with his fellows, in whom he recognizes the same kind of being as that which he is conscious of himself possessing, and which inevitably becomes his standard—at least his implicit standard—of concrete reality.

A contemporary school of philosophical theologians in Germany has done well to call attention to the experience of which the use of the second personal pronoun is the expression, and to suggest that theories of knowledge have too often tended to ignore this and to rest content with treating the apprehension of our neighbour as 'he' as our best means of understanding the spiritual nature which we share with him. With this recognition of social intercourse as supplying a plane of spiritual experience higher than that of contemplation from without, there goes naturally a parallel recognition of the relation to God expressed in prayer, worship, self-surrender, as the medium of a revelation to us of the divine nature fuller than any which could be received through speculation apart from a religious experience of this kind.

It is no doubt true that Religion uses and must use mythological imagery and language to express this experience. Nor is it Religion only which employs this mode of expression; even Science, to which of all our spiritual activities mythology might seem to be least congenial, does not on occasion altogether despise its aid. Moreover, it is to be confessed that there is a genuine danger to Religion involved in the possibility of mythology being taken for other than it is. Those who are children in understanding, if not in age, must still speak, think, and feel as such. But if, when called upon, like the apostle, to 'put away childish things' men persist in bondage to the imagination, they run grave risk of finding their faith baffled by the inadequacy of familiar language and imagery to express their mature experience. Yet may we not be 'throwing away the child with the bath' if we discard as mere mythology convictions, such as those of the reality of our own and other selves, which we do not cease in fact to presuppose, even when we affect to treat them as dissolved by philosophical criticism? It is, nevertheless, of the first importance, if not to Religion, at least to theology, and so indirectly to Religion also, that philosophical criticism should be allowed all possible freedom, and that even such convictions as I have mentioned should not be treated as sacrosanct and exempt from its scrutiny, but permitted to depend upon their own intrinsic stability for effective resistance to its dissolvent power.

Philosophy, in separating itself from its parent, Religion, and setting up for itself, is fitting itself for its own special task, which is the satisfaction of the speculative intellect. It is fully justified in jealously guarding its autonomy within its own sphere and in refusing to be turned aside by practical, moral, or religious considerations from the resolute attempt to think out the problems presented to it not merely by what may be called scientific experience, but by experience of every kind, including those kinds to which we apply the terms which I have just used—practical, moral, religious. But it is not justified in forgetting that it is itself an activity of the one self which is also active in all these forms of experience and is conscious of its unity in them all. This language is perhaps not Kantian; but the ethics of Kant rest upon his profound conviction that in the consciousness of moral responsibility, which is at least one of the roots of Religion, the human soul is aware of something in itself more fundamental than the theoretical activity which, taken in abstraction from it, is in comparison with it departmental. Moreover, Kant's view of Religion itself is, in the end,—however strange and even perverse the forms in which he sometimes chooses to express it—that here we have the necessary postulation by the reason of a unity, beyond all apparent oppositions, between speculation and practice. I have no desire to cry 'Back to Kant', or to disparage the work of his successors; but even the features of his philosophy which are most obnoxious to criticism are often traceable to a certain sensitiveness to other aspects of the problem than those in his treatment of which his critics find him deficient.

A very able writer in this country[1] has lately put forward and

[1] M. Oakeshott, *Experience and its Modes*, Cambridge, 1933.

vigorously supported by arguments a view altogether different from that suggested in my last paragraph. Utterly divorcing life or practice from truth, he describes the former as an 'arrest of experience'—of experience, which Philosophy, in its quest of ultimate truth, continues to carry on regardless of the incoherences discovered by its criticism to exist in the assumptions made by practical life (within the sphere of which this author regards Religion as falling). Truth, the aim of Philosophy, is thus placed in opposition to life, and incidentally to Religion, which is a part of life. But, even by the confession of this resolute devotee of a truth which gives the lie to life and of a Philosophy which is, in a sense far other than Plato's, a *meditatio mortis*, we must in the end—since, unless we live, we cannot even philosophize—cry *Pereat veritas, fiat vita*, and return, like the guardians of Plato's ideal State, from the vision of ultimate reality into the cave of practice—although, unlike them, without having in the least improved, by our experience of that 'happy-making sight', our capacity of dealing with the problems of every day. It would seem, on the contrary, as if the heavenly vision is more likely to have taken the heart out of our life in this world, and even out of the religion which might otherwise have put heart into that life by showing that it has issues in a higher world, beyond or within this. The doctrine is a disconcerting one, and it is not possible here to examine it as fully as the earnestness with which it is defended, and the ingenuity of the arguments by which it is maintained, undoubtedly merit. But the present writer must own himself unconvinced that the admission of inconsistency with the necessary assumptions of any life—even of the religious life, which its preachers are apt to contrast with other forms of life as 'life indeed'—can support a claim to be the ultimate truth about experience. Nor can he regard it as possible for Religion to follow the example of Science and of History, which go about their own business, justly resenting any pretensions on the part of Philosophy to interfere with it by raising doubts about the ultimate reality of an external world or of a temporal series. To men of science and to historians, as such, doubts of this kind must indeed appear irrelevant. For they are concerned with measurable motions or with successive events, whatever difficulties these may present to a metaphysical critic. But it is far otherwise with the religious man. He may be prepared to allow the inadequacy of the symbolism which shapes his language and determines the form of his worship; but, if he is not dealing with what is ultimately real, in such a sense that a further revelation of its nature will not overthrow his conviction of its intimate presence in his religious consciousness, then he must confess himself deluded and bereft of any justification for the further practice of Religion. He cannot (so far as the criticisms of Philosophy mean anything to him) consistently with loyalty to Religion admit the possibility of their justice while affirming them to be irrelevant, as the man of science and the historian can, and indeed *must*, in loyalty to their respective pursuits, affirm them to be irrelevant, however just they may be. For that of which he is in search must be *veritas et vita*.

It has already been observed that not only Philosophy but History has its roots in Religion. For, in all probability, it is in connexion with the religious practices which aim at establishing and maintaining friendly relations between a community of primitive men and the mysterious powers, environing their life, on whose operations the continuance and prosperity of that life seems to depend, that there arises in the minds of such primitive men a curiosity about the origin of these practices in the past of the community whose life they find themselves sharing but from the communications of their elders believe to embrace experiences which they individually do not and cannot remember.

Just as Philosophy has turned aside from all preoccupation with the special wants of the philosopher to devote herself to dispassionate inquiry into the general nature of reality, so History has learned to occupy herself with the whole past of humanity, so far as it is accessible to her investigation, irrespective of that sense of continuity with the particular past of a community to which oneself belongs. This sense is nevertheless, in most instances, still the original stimulant of interest in those who come, as scholars, to embrace the ideal of an objective and impartial consideration of all willed and purposed events which fall within their knowledge but were antecedent to those contemporary with themselves.

In either case one may intelligibly speak of Philosophy or of History as having emancipated itself from Religion. Neither could indeed have attained its full stature, had it remained in close association with the religious atmosphere of its youth. Yet Religion is herself interested in this very independent development of her offspring. A world-view on the one hand, on the other the consciousness of a common life, shared by each self with others and involving a past unlimited by the extent of individual memory—these are features which belong in some measure to all Religion. That is, indeed, precisely why it is within the womb of Religion that Philosophy and History first take shape. But in the end Religion cannot be satisfied with a false world-view or with a sense of continuity with a past which was never present. Philosophical and historical error can certainly coexist in the same soul with the deepest and sincerest religious faith; but only when they are not recognized as error. Religion may indeed legitimately protest that her own experience invalidates a philosophical theory which would contradict it, or an historical theory which is inconsistent with the fact of her having that experience. But genuine religion cannot accept the definition which the child is said to have given of faith, that it is 'believing what you know to be untrue'. The speculations of Philosophy and the researches of History are continually exerting upon the theory of Religion (which we may call Theology), and through it upon Religion itself, a chastening and purifying influence which Religion can recognize as a wholesome discipline, nay, as a *regia via sanctae crucis* through which it must pass to enter into a state of greater perfection than would otherwise be attainable.

It will be obvious to my readers that many hard questions might be raised about the topic of this essay which I have left altogether untouched. I have, for example, not attempted to show how I should apply the suggestions here put forward to particular cases of apparent clash between articles of religious faith and the results of philosophical or historical investigation. Nor do I pretend that only the limitation imposed by the space at my disposal has withheld me from the endeavour to grapple with difficulties from which greater abilities than mine might well be excused for shrinking. The subject of the relations of Religion and History I have lately discussed elsewhere.[1] With respect to those of Religion and Philosophy I will conclude by stating certain convictions which I have already intimated.

In the first place, Philosophy is rightly held to be distinguished from other activities of the human spirit—History and Science among them—by its refusal to make assumptions for the purpose

[1] *The Historical Element in Religion* (Allen & Unwin, 1935).

of its inquiry which are not thereafter to be called in question; and by its claim freely to examine the assumptions thus made by such other activities. But we need not go on to take for granted that Philosophy may not find among the assumptions which it thus examines some which it can accept, not as untested assumptions, but as necessary factors in experience.

Secondly, I hold that the consciousness of selfhood which is revealed both in intercourse with our fellows, in whom we recognize *other selves*, and in the sense of being in intimate relation with that all-embracing and all-permeating reality, at once 'transcendent' and 'immanent', which we divine to lie behind and within all which enters into our experience, is something which, unless it be frankly acknowledged as fundamental—not as sacrosanct from criticism, but as standing criticism—Philosophy will have on its hands as a mere enigma or surd, such as a great English thinker of the last generation, Herbert Bradley, might have called a 'scandal'; such as is, I venture to think, in his own philosophy, what he is often content to call 'a finite centre of experience'.

With these two convictions I would conjoin a third; that in the Christian doctrine which represents as belonging to the nature of the Supreme Reality that which is known to us in the mutual relations of persons, but which is apt to be relegated by theories of knowledge to a position of less importance than the relation of subject to object in mere contemplation, there is enshrined a thought of value to Philosophy. For Philosophy can never without risk of serious impoverishment ignore the testimony of the religious consciousness, whereof alone indeed, according to a remarkable saying of Bernard Bosanquet,[1] 'metaphysic comes to be little more than the theoretical interpretation'.

[1] *Value and Destiny of the Individual*, p. 230.

CONCERNING CHRISTIAN PHILOSOPHY

THE DISTINCTIVENESS OF THE PHILOSOPHIC ORDER

By ÉTIENNE GILSON

AMONG the reasons for the discredit in which the scholastic philosophy is held to-day there is none which goes deeper, or contains more truth, than the sterility of medieval thought in the scientific sphere, and the present-day difficulty of reconciling that philosophy with the conclusions of positive science. This sterility is an undoubted fact; but it was not an absolute sterility as is sometimes supposed by the ill-informed. In the thirteenth century, in the universities of both Paris and Oxford, there were men who conceived the possibility of a natural science of a type either purely mathematical, comparable with that of Descartes, or empirical, like that of Aristotle; and yet they did not for a moment doubt that such a science could be reconciled with theology. For reasons doubtless complex, the attempt was a failure; and it remains true that there is not, properly speaking, one single great scientific discovery which can rightly be ascribed to the Middle Ages, and that even if we should succeed in ascribing several, they would prove to be due to the initiative of isolated individuals whose thinking was outside the orbit of contemporary thought.

The most important consequence of this fact is that the great uprush of science in the seventeenth century, not having received its impetus from medieval philosophy, rose in direct opposition to it. Apart from the possibly unique case of Leibniz, who had a very deep and close affinity with Aristotle, there was scarcely a thinker round about the year 1630 for whom the choice did not seem inevitably to lie between science with its proofs on the one hand, and scholasticism with its uncertainties on the other. From then onwards the complaint made of the Middle Ages is not only that its speculations bore no practical fruit—an objection that we have already stated to be superficial[1] —but also and more particularly that it was unproductive in the sphere of thought: a very grave objection this time, especially as that Peripatetic philosophy which was incapable of producing modern science, fought against it from the day of its birth, com-

[1] See *La Vie intellectuelle*, 25 March 1933, pp. 181–94.

bating it in the fields of astronomy, physics, biology, and medicine, and meeting with a series of well-deserved defeats from which it has not yet recovered.

Facts such as these, of which it would be only too easy to collect historical evidence, are more than facts; they are indications of certain ideas. If scholasticism was not the mother of modern science, treated it indeed as a stepchild, it was probably not because of some kind of historical accident, but for reasons whose nature it is our task to discover. The whole question comes to this: Is its philosophic essence as such incompatible with the spirit of positive science? So the majority believe, and if it were so, we should not for a moment hesitate to abandon it; but it is our belief that the scholastic philosophy has only to become more completely true to its own essence than it has ever been, in order to be reconciled with science and even to help in its development.

If we are to grasp the meaning of this problem, perhaps the simplest way will be to go back to its original data, and try to find out what led to the break between the Middle Ages and modern thought. As we are studying it in its philosophic aspect, it is from a philosopher we must seek the explanation, and on this point no one can enlighten us better than René Descartes. The *Discours de la Méthode* appeared indeed too late to kill the scholastic philosophy, for the creative powers of thought had long since turned aside in other directions; but it remains true to say that it was Descartes who drew up its death certificate. He analysed the causes, he pointed out what was obstructing its thought and so crushing out its life; he defined the rules of a method which was productive of new truths simply because it was opposed at every point to the old method: and to do all this was to do more than abandon the old philosophy—it was to suppress it by putting something else in its place. The actual way in which Descartes replaced it is sufficiently remarkable to deserve our attention.

All Cartesianism, and in a sense all modern thought, can be traced back to a winter night in 1619 when, in a living-room in Germany, Descartes conceived the idea of a universal mathematics. From our present point of view the details of the method which he later evolved from it matter little. What was, and still remains, of capital importance is the spirit of that discovery, even, for the moment, one particular aspect of that spirit. A young mathematician in the ardour of his first scientific triumphs conceives the possibility, even the necessity, of applying generally to all problems indiscriminately the method which has lately brought him such dazzling success. Never in the history of human thought has there been known a shift of perspectives more tremendous or more daring than this, and on it we still live to-day.

It involved philosophy in a formidable adventure which, according to one's point of view, may be regarded either as the true beginning of its progress or the gravest of its crises. The first consequence of the mathematical method of Descartes, that from which all the others spring, was the obligation imposed on the philosopher to proceed always from thought to existence; even to define existence always in terms of thought. For the mathematician the problem of essence always comes before that of existence: the true circle and the true triangle are the definitions of the circle and the triangle; the figures produced in sensuous experience are only approximations to their definitions. It is not by chance that geometry is the science of sciences for Descartes as for Plato. In any case, the systematic application of the mathematical method to the real could have only one immediate result: the concrete complexity of things was replaced by a certain number of clear and distinct ideas, themselves conceived as being the true reality. To go back to the experiment of Descartes, the real from this point of view is reduced to two ideas and therefore to two substances—thought and extension. And since it is in the nature of ideas to be mutually exclusive, each containing everything that comes under its definition and nothing more, so it follows that it must be in the nature of substances to be mutually exclusive, each containing everything that comes under its definition and nothing more.

It is difficult to exaggerate the far-reaching effect upon philosophy of such a reform. Up to the time of Descartes, and particularly during the Middle Ages, it had always been admitted that philosophy consisted in the transposition of reality into conceptual terms. In this sense it is entirely just to describe it as an abstract conceptualism; but it is not just to accuse it of having *thingified* its concepts. On the contrary, the invariable method of the scholastic philosopher was to proceed from things to concepts: thus he required several concepts to express the essence of one single thing, according as he multiplied his points of view concerning it; and consequently no one was less liable than he to take for reality what he had extracted from the real. To convince ourselves of this we have only to consider the case of any substance. For the scholastic it consisted always of matter and form—that is to say two concepts—although neither was matter anything apart from form, nor form anything apart from matter. It was not St. Thomas who *thingified* concepts, but Descartes: and he could not avoid it once he began to raise our concepts to the status of Ideas. He took ideas abstracted from reality, and turned them into models: and it is not enough to say that reality must conform to them; they are the reality itself. The divergence between the two philosophies on this point leaps to the eye when one considers that for Descartes every substance is known because it is reduced to the content of his idea, whereas for the scholastic every substance as such is unknown because it is something other than the sum of the concepts we extract from it.

By turning the concrete into a mosaic of clear ideas, the mathematical method of Descartes raised difficulties whose solution was sought throughout the whole of the seventeenth and eighteenth centuries: in the nineteenth century it led in the end to despair—despair of philosophy itself. A universe of extension and thought can be expressed only in a deterministic philosophy to which corresponds an equally deterministic science: on the one hand pure spiritualism; on the other pure mechanism. From the outset nothing could be more satisfactory for science, and this is only natural; having set the method, it is bound to find itself in the results. But it is a different matter for philosophy: having given up the right to a method of its own, it must attempt to recover philosophic results with the help of a method which is not philosophic.

How can the domain of pure thought ever be in touch with the domain of pure extension when the property of substances is to be mutually exclusive? This is what Descartes does not tell us. He allows us a thought (not a soul), and extension (not a body): he is unable to account for the union of soul and body. When he offers as the solution a third idea, that of a union of soul and body whose truth may be felt but not known, he is himself contradicting his whole method of clear and distinct ideas. What Leibniz said remains true: 'At that point Monsieur

Descartes withdrew from the game.' When others after him take up the problem of 'communication of substances', they take it up on exactly those foundations laid by Descartes; consequently they involve themselves in a series of costly hypotheses, each of which, however much it differs from the rest, comes back at last to joining by a bridge fragments of the real between which the Cartesian method had dug a ditch which could not be crossed. It is, by definition, impossible to go direct from one to the other, so it is no surprise that the bridge must pass by way of God. The occasionalism of Malebranche, the pre-established harmony of Leibniz, the parallelism of Spinoza are so many metaphysical 'epicycles' to solve an ill-stated problem by rescuing, with the aid of complementary devices, the very principle which makes the problem insoluble. The great metaphysical systems of the seventeenth century are pure works of art, possibly the most perfectly adjusted systems of ideas ever produced, and precisely because, like mathematics, they deal with pure ideas, and so are entirely unhampered by the complexities of the real. What does hamper them is the difficulty of obtaining contact with reality. Having eliminated quality from extension, they are incapable of accounting for it when it reappears in thought. They set out in triumph from the idea, and in the end it is sensation they have failed to explain—that inferior act, suspect, even contemptible if you will, which yet reveals something which is not pure thought since it does not belong to the intelligible, and still is not extension since it already belongs to thought. The multiplicity of contradictory hypotheses required by the application of a principle may not be a proof of the falsity of that principle, but it is an indication of it. This is a case for returning to the rule of 'economy of thought' dear to Ernst Mach: the increasing complications in which these theories involve inquiry call us to look for simpler theories and to give them the preference.

The problem of the communication of substances raised insurmountable difficulties when it came to passing from one order of substance to another; the difficulty of passing from one substance to another within the same order was no less, for it was exactly the same. Malebranche saw this clearly, and if he radically denies all causal efficacy—that is to say, all transitive causality—in the order of secondary causes, it is precisely because, every substance being really distinct from any other, that sort of mutual participation of substances which causality is becomes in his system an impossibility. The monad of Leibniz, a simple indivisible entelechy which can begin only by creation and end only by annihilation, has 'no windows through which anything can go in or out'. Nothing could be more logical, but what follows in the history of philosophy is no less so. The lesson taught by Malebranche was not lost, and it was David Hume who took it up: if we do not understand how a body can act upon a body, or a thought upon a thought, or a body upon a thought, or a thought upon a body, we shall understand no better how it is possible for a thought, even a supreme thought, to act upon bodies; for our whole idea of God is derived from our experience, and it is impossible for us to have any idea of the causality of God when we have no idea of our own.[1] The scepticism of Hume then is in the direct line of descent from the mathematical method of Descartes: it expresses only the impossibility of re-establishing real relations between substances once we have made a radical separation between them. After Hume, if Kant was to save a causality which could not be found in things, all that was left for him to do was to make thought impose causality upon things. In this way the Cartesian cycle was completed with the purity of a perfect curve and in accordance with the demands of its original principle: starting from mind, philosophy, after several fruitless attempts to get outside it, declared its definite intention of remaining inside. This resignation must not, however, be regarded as a triumph: it recalls that of Descartes when, having given up the attempt to prolong the life of man, he declared himself content to teach him not to fear death.

We should be strangely in error if we supposed that the effects of the mathematical method made themselves felt only in metaphysics; they spread to moral science and thence to sociology. In this the initiator was no longer Descartes, but Thomas Hobbes, of whom indeed Descartes thought highly, though rather for his political philosophy than for his metaphysics.[2] What we are given in reality is a concrete complexity whose

[1] D. Hume, *An Enquiry concerning Human Understanding*, VII. i, edited by L. A. Selby-Bigge, p. 72. The whole argument of Hume in this text, which is of the first importance in the history of philosophy, is aimed directly and consciously at the occasionalism of Malebranche. Hume accepts his criticism of transitive causality, but he extends it from man to God.

[2] Descartes, *Lettre de 1643*, edited by Adam-Tannery, vol. iv, p. 67, ll. 10–26.

component parts are interdependent. Man is not only a rational animal but a political animal, because the State is the necessary condition of the perfect development of his rationality. For this reason the individual is invariably given to us in a State, outside of which he could not fully realize his essence, or even live, although the State itself has no life except in the individuals who are its very substance. It is then equally true to say that nothing is found in the individual which does not come to him from society, and that there is nothing in society which does not come to it from the individuals, since it forms them and they compose it.

Let us, on the other hand, imagine this complex reality decomposed into ideas each defining a substance: the individual would then become a thing in itself, the State would become another, and we should have a new problem of the communication of substances, as insoluble as the first. This is where Hobbes led modern thought when he defined men as isolable individuals, equal, for practical purposes, in the faculties of both body and mind.[1] As a result of this political Cartesianism, the individual found himself set up as a being by himself, and consequently an end in himself, the subordination of which to the State as a higher end became difficult, if not impossible. From that moment the political problem became what it was still for Rousseau: how to find in the individual as such, a reason for subordinating him to something other than himself—a problem even more difficult than the squaring of the circle with ruler and compasses. It is clear that for a social atom such as Hobbes's individual the right of nature is simply freedom to make use of any means he thinks fit, in order to secure his own good:[2] every man, says the *Leviathan*, has by nature a right to every thing. How, in that case, are we to reconstruct a social body with such liberties? How can it be contrived that in the name of my own right what is mine ceases to be mine? Out of this come all the 'social contract' theories which by various devices attempt to induce certain rights, laid down in the first place as absolute, to renounce themselves; which amounts to producing servitude from an aggregate of liberties.

[1] Hobbes, *Leviathan*, i, chap. 13. The early part of this chapter is simply the application to the political man of what is said about the intellectual man in the early part of the *Discours de la Méthode*. Even certain expressions of Descartes are to be found in it. The *Leviathan* was published in 1651.

[2] *Leviathan*, i, chap. 14.

Stated in those terms, the problem was so difficult that it could not fail to produce an abundance of attempts at its solution; but logically these were bound to lead to recognition of the contradictory nature of the problem, and to set up, one against the other, these two antinomic realities which can never be reconciled. On the one hand, we have the individual in the pure state; and as the definition of the individual as such is to exist by itself, so we arrive at the anarchic individualism of Max Stirner,[1] or the aesthetic individualism of Nietzsche. The Individual and his property. Nothing could be more logical; and Stirner proved himself a philosopher in his ability to push an idea to the purest formulation of its essence. If the individual is only an individual, then it is illogical to seek to produce the collective from the individual: the logical thing is the radical elimination of the State as a restraining force. But suppose, on the other hand, we take the collective as such; its very essence is the negation of the individual, and therefore it becomes a contradiction to construct it of individuals: and then it is Comte and Durkheim who are the true philosophers. 'Man is nothing; it is Humanity which is everything.' Here again nothing could be more coherent, for in a collective being as such, the individual as such can find no place; he finds himself eliminated, reduced, denied, in advance and by definition. Modern society therefore, in so far as it attempts to reform itself on the model of its own doctrines, is condemned to oscillate perpetually between anarchism and collectivism, or to live empirically by a shameful compromise which is without justification.

The cult of antinomies in modern philosophy is not a surprising phenomenon. Kant comes up against them; Hegel lives by them, and thinks that the endeavour to overcome them constitutes philosophy itself. The whole endeavour of medieval philosophy, on the other hand, was to avoid them. For St. Thomas and for Duns Scotus, the fact that they are reconciled in the real, proves that they are not insurmountable, and that if we concentrate on representing the real as it is, we ought not to encounter them. So it is actually we who introduce them by our mathematical method. If there is an initial error at the origin of all these difficulties in which philosophy has become involved, then it must be the error made by Descartes when he

[1] On this point see that remarkable work of V. Basch, *L'Individualisme anarchiste, Max Stirner*, 2nd edition, Paris, Alcan, 1928.

decreed, *a priori*, that *the method of one of the sciences of the real was valid for the sum of the real.*

Such a decision was bound to entail, sooner or later, much more than philosophic difficulties: it meant the disappearance of philosophy itself. Whatever indeed be the science whose processes are set up as a universal method, we are condemned in advance to extract from that method only what it is capable of giving; and that is science, not philosophy. Few mathematicians to-day would concede to Descartes that his *Méditations* are, as he liked to imagine, as certain as, or even more certain than, mathematics. And yet, considered in itself and without reference to the difficulties it involves, a mathematical type of metaphysics remained a possibility, because in both cases thought proceeds by construction of ideas and belongs to the order of pure ideas. It is only with the greatest difficulty that Cartesian metaphysics can recover the conclusions of scholastic metaphysics—the spirituality of the soul, the existence of God, the existence of matter; but it does in the long run recover them, and so may keep the consciousness of its own existence. It is entirely otherwise with Kant, for whom the physics of Newton provided the standard scientific method. All physical knowledge presupposes sensuous intuition; if then it is in relation to physical knowledge that we judge of other kinds of knowledge, it is clear that where sensuous intuition is absent, knowledge also is absent. At once it stands to reason that the fate of metaphysics as a science is settled in advance. Deprived of concepts, it is left with nothing but Ideas, in whose antinomies it becomes finally imprisoned.

It was from that moment when philosophy was despaired of as a science that there began the search for its justification in an order foreign to that of rational knowledge. Kant, who would not and could not do without philosophy, attempted to find a basis for the conclusions of metaphysics as postulates of moral science. Comte, who once and for all reduced objective knowledge to the knowledge of science, but who recognized the inevitable anarchy of a purely objective thought, sought to legitimize philosophy as a subjective synthesis made from the point of view of Humanity. Finally Monsieur Bergson, realizing the necessity of getting outside the limits of the scientific order if the philosophic order was to be attained, made a gallant attempt to make his way to an intuition beyond the concept.

But this very intuition—which is *experience* rather than *knowledge* of the real, and an ever fruitful method of investigation rather than a formula of discoveries—merely makes us critical of a science which considers itself a philosophy; it does not help us to construct a philosophy.[1] For although it may be necessary to achieve contact with the unexpressed, and to come back to it again and again, if we are to make any headway in philosophy, yet philosophy consists after all in what it is capable of saying about it, in spite of deficiencies of expression which have constantly to be corrected.

We cannot then be surprised to see philosophy to-day resigned to suicide and regarding its resignation as a triumph. From the method of one science, we can extract only that science and as much of the others as can be reduced to it. From all the methods of the sciences put together, we can extract nothing other than the sum of the sciences; which is all very fine, but leaves no room for an autonomous philosophy. If we take that road we come inevitably either to the absolute positivism of a Littré, which purely and simply reduces the content of philosophy to that of science, or to the idealism of Monsieur L. Brunschvicg, which reduces philosophy to a critical consideration of the stages passed through by thought in the constituting of science—the history of Mind.

Here we see philosophy arrived at a point where it seems difficult for it to go farther along the path of its own dissolution. But the last step of the outward journey is also the first step of the return, and here possibly is the point where consideration is necessary, preparatory to a new start. At first sight any idea of a return to medieval philosophy seems eminently absurd. It was that philosophy which survived with great difficulty in the dogmatic metaphysical systems of the seventeenth century; in eliminating all metaphysics, science completed the elimination of scholasticism itself. After three centuries of uninterrupted scientific progress, the same progress that relegated Aristotle's world to limbo, how could there be any question of going back to it?

And there is no slightest question of it: not only for reasons of expediency which, however compelling, would be wholly

[1] The pragmatism of James, an enterprise more complicated but less philosophic, sought to submerge both science and philosophy in the common category of efficiency. In order to save philosophy, it made two victims instead of one.

unphilosophic, but also because we are bound to condemn the scientific sterility of the Middle Ages for those very reasons which to-day make us condemn the philosophic sterility of 'scientism'. Aristotle also had exaggerated the scope of one science and the value of its method, to the detriment of the others; and in a sense he was less excusable than Descartes, for in this he came into open contradiction with the requirements of his own method, whereas Descartes was only carrying his through. And yet, philosophically, Aristotle's was the less dangerous error, for it was an error of fact, and left the question of principle untouched: to biologize the inorganic as he and the medieval philosophers did, was to condemn oneself to ignorance about those sciences of the inorganic world whose present popularity comes chiefly from the inexhaustible fertility which they display in things practical; but to mathematize knowledge entirely, and on principle, was to set strange limits to physics and chemistry, and to make impossible biology, metaphysics, and consequently moral theory. This is the point it remains for us to explain.

Since the Christian universe is a creation of God, not of man, the Christian philosophy instinctively looks on these problems from the point of view of the object. Any medieval philosopher would willingly concede to Descartes that the sciences taken together are only the human mind, always one and the same however many be the problems to which it is applied: but although the human mind in itself is always one, the things to which it is applied are not; and for this reason its methods of approaching the real must vary as much as the real itself. An Aristotelian discourse on *method* is therefore an impossibility; it is possible to speak only of a discourse on *methods*. To the order of abstract quantity corresponds the mathematical method; and even that must vary according to whether it is a question of continuous or discontinuous quantity, of geometry or arithmetic. For the order of physics its own method is appropriate, for there we have to study the movement and properties of inorganic bodies. For the order of biology yet another method is appropriate, since it deals with the study of organized beings; and so on for psychology, moral theory, and sociology. Nothing could be more incorrect than to regard these differing methods as isolated, for the method of a more abstract science dominates that of the more concrete sciences, and extends to their domain:

but they are specific methods, and remain distinct, inasmuch as every order of the real requires by reason of its very distinctness an appropriate mode of investigation. Thus Wisdom, or first philosophy, or metaphysics, lays down the guiding principles of all other sciences, and humanly depends on none of them: as the others study different modes of being, so it studies being itself, in its essence and its properties: it is the science of being as being: mathematics is the science of quantity; physics is the science of beings capable of movement, biology of living beings, psychology of rational beings, and sociology of human beings living in society. Nothing could be more comprehensive or more adaptable than such an attitude, and one fails to see *a priori* why a philosophy which adopted it need have misinterpreted one of the orders of the real.

Actually there was nothing which compelled it to do so. Aristotle's error lay in not being true to his principle of *a science of the real for every order of the real*, and the error of medieval philosophy lay in following him in this. Committing the opposite mistake to that of Descartes, Aristotle set up the biological method as a physical method. It is generally admitted that the only positive kinds of knowledge in which Aristotelianism achieved any progress are those which treat of the morphology and the functions of living beings. The fact is that Aristotle was before everything a naturalist, just as Descartes was before everything a mathematician; so much so indeed that instead of reducing the organic to the inorganic like Descartes, Aristotle claimed to include the inorganic in the organic. Struck by the dominance of form in the living being, he made it not only a principle of the explanation of the phenomena of life, but even extended it from living beings to mobile beings in general. Hence the famous theory of substantial forms, the elimination of which was to be the first care of Descartes. For a scholastic philosopher, as a matter of fact, physical bodies are endowed with forms from which they derive their movement and their properties; and just as the soul is a certain species of form—that of a living being—so is form a certain genus of soul—the genus which includes both the forms of inorganic beings and the forms or souls of organized beings.

This explains the relative sterility of the scholastic philosophy in the order of physics and even chemistry, as well as the inadequacy of Cartesianism in the order of the natural sciences. If there is in the living being anything other than pure mechanism, Descartes is foredoomed to miss it; but if there is not in physical reality that which defines the living being as such, then the scholastic philosophy will not only fail to find it there, but will never discover even what is there. Nevertheless it wasted its time in looking for what was not there; and as it was convinced that all the operations of inorganic bodies are explained by forms, it strove with all its might against those who claimed to see there something else, and clung to that impossible position until, in losing it, it lost itself. Three centuries spent in classing what must be measured, as to-day some persist in measuring what must be classed,[1] produced only a kind of pseudo-physics, as dangerous to the future of science as to that of the philosophy which imagined itself bound to it; scholasticism was unable to extract from its own principles the physics which could and should have flowed from it.

Our first duty then to-day is to restore to each order of the real what is due to it. In each order there is need to maintain the reality of form, without which it is impossible to account for structure. It is the principle of intelligibility in the real; positing the end for the manifestations of energy and the conditions for their fulfilment, it rules the mechanical aspect of everything, imposing on forces, even physical and chemical, certain structural laws which differentiate bodies, and maintain a real distinction between the energies themselves. Still more must it play this part in botany and zoology, where the *types* are facts and laws even more manifest. But *typology* is a scientific problem which is absolutely universal, and appears in the inorganic as well as in the organic; and although the sciences to-day are tending in another direction, the fact is still there, and the need

[1] It is clear that Aristotle's error, less serious than that of Descartes from the point of view of philosophy, was more serious from the point of view of science. To extend, like Descartes, a more general science to the less general sciences, leaves it possible to reach in these last what they have in common with the first; hence a mechanization, always possible though always partial, of biology: but to turn the method of a more particular science back upon a more general science amounts to leaving the more general without an object. Now, in missing the real objects of physics and chemistry, Aristotle missed at the same time all that bio-chemistry teaches us concerning biological facts—which, although it is neither the whole nor the most important part, is possibly the part which is most useful. And this, as well as being a serious gap in his theory, is the thing that human utilitarianism will never forgive him.

to reckon with it will always remain, and form is the only principle which allows us to account for it.

There is then no question of denying the hylomorphism of inorganic beings, but what does seem necessary is a radical severance of the idea of organic form from the idea of inorganic form. *Formae naturales sunt actuosae et quasi vivae*, said the Scholastics: between the Cartesian artificialism which makes animals into so many machines, and the Aristotelian vitalism which makes physical bodies into so many animals, there must be room for a mechanism in physics and a vitalism in biology. Every 'nature' requires a formal principle, but not every form is living.[1] Inorganic form is a principle of structure and of arrangement of energies, but not a source of energy which is calculable, or experimentally demonstrable, nor an inner spontaneity giving rise to observable quantitative variations.

But at the same time it becomes evident that the failure of physics in the Middle Ages does not detract from the validity of medieval philosophy: in a sense it even confirms it, since that philosophy failed only because it was not sufficiently faithful to its own principles. There is nothing to condemn it to the astronomy of Ptolemy, to geocentrism, to motive Intelligences as the explanation of the movements of the heavenly bodies; it is not obliged to believe with St. Thomas that bodies, by reason of their substantial forms, have a fixed tendency towards a certain place; nor that the reflection and refraction of light rays are

[1] It is indeed very evident that notwithstanding the error of imagination which induced certain of the Scholastics to conceive the forms of inorganic beings after the fashion of the forms of living beings, hylomorphism loses none of its value. It is sufficient to recall that every metaphysical idea arises, upon contact with the most general facts of our material universe, from a judgement made in the light of being—that is to say the light of the principle of contradiction—and that consequently any such idea is analogical, like the idea of being itself. Such is the concept of form, realized differently in inorganic beings and living beings. But since the human mind never thinks without appealing to the imagination and to sensuous experience, reason is naturally tempted to attach concepts which are metaphysical, and consequently analogical, to this or that image and univocal realization. It was to such an allurement that Aristotle yielded, his medical education tempting him to 'biologize' form in its whole extension. But let us note in his defence that if we look up the sixth book of his *Physics* and certain passages in the second and seventh books, we can see plainly that he glimpsed the part played by quantity and measure in scientific knowledge. If he did not go farther along this path, it may be simply because of his ignorance of mathematics, of which he seems to have known only simple proportion. It is possible that this fact had a considerable influence on the general trend of his labours.

metaphors of a corporeal nature intended to express immaterial realities. There is no one so absurd as not to recognize that what is false is false. And it is not only those waste products in science that must be and have been scrapped: everything in the metaphysical and psychological order which is founded on them must be scrapped along with them. So any revaluation of the medieval tradition must start with the principles, not judging beforehand what they can, or can not give, but putting them freely to the test, in order to find how far they have value in explaining the real. The problem is not to involve them in new systems with whose unstable elements they would seem once more bound up, but to restore them in their purity and their enduring fertility, and so to prevent at least the loss of the spiritual possessions which ought to remain a permanent acquisition.

The first and most necessary of those possessions is the existence of philosophy as an autonomous discipline of thought, and of a metaphysic crowning that philosophy. The old definition holds good, as even Auguste Comte came to recognize: philosophy is the study of wisdom. It includes then within itself the sum of the sciences, each of which is trying to forge the instrument adapted to the order of the real which it undertakes to explain; but beyond the problems raised by the different modes of being, there is the problem raised by being. And it is not: How does such and such a thing exist? It is: What is 'to exist'? In what does existence consist? Why is there existence at all, since that given to us does not appear to contain in itself a satisfactory explanation of itself? Is it necessary or contingent? And if it is contingent, does not it postulate a necessary existence as its cause and its explanation? Such then is the object of the ultimate science to which the human mind rises in the order of purely natural knowledge—the science of existence beyond the sciences of the ways of existing. It is called 'metaphysics'—a science which was founded by the Greeks, who clearly realized the need for it, and one which Christian philosophy will never allow to die, because it is the first and the only philosophy for which the very existence of beings seemed, and still seems, contingent—that is to say, requiring its own principle of explanation, whose nature must be studied by a science which is distinct from the other sciences, and which dominates them because its object is the problem without which there would be no other problems.

As long as there is Christianity, there will be metaphysics to link the various modalities of existence with Him *qui non aliquo modo est, sed est, est.* Every science in its own place, but, above them all, the one without whose object there would be no sciences, because there would be neither any reality to be known nor any intelligence to apprehend it.

Translated by D. A. Paton, University of Reading.

TOWARDS AN ANTHROPOLOGICAL PHILOSOPHY

By BERNARD GROETHUYSEN

THE starting-point of all anthropological philosophy, or all philosophy of man, is the ancient maxim 'Know thyself'. But what is it that man wishes to know about himself? What are the questions which he puts to himself? 'Know thyself' is the command. Is it in fact a command to know? Does man ask himself no other questions than such as can be answered by appropriate knowledge?

If we wish to grasp self-knowledge in the sense of self-reflection, we must not identify knowledge with scientific knowledge, but must give it a much wider significance. 'Know thyself', then, means not simply try to define yourself by concepts, try to determine the essential characteristics of the species 'Man', but become conscious of yourself, live in the consciousness of yourself, understand yourself, come to experience yourself, be present to yourself, live in the awareness of your present, come to yourself.

All these various interpretations of the maxim seem to lead us beyond the conception of knowledge as one in kind. Man wishes to live consciously; he wishes to know how things are with him. He is unknown to himself, and wishes to know himself. He has lived without knowing who he is, and now he seeks to become conscious of himself and his life. This striving finds expression first in the wide region that lies between life and knowledge, the region of reflection on life, of appreciation of the different values in life; it finds expression in what we may call the philosophy of life. Man makes notes, gathers experiences, reflects on the past, and seeks to express the meaning of life. He tries to hold fast whatever is of significance in the course of his life, so that by it he may interpret that life. He wishes that his life might become, as it were, transparent, that he might take possession of himself and of it. The historian finds an immeasurably rich literature of diaries, letters, autobiographies, and essays in which this striving for self-interpretation finds ever new expression.

In this literature the different tendencies that arise in self-reflection are not yet separate. Man reflects on himself and on the world. He tells of his own experiences and those of other men; he considers life in general, and comes back to his personal experiences. Many ways lead from concrete experiences to general considerations. Some particular experience is the occasion for considering life as such, and on the other hand general reflections find their justification again and again in personal experience. Thus, inasmuch as self-reflection takes the form of an undifferentiated consideration of life, the personal and the general are found in it in the closest connexion.

This is altered when the idea of man as it appears in knowledge, with its function of making objective, becomes of real significance for man's reflection on himself. We may best explain the change if we take as our starting-point the sentence, 'I am a man.' The man who strives for self-knowledge knows himself as a man. What am I? I am a man. Now the emphasis here may lie, as hitherto, on the individual 'I'. It was I myself that I wanted to know, not really man. But I can, on the other hand, ask the question about man with no reference whatever to myself. When I do so, the fact that I am a man appears to me as something accidental. I am a man among many, and the fact that I who put the question am a man is in no way significant. Even if I were not a man but some other being, I could, as it were, ask the question merely from the desire to extend my knowledge, so that my question about man would not in any way differ from a question about any other being or anything else I might choose. If, then, I try to apply to myself what I know of man, I see when I consider the real question that this is not essential to it. Although the fact that I am a man may be the reason why the question has a special interest for me personally, and why I have asked it at all, yet in the formulation of the question itself this plays no part. The very way in which I put the question compels me to give up thinking of myself as something individual. I have become, as it were, a 'he' to myself; I am an object like any other. I conceive myself impersonally like any other thing. If I wish to find the way back to myself, to re-establish myself, as it were, personally, I can do this only by rediscovering myself as an instance of a species, having no mark of the distinctive and unique.

With this, the original formulation of the question is altered. The question about myself, as I originally put it, was a question which arose in the context of an individual life. It was a personal question, a question concerning myself. Its significance lay precisely in its personal, vital character: it was its very nature to be man's questioning of himself for his own sake. This changes now that the philosopher takes my question up, and now that it is he who answers it for me. With this, the original monologue of self-reflection becomes a dialogue. On the one hand stands the individual, questioning himself for his own sake, on the other, the philosopher answering out of his impersonal knowledge. What, then, can justify the self-interest which originally moved man to obey the command 'Know thyself'? How can the individual establish the uniqueness which he ascribes to himself?

In some such way philosophical reflection leads to a transcendence of the first, naïve, human standpoint, and with it of the immediacy of the individual's relation to himself. It creates a gulf between man and himself, as he seeks to grasp himself by means of a general type, an idea. Man gives up his original self-centredness in favour of science. Original, pre-scientific reflection on the self enters, thus, on a new stage, for it is recognized that there can be no science of myself, but only a science of man. Regarded in this way, the command 'Know thyself' involves a contradiction. There is no such thing as knowledge of myself; there is only knowledge of man. If I am to reach knowledge, I must give up this immediate relationship to myself. Not as 'I myself', but only as man, am I knowable to myself.

But we have seen that self-reflection cannot simply be identified with scientific, philosophical knowledge. My need is, not merely to know myself, but to be, in some sense, present to myself as I am, to live in the consciousness of myself. I know that I am a man, and this idea of man may be constantly present to me, but I can find no means to remove the gulf which separates me from the objectively conceived being 'Man'. I am neither man, nor a man; I am myself.

The discrepancy between myself and the object of anthropological knowledge shows itself in two different ways. In the first place, there is the process whereby the 'I myself' becomes a 'he', and in the second, the process whereby that which belongs to me as an individual is universalized and deprived of value. Both of these moments in the transcendence of the naïve standpoint set limits to a philosophical self-reflection having the form of knowledge, and lead to other forms of man's reflection on himself. Confronted with the universalizing process of thinking, I cannot hold fast to the uniqueness of experiences, as they make themselves known to me in the setting of my life and that of other men. What I experience is for the philosopher only a 'case'. If I speak to him of my love, of the individual circumstances, of the object of my love, he will necessarily leave all these out of account, in order to see my experience as something typical, running its course in accordance with definite laws.

Now it is the function of art to restore the specific meaning of the experienced. It justifies, as it were, the original, vital point of view, from which the essential always appears to us only in the context of life. It preserves life in its uniqueness. Art seeks to express in some way the meaning of a particular happening, the significance for men of a given content of experience, never forsaking life for love of its idea.

Thus, in art, life comes to recognize its own concrete particularity. That which man in his individuality had experienced had somehow been destroyed by the universalizing process of thought. Where was he himself, this individual man, where was his individual life? He had, as it were, become absorbed in the idea. In art, now, significance is restored to that which concerns or happens to this or that individual. The whole content of a life, all that appears to the individual as *his* life, is made once more visible and palpable, and receives again the unique meaning which it had for the individual before any process of universalizing or intellectual apprehension.

Art in this sense is man's representation of himself, as philosophy is man's knowledge of himself. Self-reflection embraces both, but neither can be reduced to the other. Man cannot at the same time both see and know himself; seeing, he cannot know himself, and knowing, he cannot see himself. To picture man is not the same as to know him, and in the idea man loses his visible form. It may well happen that in the course of history there are poets who present man in accordance with what anthropological philosophy knows of him. This was so in the classical French poetry of the seventeenth century, when the poets made their own certain definite modes of interpreting man and his passions. It can, however, also happen that the creations of a poet cannot be traced to any determinate knowledge, that, as with Shakespeare, life itself is present, although it cannot be expressed in universal terms. What is essential is that we should recognize knowing and seeing, conceiving and representing, as two forms of self-reflection, as signifying two directions which man's reflection on himself may take, influencing each other in various ways but never becoming identical.

Both philosophy and art have thus their special place in the realm of self-reflection. To the philosopher, each experience, however important it may be for the individual, can display itself only as an instance of a general conception, and must seem in itself inessential. It is not *this* sorrow that is essential, but the fact that there is such a thing as sorrow; not that I die, but that there is death. There is no place here for the individual outlook, with its constantly changing meanings and its relation to a determinate pattern of life.

Through images, art leads man back to himself, to the unique significance of life, of his own life as well as of the lives of others. He rediscovers himself here; he lives with himself again; he lives in the presence of life as it can be portrayed but never known, seen but never conceived.

Thus man grasps himself in images, as he sought to grasp himself in ideas. The two cannot be made one. In knowing himself, man cannot remain present to himself as he actually is, as his life runs its course in the multiplicity of its individual concerns; and, on the other hand, in becoming present to himself in art, he cannot know himself. Only by philosophy and art together can he fulfil the command 'Know thyself'.

To these two forms of self-reflection may now be added, as a third, religious reflection on the self. *Anima mea*, here lies the fundamental motive of all religious reflection on the self. Neither the philosopher nor the artist can, in the last resort, speak of *my* soul. In religion man seeks to hold fast to the immediacy of the relation of his soul to itself. The soul communes with itself. What would it profit it to gain all knowledge, how could any imaginative intuition of life help it, if it were to lose itself? The soul which I seek to grasp by thinking, which speaks to me out of images, is my very self. I mean to seek myself, and nothing else; I am concerned for my soul. I seek the salvation of my soul.

This desire to hold fast to oneself is already implied in the original demand for self-knowledge. It is 'Know thyself', not

'Know him'. Man finds himself as a 'thou'. In self-knowledge this 'thou' turns into a 'he'. This, however, is no more than a special form which self-reflection takes in the course of its development. Self-reflection, as a particular attitude of the human mind, does not rest on this impersonal view of myself, but on the very being of myself, a being in which this 'I myself' does not turn into a 'he' but takes on the form of a 'thou', 'thou thyself'.

Self-reflection, in this sense, denotes a dialogue in which man engages with himself. Man speaks to himself; an 'I' which confronts itself as a 'thou'. I am this being, and this being is not just something or other taken from the all-comprehensive external world, but it is I myself. We have here a fundamental problem grounded in the very being of the self. Man remains united with himself.

This immediate concern of man with himself is the basis of all religious reflection on the self. The starting-point is not simply the 'I' but the 'self', not simply 'I am', but 'I am I' or, to put it in another way, not simply 'I am' but 'I live'.

Thus reflection on the self appears in different forms. Now one, now another form predominates in the historical development of this reflection. At one time it is religion, at another art, and at another philosophy, in which man finds the clearest revelation of himself. There have been times when man knew more of himself than he could express in art. At such times it is by means of philosophic knowledge that he interprets himself. Again, he feels constrained, not only to know about himself, but to see himself in a living representation. Life in its many-sidedness seems to him the essential thing. Then, again, he turns back to himself. It is his soul with which he becomes concerned, its longing, its destiny and its hopes; who am I myself, and what will become of me? From the manifoldness of life as it appears to him, man retreats into himself, turns back into his own soul. No knowledge and no art can satisfy him now. His question springs from his very self. He seeks his soul, his God, the 'thou' with whom his soul holds converse.

What is the attitude of the philosopher to these different forms of reflection on the self? At first sight, philosophy would seem to be itself one of the ways by which man seeks to grasp himself. Philosophy has to tell man who he is. Man has to know himself as man. Yet as long as philosophy limits itself to this task, it can perform only a partial function in the process of self-reflection. The need that is involved in the command 'Know thyself' cannot be satisfied by conceptual knowledge alone. It matters but little whether such knowledge is possible, whether it is given to man to *know* himself. What we are concerned with is to fix the limits of each form of knowing, whatever it may be, in its relation to reflection on the self. Is life knowable at all? Can man's coming to consciousness be wholly expressed in the form of a science? Is it merely by knowledge that the aim to live consciously is to be achieved? If this were true, there would be only one form of reflection on the self, the philosophical. But it is just the task of philosophy to establish its own inability to answer the question which man asks about himself, by recognizing the limits of knowledge, that is to say —its own partial function in the context of life. Even if man knew all that he was able to know about himself, the command to become conscious of himself would still not be fulfilled.

The recognition of this fact would be the task of a critical, anthropological philosophy. Not merely any particular piece of knowledge, but knowledge in general is one-sided, as contrasted with the comprehensiveness of the demands implied in reflection on the self. It cannot exhaust the totality of the given forms of man's relation to himself. Self-knowledge is only one side of man's experience of himself.

Thus critical, anthropological philosophy leads to critical reflection on philosophy itself in its relation to human life. It transcends the 'naïve' standpoint from which the philosopher sees the demand for knowledge as the demand which is universal and all-embracing. The philosopher must recognize the limits of his own problem, and the way in which it limits in advance the range of possible solutions. Even if the philosopher had found all that he sought, he would only have extended the sphere of his knowledge. The real task is to bring to consciousness the limits of this sphere, limits which are determined by the function of knowledge as such.

This cannot be done if from the outset the question is put from the standpoint of knowledge itself. For, in so putting the question, it is presupposed that it is knowledge alone that matters, and if so, our task amounts to this—to determine whether knowledge does or does not satisfy the claims which we make for it. Now the question about self-reflection cannot be reduced to a problem of knowledge. I do not aim exclusively at knowledge; if I did, and if my knowledge should finally prove insufficient, I should have to ascribe this insufficiency to the imperfection of my faculty of knowledge. Thus I shall not simply arrive at the result that there is something irrational which cannot be intellectually grasped, or that there must be something other than discursive thought, namely, intuitive apprehension. For in doing so I should not be going beyond the sphere of knowledge, but should be seeking merely to extend it. We should not be concerned with a critical insight into the limitations of knowledge as such, but should simply seek to determine whether that which we *wish* to know is actually knowable or not. Properly speaking, this would not mean that besides knowledge there is something else, but that there are other modes of knowledge besides ours.

Thus, the task of a critical anthropology will be to determine, from the point of view of reflection on the self, the limits of all knowledge. Man asks himself what philosophical knowledge can offer him, not this or that system of philosophy, but philosophy in general. It is true that all philosophy can be regarded in one way as a criticism of man, of such things as his naïve belief in the reality of the external world, his natural self-centredness, but here the relation between philosophy and man is reversed. Man criticizes the philosopher. He does not wish for more knowledge than the philosopher has been able to give him up to now; he wishes for something other than knowledge. The realization of himself, for which he strives, cannot be exhausted in knowing.

Recognizing the insufficiency of all philosophical knowledge, man turns to other spheres in which the demands of self-reflection might be satisfied. No other method of self-reflection, however, will satisfy him. In art man seeks, as it were, to draw near to himself, to perceive life in that immediacy of experience which escapes all intellectual formulation, to grasp the meaning of experience in its uniqueness. He thus tries to find in art's images what he could not find in concepts. And as every image created by art may be said to be an interpretation of life, he may rediscover himself in them all, yet not as he immediately experiences himself. In all these images he sees possible forms of life, but in none of them can he hold fast to his own reality. His reality resolves itself into a series of possibilities. He feels no longer bound to himself, and yet he cannot get away from himself. Where is he himself among the different forms which pass before him?

Now it is a fundamental characteristic of all religious reflection on the self that it seeks to lead man back to himself, that it tries to annihilate the gulf which there is in philosophy between the idea and the self, and in art between the image and the immediate reality of the self. The dynamic of all religion lies in religion's grasp of the problem of life in its original significance. Philosophy and art involve man's detachment from his self-centred vitality. Religion is concerned with *you*, not with man as such, nor with any idea in which you yourself would disappear, nor even with an image in which you would see only a possible form of your life and of life in general. Religion speaks to each one separately. The God of religion knows only you, and speaks to each individual, unlike the God of philosophy who knows only species and for whom the individual exists only in its universality. Each is alone with the God of religion: he asks the questions which concern him: he seeks the salvation of his soul. God is mindful of him, of *his* soul.

Thus man seeks in religion a place where he may hold fast to himself in the vital immediacy of experience. The religious man does not transcend the original attitude towards life; 'Know thyself' means for him, be mindful of yourself, tend your own soul, know how it is with you, do not lose yourself in that which distracts you from working out your own salvation. Seek God who sees you as an individual, while in the world and for the world you are always merely something particular and inessential.

Thus, religious reflection on the self is not a process which can be traced back to a purely intellectual effort. On the contrary, its foundation is man's longing to hold fast to himself. Yet religion, in dealing with what belongs to the sphere of concrete reality, must reduce it to the form of ideas and images, and in this necessity lies the insufficiency of all religion. The divine 'Thou' to whom man turns becomes by the processes of conceptual thinking a 'he' about whom much can be said; the individual soul places itself in a system which man tries to express in images and intellectual formulae. It cannot dwell in the religious awareness of itself, in its solitude with the God of religion.

Thus, none of the forms of spiritual life can by itself fulfil the demands of self-reflection. By different paths man seeks himself, and in the end finds only his shadow. He always becomes something different, an image or an idea. He loses himself in the very effort to hold fast to his own present.

From this dialectic, which springs from the insufficiency of each of the forms of self-knowledge and which prevents him from resting in any of them, man can rise to a new conception of the problems involved in the demands of self-reflection. On the basis of the knowledge achieved by a critical philosophy of man, a new philosophical attitude to these problems is adopted. The philosopher brings home to himself the conversation which man has held with himself throughout the centuries. He excludes none of the forms of this dialogue. For him philosophy, religion, and art are alike self-revelations of man. The philosopher does not allow himself to be bound by any of these forms, but recognizes the relativity of each of them, for each can grasp man only in its particular perspective, which is determined for each by the special conditions of the attitude peculiar to it. The object of man's search lies in the totality of these perspectives. But each perspective forms a closed system, and each system maintains its separate identity. Philosophy cannot become art, nor art philosophy, precisely because man's self-knowledge is distinct from his self-representation. The conception of man which is the product of thinking cannot be made one with the imaginative realization of life which is the product of artistic activity; idea and image cannot be reduced to one another. The same is true of philosophy and religion. What I know, I am no longer; what I am, I know no longer. Life and knowledge cannot be made one.

Thus, philosophy recognizes that in none of the forms which reflection on the self takes is the whole man present to himself. At the same time there appears a new task for the philosopher. He has to try to *understand* man's conversation with himself, and to interpret man himself by means of this conversation. He cannot confine man in an idea, for an idea can never give the whole man, the living individual, but he can try to bring man to an understanding of himself through his works, his thoughts, and his images. What man has thought, experienced, and devised is, as it were, the text to be interpreted, the text in which life appears as a never-to-be-completed whole.

If the philosopher considers from this point of view the historical course which reflection on the self has taken, he sees at once that man's effort to grasp himself is truly an activity by which man fashions his own being, and not a process which takes place outside him, a process of confronting himself and, as it were, observing himself from outside. He becomes conscious that each grasping of himself is at the same time a fashioning of himself. Self-reflection is at the same time self-formation, self-creation.

Thus the aim of an anthropological philosophy will be to make man understand himself. This understanding will embrace alike the ideas and the images of himself which man created and in which he created himself. Man sought to grasp himself, to be present to himself, but this immediate, unambiguous consciousness of himself was denied him. He can grasp himself only through the medium of his creations.

Thus the demand which anthropological philosophy makes of man is 'learn to understand yourself'. Man had asked himself the question, 'Who am I?' and had desired to grasp himself in his immediacy. In seeking himself, he saw himself and thought about himself by means of different representations. In each of these forms of reflection he was present, but in none of them could he become one with himself, in none could he rediscover his whole being. This failure was not due to any imperfection in his thoughts or images. Its real ground lay deeper—in the inability of ideas and images to represent reality and the being of the self as a whole. Because of this, man could not realize the meaning of his own life, nor could he become present to himself by means of self-knowledge.

Now in reflective, anthropological philosophy man seeks to *understand* himself. In understanding, however, man does not enter into an immediate relationship with himself. He can come to an understanding of himself only through the ideas which he himself has formed, the images in which he has given embodiment to himself, and the ways in which he has expressed his experiences and his longings. Thus anthropological philosophy, in its task of interpretation, presupposes all the different manifestations of human life. In his attempt to grasp himself in the idea and the image, man created the forms, by reflection on which he might understand himself. In seeking to know himself, he learned to understand himself.

A reflective, anthropological philosophy in this sense is necessarily at the same time philosophy of art, philosophy of religion, and philosophy of philosophy. It seeks to understand man through religion and art; it seeks to make man through them intelligible to himself. Its relation to an unreflective, philosophical anthropology is fundamentally the same as its relation to art and religion. For to it unreflective philosophy is only one of the ways by which man tries to grasp himself. It starts from the relativity, not merely of this or that system of philosophy, but of philosophy in general. Even knowledge is only a one-sided form of the realization of the self; it cannot give the whole answer to the question which man asks about himself.

In reflective, anthropological philosophy it is, as it were, man who questions the philosopher, man who from his own standpoint criticizes philosophy. Man, reflecting on himself, asks how far philosophy will take him towards that grasp of himself which he desires. Is it I whom the philosopher presents intellectually, or am I always another who will not be contained in the knowledge of the philosopher, whose being is not and cannot be identical with that which the philosopher presents, since it is not possible to reduce myself to a conception of myself?

Thus art, religion, and philosophy only point the way to something else, to man who expresses himself in them. All their utterances may be regarded as answers to man's question about himself. Yet it is denied to us to overcome the differences between these modes of answering the question. Only by a reflective understanding can man become conscious of the unity of their relations to man, and rediscover man in them, although without being able to transcend their distinctness from each other.

A reflective, anthropological philosophy cannot take the place of any of these attitudes of the human mind. It is not a new approach which seeks to take its place along with the others. It remains bound to them, and they are necessarily presupposed by it. It is an understanding of the many ways in which man expresses his experiences. It embraces them all, and because of this they find their unity in the understanding, although without losing their independent significance. A reflective understanding includes them all, and all in the same way, as expressions of human experiences.

Understanding in this sense means the unifying of these different and mutually irreducible modes of expression—the representation and definition of life. Through understanding, a unity is found in reflective consciousness, a correlate of the original unity of life, which had been given different modes of expression. It is man himself who is unified and understood. In the different languages which he speaks, I understand man, the speaker.

Thus to the unity of human experience corresponds the unity to be found in a reflective, philosophical understanding, and only in such an understanding can man grasp the totality of human experience. Here he finds a unity which none of his separate modes of expression could give him. Here he overcomes the one-sidedness of each particular attitude. But the unity which he finds exists only for reflection. The different languages, in which man expresses himself, retain their individuality. The philosopher seeks by reflection to understand them, without ever wishing to introduce a new language to take their place. He grasps the common meaning of these different modes of speech, as he seeks through them to understand man who expresses himself in them. He seeks to grasp images, ideas, meditations as words in which human life achieves expression.

Translated by Sheila A. Kerr, University of Glasgow.

THE TRANSCENDING OF TIME IN HISTORY

By GIOVANNI GENTILE

I

REALITY is spirit; and spirit never is but is always coming to be, not something given but a free activity.[1] That is what distinguishes it from nature, and, such being its essence, spirit, which is identical with reality, is history, or the process of self-realization. The truth of this is clearly seen whenever we have to study any actual creation of spirit, such as a theory, a work of art, a revolution, a reform, an institution, a law. Such a creation, as soon as we try to understand it, appears as a process, as something evolved. It has its own principle of development and a result of its own, which is the final and complete manifestation of that principle, revealing the force and significance of which it was capable. It is no doubt a unity, but a unity that can always be schematized as a trinity or as the necessary synthesis of two terms. Each of these terms exists in virtue of the other and accordingly distinguishes itself from the other, just so far as it is logically, and therefore inseparably, connected with it by a fundamental relation, a *tertium quid* essential to both.

Only by the help of this formula can we understand either the unity or the life of any great historical event, any simple thought of our own minds, or any feeling of the human heart. Nothing exists in the spirit or for the spirit but has, by that very fact, a beginning, a life, a conclusion. There is nothing which we can really regard as existing absolutely[2] either in the past or in the present.

II

But however easy it may be to recognize this relative or developing[3] character, which is what gives reality its historical nature, it seems less easy to understand the significance of that nature itself. The first result of the failure to understand it is the distinction of historical from other reality. The classical metaphysic never escaped from this distinction, and was led by

[1] *non immediatezza ma libertà.*

[2] *immediatamente esistente.*

[3] *di mediazione o di sviluppo.*

it to undervalue the conception of historical reality and, in fact, to misunderstand its essential character.

Those who make this mistake admit the historical character of all creations of the human spirit, but deny it to the conditions of the human spirit's existence. The man of science, who presupposes nature as conditioning the human spirit, thereby denies nature's historical character. The theistic philosopher, whether Platonist or Aristotelian, who presupposes God, excludes God from history. For him God is the first principle of the intelligible world, whom our thought is driven to discover in the world of experience: the unmoved mover, outside the process of cosmic evolution which derives from him. And so men of science and theologians come to speak of the eternal and immutable laws of nature, or, less naïvely, of the eternal thought of God. But such thought would be perfect, and therefore incapable of that growth and development in which human thought consists, and from which all its works from time to time proceed.

But such naturalistic or theological metaphysics are absurd in the eyes of modern philosophy. For modern philosophy, even when it does not claim that the thought in which the human spirit manifests itself is everything, at least makes the modest demand that it should be something. And it is on this something, whatever its limitations, that both men of science and theists must rely, if they are to infer an eternal reality as the presupposition of thought. They presuppose this reality as the *ratio essendi* of thought, but it drives us back to another presupposition which, though the very opposite of the first, is yet necessary as its *ratio cognoscendi*. Indeed, the first has always implied the second, even in the crudest theological or scientific dogmatism, both of which have always laboured to prove the truth of their statements, and to justify them to thought, whose authority they thereby implicitly and practically acknowledged. Thought, then, was admitted to be something, if not everything. But in fact this 'something', which cannot be denied without ceasing to think and thereby sacrificing the beliefs we may hold most necessary, this something, which is essentially thought, has its own character, which cannot be denied without denying its very existence. A man may submit himself before God or Nature by striving to conceive his thought as limited; but he cannot avoid allowing it the capacity of judging truly. And to judge truly is to submit itself to truth, to have value. And nothing can have value unless it is unconditioned.[1] Man, then, must think of himself as free, and must attribute to himself all that is necessary for such freedom. He can no longer believe himself limited, for what is limited is conditioned, determined, unfree. Limited he may be as a part of nature; which he thinks he must believe that he is. But as capable of distinguishing himself from nature, and of contrasting himself with all natural things as their superior; as the being who is here and now thinking and trying to understand exactly what he is, limited he cannot be, however sincere his professions of submission. He must be all or nothing.

Moreover, however ready he may be, in defiance of logic, to insist that spirit is conditioned, there is still the irrefutable teaching of Socrates that the only object of our knowledge is thought; there can be no actual object but an idea. We must either give up talking of God and nature, or open our eyes and confess that we can mean nothing but our ideas of God and nature. Then we shall find our theology in the history of theological doctrines; then nature, as science gradually becomes aware of its own logical procedure and of the source and meaning of its problems, will reveal itself as a product of developing human thought. Even those who insist that something exists other than spirit will have to agree that it exists for spirit as the object of thought, and that this object is one which thought strives to appropriate, entering into it, analysing it in order to reconstruct it and to breathe into it its own life. And so they will have to agree that, however much thought desires to distinguish objects from itself as an opposite, it yet assimilates them and clothes them in forms peculiar to the process of its own life.

III

The second result of failing to understand the significance of the historical nature of reality is a distinction which must be held even more false and misleading than that drawn by theology and natural science. This is the crudely materialistic distinction drawn by the philosophy of history itself. For though, as was remarked in the last paragraph, history is the denial of metaphysic, yet metaphysic, thrown out at the door, soon creeps

[1] *libero.*

back through the window and takes up its abode in the very home of history. In fact, we have not done with metaphysic merely by saying that everything is history or spirit in the form of history. Metaphysic lives so long as we allow any conditions of thought. And to deny all conditions absolutely, though necessary from the philosophical point of view, is not easy. The crux of philosophy is to define thought without presupposing any conditions. Even the theologian refuses to presuppose conditions—but only those which would limit the thought of God. For human thought he believes conditions must be retained; yet he himself, as he goes on, begins more or less to suspect that God and man, if they are to be very God and very man, must overcome their opposition and be identified, as they historically have been in the Christian church. The man of science, too, refuses to presuppose any conditions limiting nature, which he must conceive as something unconditioned, containing in itself the principle of all its works. But he confines the thought which has to recognize this nature within the limits of natural conditions. Here, too, it is thought which is being set free; but what thought?

Within thought itself it is possible, and indeed common, to make distinctions, and distinctions as metaphysical as those which make up the internal contradictions of theology and naturalistic philosophy. A distinction is easily drawn between the thought which has been thought and that which we are now thinking; between Aristotle and myself, who am not Aristotle but am reading him and who confront his thought as if it were an object, no less real in itself and no less conditioning my knowledge of it than the Nature of science or the God of theology, also supposed to be real conditions of my knowledge. A similar distinction is drawn between the historian and the Christianity or the Middle Ages of which he writes, between *res gestae* and *historia rerum gestarum*. And a further distinction is drawn between the written history and the thought which is now studying it. In short, history, whether as facts or as the account of them, is hypostatized as an object over against the subject who adverts to it, as an object supposed to exist without relation to any adverting subject now or hereafter. When that is done history is thought of as a reality mechanically related to its student, as a system already existing, and following scientific laws; as conditioning therefore our minds not only by the knowledge of it we may come to acquire in our historical studies, but also by its absolute determination of our whole personalities.

Reality in its so-called complexity is free because it is the whole of history, the whole of spirit. But this or that particular 'reality', the particular spirit which is the empirical knowing subject, who studies history and asserts it to be the essence of reality, that 'reality' is not free; for it is, in fact, not history and not spirit at all. The annalist who seeks reality in the past among the tombs is plunging headlong into the whirlpools of mechanism.

The presupposition we are concerned to deny is one which, till man becomes fully self-conscious, threatens to stifle him in the very act where he must be and show himself a man. Historical fact (*res gestae*) is not presupposed by history (*historia rerum gestarum*).

IV

The metaphysical theory of history is based directly on the idea that historical writing presupposes historical fact, an idea as absurd as those of other metaphysics, and pregnant with worse consequences; for no enemy is so dangerous as one who has managed to creep into your house and hide there.

The fundamental principle of this metaphysic is the idea of *historical truth*, which is distinguished from logical truth on the ground that the latter conforms to the nature of thought, so that thought recognizes itself in it under the guise of self-evidence. Historical truth, on the other hand, is supposed to be foreign to thought, which could never come to recognize it without going beyond itself. Historical truth demands something external to the thought which knows it, and this external object, since it conditions thought, is presupposed by it and precedes it. It is the *past*. Unless we affirmed historical truth, the idea of the past would never arise, nor consequently that of *time*, which arises from the relation of past to present. This idea, or intuition as it may be called, of time, like that of the past, on which it is founded, is among the most obscure which play their parts in the thought and life of man. It is one of the ideas which all employ and which might therefore seem one of the most obvious, but which are the most obscure, because as soon as those who use them try to understand their exact meaning they fall into the greatest difficulties. Reliance on this idea may easily plunge us in the most crucial antinomy—*Everything is past: Nothing is past.* For, indeed, everything of which we try to think as real, and as part of the real world to which we who are thinking belong, is some historical truth and presents itself to our thoughts as already existing. It must have preceded our actual affirmation of it, however immediately, if our affirmation is to be true. Yet the past *is* not; as beside the actually existing it is no longer, it is dead. Long ago or just this moment it has given place to what is now being done. It is beyond our apprehension. *Praeterit figura hujus mundi.* This ceaseless engulfing of the present by the past is the annihilation of all that thought tries to grasp as the stuff of reality. Our world melts and falls away before our eyes; merely to be thought of is to vanish.

Nor, so long as we take this abstract view of the past, can we escape from historical to logical truth, from the temporal to the eternal. Once we have taken the point of view from which thought presupposes a historical antecedent and itself thereby enters the time-series, logical truth itself becomes historical. For the eternal must now condition the temporal; we cannot exclude it from the reality which thought presupposes as its own necessary antecedent. So man is born and thinks because his birth was determined by God and by the laws of thought subsisting in God. God, therefore, may be eternal, but he is before man was or thought. And when man thinks of him, however he may once have been, he is past.

And what at bottom is the past? Thought lives by becoming conscious of itself, by realizing itself as the self-conscious ego. In the act of self-consciousness it creates itself as its own subject and object. And the objectivity of this object consists in its opposition to the subject, in not being what the subject is. The subject is consciousness, awareness; the object is, or at least appears to be, the opposite of consciousness and awareness. The things we are aware of determine our awareness;[1] by definition they are the unconscious.

This opposition or mutual negation, immanent in the act of thought, is the simultaneous creation of the two terms between which the whole world of thought has to develop. The subject is unity, the object multiplicity; the subject free, the object necessary; the subject present, the object past.

The object is past because its first opposition to the subject is abstract. The subject sees the opposition of the object to him-

[1] *è il limite del sapere.*

self, but does not see its identity with himself. Over against himself, he, who is one and must be one in the infinity or freedom of his nature, sees himself as another and does not recognize the one self for the other. And so this other seems to him something given to him, not derived from himself, something natural or external. And since it is external it must condition the very act in which he asserts its existence; and since it is a real condition of that act it must be asserted to be outside the act of assertion. It must be something merely given to him as the starting-point for the process by which he discovers it. It *was* before he was. And so we have the past. It is the unconscious being which precedes the being who is to become conscious. It is what we must have been while we were still looking for ourselves but had not found them. It is something natural, which is, when we come to think of it, the whole of nature regarded as an ideal moment in the process by which self-consciousness is realized.

The past, then, is the character of an object still affirmed in an abstract way by a thought naïvely unconscious of itself. It is the abstract *logos*[1] in which, as thought expands and builds up its world, the whole system of nature displays itself as the totality of what conditions human life.[2] Consequently it includes the whole system of history as the totality of what depended, indeed, for its occurrence upon men, but has now been actualized by them, so that, relatively to us who speak of it, it is a mere extension or development of nature. Nature, as we find it, is no longer virgin; but as a whole, however modified, it still conditions the life of the man who is now alive, thinking and acting. The molten fiery metal of the spiritual life, as it grows cold and hard in history, coalesces with sheer aboriginal nature, to form the solid mass which surrounds the human individual and confines him in time if not in space. History becomes part of nature, and the metaphysics of history[3] goes side by side with the naturalistic metaphysics which it had set out to oppose.

V

If we are to free the spirit from all presupposed conditions and to attribute to it the freedom it must have if it is to live at

[1] *logo*, perhaps 'notion', but the author has given the word a technical sense. See his *Sistema di logica*, vol. i.

[2] Cf. Gentile, *Introduzione alla filosofia*, Milano, 1933; and the article 'Genio e poesia', in the *Giorn. crit. d. filos.*, 1934.

[3] *storicismo.*

all, we must deny not only the presuppositions of theology and naturalism, but also those of historical metaphysic, and we must examine the theory of history much more searchingly than that metaphysic has done. Such an examination will insist that, when we speak of a thought free from all conditions, we should not be supposed to mean human thought in general, which is something we think of, an object of our thought. Rather we mean the only thought that really can be, the act of thinking, a definite thought, our own thought, the thought (if we are speaking of history) which is active in us while we think of history.

I have already said that the object, as we affirm it in abstraction, is multiplicity as opposed to the unity of the subject. Indeed, this heterogeneity of the abstract object does not admit of the self-identity which would make it a unity. This unity belongs to the subject, but only so far as the subject is actively self-conscious. The unity which can pertain to the object is simply that which it achieves so far as our abstract affirmation of it is absorbed in concrete self-consciousness. Accordingly, the object, as it is affirmed in the abstract *logos*,[1] is not a given, unique other, but an absolute, unrelated *other*, twice other,[2] consisting in a multiplicity whose heterogeneity is rigid and cannot be overcome. For this reason the abstract object of the materialist is atomistic, since he absolutely cuts off the object from the subject. Hence, too, the spatial particularity of all natural objects, since they are limited, and therefore other, in the absolute sense. From this also follows the multiplicity of the past, into which the object, when abstracted from the subject, crumbles away and disappears.

This multiplicity of the past is the abysm which yawns for present and future alike. For the present and the future are alike imagined as a production of the line of the past, and therefore they go along with the abstract object and come under the same logical demand for a condition of the thinking act. Time as a whole, being only a form of reality as that is abstracted in thought, does not presently condition[3] the acts of thought which think that reality, but appears to them as wholly past. The predictions of the historian, like those of the astronomer or farmer, can only be inferences from past facts according to empirical laws. And since we try to represent the future as

[1] *logo.* [2] *altro e altro.* [3] *non ha posto per.*

determined (as theology attributes such a representation to the mind of God), the very events assigned to the future are thought to have a necessity which is the property of the past, whose nature it is to be irreversible even by God. As Manzoni says sublimely:

E degli anni ancor non nati
Daniel si ricordò.[1]

As to the present, it is plain that a present which stands between past and future cannot be the present in which we see it and judge it to stand between those two terms. The first intervenes between past and future, the second includes past, present, and future within itself.

In conclusion, there is one present which does not follow the past nor precede the future, but embraces all times and the birth and death of all things, being eternal, infinite, immortal; and there is another present, the temporal now, which is never really present, but for ever eludes the grasp of thought, dies as it is born, and drags the future with it into the abysses of the past.

Clearly, the present which is really present is that of thought; the present which is past is part of the world.

VI

From this it follows that the temporal character of history is an unreal one. A reality thought of in terms of time is thereby projected into the past and so excluded from existence. Historical science, priding itself on the 'facts', the positive and solid realities, which it contrasts with mere ideas or theories without objective validity, is living in a childish world of illusion. It little knows how much these facts, so lifelike in their flesh and blood before the eyes of the historian, owe to the thought that called up their fleeting shades from the kingdom of death, to which, as facts, they had been justly condemned for ever.

In truth, facts, as a realistic theory of history imagines them, independent of the thought which has to ascertain them, facts in their multiplicity, particularity, and chronological order, are absolutely non-existent and as irrational and unintelligible as the so-called phenomena of nature. A fact is by definition *quod factum est* (*perfectum*); that is to say, it is something past and no

[1] *La Risurrezione*: 'Daniel remembered the years which were not yet born.'

longer real. To know it, in the only way that is possible, is to make it live again, to actualize it; and that means to take it out of time and free it from its chronological character, in order to transfer it from the abstract world of facts to the concrete world of the act (the historian's act) of thought, to which all facts belong in the synthesis of self-consciousness.

The realist's demand for facts is amply justified. Ideas without facts are empty; philosophy which is not history is the vainest abstraction. But facts are simply the life of the objective side[1] of self-consciousness, outside which there is no real constructive thought. This objectivity is identical with the actual concrete reality of the subject, as that presents itself to his self-consciousness. It is the object of perception as it is in itself before it has received form in perception; it is sensation. It is essential feeling, which is not, as the old metaphysic, entangled in naturalistic and materialist empiricism, imagined, the commerce of the subject with an external world; rather it is a movement initiated by the fundamental subject spontaneously. Sense perception, on which historical observation is based, is nothing but this spontaneity[2] of the subject reflected in the objectivity of self-consciousness; it is the concrete thinking which recognizes in the object the subject whose thinking it is. *Truth*, when we think of it as anything beyond the *conviction* of 'facts' in this sense, vanishes in the incoherent idealism which makes the reality of the divine world we inhabit into a coloured impression on the passive brain of a dreamer.

VII

To speak of facts is to speak of a temporal order, a succession. And this succession is a chain which we fondly imagine to be suspended by its first link from a starting-point. But no starting-point can ever be established except arbitrarily. And no starting-point for an era or a period has, in fact, ever been established except *ex parte post*, when thought has travelled far from it and is reconstructing a civilization or a past stage of itself from its present point of view. The only link of the chain which, in fact, has a relative fixity is the one we hold in our hand, not the first but the last, starting from which we retrace the course of the past, and seek the yesterday of each to-day and the antecedent of every fact. And in this we are con-

[1] *momento.* [2] *immediatezza.*

strained by the same logic which, by hypostatizing the object of self-consciousness, drives us, so to speak, to plunge from the eternity of thought into the past of time. We have not really behind the present a recent past leading us to it from a remoter past; that recent past is the first rung of the ladder by which we climb back to pasts ever more remote.

The only fixed point from which we can start is not a present following a past but eternity issuing in a temporal given;[1] that is the link to which we bind one by one all the other links of a chain producible to infinity. Thus the chronological order is constructed.

If we would understand how it comes about that this order breaks down, we must observe that order implies unity or system, and that the unity of time directly contradicts the abstract objectivity from which time is derived. This proves the inexpugnable presence of consciousness, with its synthetic activity, unifying the material multiplicity of time and spiritualizing it, by synthesis, into a system of juxtaposition with mutual exclusion of all parts, whether historical periods, hours, days, years, centuries, or moments. Outside such a system it would be vain to look for a before or after or, indeed, any arrangement of the separate parts of time. Within it, the before, like the after, only becomes so by ceasing to be so. Both must lose their successive character and be grasped simultaneously; they must put off the old chronology to take on the subjective thought-form of eternity.[2] When this has been done, the order, which appeared to unreflective or relatively unreflective thought as a succession, does not indeed disappear; rather, as we have seen, it is more firmly knit and founded. But, since in the process it has ceased to be a succession and become an inter-connexion of parts all mutually implied and conditioned in the unity of the whole, it has already passed over into the timelessness of thought.

In this transformation—a transformation *a priori* in which all intuitions of time are explained away[3]—the temporal series is made from an abstract object into an act of self-consciousness. Thereby the series collapses internally, just because it has now been ordered and intuited in its new-found unity. We may note, indeed, that every historical research, by which thought labours

[1] *che trabocca nell'immediato temporale.*

[2] *idealità tutta soggettiva dell'eterno.*

[3] *si risolve.*

to construct the temporal series beyond its own present act, is a regressive movement. The more we research, the farther back we are led. Yet the more we discover, the more closely present and past are linked; and, in the resulting historical thought, we enter on a forward process which reconstructs the discovered reality in the systematic development from its origins to our own day.

We might say that the regressive series of time belongs to the pre-history, and the progressive series to the history of thought. But, of course, pre-history and history are only ideally distinguishable. In fact, they are aspects of a single process, in which the very act that projects a past behind the present constructs the synthesis of both terms in a progressive order. The same thing happens whenever science works back from effects to causes, and, indeed, in all inductive inquiry, which, starting from judgements of experience, investigates the principles on which they logically depend. For induction is inseparable from deduction.

VIII

Our philosophical idea of the historical fact (as of all facts or concrete objects of thought and experience) retains the positive reality which is necessitated for the idea of fact by the fundamental anti-metaphysical demands of our 'positivism'. But, on the other hand, it rescues the fact from that past which is a kingdom of the dead and restores to it the reality and essential life of what is actual.

Common sense has an ironical fate when it abandons the one firm ground on which it might have relied. To escape being driven at the mercy of unbridled imagination over the boundless regions of abstract thought, it puts its trust blindly in a hypothetical world of objects. But such a trust is destined to lure it helpless into a labyrinthine series of facts and objects without logical connexion or any kinship to the spirit which tries to catalogue them. For facts can have no order or relation, not even a mechanical one, that is not derived from the system in which the synthesis of self-consciousness represents them. As soon as that synthesis is split into a dualism—as is done alike by the man of science and the historian when they presuppose the existence of facts—at once the belief in facts becomes an atomistic theory, which is essentially the negation of any order or system. So the historian and the man of science alike can find no rest. They go from fact to fact, but make no end of their seeking. The darkness, which the lamp of research was to dissipate, grows ever thicker, and, as facts pile up before the anxious gaze of the researcher, there creeps over him a sense of hopeless mystery.

But this mystery is merely the void which thought created about itself, when it formed the abstract fiction of knowable objects that are not, by imagining facts where none are. For such supposed facts, far from being the solid starting-point which scientific and historical theorists claim, are the abyss into which they plunge when they close their eyes to the reality that stares them in the face.

We may grant that, at the bottom of that abyss, the men of science, by help of that palpable imagery which naturally links men to the sensible world, escape the lingering agony of the historians. The latter, fascinated though they are by the phantom facts which they have themselves unconsciously summoned into a past series, yet cannot help once and again asking themselves by what right they lend the substance of the real world to things long ravished by the rage of time. In times past men were born and thought and laboured, suffered or were glad, conquered or were vanquished; but all these are long since dead like the flowers on whose scent and beauty in their lives they feasted, or like the leaves which they saw growing green in spring or sere and fallen in the autumn. Their memory lives; but a world remembered, like the world of dreams, is nothing; and remembering no better than to dream. Strong as is our natural tendency to trust the memory which sets the stamp upon our personality, upon our outlook on the world, and so upon the world which we call ours, yet gradually there lifts its head a disheartening scepticism, which distrusts all historical evidence and wraps every statement of the past in doubt.

For one who takes his stand on historical realism and believes in independent facts,[1] the whole world of history can have no more solid reality than the abode of shadows through which Dante's imagination roams.

But luckily the historian need not hold this metaphysic of history. The more intense and vigorous his historical activity and the greater his value as a historical thinker, the more

[1] *astratto oggettivismo.*

lively, though perhaps unconscious, is his awareness of the 'subjectivity' of the facts that interest him. They have import for him only in proportion to the interest which he is prepared to take in them. He knows that this interest of his, which gives the fact its historical significance and makes it the object of his researches, is not shared by all; it presupposes a certain culture, a certain mental disposition, that is to say, a particular kind of mind. The earth was not for Homer what it would be for Columbus; for the child the world is confined in narrower bounds than for the man, much narrower than for the astronomer. Similarly, when human thought turns its attention to the past, it develops and defines the character of that past and of itself concurrently. A past event is ancient or modern, or at least relatively so, according to the thinker's intellectual development. The historian, in short, knows well enough that the life and meaning of past facts is not to be discovered in charters or inscriptions, or in any actual relics of the past; their source is in his own personality. But this personality, too, must not be thought of in abstraction, but for what it really is, with its peculiar culture, peculiar interests, and peculiar relation to the documents, the monuments, and the excavations. Man is always a man in virtue of being a man of his own world *omnimodo determinatus*.

IX

When we have corrected the point of view from which historical facts must be appreciated, when we have explained historical reality as the concrete synthesis by which we apprehend it in an act of self-consciousness, it is clear that the facts recorded are identical with the recording of them. And that very form of reality, namely history, which seemed to invite thought to presuppose a temporal reality, is itself reduced to the instantaneous or timeless act of thought. History as it is made, not as it is abstractly imagined, the only history that really is, is not in time but in thought and of thought; it is eternal. We cannot admit the dualism, propounded by Giovanni Battista Vico in his *Scienza nuova*, between the temporal and the logical[1] or eternal history. From the only legitimate point of view, that of the actual synthesis of self-consciousness (which is itself not in time but includes time), there is but one history, which is logical[1] and eternal.

[1] *ideale*.

The time of history only lives by dying into thought and being reborn *sub specie aeterni.* If our fear of death comes from the constant spectacle of 'perished seasons'[1] which draw us after them like a whirlpool into which we must one day sink, we are frightened by a shadow. For this past, this time which is for ever being wrapped about

> l'uomo e le sue tombe
> e l'estreme sembianze e le reliquie
> della terra e del ciel,[2]

cannot be conceived as the *mors immortalis* of Lucretius. It is no death from which life will never spring again; rather it is the death of what dies by putting on eternity, and dies because it has a part in that immortality which, by including time, makes it eternal. The past is time losing itself in the eternity of the thought which grasps it.

Leopardi says that time '*se ne porta ogni accidente*',[3] and asks himself:

> Or dov' è il suono
> di quei popoli antichi? or dov' è il grido
> de' nostri avi famosi, e il grande impero
> di quella Roma, e l'armi, e il fragorio
> che n' andò per la terra e l'oceano?[4]

But his answer could only be given by one who believed in an independent world:[5]

> Tutto è pace e silenzio, e tutto posa
> il mondo, e più di lor non si ragiona.[6]

An answer which contradicts itself.

Translated by E. F. Carritt, University College, Oxford.

[1] Leopardi, *L'Infinito.*

[2] Foscolo, *I Sepolcri*: 'Man and his tombs and the last tokens and the ashes of the earth and heavens.'

[3] *La sera del dì di festa*: 'bears all its sons away.'

[4] 'Where is now the sound of those ancient peoples? Where is now the rumour of our famous fathers, and the mighty empire that was Rome, and the sound of its arms that went through every land and sea?'

[5] *astratta oggettività.*

[6] 'All is peace and silence; the world is quiet and there is no more speech of them.'

SOME AMBIGUITIES IN DISCUSSIONS CONCERNING TIME

By L. SUSAN STEBBING

THE problem of Time and Change has been described as 'the hardest knot in the whole of philosophy'. Every one is familiar with St. Augustine's dictum: 'Quid est tempus? Si nemo a me quaerat, scio; si quaerenti explicare velim, nescio.' It would be a mistake to suppose that St. Augustine knew something when no one was asking him a certain question, but ceased to know that very same thing when he was asked that question. On the contrary, what his *scio* expressed was merely his familiarity with a certain experience; his *nescio* must have expressed his inability to answer *certain kinds of questions about* that experience, and thus his inability to formulate a theory about that experience. To ask and to answer these questions and to formulate that theory is, it seems, the problem of Time. But only philosophers ask these questions; only a philosopher would formulate a theory in terms of those answers. To explain what time is is quite different from having the experience which led St. Augustine to say *scio*.

I have referred to St. Augustine's well-known dictum not merely because it is well known. My purpose is to emphasize the consideration that there are questions asked about time which might have been answered by St. Augustine or by his contemporaries. In other words, the answers to these questions are wholly independent of knowledge obtained by physicists. It may turn out to be the case that some or all of these questions are nonsensical; in that case they would not strictly be questions at all. But it is rash to assume at the outset that a question which seems unanswerable is in fact not a proper question to be asked. Even if this were so, still some account can be given of how it is that the question has seemed to be sensible. We do not knowingly talk nonsense. It may, then, be worth while to consider some of the questions which philosophers have been wont to ask about time.

The most common of these questions is whether time is real. A considerable number of philosophers have maintained that time is not real; some have been content to dismiss time as an illusion; others have granted to time a partial reality. Few have paused to ask what is meant by the assertion or the denial of the reality of time. Of these few McTaggart alone makes clear what exactly it is that he is denying when he denies that time is real. He sees that the denial entails acceptance of the following consequences: 'Nothing is really present, past, or future. Nothing is really earlier or later than anything else or temporally simultaneous with it. Nothing really changes. And nothing is really in time. Whenever we perceive anything in time—which is the only way in which, in our present experience, we do perceive things—we are perceiving it more or less as it really is not.'[1] Professor G. E. Moore, who does not deny the reality of time, agrees with McTaggart, who does deny it, with regard to what this denial entails.[2] It is important to recognize that these consequences *at least* must be accepted if time be rejected as unreal, and, further, that the acceptance of them is paradoxical to common sense. McTaggart has the unusual merit of recognizing the paradoxical nature of his view, of seeing clearly the necessity of justifying the acceptance of the paradox, and of attempting to show in detail what characteristics of the eternal are 'misperceived' when any one believes that something is in time. I shall briefly consider his argument.

Positions in time form a series which may be distinguished in two ways, viz. as past, present, and future, and as earlier and later. McTaggart carefully distinguishes between these; he calls the first the A series, the second the B series. He seeks to show that the A series is fundamental to time, and that the A series is self-contradictory and, therefore, impossible. If this be so, it follows that time is unreal, in the sense in which that statement has already been explained. The fundamental premiss upon which McTaggart's argument depends is that time implies change. Granted this, the argument may be shortly summarized. (*a*) The positions in the B series do not change but are permanent and unalterable; for example, the death of Socrates is always earlier than the birth of Newton. (*b*) The characteristics of an event cannot change; if it is ever true of an event

[1] *The Nature of Existence*, vol. ii, par. 333.

[2] See *Philosophical Studies*, pp. 209–10. Moore recognizes the importance of translating the statement 'Time is unreal' into concrete statements such as those given by McTaggart. To spell time with a capital 'T' may mislead us.

that it is the death of Queen Anne then it always was, is, and will be true of it. (*c*) The characteristics of substances, e.g. a poker, cannot change. If my poker is hot at two o'clock on a particular Monday, then it is always 'a quality of that poker that it is one that is hot on that particular Monday'.[1] (*d*) Change occurs only in virtue of the A series; the position in the B series of the event which is the death of Queen Anne does change with respect to the A series, since this event was in the remote future, then in the near future, then in the present, then in the past, and continues to become more remotely past. If the A series were real, change would be real; but unless the A series is real, change cannot be real; if change is not real, then time is not real. It remains to show that the A series is not real. (*e*) The A series is a series of past, present, and future. Past, present, and future are incompatible determinations of an event, yet every event has them all, with the possible exception of the first event (if there is one) and of the last event (if there is one), and even these have two incompatible determinations. For example, the death of Queen Anne is past, has been future, and has been present.[2] Thus the reality of the A series leads to a contradiction, and must be rejected. (*f*) The B series appears to be temporal because it is combined with the A series which alone gives significance to 'earlier than' and 'later than' (or 'before' and 'after'). When the unchanging order of earlier and later is reinterpreted without reference to the A series, then the B series is seen to be unreal, or is recognized as the non-temporal C series which is the reality of the B series.

It is not my intention to examine McTaggart's argument in detail, nor to discuss the C series, the misperception of which accounts for our erroneous belief that there is a temporal series. My interest is confined to certain points in the argument which bear upon the subject of this article. Of the ambiguities which infect discussions concerning time, some at least seem to me to be prominent in McTaggart's argument. These ambiguities are connected with the use of the words 'changeless', 'changing', 'permanent', 'timeless', 'temporal', 'always', 'never'. I believe that these words (and their synonyms and derivatives, e.g. 'alterable', 'unalterable') are used in different senses in

[1] Loc. cit., par. 315.

[2] McTaggart holds that the attempt to get rid of the *tense* in these expressions involves a vicious infinite regress or a vicious circle (see op. cit., §§ 329–33).

different contexts, that in these different contexts they may be so used as to be free from any harmful ambiguity, but that they are sometimes so used as to be susceptible of different interpretations without the possibility of these different interpretations having been recognized. In that case, of course, it is not surprising that difficulties should arise. That these words are used with harmful ambiguity must now be shown in detail.

Premiss (*a*) in the argument given above states that the *positions* in the B series do not change. (Here 'positions' can be taken to stand for either events or moments of absolute time, if such moments exist.) This must be granted. Given any one position, then every other position is either earlier or later than this position, and not both. In other words, the *positions* have a *fixed* order and the order is serial. The order is *timeless*; it is, then, equally non-significant to say that the order 'does not change', i.e. is unchanging, and to say that it 'does change', *provided that* the word "change" be used in the sense in which it is used when we say that a process 'is changing', or 'has changed', &c. The point to be noticed is that 'So and so does not change' is not the contradictory but the *contrary* of 'So and so changes'. Neither may be predicable, namely, if *so and so* does not permit of temporal determinations. It is, for example, nonsense to say 'The order of the integers 1, 2, 3, . . . (arranged in a series generated by the relation of *next successor*) does not change' *provided that* "change" is used in this context in its *usual sense*, i.e. in the sense in which it is used in the statement 'Time implies change'. I shall henceforth call this usage of "change" (its synonyms and derivatives) the *strict sense*. It is equally nonsensical to say that the order of the integers 'changes'. The point is that such a statement would be *nonsensical* and not *false*. But we do sometimes use "does not change" and "is unchanging" and "is unalterable" as synonyms for "is fixed" when "is fixed" does not mean anything to do with time or with place, but is to be defined by reference to logical relations. In this sense 'is fixed' is equivalent to 'is fixed with respect to'. Our language is full of temporal, no less than of spatial, metaphors, as is exemplified, for instance, in the phrase 'generated by the relation of'. The reasons for these linguistic forms are not far to seek. But it is a grave, though a not uncommon, mistake to take these phrases in a literal sense. So to take them is to manufacture paradoxes. Thus, from the true statement 'The death of Socrates is an event which is fixed with respect to the event which is the death of Queen Anne, as being earlier than it, and, *therefore*, as being *not* later than it', we must not infer that the two events are in *unchanging* relations to each other, for 'unchanging' in this context is meaningless. The phrase 'is fixed with respect to the relation of' means 'has a determinate place in the series constructed by the relation'. Here, 'place' (or 'position', which could be significantly substituted for 'place') has no more a temporal than a spatial significance. The series is a *timeless order*. Of that which is timeless it is non-significant to predicate either *changing* or *unchanging* in the strict sense. The order of change cannot significantly be said to change (or not to change) any more than the concept of change can be said to change (or not to change).

Similar ambiguities arise in the use of the words "permanent" and "always". Consider, for example, a statement made by McTaggart when he is distinguishing between the distinctions *earlier-later* (B series) and *past-present-future* (A series). He says: 'The distinctions of the former class are permanent, while those of the latter are not. If M is ever earlier than N, it is always earlier. But an event which is now present, was future, and will be past.'[1] In this statement 'permanent' is used as a synonym for 'unalterable' or 'unchanging' in the sense of 'fixed with respect to' already discussed; it is not used as a synonym for 'unchanging' in the strict sense. Or, if it *is* so used, then McTaggart has written nonsense without noticing that he has done so. Permanence, as commonly used, involves *persisting* through time, i.e. *continuing unchanged*, where 'unchanged' is used in the strict sense. But in this common usage 'permanence' is *not* a synonym of 'is fixed with respect to'. I suggest that McTaggart's statement is significant *only* if 'permanent' be used in an improper (or, at least, an unusual) sense. If so used, it is true. The difficulty is that he has not noticed that he is using it in an unusual sense; hence from his *true* statement, he draws conclusions that are false. He has failed to see his mistake because he has failed to notice the ambiguity.

Again, when he says that if M is ever earlier than N, 'it is always earlier,' the use of "always" give rise to ambiguities. It should be observed that I do not say that "always" as used in the statement I have just quoted is ambiguous. On the

[1] Loc. cit., par. 305.

contrary, I think the statement is clear. "Always" is here used in a manner analogous to the way in which McTaggart has used "permanent" in his preceding statement, which I have just discussed. Indeed, his statement, 'If M is ever earlier than N, it is always earlier' is certainly given by him as a further explanation of his statement, 'The distinctions of the former class (the B series) are permanent.' But, as I have already pointed out, this usage, although clear in its context, may, nevertheless, give rise to ambiguity. It is almost certain that ambiguity will result if such words as "permanent" and "always" are not used in their strict sense in a discussion about change and time. McTaggart has not avoided this mistake.

The words "always", "never", "sometimes" ought to be very carefully used when we are discussing time. There is a now familiar usage of these words in the context of propositional functions. If ϕx be a propositional function we can significantly say 'ϕx is always true', 'ϕx is never true', 'ϕx is sometimes true'. What 'ϕx is always true' *means* is 'ϕx is true in all cases', i.e. 'ϕx is true for all values of x'. The expression does *not* mean 'ϕx is true at all times', for "true at all times" is nonsensical. *True* is a timeless predicate. This usage of "always" is familiar, and is clear in the given context. But it is an unfortunate usage, since "always" is most commonly used to mean "at all times", as, for instance, in the sentence, 'He always suffers fools gladly.' Truth, however, does not admit of temporal determinations. The usages of "never" and "sometimes" can be dealt with in the same way.

That McTaggart has failed to notice these ambiguities is further borne out by another part of his argument. He says: 'There can be no change unless some propositions are sometimes true and sometimes false. This is the case of propositions which deal with the place of anything in the A series—"the battle of Waterloo is in the past", "it is now raining". But it is not the case with any other propositions.'[1] This statement involves, I think, two mistakes. The first is the mistake of supposing that "sometimes true" means "true at some times". That this is a mistake I have tried to show in the case of the expression "always true". Thus "sometimes true" means "true in some instances". The second mistake consists in supposing that a proposition could have instances, or cases. It is propositional

[1] Loc. cit., par. 317.

functions—not propositions—which have instances. Thus, for example, 'the battle of Waterloo is in the past' is equivalent to 'There is a time *t* which is later than the time *t′* at which the battle of Waterloo happened'.[1] 'The battle of Waterloo is present' is equivalent to 'The battle of Waterloo is happening at *t* and there is no time *t′* which is later than *t*'.[2] The values of *t*, in the propositional functions, which must be assigned in order that a true proposition should result are different in the two cases. The propositions are *different*; there is not *one* proposition which is true at one time and false at another time. To say that the values of *t* are different values just *means* that the values of *t* which would satisfy the one propositional function would not satisfy the other. It follows that if I say 'The battle of Waterloo is past', and again 'The battle of Waterloo is past', the latter proposition is not the very same proposition as the former. For "is past" means "is earlier than now", and "now" does not denote in the first of these propositions what it denotes in the second. But, though different, the two propositions have a peculiar kind of correspondence in that they are systematically connected. This systematic connexion is due to the serial nature of time.

In spite of what has just been said with regard to the meaning of "is past" as it occurs in 'The battle of Waterloo is past', it is not true that past, present, future are to be defined with reference to earlier than, and later than, nor that the former set of distinctions is less fundamental than the latter. On the contrary, I agree with McTaggart in holding that the A series is more fundamental than the B series. That this view is not incompatible with what has been said in the preceding paragraph I shall shortly attempt to show. But first, I wish to point out, with regard to what I have said concerning the timeless order of the terms in the B series, that McTaggart seems to me to be mistaken in holding that the following statements are all true, viz. (1) the B series is unalterable (or unchanging); (2) time implies change; (3) the B series *appears* to be temporal. Certainly the positions in the B series do not appear to be alterable; no one would hesitate to accept McTaggart's statement that they are 'permanent' (in the sense in which he must have intended to use the word "permanent"). We may, then,

[1] This statement is further discussed below. See p. 120.

[2] See p. 120 below.

accept (1). If, however, we accept (2), then we cannot say that the B series *appears* to be temporal, where this clearly means "appears to be but is not". In my opinion the B series is a *temporal series*,[1] but we must be careful to notice that "temporal", in the phrase "temporal series", is a descriptive epithet of a curious kind, just as it is in the phrase "temporal fact". The B series can be said to be a temporal series because the *terms*, arranged in the timeless order *earlier-later*, are events. It is only to events that we apply the words "earlier than" and "later than"; hence any *term* which could significantly be said to be earlier, or later, than some other term must be an event. When the terms are regarded from the point of view of *earlier-later*, they are regarded as in a serial order which it is convenient to call 'temporal' since the *elements* ordered are temporal. But the order is not temporal; it is timeless. Similarly, we speak of a 'temporal fact'. This use of "temporal" is analogous to the use of "material" in 'material fact', and to "mental" in 'mental fact', and to "geological" in 'geological fact', and so on. A *fact* is timeless. But some facts are facts about a time; such facts may be referred to as 'temporal facts' where "temporal" will be a descriptive, transferred epithet, just as "mental" in 'mental fact' is a transferred epithet. A mental fact is a fact about a mental state, or a fact about a mind, in which case the fact is a fact of higher level. A material fact is a fact about a material object, and so on. It is because the epithet is transferred that I called it a 'curious kind' of epithet.

Thus, McTaggart's argument that the B series is not really a temporal series and that the A series is unreal seems to me to amount to nothing more than a repudiation of change, combined with the fundamental premiss that time implies change. This fundamental premiss I have granted. But McTaggart has done nothing, so far as I can see, to show that change is unreal. He has failed to notice that the whole of his argument against the reality of the A series depends upon his having already accepted the premiss *change is unreal*. But if events are as such passing, then changes evidently occur; here "change" is used in that sense in which *Time implies change* must be accepted. The root of the contradiction which McTaggart finds in the A series seems to me to lie in the fact that he regards the terms in the

[1] McTaggart holds that the B series 'is really a series' but that 'it only appears to be temporal' (loc. cit., § 736). The reality of the B series is the C series.

A series as though they were timeless characteristics, notwithstanding his insistence that *if time were real*, then time would be an A series. Consider, for instance, his assertion that any attempt to explain what is meant by "has been", "is", "will be", involves a vicious infinite or a vicious circle.[1] He argues that 'M is present' means 'M is present at a moment of present time' (and similarly for past and future). But he is willing to admit that the *is* of 'M is present' is not a timeless *is*; nevertheless, he treats it as though it were a timeless *is* of predication. Provided that the *is* of 'M is present' is a temporal 'is', then I cannot see any reason for supposing that 'M is present' *means* 'M is present at a moment of present time', though the latter is certainly *entailed* by the former. The point of my criticism is that McTaggart has failed to take seriously the view that *was*, *is*, and *will be* are temporal. This statement brings me to the consideration of the very simple, and no doubt crude, way in which I should deal with statements involving the A series.

We say 'Something is going to happen', and it does happen. That something is *going to happen* is what we mean by *future*. We say 'Something is happening now'. That something is *happening now* is what we mean by *present*. We say 'Something has happened'. That something *has happened* is what we mean by *past*. *Time* covers *is going to happen*, *is happening now*, *has happened*. Apart from happenings there is no sense in the word "time". But it is a mistake to regard *Time* as a substance, or to try to use the word "Time" as a substantive. It may be supposed that no one would do so. But this would be a mistake. It is, indeed, an error so common and so difficult to avoid that it deserves to be described as 'the fallacy of the substantive'.[2] When it is asked, 'Was Time created?', 'Has Time a beginning?', 'Will Time end?', then Time is being regarded as a substantive. But these questions are nonsensical. So, too, in many of its interpretations, is the question 'Is Time real?' Properly interpreted (i.e. freed from the fallacy of the substantive) this ques-

[1] See op. cit., par. 330. The point is more clearly made in his original article in *Mind*, 1908.

[2] Prof. Cassirer has emphasized another instance of what I have called 'the fallacy of the substantive'. He says: 'Fast schien es das unvermeidliche Schicksal der naturwissenschaftlichen Weltbetrachtung zu sein, dass jeder neue und fruchtbare Massbegriff, den sie errang und für sich feststellte, sich ihr alsbald wieder in einen Dingbegriff verwandelte.' (*Zur Einsteinschen Relativitätstheorie*, p. 15.)

tion can only mean 'Does anything happen?' To this the answer is indubitably, 'Yes; something does happen and also something else.' And further, 'Something did happen but is not happening now,' and again, 'Something will happen although it has not yet happened.' These answers suggest that time and causal connexion are bound intimately together. I believe that this is so and that the causal structure of the world and its temporal ordering both spring from the essential connectivity of experience. The bearing of this upon time from the point of view of physical speculation will be briefly considered later.

My point here is that we are forced to recognize three fundamental time-determinations: future, present, past. These are mutually irreducible. Thus, *will be*, *is now*, and *was* are each unique; they cannot be analysed in terms of each other, nor in terms of anything else.[1] Moreover, *will be*, *is now*, *was*, do not involve a timeless *is* of predication. Of course, if there were a timeless *is* involved in temporal facts, then there would be the contradiction which McTaggart thought he had found. But since no timeless *is* is involved, the infinite set, which McTaggart held to be vicious, is not a vicious infinite. There is an infinite set of *entailings*, not an infinite set of *meanings*, of the same proposition. Thus, there is no reason to hold that the A series involves a contradiction.

There is unfortunately a great wealth of linguistic forms for referring to the time-determinations *past* and *future*. Thus, we can *say* "is in the past", "is past", "was present", "was"; we can *say* "is in the future", "is future", "will be present", "will be". In each case it is the last of the four expressions which most clearly expresses the time-determination in question. In some contexts one of the other expressions may be more convenient, but it is important to remember that none of the other three, in the first set, has any significance which "was" lacks (and none of the other three, in the second set, has any significance which "will be" lacks), *provided that* the expression is

[1] McTaggart himself insists that the vicious infinite does not arise because of 'the impossibility of *defining* past, present, future, without using the terms in their own definitions'. He has admitted these terms to be indefinable. His point is that the contradiction arises from the fact that the nature of the terms involves a contradiction, and that 'the attempt to remove the contradiction involves the employment of the terms, and the generation of a similar contradiction'. But it seems to me that he does regard the terms as timeless characteristics (owing to the initial repudiation of change), and that in discussing the analysis of temporal facts he falls into the fallacy of the substantive.

intended to be so used as to express nothing but *a time-determination.* If this be forgotten, ambiguity will arise and fallacious arguments may result. McTaggart has undoubtedly fallen into a mistake of this kind. In an important footnote he says: 'The past, therefore, is always changing, if the A series is real at all, since at each moment a past event is further in the past than it was before. . . . It is worth while to notice this, since people combine the view that the A series is real with the view that the past cannot change—a combination which is inconsistent.'[1] In this statement there is an ambiguity in the use of the word "past". In 'the past cannot change', the word "past" is not being used as it is used when we say 'The battle of Waterloo is past', i.e. when "past" is being used a time-determination. What do we in fact mean when we say (and, in my opinion, rightly) that the past cannot change? We mean either 'What has happened in the past has happened in the past' or, in some contexts, 'What has happened in the past cannot be altered now.' The first of these alternative meanings is a tautology; the second is a statement of the temporal unidirection of causality. It should be observed that in neither of the statements is the addition of 'in the past' required; these words add nothing to 'What has happened'. To say, 'The past is now changing', if that means 'What has happened is now happening', is not to say what is false; it is to speak nonsense. Thus, those who hold that the past cannot change and also that the A series is real are not combining contradictory statements. What these philosophers mean by 'The past cannot change' does not contradict 'The past is always changing' in the sense in which McTaggart uses these words in the statement quoted from him above. He does, indeed, leave us in no doubt as to what he means, since he gives as his reason for holding that the past is always changing, that 'at each moment a past event is further in the past than it was before'. But 'is further in the past than it was before' means 'is more past'. This is clearly not inconsistent with 'What has happened has happened', nor with 'What has happened cannot be altered now', nor with 'What has happened cannot be as though it had not happened'. But these are the only senses in which people say the past cannot change. McTaggart has taken advantage of his peculiar view that whatever can be truly asserted of a term belongs to the nature of that term. He then

[1] See op. cit., p. 13 n.

speaks of the term 'changing'. But this is not the sense of "change" required by his argument.

The difficulty of avoiding the fallacy of the substantive is likely to be greater if we allow ourselves to use 'in the past' instead of 'was', and 'in the future' instead of 'will be'. Such phrases lend themselves to the supposition of a quasi-substantive *the past*, or *the future*, and these quasi-substantives come to be regarded as having a shadowy kind of existence in which events are located. The mistake is analogous to the mistake of regarding space as a kind of tenuous box or receptacle. But "Space" is only a compendious way of referring to spatial facts; "Time" is only a compendious way of referring to temporal facts. A mistake of the kind just indicated is involved in McTaggart's argument that the past is always changing.

Neither the past nor the future has a *shadowy* existence; it is, indeed, misleading to use the word "existence" at all in this connexion, although it is sometimes so used as to raise questions which can be discussed. I prefer, however, to raise these questions in a slightly different form.

'The past and the future are equally real: both are as real as the present.' This statement comes perilously near to being nonsense, but it may pass muster if it be regarded as contradicting the statement, 'Only the present is real.' To say that the past is real is to say *something has happened*, or, in other words, it is to say that *so and so is past* is true for some instance falling under the description 'so and so'. And similarly for the future and the present. This should be clear from the preceding discussion. There is *no other* significance in the statement that the past is real; there only seems to be some other significance when we fallaciously regard *the past* as a quasi-substantive. So with *the future*.

The present does, however, seem to differ from both the future and the past. Thus, we are often told that only the present exists. Perhaps this statement reduces to the tautology 'Only what is happening now is happening now'. Its intention may, however, be to point out an important difference between the present, on the one hand, and the past and the future, on the other hand, which does give the present a privileged position in relation to us. This difference is due to two different circumstances. First, *our* activity differs in relation to the present as contrasted with its relation to the past and its relation to the future. *We* can initiate change only in the future; we cannot make the past other than it has been; we *feel* that what *will be* is not yet determined, but, in so far as we are now *causing* something, then that which will be is determined, even though it is not yet. This is, I think, a correct description of *our attitude* to the past and to the future. The justification of this attitude has an important bearing upon the theory of time, to which I shall return below. Secondly, perception is always of what *is now*; that which is sensuously presented to a percipient co-endures with his perceiving. Perhaps that which *has happened* cannot be demonstratively referred to; certainly that which *will happen* can be referred to only descriptively. We can, if we like, signalize this description by saying that the past and the future are 'constructions', but if we do so we must be careful to notice that *being a construction* does not entail *being unreal*.

It has been held that time-determinations are to be defined by reference to cognitive distinctions. On this view, the past is defined by reference to remembering, the present by reference to acquaintance, the future by reference to expecting. There are insuperable objections to this view. To mention only two. It is not nonsense to suggest that there may be direct memory of the past, just as there is direct acquaintance with the present. If so, then the difference between past and present cannot be defined by reference to the distinction between indirect and direct cognitive consciousness. Secondly, it does not seem nonsense to suppose that the world might have consisted of rotating bodies, and that when the *nth* rotation occurred the *n*—*1th* would be past. This does *not* mean that if a percipient *were* perceiving this rotation, he would judge that the *nth* rotation was later than the *n*—*1th*. I see no reason for supposing that *There are temporal facts* entails *A percipient exists*.

It is true that our *knowledge* of events as past, present, future, depends upon differences in our cognitive attitudes, so that, if we did not remember, were not acquainted with, did not expect, we should not apprehend time-determinations. But it is the temporal passing of the events which makes it possible for us to have these relations and thus to have this knowledge. Here, as always, it is extremely easy to fall into the fallacy of the egocentric predicament.

The privileged position of the present *relatively to us* makes it natural for us to attempt to analyse past and future facts in terms of the B series. Consider the two following sets of expressions:

(α) (1) 'The battle of Waterloo is past.'
(2) 'The battle of Waterloo is earlier than now.'
(3) 'The battle of Waterloo happened and is not happening now.'

(β) (1) 'My death is future.'
(2) 'My death is later than now.'
(3) 'My death is not happening now, but it will happen.'

In both (α) and (β) each of the three expressions asserts the same fact. In each set (3) is the expression most appropriate for bringing out the point that no timeless *is* is involved in past and future facts. In each set (2) is appropriate for bringing out the point that (1) is an indeterminate expression *unless* the time of predication is known. When we want to exclude reference to the time of predication, we find it convenient to divide time-determinations into the two classes *Earlier* and *Later*, just because these are *fixed*, in the sense of "fixed" discussed above. But it is just this exclusion which reveals the fact that the B series is less fundamental than the A series. There are *three* fundamental time-determinations, not only *two*. Apart from the standpoint given by *now* the proposition 'The battle of Waterloo is present' is indeterminate; it involves a propositional function. To show this I gave, on page 113, the equivalent expression 'The battle of Waterloo is happening at *t* and there is no time *t′* which is later than *t*'. The whole point of this elaboration was to show that *now* is the only value of *t* which would yield a true proposition. Thus, 'The battle of Waterloo is present' is not sometimes true and sometimes false. There is one historical event, but a different proposition on each occasion of some one's referring to it. It is *happenings* which are the concern of the historian.

If what I have been saying is correct, then there is no reason for saying that *future*, *present*, *past* correspond respectively to *coming to*, *presented to*, *passed by* some percipient. But because there are temporal facts we can truly say, 'Some experience is coming to us; some experience is presented to us; some experience has passed by us.' Time is passing. It is this which makes the A series fundamental and which renders it impossible that the A series should be a misperception of a series constructed by a purely logical relation. Time, in a sense, is fundamentally alogical. It is this which makes it difficult to give an account of the temporal series that would make it fit in neatly with our rational scientific schemes. The difficulty arises from the fact that time has not only an intrinsic *order* but also an intrinsic *sense*, or, as I prefer to say, an intrinsic *direction*. This is shown in the expressions 'earlier than now' for 'past', and 'later than now' for 'future'. In observing this direction we recognize that *now* is fundamental. In my view the essential unidirection of time is the counterpart of the unidirection of causation. It is this which makes us more ready to believe that the past exists than that the future does; it is this which makes us give pre-eminence to the present, i.e. to what is *happening now*. Not only is it true that without time, no causation; it is also true that without causation, no time.

We may ask whether there is a common time connecting, for example, my writing this article with your reading it. The answer is 'Yes'. My writing is present; your reading is future. In saying this I am assuming (as I *now* write) that you *will be* reading this article. Perhaps this article will be destroyed quite soon, unread by any one. Then this destruction is future; it assuredly is not yet. But *ex hypothesi*, you will not know of this destruction; there would be no event *your reading this article*, hence, no common time between *my writing* and *your reading*. But, provided that you are reading this article, then there is assuredly a common time; when the future event happens, i.e. when you *will be reading* this article, my writing it is past. You cannot read what is not yet written. Temporal succession involves causal concatenation. It is logically necessary that cause should precede effect; simultaneity involves exclusion of the causal relation. Just in so far as my action could not influence yours, nor yours mine, no common time connects our actions. Our common time would, in that case, be the 'objective common time' which we gain by an elaborate intellectual construction. In this short essay it is not possible to discuss this important problem.

It is at this point of our discussion, but not before, that physical speculations become relevant. The significance of the theory of relativity lies in the fact that it has shown that the possibility of establishing a causal order is the sole condition required to enable us to speak of a time sequence in nature. The limits of this essay do not permit the expansion of this statement. It must suffice to point out that in saying that widely separated events are simultaneous we imply that no causal relation could hold between them; in saying that two events are causally related we imply that a temporal relation of succession holds between them. It would be a mistake to interpret this as saying that causal connexion is nothing but invariable sequence, for "invariable sequence" is used to mean "regularity of sequence". This is a notion quite extraneous to the one under discussion. In trying to find regularities of sequence we are taking an abstract view, the goal of which is to reach expressions capable of being 'true at all times'. Such expressions (e.g. 'Iron expands when heated') do not involve a temporal *is*. So far from wishing to *define* causal connexion by regular sequence, I wish to insist that the connectivity of the fundamental elements in the world is, on the one side, causal concatenation, on the other, unidirectional, temporal succession.

In physics we are never concerned to talk about what is happening now; we want only to talk about connexions of characters at all times and at all places; the statement of these connexions involves the timeless *is*. But these statements are to be determined by what is *observable*. In discovering what is observable we depend upon what we *are observing now*. In order, however, to bring what we are observing now into a rational scheme with what we are not observing now, we drop out the reference to *now* and transform *observing now* into *observable under such and such conditions*. From this point of view there is no special relevance in Minkowski's remark that we never observe a time except at a place, nor a place except at a time. It is not from such considerations that we discover the necessity of hyphenating Space-Time. This necessity is due wholly to the nature of measurement and to the central part played by measurement in physics. Only that can be measured which is observable.

From neglect of the peculiar conventions of physics, there arise such paradoxes as the paradox of 'the time-retarding journey'. But, like all paradoxes, this paradox is due to a confusion of standpoints. The paradox is deduced from the general theory, and may be regarded as an example of an equation of the form

$$\int_{t_1}^{t_2} dt \ (1-u^2/c^2)^{\frac{1}{2}} = (1-u^2/c^2)^{\frac{1}{2}} \ (t_2-t_1).$$

It is true that $\int_1^2 dt$ is the same both for the observer who leaves the earth with a very high velocity and for the stationary observer, whereas *the time each has lived*, which would be represented by $\int_1^2 ds$, will be different. But the time is the same for the observers *not as observers* but only as *objects observed.* The whole point of introducing 'physical time', as contrasted with 'lived time', is to secure this consistency. In physics 'time' is a fourth dimension; in experience it is not: in physics time is no less relative than space; in experience there is an absolute *now* and an absolute *here.* The point of these brief, dogmatic statements cannot be properly dealt with in this short essay. It must suffice to say that the discussion of time as a problem for philosophers is largely independent of physical speculations.

It is important to insist that neither time nor causation is subjective. There may be said to be 'subjective times' dependent upon conditions relative to the percipient; there is a subjective causality also dependent upon conditions relative to the percipient. But these conditions are in the world, i.e. are really conditions. In communicating with each other, and in scientific speculation, we seek to ignore these conditions in order to attain statements of universal significance. To elaborate these points would require more than the space allotted to this essay. Nevertheless, their elaboration would provide abundant illustrations of the ambiguities which infect discussions concerning time.

THE UNIVERSAL IN THE STRUCTURE OF HISTORICAL KNOWLEDGE

By THEODOR LITT

I

IN the discussions on the logic of historical knowledge which have been called forth by the fundamental inquiries of W. Dilthey and H. Rickert, the question of the meaning and logical character of the universal embedded in the structure of historical thought constitutes one of the most debated problems. Dilthey's last and maturest inquiry into historical knowledge, the Academy dissertation on 'The Structure of the Historical World in the Humanistic Sciences',[1] gives a clear indication of the urgency as well as of the difficulty of the question. Adopting again the formulation of the 'Introduction to the Philosophical Sciences', he inquires into 'the relation in which the unique, the singular, the individual, stands here to general uniformities' (p. 87). He finds in the system of thought of the Enlightenment the grand attempt to reduce the bewildering multiplicity of the cultural achievements of man to 'laws of relation, expressible in fixed concepts which produce in all cases alike the same outlines, for economic life, for legal organization, for the moral law, for faith in reason, for aesthetic rules' (p. 97); in other words to give the leading place in the elaboration of historical material to the universal. Over against this mode of treatment he sets the contrary procedure, by which the 'historical school' tried to advance to cognitions of the universal. Rejecting 'the derivation of universal truths in the humanistic sciences by means of abstract constructive thinking, the comparative method was for this school the only procedure for rising to truths of greater universality'.... 'Universal truths are, from this standpoint, not the foundation of the humanistic sciences but their last result' (p. 99). To himself it seems advisable to supersede the two one-sided views in a higher interpretation. He denies that it is a legislation in advance either for the universal or for the particular; rather, he finds that in the humanistic sciences 'everything is determined by the relation of mutual dependence' (p. 143). When the historian tries to understand a single

[1] *Gesammelte Schriften*, vol. vii (Leipzig, 1927).

phenomenon, a person, a community, an event, he is trying to get back to the universal principles in which the experience of the nature of historical coherence is grounded. But this experience in turn extends and enriches itself by incorporating in itself the single phenomenon discovered with its help. Hence arises the thesis of the 'mutual dependence of the historical and the systematic' (p. 144). Discovery proceeds in such a way that 'universal truths and historical knowledge of the singular develop in reciprocity with each other' (p. 145).

That this relation of mutual dependence actually exists in the investigation proper to the humanistic sciences we can learn from every historical work of deeper significance. No really great historian would give up the claim on the one hand to support the study of the individual and concrete with reflections of a universal kind, dealing with the nature of historical forces and movements, and on the other hand to enrich these universal insights with the knowledge of the individuals illuminated by them. But we can assure ourselves by a very simple observation that the problem is thus not yet grasped in its full significance. If we choose an extract from any work of history which combines universal considerations with the representation of the individual, we at once convince ourselves that both the former and the latter have an essential point in common, viz. that they are both *formulated in language*. To state it more precisely, it is the same linguistic formulae that come indifferently to our service for the discussion of universal conditions and for the representation of individual phenomena. But these linguistic formulae are symbols of verbal meanings to which in turn the character of *universality* belongs. To indicate an individual is exclusively the function of proper names. These, therefore, must be present in every real historical representation, as an infallible sign that its concern is with the investigation of something unique, which cannot be repeated. But what is discovered and is to be asserted *about* this so-called unique must be apprehended in universal meanings of words, precisely in order that it may be able to take the form of distinct knowledge and be communicated. Thus the logical problem remaining for discussion complicates itself in the following way: a universal —viz. the universal meanings of words—expresses itself in statements on the one hand of universal content and on the other of individual.

The part taken by universal meanings of words in the structure of historical knowledge, which, so far as I can see, is hardly noticed by Dilthey, has, on the contrary, been of lively interest to Rickert, the specialist in the logic of historical knowledge. He sets himself the question how the appearance of this universal is reconciled with the tendency of history towards knowledge of the individual, and answers it in this way, that the universal enters here, not as it does in the natural sciences, but only in the role of an indispensable means, while the 'end' is precisely the grasping of something not universal, something unique; in order to produce knowledge at all, especially communicable knowledge, historical thinking must make use of universal meanings of words as the 'elements' out of which it 'fits together' the image of the particular to be represented.[1]

I cannot but think that in these discussions the problem is only indicated, not really solved. For all the phrases by which the ancillary position of the universal is expressed here, in contrast with the particular to be represented, are nothing more than external analogies or illustrations. Neither the pair of concepts, means and end, nor the idea of a 'setting together', a 'fitting together', a 'combining' of 'elements' into a whole, is adequate to give a clear solution of the logical problem as such. The difficulties lying unsolved in the background come out particularly clearly in a passage of Rickert's discussions on the subject. He thinks that a particular, in order to be capable of entering into a scientific judgement, must be reckoned as a 'member of a class'. In order that it could be represented in universal meanings of words, there must already have preceded it a classification, however primitive, of the phenomena to which the particular in question belongs.[2] In this thesis what remains unsolved in the problem comes out clearly. Classification means just abstracting from the particular and attending to what is common to single phenomena. But how is a combination of the 'concept-elements' arrived at in this way going to lead back again to something particular and unique? How is a 'fitting together' of pure universalities going to result in anything else than a further universal?

[1] *Die Grenzen der naturwissenschaftlichen Begriffsbildung*[5] (Tübingen, 1929), pp. 38 ff., 304 ff., 740 f.; *Kulturwissenschaft und Naturwissenschaft*[7] (Tübingen, 1926), p. 66 ff.

[2] *Die Grenzen . . .*, p. 44.

II

Thus the question arises whether the nature of the universal present in the meanings of words has been rightly grasped here. A glance back at the considerations of Dilthey given above is sufficient to confirm this doubt. The manner in which the humanistic sciences advance to universal statements he qualifies repeatedly as 'a procedure equivalent to induction' (p. 132). Now the classification as a result of which Rickert thinks he is going to get the universal meanings of words is not without further consideration to be identified with what Dilthey means here by the term 'induction'. Dilthey sees clearly how far these inductions fall short of the exactness of real class-concepts.[1] But one essential point is common to the logical methods of procedure which both investigators have in mind: their possibility depends upon the assumption that thinking surveys a plurality of single phenomena. For only on the basis of a comparative conspectus of such a plurality can inductive generalization, or the formation of the class-concept, come about. In both cases the 'universality' of what is known is equal to the 'common nature' (*Gemeinsamkeit*) of what can be stated in more or less exact form about each of the individual phenomena. Thus, to do Rickert justice, we should have to assume that the basic 'universal' which meets him in the universal verbal meanings of every historical judgement is not essentially different in its logical character from the other 'universal' which Dilthey finds in the generalizations of the humanistic sciences: the former, no less than the latter, would be the fruit of a synthetic apprehension of similar individual phenomena.

But this logical assimilation is ruled out for a very simple reason. Universal meanings of words cannot be the result of a classification, however unsystematic; for every such classification *presupposes* already the system of verbal meanings, viz. *language*, as existing and at our disposal. To apprehend a plurality of single phenomena, marked off as such, to articulate them into each other, to hold them together in comparison, and to examine them this way and that for common traits is possible only by *thinking*; but it is only *pari passu* with speech

[1] Loc. cit., p. 188: 'Die Begriffsbildung ist . . . hier nicht eine einfache Generalisation, welche das Gemeinsame aus der Reihe der einzelnen Fälle gewinnt. Der Begriff spricht einen Typus aus. Er entsteht im vergleichenden Verfahren.'

that this thinking reaches the height of development at which this achievement is within its power. It is impossible for the universal verbal meanings of speech to be reached by a procedure whose exercise is possible only in combination with a language already formed. Thus, if the expressions of developed speech make formulae available which can be used by the classifying work of thought for the symbolization of its concepts, the meanings symbolized by these words could not possibly be originally produced by just this procedure of classification. They would have to be there already in some form or other, in order that the work in question should be started at all and carried through.

What is the meaning, for our logical problem, of the argument from the philosophy of language thus indicated? There is already adumbrated in it the solution of the difficulty with which Rickert's view, already objected to, was not able to cope. If the universal meanings of words were really the result of classificatory thinking, we should have had before us in them a 'universal', from which it would not have been possible to reach in any form the concreteness of an individual phenomenon to be represented. Only because and in so far as there belongs to them originally, i.e. before their adoption and use for the ends of classification, a totally different character, could they enter also into the representation of the particular, and thus into the structure of historical knowledge.

E. Cassirer, in Chapter IV of his *Philosophy of Speech*,[1] has made a searching investigation of that form of the 'universal' by the development of which language makes possible the classificatory procedure of thought, and even in a certain sense anticipates it. He exhibits this form in such linguistic phenomena as belong to the early period of the growth of language, or to languages that have stood still on primitive levels. But for the purpose of our study it is important to state that even if the thought that is bound up with speech has risen to the highest levels of the formation of scientific concepts, these old, original forms do not altogether pass into the background or disappear. On the contrary, 'living' speech, i.e. speech not deliberately adapted to scientific ends, shows them in constant and unimpaired activity. Now it is just the representation of the *particular* in speech that gives the most convincing proofs of

[1] *Philosophie der symbolischen Formen*, vol. i: 'Die Sprache' (Berlin, 1923), p. 244.

this fact. Suppose I report something that happens with the words '*X* was very much excited'. Should we get the exact sense of this statement by interpreting it as meaning that here the behaviour of the particular individual indicated by the proper name was more closely determined by subsumption under the classifying concept 'excitement'? The character of particularity quite clearly does not confine itself to the grammatical subject indicated by the proper name, but also pervades the predicate, irrespective of the 'universality' of the meanings of the words. The meaning of the predicate does not exclude, but includes, the particularity that characterizes the excitement of just this definite subject. It is precisely the quite definitely qualified excitement of *this definite* man that is meant, not 'excitement' as a universal form of activity which he realizes just like innumerable others. That the sense of the statement is this and nothing else is obvious as soon as one sets beside it the judgement in which, say, a botanist assigns a plant put before him to a class, a judgement which leaves out of account, as totally indifferent, the particularity of the 'specimen' before him. Thus we have in the former case a universal which does not exclude particularity, but retains it within itself. Statements of this kind agree perfectly with what Cassirer argues about the universality of the original meanings of words: it is not their function to set up 'connexions of the manifold', but 'to give to each *individual impression* the meaning of something valid for itself' (p. 247). Naming 'is not a consequence of the class to which something belongs, but connects itself with some single quality which is apprehended in a vivid total content' (*an einem anschaulichen Gesamtinhalt*) (p. 250).

There is still another question to be raised, viz. what is essential for the formation of a universal of this sort? While classificatory concepts come into being only on the presupposition that the contemplating mind rises to the level of a purely objective, and thus quite impersonal and indifferently neutral, thinking; on the other hand, when the vivid impression is being determined in speech, the *personal sympathy* of the contemplator is at work not merely as an accessory motive, but in the leading place. We have known since Herder that the growth of linguistic forms can be explained only by the inner possession (*Ergriffenheit*) of the *whole* man striving towards intelligible expression. And it is self-evident that this sympathy primarily and originally belongs to what is concrete and lived with in full vividness. To grasp what is experienced in its whole determinateness, or, better, to bring it to its full determinateness in apprehension, is the tendency which not only brings the first universal meanings of words into being, but also, on the level of the fully formed life of speech, ever fulfils and animates them anew. A statement like the example given above presupposes on the part of the speaker on every occasion at least a minimum of interest, which makes the particular excitement of this definite man seem worth noticing and mentioning. There might be a question of denying the existence of such an interest if one wanted to understand the predicate of the statement in question as meaning that in its case the result was 'assignment to a class'.

We are now in a position to determine more closely the function which universal meanings of words exercise in the structure of historical knowledge, in the formulation of the historical judgement. For the situation before us is in two ways like the other, in which we saw 'living' speech building and using its universal symbols. In the first place, the task of historical thinking is to grasp and hold fast a unique form in its whole concreteness and vivid determinateness. The purpose which reveals itself at first purely externally in the use of proper names pervades also the universal expressions which are brought in to complete the content of what is indicated by the proper names. And this purpose will be realized, both in the case of the speaker and in that of him who understands what is spoken, exactly as, and only in so far as, those expressions are used and understood as indicating concrete fullness of content, without any thought of arranging things under classificatory abstractions. It is obvious that the mastery of the true historian rests not least on the art with which, by the choice and arrangement of words, he knows how to call forth this vivid fullness. But in the second place, the historical object can achieve life and fullness of content in presentation only in so far as it is met by that inner sympathy which is so characteristically different from the cool activity of abstract thinking. It is only if this kind of relation to *life* exists or arises that the universal expression can set up a concrete image.

Thus we come to a result already stated by Rickert,[1] but

[1] *Die Grenzen der naturwissenschaftlichen Begriffsbildung*, pp. 496 ff.; *Kulturwissenschaft und Naturwissenschaft*, pp. 67 ff.

obscured by his bringing in the classificatory universal: even if the historian does his work with a scientific mastery which cannot be surpassed, this perfection can never include the power to carry over the universal verbal meanings brought by living speech into the logical form of classificatory concepts for the sake of scientific 'exactitude'. For by this transformation he would deprive them of just that property by which they were fitted to serve for the construction of concrete historical images. It is a complete misunderstanding of the problems of historical knowledge to attempt to push the endeavour after 'exactitude', in itself quite justifiable, into the inner nature of linguistic symbols.

But what is the position now of that other 'universal' whose reciprocal relation to the individual has given a man like Dilthey so much trouble? It has already been stated that the same verbal meanings which we meet in statements about individuals enter into the universal statements of the humanistic sciences. Surely here, where the universality of verbal meanings really serves for the rendering of a universal (i.e. a universal insight, experience, &c.), it should have been possible, and even imperative, to build up that classificatory exactitude which is impossible in the representation of the particular? This question is undoubtedly to be answered in the negative. For how could the logical elements of a generalization, which comes into being and realizes its content in the constant intercourse discussed above with single pieces of knowledge, bring about an 'exactitude' which, in turn, has no reference to these? Obviously the question here is about generalizations whose logical character would be rightly designated, in the term invented by H. Maier,[1] 'intuitable generalization' (*anschauliche Verallgemeinerung*). The concrete liveliness which belongs to the individual cases lying at the basis of induction must pass over into the content of universal statements, in order that in these there should be found any meaning that can be actually realized.

III

From what has been established, it looks as though every universal that can be discovered and asserted about life and the structure of the historical world must consist of generalizations of the kind discussed. Dilthey, in fact, seems to have held this

[1] *Das geschichtliche Erkennen* (Göttingen, 1914), pp. 21 ff.

view. If it were right, we should have to admit that our universal knowledge about the nature of the reality around us, which forms the subject of the spiritual history of reality, has a very vague and uncertain character. For it is quite clear that every new unique experience that is given to us might make necessary a revision of the universal statements so far accepted. A reciprocity of the sort represented, never reaching a conclusion, can never produce anything but a quite undetermined and even provisional knowledge. But we need not resign ourselves to that. Our universal knowledge of the structure of the spiritual world is by no means exhausted by empirical generalizations of the kind so highly esteemed by Dilthey. What a man like *Hegel*, among the classical thinkers, has undertaken and carried out on the grandest scale, the self-illumination of the spiritual world in 'strict' (*strengen*) concepts, constitutes a possibility and a problem that remain for us. It would be going much too far to enter upon the logical discussion of the universal that comes in sight here. It must suffice to draw attention to the fact that, and the extent to which, this universal appears even in the studies of Dilthey himself, whose logical analyses have regard only for the universal of the kind spoken of above.

Dilthey sets himself the question, 'How does historical experience arise, i.e. as a universal knowledge of the outlines of historical existence?' In answering this question he starts, quite rightly, from the way in which the so-called 'life-experience' (*Lebenserfahrung*) of the individual man arose. He knows how to make a vivid picture of the manner in which personal 'experience' (*Erleben*), the elaboration in thought of what is experienced, and the 'understanding' of what goes on for and in the conscious beings around us, give rise to and progressively confirm the certainty that in all this process there prevail certain *uniformities* which might be laid down and retained in universal statements. All very well! But there is still the further question to be raised whether, while we are in the manner represented putting together our own experience and that of others in universal judgements, we are not already making certain presuppositions about the structure of the spiritual universe, which cannot in their turn be reached and established by the same procedure: to put it in other words, whether the material which lies at the basis of the above-mentioned generalizations cannot be recognized as available for the end aimed at only under the presuppositions mentioned. What do I presuppose when I examine my experiences according to their inner coherence and the uniformities that appear in them? I presuppose that I am a being who is capable of holding a series of experiences together in one thought that is not illusory, can reproduce them faithfully in acts of memory, arrange them and sum them up in accordance with certain guiding 'points of view', and present them in linguistic form adequately and intelligibly. What do I presuppose when I hold together for comparison the fruit of these experiences of mine with what others have done, experienced, and suffered? I presuppose that I am a being who is able by means of observation, intercourse, communication, &c., to reach, from what goes on for and in other beings, a knowledge at least in some degree adequate. When we accord belief to those empirical generalizations which arise in the experience of ourselves and others, we already presuppose the above-named conditions to have been fulfilled. We cannot possibly assure ourselves of them by the same kind of generalizations: for every single generalization rests in turn upon the self-same conditions. Now it might be objected that this is to say something self-evident. *Every* effort of thought without distinction would rest upon this presupposition. To have faith in the validity of thought, in the power of thinking, in the ability to understand and communicate, &c., must be granted wherever a man ventures upon a problem of knowledge. But this contention, undeniable as it is, would forget that the complex of these universal presuppositions, as soon as it is made the presupposition of the investigation of the '*spiritual* world' acquires quite a different meaning from that which it has when, e.g., the investigator of 'nature' uses it. For in the former case, and in it *alone*, what the thinking mind presupposes forms at the same time a part of what it wants to investigate. The 'spiritual world' whose nature the investigator would like to determine in universal statements includes *in itself* all those spiritual attitudes, actions, and abilities which are presupposed, and that not as merely incidental motives, which can perhaps be dispensed with, but as quite fundamental and ever-present functions of spiritual being and doing. It is thus really not a question of a *part* of what is to be investigated, but a question of its constitutive and fundamental motives. If, however, one takes the trouble to unfold all that is included in those presuppositions, apparently so harmless and 'self-evident', one finds that nothing less is contained in them than *the whole framework of spiritual being*, down to its spatio-temporal presuppositions (e.g. language). So that every attempt to fathom the spiritual world presupposes at the outset what is to be fathomed, and so to carry out the attempt must be in the first place to illuminate this presupposition to its depths and make it self-explanatory.

This self-enlightenment, however, comes about in the form of universal concepts, which, though not in the least inferior in strictness and certainty of inner grounding to the abstractions of classifying thought, by no means achieve their content by revealing what is 'common' in a multiplicity of phenomena: they rather bring to expression a universality, resting on itself and providing its own ground, that can be grasped, if we look in the right place, for and in every 'particular' of the spiritual world. It is precisely the 'identity' of the particular and the universal which Hegel, from the standpoint of classifying thought, called inadmissible that becomes in those concepts certain of itself. From this it is intelligible without more words that universal verbal meanings, which we have already learnt to recognize in such diverse logical functions, answer particularly readily to just *this* way of forming concepts. It is indeed, as we saw, these verbal meanings, in the original and actively persisting use that is proper to them, which, in contrast with the divisions of a classifying abstraction, grasp and fix the universal in the uncurtailed concreteness of the particular, and not as something sharply distinguished and externally separable from it. In the method of forming concepts that is here discussed this original tendency of speech finds its logical completion, while the classifying abstraction, which is often wrongly looked upon as the standard form of abstraction, if not the only possible form, presents a logically lower level (as Hegel[1] also had already seen quite clearly).

With the outlook on this new, third form of the universal we might close the matter. For with this outlook it has already become clear how richly articulated is the logical structure to which we are led by the question about the universal in the structure of historical knowledge. Empirical generalizations, universal meanings of words, *a priori* fundamental concepts—each of these forms of the universal presents in itself a special

[1] *Wissenschaft der Logik*, herausg. v. G. Lasson (Leipzig, 1923), ii. 290 ff.

complex of logical relations. To make clear their inner coherence, it might be sufficient to remember that all that we can know and assert about the nature of the universal meanings of words, on the one hand, and, on the other, of the classifying abstraction, and finally of *a priori* fundamental concepts, appears in the logical forms of these last named.

Translated by George Brown, University of Glasgow.

ON THE OBJECTIVITY OF HISTORICAL KNOWLEDGE

By FRITZ MEDICUS

WHERE we are fully entitled to speak of the *objectivity* of a piece of knowledge, the knowing subject knows an object before him, independent of himself; the personality of the knower has no significance for the content of the piece of knowledge. The knowledge originates in selfless devotion to what is actually found. It thus claims to be valid of this, of the 'object', and so to be valid in precisely the same manner for every subject. When an experiment is demonstrated in the lecture-room of a department of physics, the visual impressions are different for every spectator: each sees what goes on from his own situation, but these individual differences do not enter into the piece of knowledge itself: what is to be understood has no reference to the accidental circumstance of this or that observer.

The objection is often brought against the *Critique of Pure Reason* that the Transcendental Analytic is directed one-sidedly to natural science. If the book aimed at a theory including every kind of knowledge, the criticism would have to be allowed. But the book attempts to deal systematically with the problem of knowledge only in so far as knowledge is in a strict sense *objective*; it identifies experience with 'all our objectively valid knowledge'.[1] But Kant is aware that there is also a knowing that is not objectively valid—a knowing in which there is no object independent of the subject, standing before him. It is of this kind of knowing that he speaks especially in the *Critique of Judgement*. Here the Introduction postulates 'a ground of the *unity* of the supersensible, in which nature is founded, with what the concept of freedom contains practically'; and thus points to an original condition prior to the sphere of objective experience. The second part of the work, the *Critique of Teleological Judgement*, then introduces what Kant has to say about *biology* and *history*—about those sciences in which the contents of the subject's theoretical interest do not become independent 'objects' standing before him, because the questions that refer to the *living* as such claim that unity, grounded in the super-

[1] *Critique of Pure Reason*, B 722.

sensible, of objective and subjective (which is not itself an 'object' of knowledge). The life of organic nature and the life of history may well be merged in our experience (*Erleben*) in such a way that we feel ourselves one with it, and we may also give ourselves an account of the rational necessity of asking about reality questions which are governed by thoughts of that 'real ground, to us unknowable, supersensible, of the nature to which we ourselves belong as a part'.[1] But our statements about life are not 'objectively' valid: life does not stand over against the subject who craves for knowledge as something independent of him; the inquiring subject is life itself, it stands in the midst of life—a position which cannot be stated objectively, but at the same time has no need to be stated objectively. The certainty that life has of itself is immediate; and in so far as other certainties build on this one, they are the results of subjective reflection.

Kant's more detailed arguments about the sciences of life cannot be compared with what the *Critique of Pure Reason* has achieved for the solution of the epistemological problems of the objective sciences. It appeared to him self-evident that objectivity is the measure of scientific earnestness, and he therefore undervalued the scientific status of the biological and historical sciences.[2] As 'the highest point to which transcendental philosophy can ever attain, and to which also, as its limit and fulfilment, it must be carried,' the question presented itself to him: 'How is nature itself possible?'[3] and in this question he understood 'nature' as experience (*Erfahrung*), in the sense of a totality of objectively valid synthetic judgements.[4] The complaint about his all too one-sided orientation towards the science of Newton is not altogether unjustified.

Yet the systematic start given by the *Critique of Judgement* ought not to be underrated. In *the objective sciences* (a problem of the *Critique of Pure Reason*) the self becomes mute before the factual existence of the natural object; where a definite object is to be known, the subject directs itself towards it, striving for objective validity. In the sphere of *freedom* (the problem of the *Critique of Practical Reason*) the self claims its autonomy: here it does not bow before nature, but nature rather is to be bowed

1 *Critique of Judgement*, § 77.

2 Cf. Ernst Cassirer, *Philosophie der symbolischen Formen*, iii (1929), pp. 9, 16 f.

3 *Prolegomena*, § 36.

4 Cf. Ernst Cassirer, *Das Erkenntnisproblem in der Philosophie und Wissenschaft der neueren Zeit*, ii (1907), pp. 540 f.

under moral ends. The *Critique of Judgement* faces the final problem in the system, that of the *unity* of object and subject, of nature and freedom. Here Kant accentuates again and again both the subjectivity and the rational necessity of the spiritual function; i.e. the question now is (not objective validity but) the taking of a *subjective* position towards nature (or the real), yet in such a way that the self in this taking up of a position *asserts* itself. Indeed, the investigator of life is unable to efface himself in devotion to his object in the same way as the physicist: while the biologist is tracing the facts of the world of life, his own belonging to it makes itself relevant; no other possibility of knowledge is left to him than a *perspective* one, determined by the peculiarity of his being involved in the whole. That applies to the biological sciences: one who wishes to understand the life of ants or dogs must see it from the human perspective. And it applies to the knowledge of historical facts: one who wants to understand the Roman civil wars does it as an Italian or as an Englishman, as nobleman or commoner, of seventeen or seventy years old, in the year 1822 or 1934, living in wealth or pinched for lack of money—in any case under conditions relevant for the setting of his questions, and so for the result of his research, conditions incapable of being repeated in exactly the same form. The subject of historical knowledge is not the timeless reason; for while reason undertakes to discover the historical, it stands itself under historical conditions. And even when we see that these conditions need not be a dead weight of compulsion, that they appeal rather to the will's responsibility to truth, they still indicate something positive, something concrete. And this concreteness is decisive for the particular perspective under which the historical is known. Human life has in a *special* way a part in the whole life of *nature*; the life of every individual man is articulated in a *special* way into the life of humanity as it is *historically* determined. Wherever knowledge has for its content comprehensive life in any of its forms, it is a modification of the self-consciousness of this life: in historical knowledge (to keep to that from now onwards) there is—to use an expression of Cassirer—'no antithetical relation' between self and world;[1] knowledge of the world is here knowledge of the self. In the German language one speaks of historical pictures (*Geschichtsbilder*). A picture

[1] *Formen und Formwandlungen des philosophischen Wahrheitsbegriffs* (*Rede, gehalten beim Antritt des Rektorats an der Universität Hamburg*, 1929), p. 29.

painted on canvas—in so far as it is not an object of knowledge, as it may also quite naturally be—is not set before the spectator as not-self, but becomes an inner experience (*Erlebnis*) to him—he experiences himself (*erlebt sich*) in it with the whole individuality of his personal being. So also the historical presentation wants to be experienced (*erlebt*) by the reader and to offer him cognitions to which his self is not related externally, as it is to the amplitude of a vibration or to the model of an atom, but which, in so far as they bring him information about long past events, fill the self with more precise consciousness of its own concrete existence.

The knower has his existence only as taking part in the life around him. But what is decisive for historical knowledge is not yet fully stated. 'Taking part' here does not mean mere articulation in it, as something to be merely accepted (as would be the case if it were a question of comprehending the whole of life in a merely biological sense); we must understand by the term a spontaneous relation of the self to the contents which are of interest for the time being. Thus they acquire, in becoming contents of knowledge, a *personal centre* to which they tend, and are thus determined, not by a relevance which belongs to them objectively on their own account, but by the sovereign, though of course not at all arbitrary, decision of the subject craving for knowledge, a subject who here allows relevance, because of his own personal consciousness of responsibility, and there denies it. A given event may be treated by one historian as of the greatest importance, and by another as quite incidental for the knowledge of a certain group of facts: each of the two historians is facing it with the experience of his own personality, i.e. as an Italian or an Englishman, as a nobleman or a commoner; he cannot understand it except in relation to what gives concreteness to his life. But, in the concreteness of what their personal life-history has produced for them, the two historians are different from each other. When they introduce their personality in order to understand historical fact, they are introducing something different; and that is why the pictures which they achieve by means of their honest efforts after the truth of history turn out differently. It may very well be the case that both historians are right, the one finding the fact in question relevant to *his* picture of history, the other finding it indifferent for *his*. Neither of them can exhaust historical reality, just because each sees it only from his own standpoint; but each of them can know it, assuming intellectual honesty, as what it needs *must* be at the moment for him. The special way in which his existence belongs to the whole, the fact that he cannot exchange the conditions of his existence, guarantees him conditions and possibilities of knowledge that cannot be exchanged with those of any one else.

Something of this is applicable also to objective knowing, but there this matter of personality has only a significance in relation to the *extent* of the knowledge that can be attained: the *content* of objective truths is determined exclusively by the objects. The physical concept 'X-rays' means more to one man, less to another; but the content of the concept has its only standard in the properties and the behaviour of the objects which it denotes. Goethe has noted the statement of Voltaire 'que la géométrie laisse l'esprit comme elle le trouve': in the progress of objective knowing (for Voltaire's remark can be made about all objective knowing) the mind grows quantitatively, but in this way it grows neither more profound nor more mature. Every piece of historical material, on the other hand, means for the man who comes across it the challenge to measure against it the meaning of his own life. Goethe had arrived at the discovery of the special cultural value of history through Herder, in whose work *Auch eine Philosophie der Geschichte zur Bildung der Menschheit* ('A Philosophy of History for the Education of Mankind') he has 'delighted' (*erlabt*), as he writes to him in May 1775. What Theodor Litt says of this 'rhapsody of humanity'—'it must be understood by contemporaries as a summons to the performance of their own task'[1]—expresses exactly the opposite of the relation stated in that remark of Voltaire between the objective sciences as such and the life of the mind. Goethe, in the letter referred to, calls the vision opened to him by Herder 'a world grasped in feeling' (*eine gefühlte Welt*), and he praises his friend because 'he does not sift gold out of the rubbish-heap but regenerates the rubbish anew (*umpalingenesieren*) and makes it a living plant'. History does not take its stand on cold objectivity, as totality of external facts, over against man, but it claims his life as being itself alive. Ernst Cassirer, in his Rectorial Address at Hamburg of 7 November 1929, expresses this point with great lucidity:

'As Goethe felt before the work of Herder, so we feel as we stand before any really great historical achievement. What grips us in it

[1] *Wissenschaft, Bildung, Weltanschauung* (1928), p. 88.

is not the report of what has happened in the past, nor is it the rendering of something merely factual; rather, we feel in it a genuine rebirth—a remoulding and revivifying of the world, something which cannot result from anything but a peculiar spiritually personal centre of life.'[1]

The 'vision' of what has happened, which is essential to every piece of historical knowledge,[2] does not occur to the mind of man in passivity: it includes in itself a synthetic act that is of greater fullness and adequacy in proportion as the spiritual life of that in which it realizes itself is comprehensive and clear. Hence the content of historical knowledge is determined, in a way not at all merely quantitative, by the individual possibilities of knowledge open to the knower (i.e. by conditions of existence that cannot be exchanged). If it were not so, if the different ways in which different persons, and even the same person at different times, think of historical concepts (e.g. tribune of the plebs, the adoption of Roman law, Queen Elizabeth, 30 June 1934) also were to be understood in a merely quantitative way, and if there were to be found one objective norm laying down definitely the meaning of these concepts (however difficult it might be to use), the principle *determinatio negatio est* would be the whole truth without remainder. The fact that one and the same reality is apprehended in different ways would under this presupposition reveal only the *limitations* of the individuals, to all of whom nevertheless the supreme aim of knowledge would be wholly common, i.e. what really happened. But that formula of *Spinoza*[3] has only a conditional validity. Long before Spinoza, Nicholas of Cusa had gone beyond it in teaching us to estimate *positively* things found in an individual form, and thus of course every personal perspective. The special qualities are not negated, he says, by the infinite unity (*unitas infinita*), but they are there in their complete truth (*verissime ibi sunt*).[4] 'Every spiritual being', as Cassirer, in his distinguished work *Individuum und Kosmos in der Philosophie der Renaissance* ('Individual and Cosmos in the Philosophy of the Renaissance') (1927),[5] interprets the teaching of Cusanus, 'is centred in itself; but in this very centring, in this indestructible individuality, it has its

[1] p. 30; cf. also Cassirer, *Die Philosophie der Aufklärung* (1932), p. 481.

[2] Cf. Benedetto Croce, *Logica come scienza del concetto puro* (1917), pt. II, ch. 3, p. 190f.

[3] Epist. L (2 June 1674).

[4] *De Docta Ignorantia*, i, cap. 24, ed. Hoffmann-Klibansky (Lips., 1932), p. 49.

[5] p. 30.

participation in the divine. Individuality does not constitute a mere *limitation* but represents a special value which cannot be levelled or blotted out.' Later, in connexion with a passage from the *Liber de mente* of Cusanus, Cassirer indicates the development of the doctrine through Leibniz.[1] Leibniz's work is carried on in Herder, Jacobi, Fichte, and Schelling, and through them influences the later ways in which the problem is apprehended.

Every individual being is intransferably himself, and in the sphere of responsible existence, i.e. in the sphere of mankind, the intransferability of the position at which any individual comes to the consciousness of himself is indicated by a *task* answering to his individual capabilities and to these alone, a task which no one can take from him and which remains unaccomplished unless *he* applies himself to it. Intransferable uniqueness does not mean isolation: the task of each person is articulated into the task of the whole social system in which his life is spent. Similarly every age has *its own* task, and in that it has its historical individuality. But only at rare moments are the tasks of individual men unambiguously defined, and never the tasks of larger societies or of whole ages (where a dictator's commands, however unambiguous, are obeyed, the depth of human existence always remains unsatisfied): to seek the precise determination of the tasks set at any time by the situation given is a matter left to the free responsibility which man bears for his humanity. Hence there break forth out of the consciousness of being involved in tasks which ought to be accomplished *questions*—questions of the most personal kind which make their claim upon *the individual man* and on which his spiritual attitude is formed—questions by which *communities* let themselves be moved in their affairs—comprehensive questions which indicate the efforts of the *age* after an understanding of its tasks and thus determine its distinguishing character (and which find their ultimate form in those questions which the individual cannot avoid asking in order that he may be spiritually free and fit for his personal task). The oppositions by which every historical life is urged on are, in the last resort, opposite ways of asking questions: life asks for solutions of its problems. Every man, every people, every age stands in history with tasks and questions shared with no other. And this historical *determinatio* is something eminently positive; for what is essential in its function is

[1] pp. 136 f.; cf. pp. 280–1.

not to set limits, but to give to the self (individual or collective) the certainty of itself and the consciousness of its problems (*die Gewissheit und die Problematik seiner selbst*), and thus advance it to ever more effective disentanglements, towards an existence ever more substantial, ever more charged with value, ever more full of reality. This positive side does not indeed under all conditions obtain its rights: where dissolution prevails, where the consciousness of responsibility lacks power or depth, or lacks both of them, self-seeking tendencies obscure the tasks, and with them the questions in which the consciousness of humanity buds out; and individual men, peoples, ages miss the sense of their existence more or less fundamentally, because from greed or thoughtlessness they misunderstand the tasks and the problems which must, by the profound necessity of the historical situation, be their tasks and their questions. They misunderstand the true sense of the historical destiny of their existence, leave their tasks undone, and experience, in the unwholesome perplexities in which they entangle themselves, the vanity of subjective wilfulness.

Now these questions—be they grasped in their substantial meaning or distorted by subjective wilfulness—these questions, which determine the typical attitude in face of *actual* circumstances and affairs, are decisive also for the attitude to the forms of the *past*. Anybody who endeavours to understand historical forms and historical relations proceeds by the questions which he puts to his material, starting from the questions which determine his personal life. The form in which alone historical reality is accessible to the understanding is individually conditioned. As the picture that a man makes for himself of the character of his acquaintances necessarily gets its direction from the questions which give tension to his own life, so it is also (perhaps after some intermediate reshaping of the questions) with the examination of historical documents on the part of the historical investigator, and in turn with the interpretation of an historical presentation on the part of a reader. This personal form of the understanding is not rigid: the historical investigator has in the documents of the past rich possibilities of widening his horizon and of giving to the questions of his personal life a deeper and more liberal meaning; and similar possibilities are guaranteed for the reader by a good presentation of history. But even the ordinary incidents of every day offer a wealth of such possibilities; they often even oblige us to enter into the perspectives of other men and thus widen our own: and anybody who is devoted to spiritual things must think it important to let nothing human be alien to him. Of course the farther the problems of another life are from one's own problems, the less is the likelihood that the connectedness of all the expressions of the other life will be able to be reproduced in our own inner experience, and that this other life will be thus intelligible. Historical investigation and even the reading of historical works presuppose a certain experience of life. The mere getting of information about the external phenomena is not yet historical understanding. For that we need inclusion within the horizon determined by the questions which our own life asks.[1] But these questions may also be too fine or too coarse in their mesh, too indistinct, to let us grasp what is essential in any other life: in the former case the aim of knowledge is missed in blind presumption, and in the latter in unquestioning enthusiasm. In order to put the right questions to history, no one can do more than arrange himself in the systems of the life of his time with the questions satisfying to that life: starting from these, where a period of the past has awakened his interest, he will grasp its nature in a way in which it can have meaning for him and for his time. 'For, after all, the measure of life is the measure of knowing.'[2] A man who, from disregard of the substantial task to which his destiny has led him, shirks the questions that life demands of him, and wilfully trumps up easier questions, flattering to his inclinations or passions, must, as he misunderstands his own life, misunderstand history also. Now since every able writer of history will influence his readers, there is the possibility that through a subjectivistic tendency in his presentation wide circles of readers will be led astray in their historical judgement. The close connexion between history and politics may turn this possibility into a serious danger. And this danger is especially great if, in a people, universally extended temptations produce the effect that one gets confused about one's own part in the political systems, and if the writing of history turns into a support of these temptations that masquerades as science.

The historical *investigator* has a different relation to historical

[1] Cf. Th. Litt, *Wissenschaft, Bildung, Weltanschauung*, p. 95.

[2] Rudolf Eucken, *Prolegomena zu Forschungen über die Einheit des Geisteslebens* (1885), p. 110.

reality (or more precisely to the piece of it that he is personally investigating) from the mere *reader* of an historical work. The reader meets in Thucydides and Tacitus, in Jocelin of Brakelond, in Guicciardini, in Ranke and Macaulay and Taine, writers who *in their perspective* convey the facts of history. The great historian teaches his contemporaries (and since he will write in the language of his people, he teaches his own people especially) how starting from the tasks and problems governing the present the epochs of the past are to be understood: read Benedetto Croce's excellent history of historiography. 'Every history and every human thought is always adequate to the moment at which it emerges, and always inadequate to the moment succeeding.'[1] But no guarantee can be given that the thought of the historian will be on the pure heights of its time. The leading historians lay down in firm lines the perspective in which a period understands its past, and their leadership consists in the very fact that the perspective which they open up is found convincing by their contemporaries. If the surrounding world is spiritually healthy, these are convinced because what is peculiar to that perspective is grounded in a profound experiencing of the problems of the present. Yet the perspectives do not convince all men in the same manner. Rather, each reader of a work of history gains something different from it; for each brings with him his personal life, reaching up to the moment of reading, as his very own presupposition for the understanding of the book, and thus the book says something different to each one. This is true even if it gives readers no occasion to suspect the work of being prejudiced and to call upon the consciousness of their own perspective for a critical attitude of defence. It is always according to the wealth and the intensity and the quality of his experiences of life that each reader will accept what he reads. We might be right in saying that we had learnt from a certain historian to understand the French Revolution; yet we have not at all then made the author's perspective our own, but formed our own perspective by getting in touch with that of the historian.

The historical investigator, then, goes straight to historical 'reality' itself. He builds his presentation on what remains of that life which he is striving to understand. Narratives about the past, to quote Benedetto Croce, have value for him only

[1] *Teoria e storia della storiografia* (1927), pt. II, ch. 3, p. 184.

if they are authentic, i.e. only if it may be assumed that 'they bring him into immediate touch with what actually happened, which they draw forth, and resurrect, out of the dark abyss of memories which mankind bears in itself'.[1] But even the historical investigator cannot grasp reality as it was experienced by those in whom he is interested. Nor can he even wish to do so if he remains clear about his task. With his work he belongs to his own time, and the material of a distant past must have a meaning to him other than that which it had to those who had joy and sorrow over it as their present, or even to the historians of an earlier or later generation. No writer of political history in modern times can have such an experience of the despotisms of antiquity as the ancient despots or their subjects had; no modern historian of religion can penetrate into the belief in the Olympian gods, forgetting himself to such an extent that they could mean the same to him as to one of those Greeks who believed in Apollo or doubted him. Even if we have the most precise knowledge and understanding of an ancient cult, we have no possibility of its immediate, unfictitious affirmation. We exist under different historical conditions from the men of the past, we stand before different tasks and have other questions to ask of life, and it is only from these tasks and questions, which govern the concrete reality of our life, that we can make our own the remains of the life of an earlier age. What has happened comes to life again, to be sure, in the consciousness of the historian; not, however, as it happened in its original life, but formed anew through the relation to a later present.

Every present allows of a multitude of reconstructions of the past, each with a different perspective. Presentations of the same material can diverge without really contradicting one another;[2] but they can even be mutually contradictory without one refuting the other. To take a single case, a certain document, e.g. Luther's letter to Spalatin of 16 April 1525, may be important to one historian because by giving a *literal* interpretation of it he can add a distinctive trait to his historical picture; another historian, seeking the unity of the history in another direction, will find only a *humorous* interpretation appropriate to *his* picture. In such contradictions there is expressed something of the still unsolved questions of the time: the task

[1] *Logica come scienza del concetto puro* (1917), pt. II, ch. 3, p. 189.

[2] Cf. above, p. 140.

that governs the time insists on being attacked from different and partly opposed sides (to keep to the last example, from the Catholic and from the Protestant, as well as from many more), and these different aspects, which present its special problems to the time, compel us to adopt different interpretations of history.

In a society that has pretensions to culture every tendency of practical life aims at an historical knowledge of itself (i.e. a knowledge of the world). It is not a mere will to truth that is at work in such an aim: the tendencies of life—tendencies of certain groups—demand the support of history. Franz Oppenheimer was right in saying that history is written 'always from the standpoint of a certain group'.[1] There is a danger that the historian may become a servant of the interests in power, and as such may help to pervert the problems of the time, the mutual relations of groups, and that fatally. The stronger a group, the easier it is for it to find accommodating 'spirits'—traitors to the spirit. But to the spirit the danger is not insuperable. While the historical researcher serves the tendencies of practical life, to which he is bound by the ties of feeling, he can none the less be exerting himself with the strictest self-discipline to find truth and to present it unveiled. Now the services which he does to his group (his country, his party, his creed) aim immediately, not at their power, but at the satisfaction of what he supposes to be their desire for knowledge; and only in so far as their will to power can be served by an honest exposition of the situation will his work aim at and succeed in being also for the good of that will. At the points decisive for the questions of the time, his presentation will endeavour to set out clearly the points of controversy, without concealing the reasons on which the opposite interpretation is based. In this way it does what it can to give the mind of the reader its freedom, and to prepare the way for the removal of the obscurities present in the consciousness of his time. To the love by which such a presentation may be inflamed, country, party, creed, &c., are not merely a positively present *power* which includes his own life, but a moulding of the *humanity* of life. Humanity is the unending task of mankind. Historical research serves it in so far as it strives after truth, checks it where it adapts its own ends to the efforts of the authorities as such.[2] But it belongs in no way to the service of truth

[1] *Soziologische Streifzüge* (1927), p. 9.

[2] Cf. Th. Litt, *Wissenschaft, Bildung, Weltanschauung*, pp. 102 f.

and humanity that the historical presentation should be colourless and neutral, that it should be 'impartial'. The spiritual life of every time has in its questions indications beyond the present. The heights of life are those at which serenity has not yet been reached, where there is not yet any unequivocal decision, but where contradictions are still to be fought out, where—always with the clear consciousness of the value of what has been accomplished in the past—responsibility is borne for what is coming to be, what is still uncertain. An historical presentation is on the height of its time if it bears a share in these questions and thus 'takes a part'. Its one-sidedness is not yet overcome in the consciousness of the time; it is still possible, even necessary, to see history also under its aspect which helps to produce the spiritual height of the age. To be conditioned by the questions of the time (which are absolutely nothing objective, and which have their reality in the immediate experience of contemporaries as a factor which gives tension), and thus to be one-sided, to be partial, is something from which no historical work can escape. But not every such work, with its one-sidedness, does reach the summit of its time.

Obviously it is to be demanded of the historian that he offer something better than a work bound to a party. Oppenheimer requires of him (relying on a dictum of Spencer) that he know his own personal equation just like an observer in astronomy.[1] The partiality which is to be allowed him is articulation into the spiritual movements of the time. It is not the taking of a part for or against individual characters of the historical past. Consequently it must not express itself in judgements of value, but in the *setting of the questions* by which the historian approaches the material of his research. It cannot injure the clarity of these problems if he takes a definite position in the spiritual movements of his own time. For we are able to *understand* history only because it has for us no existence of its own, i.e. *because we are ourselves history*; history shapes itself in and through ourselves. A clearly conscious position in the movements of the present time cannot mean that we are above the oppositions by which these movements are determined: the writer of history always belongs to his time. He can be superior to the mass of his contemporaries (and we hope he will be), but his distance from the masses belongs itself to the character of the epoch. The general

[1] Loc. cit.

problem of the time comprehends the masses and the men of exceptional ability.

In the work of the historical writer the standpoint of his party (national, religious, or whatever it may be) is justified in so far as his 'party' takes a share in the struggle for the spiritual height of the time. It would be quite unjustified in so far as his party takes part in the struggles for *power*. Where an historian engages as a publicist in a struggle for power, he will feel the temptation to suppress the arguments which are hostile to his partisanship: so he is faced with the decision either to carry the struggle to a higher level through a clarification of the real situation or to be a traitor to the spirit. Where he knows the arguments of the opposite party to be the better, he cannot, as an investigator with spiritual obligations, desire the victory of his own party: if nevertheless he struggles, by means of omissions, distortions, falsifications of his insight, in favour of the questionable claims of his party, its power or prestige may be the end which he serves; but he is working against the clearing of the situation, and the more success attends his sinister endeavours the more he lowers the spiritual pitch of his time, especially that of his own party. It is a matter of self-discipline on the part of the historian to make ineffective the limitations that threaten his work, not because of his belonging to determinate groups, but because of the impurities in their desire for power. To be fettered to a social organization by the passion for power is to belong to the *masses*. Ortega y Gasset reckons with the masses all those who require of themselves nothing out of the ordinary.[1] He alone is able to require of himself something out of the ordinary who does not surrender himself to the impulses of his own nature. Passions for power are always naturally conditioned. While they are active in a society they claim the dull, unfree life of every individual. And where they determine the conduct of a man, he is without the will for *free responsibility* which alone could lift him out of the masses. An historical work on whose standpoint a nation's instinctive, i.e. ungoverned, craving for power has influence can never be on the highest level accessible to its time. Its perspective is limited. The longest view is always from the heights. But it is possible that in decadent nations the craving for freedom, and thus for humanity generally, falls asleep, so that in them life remains without a real high level. Much of

[1] *La Rebelión de las Masas* (1930), especially chs. i and vii.

the responsibility lies with the writers of history for seeing that in their time the consciousness of a level to be reached is kept alive.

Every historian writes in the first instance for his contemporaries: the questions with which he approaches his material have been made concrete for him by the system of problems current *at his own time*, and his work makes this system more conscious by relating the *past* to it. It is *the tensions in the self-moulding of humanity* that constitute the theme of historical research, a theme that is always renewing itself and in each new form offering new interest. The writer of history has grown so much the better at his task, the less he allows himself to be captured by his material, and the more freely he can grasp it in the sure consciousness of humanity. Only as the *heir* who in his time inherits those values of humanity at the building of which the ages have laboured has posterity the possibility of understanding the past historically. A man in the grip of atavisms, e.g., a man who pleads to-day for a return to savage punishments, surely has no understanding of the history of modern criminal law: he may get information about the external facts of this history, but its meaning remains hidden from him. Similarly we are incapable of understanding those survivals of the past which we know to have once had a definite legal (ethical, aesthetic, scientific, religious) significance, but whose inheritors we cannot feel ourselves to be. We may come across the idea that the 'objectivity' of historical knowledge is the better guaranteed the farther the historian stands from the forces whose conflicts he desires to investigate. But he has no understanding whatever of this history if he does not bring the conviction with him to his work, or get it as he works, that these conflicts have some personal concern for him, because as he discovers them there become clear to him decisions which have been and are being arrived at about the conditions of his own humanity. But if he understands it and recognizes himself as its heir, then he has a perspective view of it from his particular interests, from his particular present time.

The idea of humanity is the transcendental principle of all historical knowledge. It is through it alone that historical knowledge acquires unity. Not of course the unity *of an object*. The contents to be known become the possession of the knowing self in a *perspective* way. They thus partake in the whole system of problems by which the idea of humanity is always being determined. We all carry this idea in the immediacy of our felt responsibility (this expression to be taken in its most general sense, not in the narrow ethical meaning). It is in this that we come face to face with the tasks of our present-day life. As the heirs of a long past, it is true that we have inherited a rich treasure of life-values; but in presence of the tasks of our own time, what is inherited or learnt always becomes a new problem: the very depth of our self has to stand the test. The idea of humanity calls for a *new* mould. It cannot be held fast or defined objectively and unequivocally.[1] Being concerned with new tasks, it defies every fixation. It is *supra-temporal, supra-historical*. It does not proceed from historical movements as their product, but rather first makes these movements historical, first makes possible the knowledge of reality as an historical reality. History only exists in so far as it is based upon this supra-historical (transcendental) principle. What can be exhibited in experience as something temporally determined has historical meaning in so far as it has a relation (helping or hindering) to the self-moulding of humanity; it is grasped as historical reality when there come into force the standards according to which the accomplishment of the specifically human is judged.[2]

Aristotle, who dealt with the question of the *categories* without limiting it, as Kant did later, to the problem of *objective* validity, but concerning himself generally with the meanings that 'being' assumes,[3] names in his enumeration of the categories the pair of concepts 'doing' and 'suffering' (ποιεῖν—πάσχειν). (In consistency with his general theory, Kant omitted these concepts, which indicate the manner in which the *living* being functions; for their meaning cannot be exhibited objectively but only immediately experienced (*erlebt*): in so far as doing and suffering can be stated objectively they belong to the neutral process which is comprehended by the categories of causality and reciprocity.) But for *historical* life the Aristotelian categories of 'doing' and 'suffering' would be too wide, too indefinite: they are appropriate to the life of *organic nature*—one may think for example of the sprouting of a seed or the onset of an illness. Compared with the life of history the life of nature is a life

[1] On the limits of defining, cf. Th. Litt, *Führen oder Wachsenlassen* (2nd ed., 1929), *ad init.*

[2] Cf. Jonas Cohn, *Wertwissenschaft* (1932), p. 518.

[3] *Metaphysics*, p. 1017, a 22.

without decisions, a life without responsibility. Over against the Aristotelian categories of organic nature we might set the categories of history as *responsible doing and suffering.*

The meaning of the historical categories becomes clearer when we take into consideration that history moves in conflicts—with or without bloodshed—in which enemies are vanquished, competitors outstripped, even friends insulted and turned into enemies. To struggle and to advance is a *doing*, but —in the interconnexions of human history—always in some measure *at the same time a suffering*. And what is of importance here is not suffering under the blows of the enemy (even in a cockfight the winner usually loses a few feathers) but the inevitability that forces us into conflict against an enemy: humanity is suffering. But this same humanity requires of us also that we be true to the spirit of our actions, identify ourselves with them in new actions, accept the consequences that arise for us out of them even when these consequences involve distress. And to succumb in a struggle is not merely a *suffering*, but is *at the same time a doing*. It is not a question here of the resistance that was offered before the defeat (for in this case too there would be no reason for distinguishing it from a fight among beasts): the point is this, that defeat itself makes demands upon humanity, on human maturity, on the human dignity of the man who must endure it. Not only suffering but bearing suffering, and to that extent remaining at the same time active in suffering, is the proof of humanity demanded by every unhappy fate. And so these are the names for the categories of historical life: *to answer for one's own doing—to bear suffering.*

The *subject* of historical life, and so of responsible doing and suffering, of the voluntary taking of one's place and bearing of the suffering inflicted by fate, we must think of as the *community* (*Gemeinschaft*), the community in all its forms; and every human existence, in so far as it partakes of the life of the community, is from its own place responsible for it. It is true that every man has his own personal history, but only in relation to the systems of the community. His merely individual life he has as a specimen of *homo sapiens*; just as every plant, every animal, has an individual life which exhibits the properties of the species— but not an intransferable place in systems which are held in tension by supra-individual tasks. It is in relation to supra-individual tasks that the individual man first receives what can make his life substantial; if he is to answer for what has hitherto given direction to his acting, what he cannot do otherwise than affirm as the spirit, as the justification of his acting, he has the experience of being a member of a community—be it even one which at present has only a problematical existence and may exist only as an aspiration for the future (one thinks of the harassing loneliness of Nietzsche), but in which nevertheless the relation to the future cannot be separated from its connexion with the past: there is no real future without an historical preparation. No one affirms as a mere individual the strength of purpose in his action, his struggle for freedom; with what we can call in a substantial sense our own we stand in historical systems, we are the heirs of former generations—in the whole scope of our responsible life, political, religious, scientific, &c. The conflict in which the individual ventures himself is laid upon him by the binding inheritance which gives to the community a consciousness of solidarity. And where a man appears to endure his suffering as an individual, there his endurance as a proof of humanity has a meaning which is *universally* human (not as a general characteristic but as a universal connexion). So it is in the profoundest religious myths.

It is the *problems* of every age that are indicated by the task of answering for one's doing and bearing the necessary suffering: the scientific historian can do nothing else than make these categories the standards for the material of his research. They neither limit him to the neutral course of events, indifferent to value, and to merely natural life, nor do they impose upon him a definite creed, an attitude bound by partisanship; the former would be too little, the latter too much. But they characterize *man*—man *in his relation to humanity*. It is just this, the concreteness of man (for biology understands man only *in abstracto*), that is the eternal theme of history.

Wherever this theme is grasped, wherever historical research is exercised, there it is done on the basis of the *personal history* of the man who is striving after such knowledge. Knowledge of the mathematical sciences of nature is separable from the individual who knows it: as objective knowledge it claims to be valid for 'consciousness in general' (*Bewusstsein überhaupt*) and so for every subject in the same way. But on the other hand, the Treaty of Versailles and the Reformation have a different meaning, not only inasmuch as they are understood by men living to-day as calls to pledge their lives and to suffer with a full sense of responsibility, and thus determine their historical existence, but also inasmuch as they become contents of historical knowledge. Every one who wants to know them brings with him his personal experience of life, his maturity in life, his individual life-history down to the moment of the historical discovery; and he understands them just to the extent to which, on the basis of this personal life, he can understand them. Only a self matured by its own responsible doing and suffering to some degree of personal self-realization is the subject of historical knowledge, and in the very process of discovery it will become more mature. Only as a subject itself historically determined and thus taking its orientation from a determined present (not as timeless) can it make discoveries in the world of history, i.e. give itself an account of the meaning of certain events in the infinite systems of life in which it stands itself.

But in the concept of knowledge (of validity) there lies always the presupposition of *superiority* to what determines and conditions. (Knowledge must be more than mere reaction: it cannot be conceived without the freedom of the knowing subject.) Therefore though the subject who knows history is himself historically conditioned, the categories of this knowing at the same time signify the power of the unconditioned—the unconditioned inasmuch as it is related to the knowledge of the *historical* world. As categories they set him free from the compulsion of the conditioning, give the self superiority to the contingency of the contents offered to him, in that they exhibit themselves as forms of *unity* in which the manifold acquires its synthesis (a synthesis not indeed objective, but perspectively *necessary*). They are appropriate to this function because they mean just what characterizes historical existence as such. Every community at every time stands before the task of moulding itself to one form of humanity corresponding to the possibilities open to it, and so, in consciously responsible acting and suffering, of rising above the conditionedness of its existence. History is governed by the destined, but of course not assured, progress of mankind towards humanity: in history that destiny is incessantly renewing itself.

The historian will require of himself that he understand the period whose history he is writing: the wealth of facts that spreads itself before him has to be arranged by the distinction of the *essential* from the unessential—of the essential precisely for the period in question. We know quite well that he must ask his questions as a child of his time, that the problems of his own generation, and especially his personal position in the various systems of it, determine the form of his questions. But although there must be differences between the personal perspectives of writers of history living in different lands and at different times, they are all concerned with what is essential *in the periods to be investigated*, i.e. with the knowledge of the peculiar form that humanity has achieved in them. They all desire to know why and how the men of that former day have struggled and suffered. But even this question, since it requires a personal self-surrender to the historical material, admits only of *perspective* answers.

The different perspectives of historians living as contemporaries in the same circle of civilization are not of equal value. To make an exact assessment of them is impossible. Yet it may be said generally that an historical perspective will be more free and open for the understanding of every height and depth of man in proportion as it realizes contemporary humanity in itself with more purity and strength. If one wishes to speak of the *objectivity* of historical knowledge (we need no longer say that the expression is a dangerous one), this would be possible in the first place because the idea of *humanity* guarantees the meaning of the end striven after in all historical research.[1] From this point of view the want of objectivity would be a reproach to every presentation of history whose perspective falls below the standard of pure humanity which the age as the inheritor of its past is bound to possess. The temptation to remain behind, below the required level of humanity, will in general be the outcome of some tendencies towards power on which the historian's perspective has become dependent. But wherever power as such is glorified as an end in itself, the idea of humanity is disgraced.

But there is to be contemplated also a quite different grounding of the concept of historical objectivity. Every historical narrative must be founded on *facts*, and the word 'objectivity' in relation to a certain presentation might mean that everything that is communicated in it as fact stands up to strict testing. A relation to the meaning previously given to the word is, however, to be found: for an historian's dependence on unspiritual ten-

[1] Cf. Ernst Cassirer, *Formen und Formwandlungen des philosophischen Wahrheitsbegriffs*, p. 29.

dencies in public life leads readily to the intrusion of his own wish-fulfilling fantasies into his presentation of history: inability to grasp historical reality 'objectively', i.e. in pure humanity, drives him to inaccuracies that give a false impression, to defective 'objectivity' in documentation. Meanwhile, against this second terminology we must remember that the statement of facts is never by itself historical knowledge, is never the answer to an historical problem: the shaping of the material to the picture seen from a certain perspective—or to part of such a picture—is the act that gives it an *historical* stamp.[1] But since it would be bad terminology if one tried to look for the material of historical knowledge anywhere but in itself, the objectivity of factual statements should not be called the objectivity of the historical material. (The conceptual distinction between history and its material would on the other hand be useful in cases where historical researches are in dispute; thus it could be said that St. Ignatius is a material in which Catholic as well as Protestant historical writing has an interest.) To speak of the objectivity of factual statements is not really to speak of (living) 'history' at all, but of the 'chronicle', i.e. of the desire to preserve in abstract words the past, the dead, what has lost its living meaning.[2]

Objectivity of knowledge, in the sense of being valid of the object by means of a stripping off of all relations to the peculiarities of the knowing self, does not lie within the sphere of the historian: it can only be aspired to where the investigation is determined not by the *supra-historical* idea (the idea that governs historical life) of humanity but by the *timeless* concept of the 'transcendental object' (a concept that includes in itself no relation to time and history). Histories, as every lover of history knows, must always be rewritten; they are not concerned with an object in abstraction from the knowing self, and therefore they belong to their time (and with it to the supra-historical).

But, finally, does not this still imply the admission that in *truth-value* and *scientific status* the historical sciences are inferior to the objectively directed mathematical sciences of nature?[3] The affirmative answer to the question would have to be taken into serious consideration, if the claim to timeless universal validity which these sciences make, and which they always must

[1] Cf. Th. Litt, *Einleitung in die Philosophie* (1933), pp. 302 f.

[2] Cf. Benedetto Croce, *Teoria e storia della storiografia*, pt. 1, ch. 1, p. 10 f.

[3] Cf. above, p. 138.

make on the ground of their abstract logical structure, carried in itself the guarantee of its being saturated with content. In truth the claim of timeless eternity in every single case endures just as long as the usefulness of the theory in question. If this is superseded, its claim to be valid of the object and so for every subject is at an end: a new theory has taken the place of the old: it too seems to want to be timelessly valid, but it too will yield in turn to a better, and experience the power of time. For the doctrines of mathematical science are themselves on their side historically conditioned, and any one who wishes to understand them, not merely in their limitation to the immediately present situation of their science, but in their cultural significance, must understand them historically. Like a victorious war or an alteration of the constitution, while they appear and enforce themselves they bring decisions of unsettled questions, and it is by these decisions that the life of science is nourished until difficulties arise requiring new and revolutionary decisions. The claim to timeless validity (founded by the formal relatedness of these cognitions to independent objects) is secondary: the deeper meaning of scientific concepts and judgements becomes clear from their task of satisfying the coherence of nature revealed at an *historically* determined stage of scientific knowledge, and of helping in the effort after a wider development of this knowledge. One day their claim to timelessness breaks down; but the service which they have rendered to the historically conditioned stage of civilization remains. That every stage of civilization is historically conditioned is the sign under which all human existence stands. Humanity has tried since an early stage to lift itself above the conditions of its existence in looking up to the 'eternal stars'; but it has gradually discovered, not only that the stars are not eternal but that all *knowledge* of them and of everything that is related to them stands in history and participates in it at the cultural level of the time. There is timeless eternity only as something abstractly thought in dependence upon historically conditioned cultural achievements; where its derivation is misinterpreted and it is taken to be without origin, illusions come into being. The substantial depths of eternity reveal themselves to humanity only in the overcoming of adversities, in which it becomes aware of a supra-historical destiny, the direction towards humanity.

Translated by George Brown, University of Glasgow.

THE FORMATION OF OUR HISTORY OF PHILOSOPHY

By ÉMILE BRÉHIER

WHILE the history of philosophy quite rightly determines for itself how the ordinary rules of historical criticism should be applied to philosophical texts, it must be said that it is not as history that the past of philosophy first aroused the interest of philosophers. It was not so much true and accurate information about what men thought and believed that they hoped to find in it, but rather a truth rooted in the tradition to which they were bound, and the means of defending such a truth. This attitude of acceptance or hostility with regard to the past is very different from the historical attitude. What I want to try to show is how the historical attitude has gradually emerged by a process of development which is still not complete.

It was not born of a methodical and consecutive effort, but by fits and starts, by a series of actions and reactions, in which chance has played some part. We have simply to consider the content of our representation of the past of ancient philosophy to see by what a series of accidents it came about that Aristotle was known in the thirteenth century before Plato and before the majority of the Neo-platonists disclosed by the Renaissance, and Plato before the pre-Socratic schools and before the Stoics, Epicureans, and Sceptics, on whom attention was not really directed until the end of the sixteenth and the beginning of the seventeenth centuries. Further, whatever the number of the documents available, history could only really begin when these were considered in a critical spirit. What I want to do in this article is to leave on one side the details of the history of the works on the history of philosophy which I have discussed elsewhere,[1] and to show how, in the seventeenth century, men began to acquire the critical spirit which made possible the birth of the history of philosophy, and how at the end of the eighteenth and the beginning of the nineteenth centuries the historical reconstruction of the philosophical past came about; and how, finally, down to our own day, the revival of

[1] *Histoire de la philosophie*, vol. i, Introduction.

philological studies has discredited this reconstruction and has compelled the historian to extend and render more complicated his views on the past.

I. *Historical Pyrrhonism*

The seventeenth century has long been considered an unhistorical century. This, as Ernst Cassirer says in discussing the eighteenth century, is 'une fable convenue';[1] it is even fairly easy to show the origin of this interpretation; it is the watchword of nineteenth-century Romanticism against the philosophy of enlightenment; Taine completely inherited this spirit in his well-known conclusions to the first volume of his *Origines de la France contemporaine*, where he is representative of the Rationalists of the seventeenth century with his consideration of an abstract man, independent of all historical tie. The truth is that historical criticism was born in the seventeenth century from the same intellectual movement as the philosophy of Descartes. The reason for the unjust valuation of the Romantics was that they understood history in the same sense as the traditionalists, that is to say, as a discovery of the truth (albeit suppressed truth as in Hegel), which is simply turning one's back on history as it had been understood in the two preceding centuries, that is to say, history based on historical criticism.

For it is easy to show the complete solidarity of historical criticism with eighteenth-century rationalism; it merely carries the same principles farther. It is true that reason, in the Cartesian philosophy, had set the ever-present evidence of its concepts in opposition to the persistence, through inertia, of tradition; but it should be noted that it attacks tradition, not in itself and for its content considered as an exact representation of the past, but because of the function which it has been given in the knowledge of the real, and because of the value, as truth, which it claims. Tradition thus becomes a doctrine which 'preoccupies' the mind, which interposes its prejudices between us and things; it is an obstacle which must be got rid of, and it is, in part at least, the object of the methodical doubt of Descartes. But while doubt, in the Cartesian philosophy, prevents tradition from upholding the past simply because it is past, it leaves intact its claim to give a faithful representation of the past. It is this claim which criticism submits in its turn to examination:

[1] *Philosophie der Aufklärung*, 1932.

tradition (that is to say, documents of the past and their accepted interpretation) puts itself between us and the past, in the same way as it puts itself between the mind and the object of proof. It renders or may render impossible the true knowledge of the past: hence Bayle's 'historical Pyrrhonism' which carries on the methodical doubt of Descartes. This Pyrrhonism is concerned with tradition itself and with its assertions regarding the past. There is possible in historical knowledge a kind of accuracy which is not proof but which makes demands no less severe than those made by mathematical knowledge.

It is true that historical criticism did not begin by attacking the past of philosophy. It began with spheres of the history of thought, where the nefarious role played by tradition was most manifest: hence originated the criticism of the text of the Scriptures which has continued to our own time. As early as the beginning of the seventeenth century the knowledge of Oriental languages was beginning to spread and was making it possible to estimate at its true value the Vulgate, the Latin translation of the Bible which had been proclaimed canonical by the Council of Trent. It is curious to follow the polemic, made public by the recently published correspondence between Father Mersenne and the Dutch orientalists who were correcting the text of the Vulgate.[1] The problem for these scholars was to distinguish the authentic text from the tradition and from the traditional interpretations so as to get back to the actual past; to separate that part of theology which is founded on the only real authority, that of the Scriptures, from that which derives from Aristotle, Peter Lombard, or St. Thomas; and finally to dissociate the sincere and true interpretation from the fanciful one introduced into it by the allegorical method. Mersenne attacked his opponents violently, and emphatically maintained the uselessness of the knowledge of Oriental languages. Yet the Dutch professor Sixtus Amama, writing in the year 1628 to this future friend of Descartes, offered advice which makes one think of the yet unpublished *Discours de la Méthode*: his readers, he said, would derive profit from his labours, *modo cereos adducant animos et pertinaciae causas procul habeant*.

This submission to pure fact (*mitte male loqui*, he again wrote to Mersenne, *et rem ipsam dic*), so different in many respects from

[1] *Correspondance du Père Mersenne*, vol. i, 1934, pp. 527–32.

the learning of the Renaissance which readily sacrificed accuracy to the taste for unity and agreement, is an essential aspect of the intellectual probity which characterizes the great minds of the seventeenth century. Spinoza's *Tractatus Theologico-Politicus*, which is one of the finest fruits of this probity, was responsible for the inauguration of a history of religion and a history of philosophy completely free from all subjection to philosophy. Spinoza achieved this result by a complete change of point of view, quite comparable to the Cartesian method of doubt: instead of subordinating historical truth, in interpreting the Scriptures, to rules previously laid down, he submitted himself unreservedly to what is given: *Plerique tanquam fundamentum supponunt (ad Scripturam scilicet intelligendam ejusque verum sensum eruendum) ipsam ubique veracem et divinam esse; id nempe ipsum quod ex ejus intellectione et severo examine demum deberet constare, in primo limine pro regula ipsius interpretationis statuunt;*[1] whereas the theologians were primarily concerned with how they could extract from the Scriptures 'their own "fictions" and opinions', the rule laid down by Spinoza was to allow as the doctrine of the Scripture only 'what he could very clearly (*clarissime*) derive from it', derive, that is to say, from the knowledge of the language, from the meaning of phrases in the light of their context, and from the special circumstances in which the documents had been written. This is the opposite process to tradition: tradition upholds as actual what history maintains belongs to the past. 'I learned in this way', wrote Spinoza, 'that the commandments God revealed to Moses were simply the Law which was peculiar to the Empire of the Hebrews, and was therefore meant only for them'. In documents of this kind we must look for no philosophical truth; we do not find the Scriptures teaching anything which agrees with the understanding, nor anything which disagrees with it; they leave reason complete freedom and have nothing in common with philosophy.

These considerations seem at first to affect only Biblical criticism; yet they are applicable also to the history of philosophy on account of the close connexion it had hitherto enjoyed with religion. Is it necessary to recall how, down to the sixteenth century, no philosopher was studied without inquiry being made into how far his thought was in agreement with dogma? The Christian Aristotle of St. Thomas, and the anti-Christian

[1] Ed. Van Vloten minor, vol. i, p. 363.

Aristotle of Siger de Brabant fought for pre-eminence for nearly three centuries, before any one tried to find out what sort of person Aristotle really was. The Renaissance studies of Plato suffer from the same mania of trying to find in a philosopher answers to questions he had never asked. Spinoza put an end to this situation with one stroke when he wrote of the theologians: 'They marvel at the profound mysteries of the Scriptures; but I cannot see that they teach anything different from the speculations of Aristotle and Plato; and, so as not to appear to be of the party of the Gentiles, they have made the Scriptures correspond with these speculations.' Thus the history of philosophy was at the same time freed from the authority both of the Scriptures and of philosophy itself.

From these premisses it follows that the natural tendency of historical criticism in its presentation of the past runs contrary to unity and in the direction of variety and dispersion. The object of history is human imagination, with all that spurious wealth which Spinoza denounced in it, that crumbling into pieces which submits to no rational unity. This is why historical criticism is so different from scholarship of the kind attacked by Malebranche, and why it is not in the least affected by such attacks. Malebranche's scholar, who confines himself to one author, and becomes infatuated with him, behaves in exactly the opposite way from the critic who follows the dispersion of facts. History is a direct method of curing the scholar of his infatuation. It is in Bayle's *Dictionnaire historique et critique* (1697) that we can best see the development of the results of that crumbling to which reference has been made. His historical Pyrrhonism has the same destructive effect on what we have been given by tradition and on the evidence for it as that produced by the Cartesian 'doubt' on the constructions of the imagination; and just as, in Descartes, the *cogito* is the residuum left by doubt, so, in history, there remains as certain fact whatever criticism has been unable to demolish. Bayle's *Dictionary*, as has been admirably pointed out by Ernst Cassirer[1] following Jean Delvolvé,[2] systematically carries out the unsystematic juxtaposition of facts; the most insignificant facts are dealt with in the greatest detail; there is a love of fact for its own sake; in the words of Cassirer, 'fact, for Bayle, is the *terminus ad quem* not

[1] *Philosophie der Aufklärung*, 1932, pp. 270 ff.
[2] *Essai sur Pierre Bayle*, 1906.

the *terminus a quo*'. It should be added that there is the same reversal of procedure here as has already been noted in Spinoza; historical truth is based not on a dogma discovered in history but on its own origins and subjective conditions. From this universality the history of philosophy itself benefits also; after a discussion about the date of the death of Anaxagoras, Bayle writes: 'This is the pitiable condition in which the greatly vaunted ancient philosophers have left the history of philosophy—everywhere thousands of contradictions, incompatible facts and wrong dates.'[1] He is too well aware to what an extent error is fabricated and how easily it spreads, to follow tradition blindly. 'There is no chronicler so paltry but that he can secure himself immortality for all the gross errors he makes up in an idle hour. They will be copied three months later by some author or other, and repeated from time to time by others as they are wanted; and, if public or private interest requires it, in some two or three hundred years' time they will be discoverable stowed away in libraries.'[2]

Thus it may be said that it was the long struggle of the seventeenth century which disciplined the mind to the critical spirit as regards the history of religious or philosophical doctrines. People were becoming used to the view that *historical truth*, which is concerned with the fact that men have had such-and-such thoughts, in no way involves the truth of the thoughts and opinions in question. The necessity for distinguishing between the truth of ideas and the fact that they have been held was later given admirable expression by Lessing:

'That Christ, against whose resurrection I can find no good historical ground, announced Himself on that account as the Son of God, and that His disciples held Him to be so for that reason, I believe from my heart. For these truths, as truths of one and the same order, follow quite naturally from one another. But to leap from that historical truth into an entirely different order of truths and to demand of me that I should reconstruct all my metaphysical and moral concepts on that account; to counsel me because I can oppose no credible witness to the resurrection of Christ to revise all my fundamental ideas on the essence of the deity; if that is not a *μετάβασις εἰς ἄλλο γένος* I do not know what else Aristotle can have meant by that term.'[3]

[1] Article 'Archelaüs', Remarque A.

[2] Article 'Bolsec', Remarque O.

[3] *Ueber den Beweis des Geistes und der Kraft*, ed. Petersen, vol. xx, p. 48.

II. *The Construction of History*

One of the great problems at the beginning of the nineteenth century was whether it would be possible to maintain the distinction so forcibly pointed out by Lessing. The solution of this problem in the negative brought with it, by contrast to the breaking up of the method of criticism, the construction of the history of philosophy in the manner of Hegel or of Auguste Comte. Historical criticism, which attaches opinions to a period and to conditions which are more or less transitory, tends towards a relativism in a way which is disturbing to the philosopher. It is true that Spinoza safeguarded philosophy by showing that it is only the products of the imagination that are relative to changing conditions and not philosophy itself, the product of pure thought. There can thus be a history of philosophy just in so far as there are images intermixed with pure thought; it is the history of whatever in philosophy is not pure thought. A thesis of this kind was bound to share the fate of Descartes's confident faith in clear and distinct ideas; Kant shows that reason allows the possibility of a multiplicity of divergent metaphysical theories; consequently there is a genuine history of philosophy, and the question arises as to how the fact that philosophy has a history is compatible with its being true. Perhaps, and this is what Kant held, we should seek the ground for the diversity of philosophical doctrines in the *a priori* possibilities of thought, as they are given us by reason; this is his method in the short section of the *Critique* entitled *History of Pure Reason.* The knowledge of the past would in that case do no more than reveal actual examples of types of thought which we could in the last resort have discovered without history, since they arise from the natural laws of the mind. Contingency and the character of having a history would in this case belong, not to the doctrines themselves, but to their appearance at a particular time and as a result of favourable conditions; but these are characteristics which do not really concern the philosopher at all. This is a difficult attitude to accept. Can it be maintained that philosophical systems are as little connected as Kant says with the conditions of period and civilization in which they appear?

This feeling that philosophy essentially has a history was intensified when, in the eighteenth century, it was recognized that there is a solidarity as between the various periods in human development. Spiritual life can only be described as a reality which has developed gradually: the typical example of this spiritual history is found in sacred history known by revelation, which is made up of spiritual happenings which are ordered and conditioned by one another—the creation, the fall, redemption, salvation or damnation. This history known by revelation is the only type of history of spiritual matters which Malebranche allows; for according to him the past can only provide us, in the case of philosophy or science, with opinions which it is not only useless but exceedingly harmful to study. Now in the eighteenth century there arose a history of the human mind or human reason which was conceived on the model of sacred history, designed like it to show man's progress towards blessedness, yet making such progress dependent not on transcendent grace, but on an internal and immanent law. 'This picture', writes Condorcet, at the beginning of his *Tableau des progrès de l'esprit humain*, 'should exhibit the order of changes . . . and show also, in the modifications which the human species has suffered in the course of its ceaseless renewal amid the vastness of the ages, the course it has followed, the steps it has taken towards truth and happiness.' Here is the same faith in the future as in sacred history, which in its function of assigning a purpose to man should be replaced by profane history. 'The result (of the work) will be to show, by reasoning and by facts, that nature has set no limit to the development of human faculties. . . . These observations will lead to the means of assuring and speeding up the fresh advances for which man's nature still allows him to hope.'

This faith in progress is quite distinct from the belief in intellectual progress which finds expression in Pascal and Malebranche; for them, progress is above all a reason for shaking the authority of the ancients in scientific matters. But for Condorcet, history serves to demonstrate progress, and above all to give faith in the future.

The tendency represented by Condorcet's work had a great influence on the construction of the history of philosophy which was at this time struggling to unite, concentrate, and unify what appeared scattered and incoherent. For a long time it really did provoke and organize research. It led, in the first place, to the assertion that there is a unity in the evolution of the mind which makes all doctrines necessarily successive aspects of the same idea. Between them no real and complete conflict is possible: their diversity and opposition are reabsorbed into the unity of history. It is a fact which we may repeat at the risk of labouring the obvious that the great speculative minds of the beginning of the nineteenth century, Hegel and Auguste Comte, sought in their turn for the rhythm and cadence of this evolution; for, in history as they conceive it, a doctrine does not mean the same as an absolute affirmation: it is a moment, but a necessary moment, in the evolution which produces it and which carries it away.

The theory of progress, by asserting the principle of continuity, also provokes historical researches which attempt to base this ideal principle on the facts. Thus we find ourselves faced with two great problems which are entirely new, the problem of the philosophy of the Middle Ages, and the problem of the interpretation of modern philosophy. After the criticisms of the sixteenth and seventeenth centuries, the thought of the Middle Ages was in general regarded as the result of a decadence and of a corruption of the thought of the Ancients. Did there, then, really occur in the Middle Ages a break in the continuity of progress? Such a view seemed absolutely impossible to minds cast in the mould of Auguste Comte; for it was he, above all, who displayed the immense superiority, from the intellectual point of view, of medieval Christendom over Antiquity; and Hegel, for his part, saw in Christianity, from the time it first began, the essential principle of modern philosophy. It was at this period and under these influences that the idea was introduced of an intimate fusion of rational thought and Christian revelation. This idea had already made some transitory appearances, but had in general been most carefully avoided by the majority of philosophers. If we add that medieval research was at this time favoured both by the beginning of national histories, which sought in the Middle Ages for the origin of modern nations, and by the traditional schools which saw in medieval Christendom the only conception of a political order capable of putting an end to 'revolutionary anarchy', we shall see how many reasons there were for allotting to the Middle Ages an important place in the construction of the history of thought.

With regard to modern philosophy since Bacon and Descartes,

the attitude which was beginning to be adopted (this too for the first time) was that of the historian who wants not to choose one doctrine from among others, but to grasp it in its historical continuity. From these new researches, guided by the *a priori* idea of progress, sprang a history of philosophy that aimed at unity and completeness.

Yet the notion of progress, which was inherited from the eighteenth century, underwent a profound transformation during the first half of the nineteenth. Condorcet thought of progress as an indefinite evolution, according to a model borrowed from the abstract sciences: this conception makes it impossible to achieve a doctrine which can organize and define, and be capable of providing history with an end and a purpose. It is in these respects altogether opposed to the tendencies of a period which is passionately devoted to order. It is these very tendencies which are satisfied by the new way of conceiving progress; a way which is no longer borrowed from the mathematical and physical sciences, but from the real evolution within settled boundaries studied by the organic and social sciences. In the same way as the progress of a living being is knowable only if it is considered when it has reached a full-grown and perfect state, so likewise knowledge of the progress of the mind is possible only if its history is complete and terminated; this is why the history of philosophy in Comte and Hegel (and the same characteristic is to be found in much later historians) is an inverted history, which really begins at the end, and disposes all its content in time according to its view of the issue of the process. It is in the philosophy of mind of Hegel and in the positivism of Comte that we must seek the explanation of the riddle of history, or rather, the authority for treating history as a riddle to be solved. The critical attitude of the seventeenth century had no knowledge of an explanation of history in terms of purpose, except when facts were considered from a theological and supernatural point of view—a point of view which became very common at that time and is still perhaps to be found in many historians. They always write history as if we had arrived at what the Apocalypse calls the 'end of time'. This allows the Hegelians to treat the history of philosophy as a revelation of the mind to itself, and to approach the history of thought with the respect which the theologian shows for the Scriptures: the *Entwicklung* is a *Selbstoffenbarung*.

III. *Criticism and Construction*

We have seen the ideas (prejudices we may even call them) round which the history of philosophy, considered as a whole, was for the first time organized. Yet it would in all probability have continued to take the form of dictionaries and compilations had it not been for the constructions of Hegel and Comte. It is no less true that in their day the critical spirit was dormant, or else that it was frankly sacrificed to the desire of welding historical documents into an organic whole. How to reconcile this desire with the exigencies of the critical spirit is the problem imposed on every historian since the fall of those vast structures which are called the philosophy of mind and positivism.

These structures were based, in effect, not on the critical study of texts but on the profound conviction that it was possible, by a kind of intuition of genius, to arrive at the law of evolution of the mind in accordance with which doctrines necessarily follow on one another. The criticism of this intuition, towards the beginning of the nineteenth century and in particular in Renouvier, marked the prelude of the reorganization of our history of philosophy. This law of evolution or progress presupposed, as Renouvier showed, two postulates, the first of which is apparent in Hegel and the second in Comte. The first is that philosophical systems are never mutually contradictory but at most contrary; contradiction in fact would put a stop to the reconciliation of the thesis and antithesis in a synthesis, and consequently to the gradual progress and enrichment of thought; the existence of contradictory systems would be fatal to the system which sees in history continuity of one and the same thought. The second postulate is that in philosophy there is no real recurrence; otherwise the evolution would not occur in one single direction, as the theorists of progress maintain. Now Renouvier, who adheres on this point to the view that had always been held before the smoke of Romanticism had clouded the mind, believes he can prove these two postulates false. In the first place there exist systems which are contradictory, systems that is to say which reply *yes* to the questions to which others reply *no*; there are some which affirm free choice and others which deny it; some affirm and others deny the creation. The second postulate also is false: the past does in fact supply us with the same contradictory answers endlessly recurring under different forms. We have but to set aside these forms, which are due to accidental differences of language and to the many methods which more advanced knowledge has provided for the expression of ideas, to recognize the same doctrine in Spencer's evolutionism as in the physicists of Miletus. There would thus be conflicts in philosophical thought, as was claimed in the ancient world by the Sceptics, which no arguing can solve and which no progress can succeed in dispelling; there can be no decision in favour of one of the two possible alternatives, except by a free choice, to which our will is determined by motives of the same kind as those which make us prefer one action to another.

What was completely transformed by the views of Renouvier was the perspective in which the historical past was seen. If there really is freedom of choice as between systems, we must be prepared for the succession of doctrines to be fundamentally contingent; this succession is historical in the fullest sense of the word, in the sense that it can be recounted but not explained; in history we have to deal not with pure ideas linked together, but with persons who make decisions. It is not due to an idle curiosity for biographical detail that the actual historian of philosophy does not confine himself to the abstract formulae of a doctrine, but concerns himself with individual thinkers, but because it is only in them that he finds that living thought of which philosophy really consists.

Positivism and the philosophy of mind, considered as history of philosophy, suffer from a further serious fault. They had established themselves in opposition to that discursive scholarship the result of which we saw in Bayle. In these histories everything was deliberately excluded from the field of vision which did not appear to be embraced by history as they understood it, that is to say as the advent among mankind of western man. Hence arose, particularly in Comte, that narrow conception of the West as evolving of its own accord with no other connexion with the rest of mankind than that of a master guiding all men towards the future. But this is not all: not only did Hegel and Comte exclude from history whatever did not humour their philosophical Messianism, but in their own preserved spheres they were hostile to those detailed researches through which questions have new light thrown upon them. Thus they put a stop to science and scholarship at a certain point, at the point, that is to say, at which their *a priori* ideas were proved. Here we are poles apart from Bayle's submissive attitude to facts.

This is the reason why, in spite of the brilliance of Hegel's gifts as an historian of philosophy, in spite of the fact that many of his views still command admiration to-day, in spite even of his great personal learning, the history of philosophy could only advance if it freed itself from a master of such formidable genius. It followed the course imposed upon it by that development of scholarship which characterized the end of last century and our own: it is by this collective philological work, pursued without intermission, that we succeed in getting at the details of history. I cannot here give even an approximate idea of this work, whose effect is revealed only gradually: gradually the inadequacy and poverty of the frames within which we have thought of the past becomes apparent. This is very important, because the idea we form of the human mind depends, to a great extent, on what we know of its past. Quite recently it was possible to say of the Middle Ages: 'Here is a vast world which has not yet been explored.'[1] This exploration, like that of many other spheres, is long and difficult, not only because it requires specialized workers, but much more because it demands from them a philosophical acumen which makes it possible for them to grasp the significance and value of documents. To what an extent the historian of philosophy could profit from the researches of Orientalists when philosophical intelligence is allied to the precision of learned research is shown, for instance, in the fine articles published by René Berthelot in the *Revue de Métaphysique*, under the title 'Astrobiologie et pensée de l'Asie: Essai sur les origines des sciences et des arts'. According to these researches Greek science, and with it the whole of Western philosophy, seems to depend on that vast movement of ideas which, in about the sixth century B.C., was radiating from Iran eastwards and westwards simultaneously. More and more it is being recognized that modern discoveries do not only add to what is known, but transform the frames within which we set out the events in the history of the mind. Thus a history of philosophy is taking shape which is now neither the scattered and dispersed history of Bayle's *Dictionary*, nor a kind of enthusiastic annunciation of the birth of the mind in the manner

[1] M. Gorce, *L'Essor de la pensée au moyen âge*, 1933.

of Hegel. This new history of philosophy is passionately devoted to exact and minute researches only because they alone can transform our picture of the human mind, just as, retaining the right proportions, it is by pushing the preciseness of his experiments beyond the limits hitherto known that the physicist has transformed his view of the universe.

Translated by Mary Morris, Oxford.

PLATONISM IN AUGUSTINE'S PHILOSOPHY OF HISTORY

By ERNST HOFFMANN

I

AUGUSTINE is for all centuries of Christian thought the founder of Christian philosophical ideas (*Bildungswelt*). He was this (1) inasmuch as all his successors drew principally upon him. And he was this (2) inasmuch as his *Civitas Dei* afforded foundation and inducement to a new conception of Christian civilization.

No doubt there seems much to be said in advance against the possibility for Augustine of a philosophy of civilization or of an attempt to explore the world undertaken by any sort of learning (*Wissenschaft*).

1. We are already living in the Sixth Age, i.e. in the last before God's Sabbath. In essentials, history lies behind us. The World-Week, which God has appointed to humanity for their existence, has for the most part already elapsed; thus there remains but little still to be done.

2. There can be no question of a systematic philosophy of civilization, since for Augustine there is primarily no question of learning at all. He deals with learning only because the opponents of Christianity appeal to learning. He cannot get at these unbelievers with Christian 'experience'. He gets at them therefore with learning; i.e. the Christian, with his supernatural consciousness through faith, takes into service the alien weapons of natural *ratio*. But *ratio*, according to Augustine, can strictly give no perfected system; for all perfection comes from love, which is above all reason.

3. A philosophy of civilization could only be philosophy about the *civitas terrena*; but this is something corrupt. *Civitas terrena* and *divina* constitute an absolute opposition. The τμῆμα of Plato between the world of Ideas and the world of appearances is transformed into the sharper τμῆμα between God's grace and God's wrath. Here there is no proportional connexion and no mean. There are two quite different historical communities: the earthly states based on force, which, being born

of sin, of necessity go to meet their fearful end at the day of judgement; and the communion of saints, which makes its pilgrimage invisibly through temporal history, to be admitted at last through the grace of God to the eternal *frui Deo*. There is no question of an antithesis between 'Christian' state and 'unchristian', nor yet of the antithesis between 'state' and 'church'. Rather the question is about the antithesis: 'invisible divine city', 'visible worldly city'. The country of the one lies in the world above; the other has its roots here below. Above all, visible and invisible. Not one of us knows whether he is a citizen of the divine city. Not even he who receives the sacrament knows whether he really receives it. For all human knowledge the question of citizenship remains open. Both historical communities pass through time.

4. Earthly life in the earthly city is corrupt in principle by sin since the fall of Adam. Not merely blemished, but corrupt. Hence the whole of empirical history deserves to perish. Out of a vessel which the potter has shaped for dishonour a vessel of honour cannot be made. Augustine's Tmematism can never be too sharply, never too radically interpreted.

And yet it was worth while for Augustine to write a kind of Christian philosophy—*Doctrina Christiana*. And to each of our four objections he has given an answer:

1. The history of the world is no doubt nearly over. But just as on the sixth day of the week of creation God wrought upon the world, so on the Friday of the world's history He still works upon us, in order then to rest. God had a purpose with the world and with us, and this purpose, for all those who believe in Him, is never done. Every endeavour, so far from slackening just before the goal, must rather, just before the goal, strain every nerve. The farther history has proceeded, the more irreparable becomes the historical event. The ideas of the ancients about the revolution of the ages, the transmigration of souls, &c., are for Christianity done away. History has become linear: a beginning, Adam; a central datum, Jesus; a uni-dimensional movement in time with a single goal, the day of judgement. We do not know the duration of our sixth age, but it is the age of the final decision. If we ourselves can do nothing for the decision, surely we stand as means in the service of God's decision. And that suffices. Not although, but because, it is the eleventh hour, the work is now of special importance. There

can be no time to be lost. The eschatological consciousness is a hindrance to Augustine as little as to Paul. On the contrary.

2. No doubt for Augustine it cannot be primarily a question of philosophical (*wissenschaftliches*) interest; his motive is not a systematic one. But he makes bold to smite the heathen systematists with their own weapons. The heathen philosophers deride the Christian because he believes, e.g., in the resurrection of the dead. But in what then does the Platonist believe, or the Aristotelian? E.g., in the combination of body and soul in the individual man. Augustine asks: Which, then, is the greater marvel? Is it a greater marvel that a body should once for all rise in spiritual glory, than that the spirit appearing for a lifetime in bodily form has knowledge of truth? Thus the Christian needs learning not for the sake of Christianity, but in the interests of apologetics.

3. The opposition between earthly and heavenly is absolute. But there is a kind of opposition which makes possible a triadic division. The great prophets, for example, have said much about Jerusalem which can only be interpreted allegorically, and thus is only to be applied to the heavenly Jerusalem; much else, which applies only to the earthly Jerusalem and is to be taken literally; but, thirdly, much which relates to both. In the Bible, therefore, we must not only think of the heavenly and of the earthly Jerusalem, but we must see the heavenly in a particular relation to the earthly. This principle of scriptural interpretation is significant for the interpretation of being in general: learning is the interpretation of signs, traces, symbols. The result of this is as follows.

4. There is, after all, a certain possibility of diminishing the effect of sin in the earthly city, of ameliorating the course of history, of uplifting civilization. Instances:

a. Servitude has come into being through sin; God's creatures have come to be slaves of men. Nevertheless, even out of servitude something serviceable to order can be made through legislation.

b. Money is the invention of covetousness, soldiers the creation of the lust for power; yet money can be used for charitable works, armies for the security of peace. Sexual desire is bondage to concupiscence, nevertheless it can be brought into service for the founding of the Christian family.

c. Even about peace itself we see that at bottom there is only the peace of the world above, the struggles of the world below. But are there not strivings after peace in the world below? The problem of the Platonic μεταξύ is renewed on a Christian basis.

Thus, even in the earthly there is to be a striving after perfection, and there are in Nature 'signs' that it is to be so: there is the perpetuation of the species in reproduction; there is fitness for purpose in the organism; there is healing and help in the art of invention. Whence comes it? From the fact that before the state of sin there was a primitive state, and then the world was in that state of perfection which corresponded with the will of God. There is in fact not only the dualism between the earthly city and the divine city. This dualism is absolute in the same sense as wrath and grace, perdition and redemption. But there is in addition the dualism between primitive state and state of sin, and this has a different structure.

Whether we are citizens of the heavenly or of the earthly city we do not know, and it is not our affair to know. God has reserved this knowledge for himself; surely he has decreed it from eternity; and we are not able to influence his decree in the least, for there is no merit in the sight of God. It would impair the majesty of the Augustinian conception of God if God could be moved from his purpose by human power. All this is fundamental fact of Augustine's religious experience. But it is one thing to wish to obtain the grace of God, another to wish to show oneself worthy of the grace of God. And this means that, taking as our pattern that earthly perfection of the primitive state, which once was, before human guilt corrupted it, we must seek to diminish the corruption of civilization. Sin was indeed mortal for human history, but death itself cannot ruin all. As the divinely willed bloom of the body is often visible even in death, so we can and ought even in the mortal sickness of human civilization to heal, cherish, amend as much as stands in our power, not for the sake of the patient, but for the sake of that which the world ought to have been, and could have been, according to the will of God. It is not enough that the Christian —as though he were certain of his citizenship in the *Civitas divina*—lives religiously in the world above instead of in the world below; rather, he must seek, in spite of the state of sin, to bring the earthly city once again nearer to the primitive state. And here Augustine thinks never of institutions, but always of the heart. He issues no external precepts; rather, my duty lies between the world below and the world above—to bring into consciousness the primitive state, and thereby to lay hold upon the only means of avoiding the adoption of that which is unworthy in the sight of God as something willed and promoted by me.

Historically considered, this whole conception of Augustine's rests chiefly on the Stoic adaptation of Platonism. The primitive state in Paradise is the *aurea aetas*, in which the Ideas of God entering into the world were as yet clearly and uncorruptedly immanent in earthly existence. But for the Stoa this primitive state is in some respect to be recaptured, through *medicina animi*, through the invisible city of the wise, through philosophy. The pattern is for the Stoic visibly there—the Cosmos, the divine universe. We see in the visible universe the objective Logos, and can make the God in us become the subjective Logos, by creating the moral Cosmos of civilization as a second world in addition to that of nature. On the other hand, Augustine's philosophy of history appears almost negative: in principle there simply is nothing to be done. Civilization is for him not work upon the world, but work for the glory of God. For Augustine the world was in principle finished when God had created it in its perfection. For the Stoa it was not finished when the Logos became immanent in it; but in the course of history a second world was to be brought into being. Thus the first philosophy of history springs not from the Stoa, not from Augustine, but only from both together. For the decisive marks of the concept of history are (1) that the world was not finished; (2) the linear dimension, which the Stoa does not know. For it there is only the cycle of the ages, the periodic conflagration of the world, i.e. history as the circular revolution of a cosmic aggregation, in which end and beginning fall together in a single fire, in which the old is consumed and the new flames forth. For Augustine there is only a single history, because Christ has come once only; and that the course of history has only one dimension appears from the fact that our sense of history has only one dimension.

II

About the turn of the eighteenth and nineteenth centuries there was a time in which books were written about the so-called Platonism of the Fathers, which, it was thought, attained its zenith in Augustine's *Civitas Dei*. At that time theologians held the view that Augustine knew Greek, that, further, he wrote his *Civitas Dei* as a Christian counterpart to Plato's *Republic*, and indeed that Augustine found his individual way from his heathen youth to his later conversion along the by-road through Plato.

But these assumptions have not stood their ground. Augustine was unable to read any Greek texts: he knew Greek only in Roman tradition, in Latin digests. Hence, Plato most probably was known to him through Cicero almost alone, and consequently in a transformation which had undergone in the schools the alterations of three centuries. And the *Civitas Dei* has no relation at all to Plato's *Republic*. For the doctrine of the *Republic* means to save the empirical city through participation in the Idea of Justice; the *Civitas Dei* does not mean to save the earthly city, but to utter a warning against it. And Augustine came to Christianity not on the by-road through Plato, but through Neoplatonism. He had attached himself at first to the Manichaean sect, i.e. to a particularly crude form of Gnosticism which teaches that there is a good and an evil God, a principle of light and a principle of darkness, which are in a state of war against one another. Then he had gone over to the school of the Sceptics, who were then called 'Academics', and hoped to obtain from suspense of judgement some satisfaction of his longing for quiet and peace. But it was only the third and last phase of his heathen period that brought him, at least for a time, philosophical satisfaction. This was the time in which he attached himself to the Neoplatonists. Not two Gods, One only, only the Good. Not Gnostic magic, which in reality was materialism, but Plotinus' world of thought, his spiritualism, his life of the spirit, his sense of being at home in a world of spirits. And not sceptical renunciation, but the kindling of that longing after truth, which then became a preparation to make Augustine ready to receive Christian baptism. His course of development, then, had nothing to do with genuine Platonism.

But in a deeper sense Augustine is a Platonist. Neither as a Platonizing Christian nor as a Christian adept of Platonism, but as the Plato of Christianity. What is fundamental in Plato's philosophical thought lies in the fact that he makes the starting-point of his whole philosophy the conviction that there is one unconditionally right way of thinking; hence *only* one (for truth is one); hence outside of this only false ways. That alone is true which can be legitimated by that one right thinking. And right thinking consists in our affirming the being of that which is, i.e. the being of the Ideas; for that alone which is thought as Idea is thought as 'being'. Thus the sphere of becoming is *beneath* being, for it does not satisfy the demands of true thinking; and just as surely God is *above* being and becoming, for He draws becoming towards being. In the fact that this principle (to hold fast to the one unconditionally right way of thinking) is fundamental, and that the three theses which follow from that way of thinking (viz. God, the world of Ideas, and the world of appearance) are fundamental, lies the essence of genuine Platonism. But in this sense Augustine is a genuine Platonist.

For there is for him only one unconditionally right way of thinking. *Divinum* and *terrenum*, grace and sin, heavenly and earthly, holy and unholy, are absolute contradictories. There is only one point of section, and to go beyond it is a sign of false thinking. And from this one right thinking there result the three fundamental theses of Augustinianism: there is God; there is the divine city; and there is the earthly city.

Augustine's God is not the Platonic ἀγαθόν, Augustine's divine city is not Plato's sphere of Ideas, Augustine's earthly city is not Plato's world of sense. But where Plato muses on εἶδος and εἴδωλον, there Augustine muses on the near to God and the far from God. Where Plato muses on the formative function of the Good, there Augustine muses on the wrath and love of God the Father. But the philosophical teaching of both thinkers has the same structure: a doctrine of two worlds, and God. And as this structure of Platonism first set Greek philosophy its problem, so Augustinianism with its analogous structure first set Christian philosophical thought its problem. Seen against Greek philosophy as a whole, even thinkers like Heraclitus and Parmenides are only forerunners of Plato; for the critical illumination of the antithesis of νόησις and αἴσθησις is as yet foreign to them. And seen against Christian philosophy as a whole, even thinkers like Clement and Origen are only forerunners of Augustine; for they philosophize about God and human nature, but not about the divine sphere, the sphere of communion with God, which did not exist as a problem for the philosophical consciousness before the *Civitas Dei*.

Indeed, I will go further. Just as Platonism allows us to understand the whole of subsequent Greek philosophy as the development of a problem from a single root, so it is in turn with Augustinianism and the whole of Christian philosophy.

Plato's triad of theses leads fundamentally to three solutions. Plato himself abides by the tmematic. He prefers the creation of fundamentally unphilosophical forms of exposition (μῦθος) to the surrender of the tmematism in his philosophical doctrine. But Aristotle passes over to the continuity of thought; thought conforms to objects, and objects constitute that great series which is called the world. This is the second way, leading to intellectualism. The essence of the world is inferred from the way in which the intellect represents it. And the Hellenistics go the third way, the mystical. They set out from Plato's tmematism, but posit the uninterrupted transitions of Aristotle, and allow the transitions between the conditioned and the unconditioned to become at last a mystical union of both.

So too Augustine's triad of theses leads to three solutions. He himself abides by the tmematic. He prefers to allow the grossest contradictions to remain in his doctrine (especially those between the doctrine of grace and the doctrine of sacraments) rather than to bridge the gulf between God and the world. But Scholasticism passes over to the continuous thought of Aristotle. The realm of *Natura* has its upper limit at the point where the ecclesiastical realm of *Gratia* begins, and the realm of *Gratia* ascends hierarchically to end where God's *Gloria* begins. This is the second way, leading to the rationalism of the Scholastics, with its culmination in Thomas. But even in Christianity Mysticism takes a third way. It does not set itself in opposition to Scholasticism; even Meister Eckhart was a Scholastic as much as any one. But what appeared to the merely Scholastic philosophy as an uninterrupted syllogistic sequence of finite steps in thought leading from the earthly to the heavenly becomes for the mystic a momentary and immediate intuition of God in the depths of the soul.

In this way I have tried to indicate in what sense the appearance of Augustine in intellectual history stands under the sign of Plato. Just as Plato made the problem of form into a canon, starting from which philosophical thought may reach to God and to the world, so Augustine's divine sphere of the *Civitas divina*, the realm of eternal communion with God, becomes the stimulus to the raising of all further problems. This can be expressed also as follows. Plato's peculiar victory was a victory on two fronts: over the Sophists and over the Orphics. It was the relativism, the scepticism, the nihilism of the Sophists against which he contended. They denied being, knowledge, permanence. They splashed about in a sea of liquefied concepts. Over against this he set his postulate of the Ideas: Being is accessible. And against the Orphic he maintained: the Good is accessible. The Good is not annihilated by the original sin of humanity, but it acts as a sun in the realm of Ideas, and thus indirectly in the world of sense. Augustine's historical achievement for Christian thought was wholly analogous—against Manichaean Gnosticism, which taught that there is a second, evil Demiurge; and against the Academic Scepsis, which took its stand upon suspense of judgement. Directed against Gnosticism—his radical Monotheism of the Good; evil lives only as ungodliness in the corrupt state of the human will. Directed against the Scepsis—the conviction of the existence of the divine sphere; there is not only God and his absence in the evil will, but there is also his presence in the heavenly Jerusalem. That is the chief thing. Shortly before the Greek πόλις was shattered for ever,[1] Plato had given to Greek philosophy that structure which defied all decay. Shortly before the Roman Empire of the West was shattered,[2] Augustine (*d.* 430) had through his philosophy so established Christianity on its intellectual basis, and had given the Christian theory of civilization (*Kulturproblematik*) a structure so filled with the devout life of thought, that the Church stood fast when the Empire was shattered.

The analogy, which from the point of view of the history of philosophy exists between Platonism and Augustinianism, must be guarded against misinterpretations.

1. The cultural roots of Augustine were of course not in the classical text of Plato, but wholly in the philosophical ideas of imperial times, with their Hellenistic foundations. His Latin was schooled in Virgil; his calling before his conversion to Christianity was that of a Rhetor; hence his eloquence is that of the Roman Neo-Sophists. All that he knows of Plato is the

[1] The battle of Chaeronea was in 338, nine years after the death of Plato.

[2] In 476 Romulus Augustulus was deposed and Rome came under German sway.

tradition of the Roman Stoa, of the late Scepsis and the school of Plotinus. All that he knows of Aristotle is some part of the *Organon* in a Latin translation. The ideal of the Platonic-Stoic sage is known to him from Cicero's *Hortensius*. The primitive state is conceived after the fashion of the Stoic *aurea aetas*.

2. In speaking of cultural 'roots', we must think in the case of Augustine only of the so-called heathen culture, not of a Christian one. As yet there was no Christian culture such as there was later, in the Middle Ages, when for instance the thought of the Church and that of the Empire interpenetrated, when ecclesiastical and worldly culture were mutually complementary, and when 'history' extended before men's eyes. Augustine is conscious of standing at the end of heathen history, and consequently at the end of history in general, not, like Plato, at the beginning of a new era. And Augustine clings to heathen antiquity with great love in spite of all his hatred. It is with pride that he speaks of the virtues of his Romans, although they belong to the earthly condition. Even as a Christian, he has no thought of repudiating the technique of heathen oratory of which he was a master, but rather he makes full use of it. If he believes that in the resurrection of the dead man is to rise in the form which the body had in the time of its prime, that is the Greek ἀκμή. The whole world of antiquity is still alive around and in Augustine, even along with the numerous Oriental influences, which from the second century B.C. flowed into it in increasing measure. And Augustine developed away from Oriental Gnosticism to Greek learning, precisely like the Apologists and Fathers before him. Christianity will not allow the reproach to lie against it that it is irrational, hence it seeks to attach itself to genuine Greek philosophy, and holds Gnosticism at arm's length all the more stubbornly, the more the latter reaches the philosophers of the late antiquity of heathendom. But against all this, against Augustine's Hellenic culture and against his Roman pride, there is arrayed the consciousness of an idea wholly new and growing only out of his Christian experience.

He sees that the whole of antiquity with its wisdom and knowledge is, for those decisions which the Christian as a Christian has to make, inessential. The philosopher of antiquity denies error and affirms the truth. The Christian affirms error as well. Error even acquires a meaning. To err is indeed the life of our individual souls. Of themselves, our souls can *only* err. But in the midst of our error we are called by God. In the midst of our erring soul falls the decision which sets the standard for our life. For this reason Augustine writes the *Confessions*, with which, making as it were a clean break with antiquity, Christian literature begins. Autobiography as the history of an erring seeker after God. Evil and error are no longer thought away, as is done by the Stoics and Platonists; but they are also not ascribed to any second God as their *causa*, as in Gnosticism. But neither were they, as by the Sophists, relativistically put on a level with truth. Rather, the heart reveals its erring, in order to make visible the grace of God in the error. God does not make the μέθεξις in the Good dependent—any more than with Plato—either on the natural structure of things or upon the striving after knowledge by the rational part of the soul, but rather God allows himself to be found by those whom he has called. This may happen at any moment; nothing depends any longer upon degrees of knowledge, but everything upon grace. *Plato* traces the degree of μέθεξις attained, *Augustine* traces the soul's erring ways so long as God was absent. The world and man become in a wholly new sense the object of a study: man as *erring* man; the world as *sinful* world. That is Augustine's way to history.

III

The problems set out for solution in Augustine's *Doctrina Christiana* are as follows:

How can hermeneutics be divine and yet capable of being learned by men?

How can truth be absolute and yet contained in knowledge which is relative?

How can learning bear a Christian character and yet be learning?

This is the third form in which the old dualism between the sphere of the divine and absolute and that of the earthly and relative recurs in Augustine. We found it, in the first place, in the two historical communities which pass through time. This antithesis remains radical. We found it, secondly, in the going astray of the soul and its being called by God. This antithesis too remains radical. We find it, thirdly, in the absolute character of the meaning of God's Word, and in the enterprise imposed upon us of fathoming this meaning. The question is: Does the antithesis, here also, remain radical?

Augustine replies: For the work of divining the sense and expounding the text of Scripture two maxims hold good: (1) to him that hath, shall be given; (2) the loaves of Jesus increase while they are shared out. That is, the interpreter must himself have a gift which comes from God, but he does not possess this gift until he shares it out: through being passed on it is increased. The Christian is thus for Augustine something active. He must be active, in order to be an instrument for God's activity. The working of God affects only the doing of something. God does not cease to give us the gift, if we apply it. The bread grows while it is broken. *Ministerio abundantia gaudemus.* In serving we attain to abundance; in sharing out we increase the substance. How, then, does the antithesis present itself in this third respect?

Every one thinks of Plotinus, of the substance which does not lose by giving away, of the superabundant spring which does not become poorer through emanation. But while we think of Plotinus, we see at the same time the change that has appeared with Christian thought. The ἕν of Plotinus flows forth into empty space: the God of Augustine will act only if he lights upon activity. Plotinus' conception of emanation is still purely cosmological. The Cosmos, as the emanation of God, is the performance of a play of which the author is God. The Cosmic drama of the world, as a performance, is in every part as inactive as what takes place before us on a stage. According to Plotinus, indeed, the beauty of this drama of the world lies precisely in the fact that it is written by the best author, who very well knows what he is doing when, for the sake of dramatic effect, he avoids merely bringing on the stage so many heroes of virtue, and introduces evil as a counterpart. On the other hand, to Augustine's transformed idea of emanation, as to everything Christian, the word applies, 'Behold, I make all things new'. Our function is not to play a part written by God, but 'what he has entrusted (*praebuit*) to us, that we must actively spend, in order that we may ourselves attain to a *mirabilis abundantia*'. In Plotinus only God's idea of his drama is 'good', the performance is a mere copy. In Augustine the good is to be actively created in the world. The wholly new stamp of 'historical' thought is seen in the *Doctrina Christiana.* In the Cosmos of Plotinus it is of no importance whether anything new comes into being. Rather, nothing new would have any place there. Whether it is through semination or explication or emanation that the One becomes the multiplicity of the world, it must be a matter of indifference to God (i.e. it does not touch his own being) what the multiple does. Whatever God gives forth, whatever comes from him, the *αὐτόγραφον* of his play, was and is good. It is only to *our* interest that we play well our prescribed part, for the sake of the universe (in order that the Cosmos should be fair). Contrariwise in Augustine God works in us, in order thereby to work farther afield. He shares out in order to augment by sharing out. He aims in history at a definitive meaning, at a decision, at a victory; and this He will in His omnipotence accomplish; the decision will fall out as He wills. It will so fall out that earthly history, be it as example, be it as warning, be it as it may, shall prove itself to be the prelude to eternity. And God has resolved so to order it that this decision comes about not through outward events but in human souls. It is in souls that there is fought the fight for and against God, for and against the divinely willed meaning of history. God needs and means to need fighting, striving, active souls. These alone are worthy of the *pax aeterna*. But above all—the fight in ourselves. That is the new thing, the Christian thing. God needs no players for His play, but He will have warriors for His purposes. Why? Because for Augustine the divine sphere is from the beginning a sphere of communion. God will have around Him such as He has created after His own likeness, and such as have not fallen away from this likeness. Just as God's life is the life of a trinity, and thus of a community, so also the *Civitas divina* belongs to him. God is no longer the thought that thinks itself; no longer the One which remains beyond all number-series. But God is the Love which wills to love, and therefore wills communion, and therefore is surrounded from everlasting to everlasting by the *Civitas divina*. The devout hope of the *anima Christiana* rests on the fact that the sphere of the Absolute is not only a Platonic Beyond, but an Augustinian Future. And starting from this conception all philosophical ideas have been transformed: (1) the meaning of the earthly in history (*Civitas Dei*); (2) the meaning of the soul (*Confessions*); (3) the meaning of learning (*Doctrina Christiana*). In all three we have the same radical dualism of the Either-Or.

1. If we are chosen citizens of the *Civitas Dei*, we never come

to feel at home on earth, whether we be king or beggar or bishop. We go on pilgrimage through a strange land, and every attempt to settle goes amiss. If we are citizens of the earthly city, then it is all in vain that we urgently propose to God the surrender of this citizenship. The enjoyment of earthly goods is our very self. No philosophy can venture to penetrate into the mystery as to why this is predestinated. Faith in God's grace is the Christian *a priori*. That everything proceeds only from grace cannot be disputed. But according to Augustine we have understood not even a line of the gospel, if we believe that the harshness of this dualism leaves no opening for our individual efforts. A heathen may and must think thus. But if God is Love, if the divine sphere is communion, then the fact that we are bound to God already exists; and if I am bound to God, then I leave to Him the decision whether my effort shall bear fruit: only the effort is my affair. And for that I am able, because I have the primitive state above me as an ideal, and victory, eternal blessedness, eternal life before me.

2. It is not otherwise in the sphere of the soul. The going astray of the soul and her being called by God is again conceived in terms of a rigorous dualism. But for Augustine there follows from this no mere waiting, no expectation of ecstasy, no Quietism. Rather, the state of error and the call are related as seeking and finding. No seeking avails if God does not let Himself be found; but He does not let Himself be found if I do not seek Him. He wills my warfare, my endeavour, and my devotion not although, but because, He Himself is Love. He will not love the unworthy, therefore I must seek to prove myself worthy of Him. His will is to work through me: I must show that my will is that He should work through me. Therefore the case is the same with psychology as with history. Augustine writes the history of the earthly city, because we must know the earthly city if our effort is to have an opening to save in the state of sin so much of the primitive state as is still to be saved. And he writes the *Confessions*, the history of his own soul, which is the history of every soul, because we ought and need to know about our erring soul, if we will that God should let Himself be found by the soul. We must first enter into the consciousness of sin, in order to be able to get out of it. Augustine's *Confessions* reverse the method of all earlier psychology. He does not start out from Plato's innate organ for the good

and rational, from which according to Plato evil and irrationality come into being only through misdirection and being led astray. He does not start out from Aristotle's psychology, with its history of development, which understands the psychical as always an instrument adapted to the end of concrete living. Rather, Augustine starts out from the secret places, from the hidden things in the soul, in which evil has made its nest and become a second nature. First we are to understand that our purposes and desires are evil from our youth up. It is only in the consciousness of sin that we find the signs and traces of the working of the divine will in us. Psychology too must be history. Just as for Plato soul and city are connected, so for Augustine are soul and history. Plato brings soul and city to the common denominator of harmonious structure. The city is the soul in large, and the soul is the city in little, because both—thought of as perfection—represent the inward combination and the accord of those who rule and those who serve. Augustine, on the contrary, starts out, not from the assumed state of perfection, but from the actual state of misery. For the Demiurge of the *Timaeus*, Cosmos and soul have remained in the state in which God bestowed form upon them. For Augustine contrariwise the earthly city and the soul have not remained in the primitive state. And for this reason the start must be made from the evil and the depraved. For 'Nature' no longer means 'whatever has persisted in accordance with the divine will', but rather 'whatever has become depraved contrary to the divine will'. The imperative in turn has acquired through Augustine its incomparably more radical, its categorical form. For Plato, evil has no being at all, none that is enduring and subsistent. Evil only arises ever again from the misuse of human freedom of choice. There is no evil in itself, but only the good, which is represented by the Ideas, and alongside it our freedom to act according to the ideal or to fall away from it. But according to Augustine the consequence of Adam's fall has been precisely this, that evil has become existent, and that our function is not, primarily, to make this or that decision, but, primarily, to annihilate the evil which has become radical. There is no decision for the good without warfare against evil, and evil is nowhere else but in ourselves. And it is only as proceeding from us that it is in the earthly city. The Platonic dualism has thus become so much the more rigid because it goes through and through us. The soul is no longer the original thing of beauty and singleness—now become overlaid and encrusted with dross, the removal of which is a negative undertaking; rather, it is an organism sick in its principle, the treatment of which rests on the presupposition that those parts which by God's grace have remained whole should be found out by the study of the sick organism. These parts are the signs and traces of God's grace. It is there that the *nova vita* must make a beginning. Here too we see that the moral imperative has become categorical, just because the dualism is radical. The worse the disease, the more radical the cure. And the fact that the decision lies with God does not take his office from the physician.

3. Precisely analogous is the transformation of the conception of learning through the Christian principle that between the Bible as the object of Christian learning and us as the readers of the Bible is fixed that gulf which is absolute. God's word is of such majesty that in comparison every word of man becomes nothing. But again there is as our function—quite without regard to the chance of success—the striving after understanding. What the earthly is for is not to extort anything, but to become worthy of an act of grace. To learn, to labour, to be active are divinely willed because God is a father who of his own will needs his children. Our heart not only *is* restless until it finds rest in God; but it *must* be restless, in order to find rest in God. Even learning, interpreting, striving after the meaning of God's word is enjoined and may not be got rid of by any spiritual exaltation. What God gives us in ecstasy is his affair. It is not our affair to prepare ecstasy, still less to set up the mystic in the place of God's word; but rather through labour to become a willing child of God for the purpose of His work in us and through us.

Thus through Augustine there comes into Christianity the motive of labouring at the cultivation of the mind (history, education, learning), not for the sake of the cultivation of the mind, but for the sake of the divinely willed fact that God is surrounded by the *Civitas divina* as his eternal company. We can do nothing in order to belong to it; but a great deal in order to be worthy of it, in case we do belong to it. We can bring home to the earthly city the consciousness that there is a divine city. We can reveal human error as the ground where God implants His grace. And we can establish Christian learning in order, by interpreting the Word, to labour along with the working of the divine Word.

All this is for the heathen 'a preaching of foolishness'; all this, for the heathen, paradox. Why? Because it is in principle irrational. Because the obligatory follows not from a rational syllogism, but from a metaphysical consciousness. The *sapiens* of antiquity says indeed: Whatever is neither deductively demonstrable nor inductively certain, must in accordance with natural logic be held for unreal, therefore the character of actuality is missing from the Augustinian construction. But Augustine, who always studies to refute the objection that for Christianity the will is not rational, could appeal precisely to the logical character of the imperative, which enters into the system neither of deductive nor of inductive analytics. As a whole, the ethics of antiquity—so he might have said—can legitimate only hypothetical imperatives; if something exists, something else ought to exist. That is the limit of the ethics of antiquity, because—like all the learning of antiquity—it sets out from being. Only Plato had removed the Good as the supreme conception of pure obligation from the sphere of being; but he himself had not, in Augustine's view, drawn the correct conclusion for ethics. He has founded ethics upon Ideas, and hence in turn upon being. Ethics teaches us how, in the moral sphere, we must copy and imitate, so far as is humanly possible, the pure forms which are set up as patterns. Plato's ἀγαθόν, in fact, does not speak; it builds, forms, shapes. Augustine's God, on the other hand, has spoken. Christianity is not natural religion, but book-religion. There is, in fact, a difference between the sculptor-God of the *Timaeus* and the creator-God of *Genesis*. For God *said*, 'Let there be light'; and there was light. God's deed was the creative Word; even from the beginning of the world onwards the being of the world was bound to the *word* of God. In the creative Word the first imperative lay implicit. And for that reason every word of God directed to us appeals primarily not to our reason but to our will. Christian ethics is thus not deduction transferred to the sphere of obligation, but obedience from the first and independent of all logic; it has a voluntary, not a rational character. Before the world that exists there was the word of God, which said how it was to be. Just as God (according to Plato) is above being, so (according to Augustine) must also our will have the primacy over our knowledge. That is the only thing that matters in the Christian ethics. Not the immanent goods, the values, the purposes of human civilization matter, but the quality of our will, the direction of our intention, the fundamental obedience towards the word of God, which is always to be a creative Word, so far as in us the hearers it is to be more widely effective, to be dynamic, to work in time towards the decision about the destiny of the world. Just as Plato laid the foundation for knowledge, when he took up a position as far removed as heaven from the tangible objects of sensuous knowledge, so Augustine became the first philosopher of civilization, because he derived its meaning from the absolute nature of the moral imperative, not from that which can be relative in respect of time and situation.

Translated by D. R. Cousin, University of Glasgow.

THE CARTESIAN SPIRIT AND HISTORY

By LUCIEN LÉVY-BRUHL

DESCARTES spoke of history in the 'Considerations concerning the sciences' which form the first part of the *Discours de la Méthode.* He recognized that 'the memorable actions in history elevate the mind, and if read with discretion help to form the judgement'; but when he passed on from this to criticism of what his teachers at the college at La Flèche had taught him, he laid emphasis on the reservations which he had already indicated in the passage just quoted. 'Even the most reliable historians, if they do not alter or enhance the value of things to make them more deserving of being read, at least almost always omit from them the most lowly and least notable circumstances; which means that the remainder does not appear as it really is, and that those who regulate their behaviour by the examples they derive from history are apt to succumb to the extravagances of the paladins of our story-books, and to conceive projects which exceed their powers.'

Thus, history cannot claim to be exact. Since it does not say everything, it falsifies the perspective of the past; it is nearer to romantic fiction than to scientific knowledge. On this theme Descartes's successors have written plentiful variations. They rarely missed an opportunity of showing historians and scholars that they had an extremely low opinion of the matters with which they were concerned. Malebranche, in particular, did not spare his epigrams, jeers, and even sarcasms at their expense. His example was followed by a number of Cartesians.

What is the explanation of this disdainful and hostile attitude to an order of studies which to-day seems to us indispensable to the knowledge of mankind, and which, since the beginning of the nineteenth century, has so widely developed? The question would undoubtedly require a profound investigation. I am afraid I can only give here some brief indications of a general nature.

In the first place we must remember that when Descartes wrote, what was called history was very different from what is called by that name to-day. History was not expected to strive to follow a strict method, to conform to the rules of a compulsory technique. It was 'a species of literature'. The best historian was he who showed the greatest talent as a writer, who had the greatest gift for composing the speeches which he put into the mouth of his characters, with the most pleasing and eloquent style. Did not Descartes, without any sense of irony, put the historian beside the writer of romances? Not that historical criticism was altogether unknown. But it found its employment elsewhere, for instance, among the great philologists who produced such fine works on the literary and philosophical texts of antiquity. These scholars were working for their peers, who alone were capable of appreciating them. They troubled little about the public at large, which for its part ignored them. They were specialists and they held themselves apart. From principle, as much as from taste and temperament, they wished to have nothing in common with the history which was 'a species of literature'. This is the only kind of history which Descartes had in mind in the passages I have quoted.

He was seeking, he tells us, among the sciences which he had been taught for those in which his reason could rest satisfied. History, an exercise in eloquence, without serious criticism of its sources, without curiosity, and making no effort to attain facts which were a little hidden, or to be at least relatively accurate, could not but be immediately set aside. Descartes had no need to emphasize the reasons which he gives, nor to add others to them, to justify an exclusion which, so to speak, goes without saying. But if he had been faced with historical works of a different spirit, based on a methodical and profound study of sources, would he have shown himself more favourable? The dominant tendencies of his thought, and his constant attitude in regard to the philosophy and science of his time, do not allow us to think so. They imply a lack of sympathy, one might even say a kind of aversion, or, if it is preferred, an absence of comprehension, in relation to researches of an historical nature.

One of his most cherished desires, an end at which he aimed all his life and which at times he thought himself near to attaining, was to substitute his own philosophy (understood in a wide sense as embracing the sciences of nature) for that which the scholastic tradition was teaching in the universities—for example, the philosophy of the teachers of Coimbra. It was his ambition to replace a body of doctrines which were almost all verbal by a philosophy based on rational principles and strictly demonstrated. At the same time the method of authority was to disappear. This is why, in spite of the traces of scholastic thought and language that commentators have been able, quite rightly, to point out in the writings of Descartes, he appeared to his contemporaries and successors as a reformer and even as a revolutionary. To listen to Descartes was to break with tradition, to consider it, as he did, as at the same time inadequate and injurious, and to join in the struggle to get rid of it. This struggle was not without danger, since, in spite of Descartes's precautions, and in spite of his efforts to win the support of his former teachers, the Jesuits, it was impossible for him to live in France. Holland, in the end, no longer gave him hospitality, and he had to accept the invitation of the Queen of Sweden. Here the climate, in less than a year, got the better of him.

Now the method of authority, which he was attacking, has the closest connexions with history. If the problems of philosophy can be studied, and solved, only in conformity with the principles transmitted by tradition, it will not be possible to dispense with history. The first condition of a good philosophy will then be to possess an irreproachable statement of these principles and therefore to procure the best possible text of the writings in which they have been formulated; and this text must be freed from the additions and alterations that may have crept into it in the course of time. This preliminary historical task is indispensable. The method of authority, unless it cynically imposes itself by force, therefore needs history to make it legitimate. This may be dangerous to it, in more ways than one, as Bayle undertook to prove.

Descartes himself, when he observed that historical knowledge must always be uncertain and consequently open to suspicion, and that it is of its very nature always subject to doubt, was indirectly striking a blow at the method of authority. For the certainty of tradition implies an historical element. If this element compromises that certainty, tradition loses its power, and the method of authority no longer has an uncontested value. How can we enforce the principles of the great teachers when we are not certain what the great teachers said?

It may be possible that Descartes and his followers held it preferable, for obvious reasons, not to join issue openly with the method of authority. Instead of attacking it directly, it would be easy enough to destroy it without even mentioning it, by showing the impossibility of relying on what is established by history. This is the method which was adopted with regard to the particularly delicate philosophical questions on the margin of theology. Consequently, the Cartesians were led to consider the cause of the method of authority and the cause of history as closely connected together, and so came to adopt an unfriendly attitude to history. They found that they were obliged to make history share the disgrace of scholasticism and to involve both in the same condemnation, in order to clear a place for, and to be able freely to build, a philosophy that was well founded and certain.

These reasons are reasons dictated by circumstances, not to say tactical reasons; and they might be held to be inspired, at any rate in part, by the needs of the struggle against scholasticism. There are others also which are of a more philosophical nature and touch the very foundations of Cartesianism. They appear already in this same first part of the *Discours de la Méthode*, where history is not the only thing to be judged severely. Descartes there reviewed all the 'disciplines' which he had been taught, so that he might estimate their value and discover whether there was any one of them which deserved his continued study. None of them survived the test even of a summary criticism. None therefore found favour in his sight except the mathematical sciences. These sciences alone admitted of rational intuitions and strict demonstrations. Up till that time geometry and algebra alone had satisfied his reason. The use made by scholasticism of the syllogism and its dialectical argumentations were but games with abstract concepts, a kind of purely verbal gymnastics. The most that we could hope to attain by this means was a probability of which there was no guarantee, and which had nothing in common with the truth on which the mind must feed. Nothing deserved that name except what was evident (to the eyes of reason), that is to say, the object of intuition and of demonstration. From the point of view of science and of philosophy everything else is suspect, more or less given up to the delusions of the imagination, to the suggestions of the desires and the passions, and therefore an easy prey to error. When Spinoza said, 'If mathematics did not exist, men would not know what truth is', he was expressing an essentially Cartesian thought. The only thing that counts in science and philosophy is what can justify itself in the eyes of reason. Was it not Spinoza too who said, in true Cartesian vein, that 'demonstrations are the eyes of the soul'?

Are there any demonstrations in history? Yes, certainly, our present-day historians will answer. They will show that the critical method which they use leads to conclusions which cannot reasonably be contested. This is true; but those conclusions do not, for all that, rest on proofs in the sense in which Descartes, Spinoza, Malebranche, and the other Cartesians understood the word—that is to say, on ratiocinations which have a rigour equal to that of mathematics, and possessed of rational evidence. For them history could never be other than a 'poor little conjectural science', as Renan put it. Moreover, they would have thought it unsuitable to use the term 'science' in this case, since even the history which is most anxious to be accurate never deals with anything but testimony. It cannot even, as can the experimental sciences, arrange for empirical verification.

Thus, even if we leave out of consideration the circumstances we recalled earlier and consider only the Cartesian doctrine of certainty and the conception of philosophy which went with it, we see at once what the Cartesians' attitude to history was bound to be. It was the immediate consequence of their uncompromising definition of truth, which excluded whatever was not rationally evident. No doubt as soon as it is a question of action, men are for the most part obliged to be guided by mere opinions, by traditions, and by probabilities and appearances. What we know of the past, even in an imperfect way, may then be very useful to us. But here we are no longer in the realm of true knowledge.

It is thus, as Malebranche delighted in repeating, the height of futility, not to say madness, to spend long years over texts which are more or less incomplete, mutilated, and contaminated, in order to try to extract from them an historical truth which they perhaps never contained, and which can have no scientific value since it cannot be demonstrated in the proper sense of the word.

Quite recently, M. Paul Valéry has roused some pretty strong feeling in the camp of the historians whose numerous troops occupy, as we know, a vast province, or rather a whole group of provinces, in the empire of science. He has directed against the very conception of the science of history a series of pointed witticisms and penetrating criticisms. They must be taken *cum grano salis*. But it is true that this fine poet is a spirit who is enamoured of precision and accuracy and is of a Cartesian temperament. If he is found in company with Malebranche jeering at history's pretensions to the dignity of scientific knowledge, this is no chance coincidence. This incident proves once again that there is in the Cartesian mind a kind of natural distrust, almost an antipathy, for history. We have just seen the chief reasons for this.

Leibniz, who had a very lively taste for history, and devoted to it a good proportion of his time, which was so wonderfully well spent, did not fail to notice this feature. And as he was never sorry to find a flaw in the armour of the Cartesian doctrine, he emphasized how much it was losing by this exclusion of the whole body of historical research. His own tendency was quite different. His was a spirit of a different order.

Translated by Mary Morris, Oxford.

VERITAS FILIA TEMPORIS

By FRITZ SAXL

§ 1. *Pietro Aretino*

FEW tyrants in history have come to an end at once so dreadful and so well deserved as that of Alessandro Medici. He was murdered by his intimate friend and kinsman, Lorenzino, on 5 January 1537, while awaiting the pleasant outcome of an amorous adventure. Six months before the assassination of Alessandro, on 1 July 1536, the Venetian publisher, Marcolino da Forlì, dedicated to him an edition of the *Cinque Messe* composed by the celebrated Netherlands musician, Adriaen Willaert. Marcolino, in his preface, gives as his reason for dedicating the work to Alessandro the latter's character of *osservatore et esecutore fedele del culto di Christo.*

Pietro Aretino, the close friend of Marcolino, was one of those who admired the works of Willaert and also one of those who esteemed Alessandro Medici; so he may very probably have put the idea of the dedication into Marcolino's head. This hypothesis is confirmed by the publisher's preface, in the first sentence of which the name of Aretino occurs:

> 'Mentre le lingue veraci dei buoni, converse in squille dai superni meriti di vostra Eccellenza, rimbombano in tutte le orecchie del mondo il fatale ALESSANDRO, Ecco la terribile tromba del mirabile Aretino, che non pur da le città, e da le selve, ma dai monti, e dai mari, fa spondersi il nome reverendo. . . .'

Alessandro Medici, violently attacked by the Florentine *fuorusciti* in Rome, stood at the apex of his power; for he had just come successfully out of negotiations with his enemies held in Naples before the Emperor, early in 1536. Charles V was just then striving earnestly to unite all the forces of Christendom against the infidel, and firmly resisted the influences which made war with France seem inevitable. Pope Paul III refused to take any strong stand in the matter, and the Emperor was inclined to come to terms with the Florentine duke, the adversary of Rome. Alessandro was married to the illegitimate

I am much indebted to my friends Professor D. V. Thompson and Dr. G. Bing for the translation.

daughter of the Emperor, Margarita, in the spring of 1536. Aretino kept a close eye upon this game of policy, and sided with the Emperor and the Medici. A few days after the date of Marcolino's dedication, he himself addressed a complimentary letter to Alessandro.

Now, he wrote, that all the uncertainties of Alessandro's fortune had been settled, and the difficulties that *Invidia* had been preparing for him had been eliminated; now that this sacred bond with the Emperor's daughter had been tied—now, at last, he would venture to address him. Otherwise, if he had written before, every truth that he might have ventured to predict in respect to Alessandro's marvellous future would have been looked upon as flattery, insincere, untruthful. *Verità, bugiarda adulazione, invidia*—these are the keys in which the letter is pitched.

The Truth that Aretino celebrates is the success of Florentine policy in the support of the efforts of Charles V to ensure a Catholic union. Aretino's *tromba* proclaimed the victory of Alessandro, announcing that his good qualities had brought him *tanta grazia appresso Cesare, quanta Cesare appresso a Dio.* Charles V held Aretino in high esteem. When Francis I of France turned against the western world, Aretino lifted his warning voice. In a letter dated September 1537 he writes: *Ahimè pessima sete del dominare! Ahì crudele volontà della vendetta . . .! Dove è, Francesco, la prudenza valorosa . . .?*

In a certain sense this commendation of Alessandro, the ally of the great Catholic Emperor, with which the preface to the *Cinque Messe* opens, is underlined by two woodcuts which were prefixed to Marcolino's book. One of them illustrates Pietro Aretino's motto, *Veritas odium parit.* Aretino tells the truth about Alessandro regardless of his opponents' hatred. The second woodcut, with the inscription *Veritas filia Temporis*, represents the liberation of the truth that Aretino and Marcolino both profess. The truth of their prophecies for Alessandro could no longer be mistaken for eulogy with flattering intent; for every difficulty that *Invidia* had raised seemed, in 1536, to have been overcome at last.

These two woodcuts appear here for the first time in combination. Each reappears often in later years: the one as Aretino's emblem in editions of his works, upon his medal, and elsewhere; the other as the conventional imprint of Marcolino's press. They

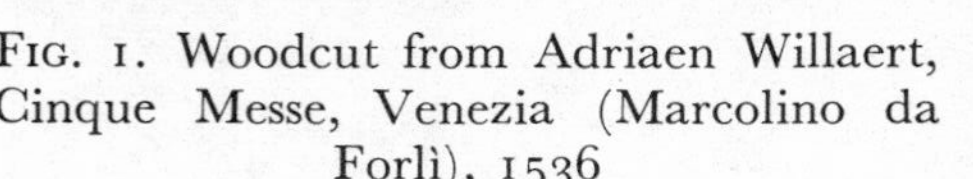

Fig. 1. Woodcut from Adriaen Willaert, Cinque Messe, Venezia (Marcolino da Forlì), 1536

Fig. 2. Woodcut from Adriaen Willaert, Cinque Messe, Venezia, 1536

Taken from the copy preserved in the Proske-Bibliothek at Regensburg, by kind permission of Msgr Poll

are used here as slogans, applying to the political situation which prevailed. They have, perhaps, some personal significance as well; for neither Marcolino nor Aretino expected Alessandro to reward such praise with mere idle appreciation. Later on these designs became the usual personal devices of the two men. In this quality they must now be examined more closely; and we shall see what part the motto, *Veritas filia Temporis*, was destined to play in contests for European hegemony.

The first woodcut, with the legend *Veritas odium parit* (Fig. 1), shows the figure of a naked woman, Truth, placing her foot upon the thigh of her adversary, Falsehood, who is represented in the form of a satyr. In the sky above Jupiter appears, and threatens Truth with his thunderbolt; but she tries by her gesture to divert his wrath to the satyr, the real sinner. Another figure stands behind Truth, holding a wreath, to indicate that in the end she is to be acknowledged as the victor.[1]

The second illustration, the one (Fig. 2) with the legend *Veritas filia Temporis*, shows Truth rising from an abyss towards Heaven, while Saturn in the person of an old man with an hourglass takes her by the arm to save her from the danger of falling back into the pit and at the same time from the onslaught of a creature with a dragon's tail who pulls at her hair and beats her with snakes.[2]

Truth was a watchword of Aretino's life, as we know from many passages in his correspondence. He was the *professore della verità*, the *oracolo della verità*, *acerrimus virtutum ac vitiorum demonstrator*; and as he also called himself *flagellum principum*, as he was proud of being the only man to tell the great ones of the

[1] If we assume a more literal interpretation of the text, *Veritas odium parit*, the satyr may be taken to represent Hatred, born of Truth. When Jupiter threatens her, Truth makes a gesture to signify that her repugnant offspring is her fate rather than her fault. The wreath which awaits her may then be supposed to stand for her ultimate absolution from the charge of bearing evil which she has involuntarily incurred.

[2] This woodcut enjoyed a vogue throughout Europe, for two reasons: first, that Aretino's writings which bear the *impresa* were read eagerly, far and wide; and second, that Marcolino's books stood high among the publications of their time in beauty and reputation. (They included the works of Doni, Cartari's handbook of mythology, Serlio's architectural treatise, and Marcolino's own production, a *Libro dei Sorti*, in which Truth appears as one of the first of the fortune-tellers.) Marcolino was acquainted with Vasari, and Titian used to design illustrations for him; so we need hardly be surprised to find this woodcut copied on Italian pottery, on German medals, in German woodcuts and engravings, and in French book illustration.

earth the plain truth, he was certainly prepared to risk incurring their hatred. It was as *Signor Pietro Aretino, per gratia divina huomo libero—che lodava chi lo meritava, e biasimava chi n'era degno—che colla verità in boccha sarebbe morto* that he wanted his contemporaries and posterity to think of him, even if it meant reaping hatred from the cruel truthfulness of his aggressive sowing.

The second motto and design are obviously less intimately suited to the character of Pietro Aretino than the first. His mind is bent upon the present world and its shortcomings, not upon some ultimate era of absolute truth.

Moreover, the text, *Veritas filia Temporis,*[1] is in itself an insufficient basis for the woodcut; for it contains no allusion to either of the perils which beset the heroine, the abyss below and the attacking monster above. To discover the special meaning which will explain the illustration and account for the revival of the theme in this Venetian circle, we must turn to another publication of Marcolino's press, the *Immagini degli Dei* of Vincenzo Cartari. In this we find combined the Greek idea that Truth must be brought up from the depths, and the Latin that Saturn is the father of Truth.[2]

Even these accessory quotations, however, do not account for the presence of the third figure in the woodcut; but another

[1] It comes down immediately from Gellius, *Noctes Atticae*, xii. 11, 7. Gellius, strangely enough, confesses to having forgotten the source from which it came to him. The notion on which this quotation is based was, my learned friend Dr. Klibansky informs me, of old common property in Greek tradition, where two different versions are prevalent: Time reveals either guilt and its punishment, as in Aeschylus' tragedies, or it reveals true valour and the honour due to it, as in Pindar's aristocratic poetry. Sophocles uses it to express his humble faith in the justice of divinity (*Aias* 646 sq.; *fr.* 280 Nauck; *fr.* 832 Nauck). After him, the idea of Time leading Truth to light becomes a literary commonplace of the new Greek comedy (Philemon, fr. 192 Kock; Menander monost. 11 and 459), thence finding its way into later Roman philosophy (Seneca, *De ira* 2, 22, 3: *dandum est tempus; veritatem dies aperit*), into the writings of the Fathers of the Church (Tertullian, *Apolog.* 7), and into the Byzantine collection of proverbs (Michael Apostolios, Cent. XIII 86 c, *Corpus Paroemiogr. graec.* ii. 599, ed. Leutsch, Göttingen, 1851). It is a remarkable fact that the version discussed in this paper, Gellius' terse formula, transmitted as he says from 'an ancient poet', can neither be identified nor traced elsewhere. In later times the saying is propagated by Erasmus' insertion of Gellius' quotation into his collection of proverbs (*Adagiorum opus*, Basileae, 1526, p. 436), his paraphrase being worthy of special attention ('. . . *quendam veterum poetarum Veritatem Temporis Filiam vocasse, quod licet aliquando lateat, temporis progressu in lucem emergat.*')

[2] Vincenzo Cartari, *Immagini degli Dei*, Venice, 1556, p. lxxiii^v. The author quotes as his authorities Democritus (Fragm. B. 117, Diels) and Plutarch (*Aetia Romana*, § 11, p. 266 E). The philosophical formulations, however, proved on the whole less influential than the poetical one, coined by Sophocles.

contemporary source[1] enables us to identify it as *Calumnia*. This extension of the basic theme, that Truth is the child of Time, brings it into association with one of the most celebrated of the Renaissance allegories, the traditional Calumny of Apelles. The design is, in fact, essentially a modified *Calumnia Apellis*. According to Lucian, Calumny drags her victim by the hair into the presence of the Unwise Judge, and Truth stands in the background, raising her eyes towards Heaven. In Marcolino's *impresa* there is no Judge. Of all the base figures of Lucian's account, only Calumny remains; and it is no mere mortal, but Truth herself, who is the object of attack. Time comes to her aid in her affliction.

The circulation of a forged letter in which he was made to slander his own patrons threw Aretino's reputation and position into jeopardy; and in the precarious situation which resulted, Aretino, inspired by both indignation and alarm, marshalled up against his enemies the figures of the ancient moral allegory,[2] investing them with such vitality that they did battle for him like living champions. For him, old Lucian's fable was no mere antique tale, the sport of fashionable erudition. It was, on the contrary, an essential canon of his creed; and the basic theme of the classical account—that the courts of princes are the seats of Calumny, where to speak honestly is to invite indignity, and truth and repentance follow slowly—is in no small degree a factor in the literary life of Aretino.[3]

The idea of using this humanistic version of the conflict between Truth and Calumny as the trade-mark of the newly established publishing house subsequently called the *Bottega della Verità* is not out of character with Aretino's mind.[4] The

[1] 'Verum cum fabulatores illi [i.e. *his enemies*] . . . libellum nostrum Aetiope aut diabolo nigriorem proditurum et eam ob causam contemnendum dixerint, volui ego eam deformitatem (si tamen deformitas nominanda est) candidissima veritate temporis filia, cum Saturno patre et Calumniatore, huic libello additis imaginibus pensare. Eam figuram, ubi volent mei Censores vel de propriis factis suis, quae Venetiis exercuerunt, exponere poterint: Quid Saturni nomine intelligatur; quae ista veritatis sit ratio; et quinam illi sint qui diaboli partibus veritate obruenda perfuncti sint.' (Johannes Muslerus, *De liberalibus disciplinis cum iurisprudentia coniungendis*, Venice, 1538; *Victoriae dedicatio*, fol. λλ^v; the woodcut on fol. 17.)

[2] *Lettere*, a cura di F. Nicolini, Bari 1913, vol. 1, p. 125.

[3] It was perhaps less influential upon his personal behaviour; but the facts which governed that are not so simple as his eighteenth- and nineteenth-century commentators would lead us to believe. Aretino was certainly above using his powers of praise and condemnation for purposes of blackmail only.

[4] The text is, however, too optimistic for his taste. It is perhaps more likely that

basic text, *Veritas filia Temporis*, is given a new inflexion: Time conquers Calumny; Time is the deliverer of Truth from persecution and oppression, and in the end brings honour and reputation.

Time, these men of the Renaissance believe, will also demonstrate the sincerity of their works; and their honesty will eventually triumph over the baseness of their enemies, and bring the fame that they deserve.

This interpretation, however, even if it applied to the circumstances of those days, had to be dressed in dignified habiliments, endowed with classical authority, weighted with philosophical and religious importance. To lose sight of this would be to overlook a fundamental characteristic of the Renaissance mentality. The minds of men like Aretino and Marcolino were concerned with the cares and conflicts of their world; but looked upon them *sub specie aeternitatis*. If they thought of their present-day problems in classic metaphors, it was because they conceived of their actions as belonging to the world of the classic, the general, the broadly significant. The allegory of ancient wisdom was the proper expression of the dignity and significance with which they regarded their own behaviour to be fraught.

§2. *Early Protestantism*

From the worldly atmosphere of Venetian Humanism, the pursuit of this theme leads us northward into the thick of the battles and dissensions which accompanied the proclamation of a new religious truth. As early as 1521 Truth was made the battle-cry of one of the heralds of religious enlightenment, John Knoblouch of Strassburg, who published writings by Luther, Melanchthon, and Erasmus, and whose name was consequently entered in the Roman *Index*. As his printer's mark Knoblouch chose an illustration of a text from the Psalms (lxxxv. 12), *Veritas de terra orta est*. In its original context this verse refers to an age of final peace in which Truth is to blossom from the ground like a flower. The Knoblouch imprint (Fig. 3), however, interprets it somewhat freely: Truth is personified as a harassed woman, who issues naked from a rocky cave, plead-

the *impresa* was evolved by Marcolino himself under Aretino's influence, even with his collaboration, than that Aretino was (as has been suggested) the originator of the publisher's device.

ing for help and waiting to be rescued.[1] Time is not represented in the cut; but the inscription promises that Time will bring Truth to light. There can be no doubt that this work alludes to the coming reform of faith.

Fourteen years later (1535) the motto to be used by Marcolino enters the literature of the Reformation. It is illustrated on the verso of the title-page of William Marshall's *Goodly Prymer in Englyshe*, issued just at the time of Henry VIII's breach with Rome (Fig. 4).[2]

FIG. 3. *Printer's mark of John Knoblouch of Strassburg.*

Its essentially polemic intention is expressed in plain and forceful language on the opposite page, at the beginning of the Preface.[3] There is no question here of fame or calumny. The drawing stands for the liberation of Christian Truth (as seen by Protestant reformers) from her captivity under the monster of Roman Hypocrisy.

Its significance therefore differs widely from Marcolino's treatment of the same theme in the following year. *Truthe, the doughter of tyme*, is seen with different eyes in England in 1535 from those which represent *Veritas, filia temporis* in Venice in 1536; and she conveys a different message. It is the more

[1] I owe my acquaintance with this significant early woodcut to the helpful interest of Mr. Campbell Dodgson.

[2] This cut appeared in all the quarto reissues of the second edition of the *Prymer*, 1535 and *c.* 1537. My attention was first drawn to the work by Mr. Edwyn Birchenough, whose forthcoming volume, *The Prymer in English 1385–1651*, will supply further information about it. William Marshall was a fanatical reformer, the editor of several polemic works, and an agent of Thomas Cromwell, the Vicar General (*D.N.B.*).

[3] This is an expansion of the Preface to Luther's *Enchiridion Piarum Precationum*, 1521. So I am informed by Mr. Edwyn Birchenough.

striking, therefore, to discover in these divergent representations two common characteristics: (1) That both render the classical text by three protagonists in conflict, and (2) That both introduce an enemy of Truth in the form of a winged monster brandishing serpents. Since the third protagonist, the enemy, is in no way suggested by the text of the motto, and still less the form which he shall take, the conclusion is inescapable that these two treatments of the theme are not independent of each other as might at first appear. It would be trying the powers of coincidence too far to question the obvious conclusion that, different as these two woodcuts are, they are descended from some common graphic archetype.[1]

The composition of the English woodcut is clearly based upon the late medieval treatments of Christ's Descent into Limbo. In this allegorical adaptation of the Limbo theme, Time takes the place of the Redeemer, and Truth that of the waiting Adam. The enemy of Truth, labelled *Hipocrisy*, forms the counterpart of the subdued guardians of Limbo, and is shown as a bat-winged monster, hovering in the air, brandishing four serpents in his right hand, and spouting streams of venom upon the figure of Truth below. Time, supported by auspicious wings upon his feet and shoulders, leads timorous, naked Truth up from the rocky depth in which she has been confined into a world of flowers, and calmly secures her against the frenzied efforts of her enemy to prevent her release from subjection.[2]

[1] What this archetype may have been, and when and where created, are questions for surmise. So also is the mechanism by which it may have been transmitted. Erasmus, who in his *Adagia*, many times reprinted by this date, had collected and grouped with other classical traditions the proverbial conceptions of Time and Truth among the Ancients, lived for some time in Venice and Basel, great sixteenth-century centres of publication, as well as in England. Holbein, his friend and collaborator, studied in Italy and came to the English court from Basel. (There is a Holbein drawing of *Veritas* and *Tempus* in the British Museum, without the figure of the demon, but with the text from Matthew in Latin, *Nihil est tectum*, &c., which appears in English under the woodcut in the *Goodly Prymer.*) These considerations, coupled with the Knoblouch illustration of the Psalm text from 1521, suggest that the archetype of the 1535 English and 1536 Venetian renderings may be sought in the sphere of Erasmus's influence in southern Germany.

[2] I am indebted to Mr. E. P. Goldschmidt for a reference to the following passage describing an entertainment at Richmond in 1513:

> 'Inglyshe and the oothers of the Kynges pleyers, after pleyed an Interluyt whiche was wryten by Mayster Midwell but yt was so long yt was not lykyd: yt was the fyndyng of Troth who was caryed away by ygnoraunce and ypocresy. The foolys part was the best, but the kyng departyd befor the end to hys chambre.'

A. W. Reed (*Early Tudor Drama*, London 1926, p. 95 sq.) has pointed out that

FIG. 4. *Woodcut from William Marshall's* Goodly Prymer in Englyshe, 1535.

The English artist applies the motto, *Truthe, the doughter of tyme*, to the defence of a new religious conviction, a Christian ecclesiastical theme; and in doing so turns naturally to a type of representation already established in Christian iconography for the treatment of the closely parallel subject, Christ's descent into Limbo. To Protestant eyes this parallel was complete and telling; and the artist was justified in pointing it out by the selection of the standard convention of the Roman Church for representing the Limbo story. In the Venetian application, however, there is no specifically Christian element; the emphasis is philosophical and secular; and the Limbo composition, as the underlying pattern of the representation, only becomes discernible through the comparison with the *Prymer* woodcut.

In Italy, and as we shall see in France, this tag of Latin continues to be understood in a secular sense; in England it retains the ecclesiastical application of its first employment. The phrase is used in controversy about the Confession through the century, and both friends and foes of the new dispensation use it for their own purposes.

§3. *Mary Tudor*

Seldom has a momentous event in the history of England been so startling to the world at large as the coronation of Mary Tudor as Queen in 1553. Daughter of Henry VIII by a Spanish princess, she had supported the Catholic faith in her household through her brother's reign. Her policy was widely opposed in England, but supported by the ministers of her kinsman, the Hapsburg Emperor. Profound wonder at the amazing turn in the fortunes of the Queen—and with hers, those of the whole Christian world—is expressed in the letters of diplomats and in the reports of ambassadors.[1] None, however, was more deeply

Collier's *History of Dramatic Poetry*, London, 1831, is our only source for this information, as to-day there is no trace, in the Record Office, of the '*folded paper*' document referred to by Collier. In consequence Mr. Reed writes: 'I would suggest, therefore, that it is wise to treat the story of the folded paper with suspicion.' But the fact that in our woodcut the Enemy of Truth is also called Hypocrisy makes it not improbable that Collier's information may be genuine. In our context it would be interesting, as it would show that the subject, the Finding of Truth attacked by Hypocrisy, was already at the beginning of the sixteenth century in vogue in England. It seems, however, remarkable that the figure of Time is not yet mentioned here.

[1] See, for example, the letter from Peter Vannes to Queen Mary, dated Venice, 13 August 1553, or that of Charles V to the ambassador Renard, 20 September 1553, in *Papiers d'État du Cardinal de Granvelle*, iv. 109.

affected by the turn of events than Cardinal Pole, the friend and confidant of the Queen, upon whose shoulders fell the task of re-establishing papal authority in England. On his return from exile, he greeted her as follows:

> 'And see howe miraculouslye God of hys goodnes preserved her hyghnes contrarye to the expectacyon of manne. That when numbers conspyred agaynste her, and policies were devised to disherit her, and armed power prepared to destroye her, yet *she being a virgin, helpless, naked, and unarmed*, prevailed.'[1]

Mary Tudor, as naked, virgin, and defenceless as the Truth that she had spent herself to find and to protect, was at last triumphant. '*Veritas*', the Bishop of Winchester said of her, '*iam proxima est*'; and one of the allegorical figures exhibited at her marriage festival represented Truth 'with a boke in her hand, whereon was written *Verbum Dei*'.

Contemporary estimates of the importance of this time were not exaggerated. With Protestantism established in Germany, Mary Tudor's accession to the throne seemed to renew the lost hope of world-wide Catholic dominion, and the institution of a final reign of peace such as the world had not known since the days of Augustus. It evoked the dream of England ruled by Queen Mary as a Catholic province of Spain, the Netherlands secure, and the Hapsburgs, with only an encircled France against them, free to unite the world under Catholic sovereignty. The same policy had led Charles V to make Alessandro Medici his ally some fifteen years ago, at a time when also Mary Tudor's marriage had already figured as an item in his calculations. There was no doubt of Mary's sincere co-operation in this dream of Catholic empire; and a decision of the destiny of Europe was momentarily expected. Of course, this decision did not come in Mary Tudor's short reign after all, but awaited Elizabeth, and the days of Richelieu.

This review of well-known facts has been undertaken in order to explain the significance of Mary Tudor's choice for her personal device, for the legend on her crest, on the State seal of her reign, on her coins, of the Latin motto *Veritas filia Temporis*.[2]

[1] Quoted from John Elder's letter describing the arrival and marriage of King Philip, London, 1555, in John G. Nichols, *The Chronicle of Queen Jane and of Two Years of Queen Mary*, Camden Society Publication No. 48 (1850), p. 157.

[2] Francis Sandford, *Genealogical History of the Kings and Queens of England*, London, 1707, pp. 499, 500: 'When she [Queen Mary] came to the Kingdom, by persuasion

Time was fulfilled, and had brought with it Truth, long banished from the realm. 'I could not believe that the blood of those to whom God had given the grace to die . . . should not prove efficacious, when to His providence the time seemed opportune. That time is . . . now come . . . in order that . . . the true religion and justice return . . . into the kingdom.'[1]

The old phrase had taken on a new and glorious meaning. This victory of Truth did not lie for Mary in mere personal triumph over jealous enemies, or even in triumph over their spiteful attacks upon what they thought of as idolatry in the Roman Church. The ancient saying of the long-forgotten poet had become a paean of thanksgiving, expressive of the humble devotion of a sovereign to her severely tested faith.

§4. *Queen Elizabeth*

In a procession which took place the day before her coronation in 1558 Elizabeth is said to have seen an allegory representing Time and Truth, and with the motto of her predecessor fresh in mind, cried out, 'And Time hath brought me hither!' If this reaction is reported truly, it indicates a widely different state of mind from that in which Mary Tudor received the news of her accession. To Elizabeth, Time has established not abstract religious Truth but her own personal success. Her religious convictions, shared by those who prepared festivities for her reception, are diametrically opposed to those of Mary. This is shown clearly by the allegorical side-show of Time and Truth past which the procession moved:

'Between . . . hylles was made artificiallye one hollowe place or cave, with doore and locke enclosed; oute of the whiche, a lyttle before the Quenes Hyghnes commynge thither, issued one personage, whose name was Tyme, apparaylled as an olde man, with a sythe in his hande, havynge wynges artificiallye made, leadinge a personage of lesser stature then himselfe, whiche was fynely and well apparaylled, all cladde in whyte silke, and directlye over her head was set her name and tytle, in Latin and Englyshe, "*Temporis filia*, The Daughter of Tyme". . . . And on her brest was written her propre name, whiche was "Veritas", Trueth, who helde a booke in her hande,

of the Clergy, she bare [as her device] Winged Time drawing Truth out of a Pit, with Veritas Temporis Filia, which Motto adorns her first Great Seal.'

[1] Cardinal Pole to Queen Mary, 27 August 1553; quoted from *Calendar of State Papers*, ed. R. Brown, *Venice*, v (London, 1873), pp. 396 ff.

upon the which was written, *Verbum Veritatis*, the Woorde of Trueth."[1]

There were also explanatory verses which showed in what sense the allegory was to be understood:

This olde man with the sythe, olde Father Tyme they call,
And her, his daughter Truth, which holdeth yonder boke,
Whom he out of his rocke hath brought forth to us all,
From whence for many yeres she durst not once out loke.

. . . . . .

Now since that Time again his daughter Truth hath brought,
We trust, O worthy Quene, thou wilt this Truth embrace.

The book in the hand of Truth was the *Verbum Dei*, exactly as it had been in the allegory held at the wedding of Mary. Elizabeth accepted it as a gift, and eye-witnesses inform us that it was the book that Mary had banned, the *Byble in Englyshe*.

In the militant days of Henry VIII, the old motto served, as we saw it in the *Goodly Prymer*, as a rally-cry of Protestantism. It was revived by Mary Tudor to sum up her joy in the triumph of Catholicism at her coronation. In Elizabeth's first public procession it reappears in a new and contrary significance. In less than twenty-five years it has reversed its meaning twice, and has been made the vehicle three times of strong emotion.

Thirty years later comes a decisive moment in the history of Europe: the Spanish Armada is defeated. The disturbance of the balance of power began with the assassination of the Prince of Orange; and shortly afterwards Time and Truth make their appearance again, this time on a controversial broadside.[2] The point of the satire in this engraving lies in its model: it is a paraphrase in political terms of one of Titian's erotic designs: *The Discovery of the Fault of Callisto*. In Titian's work the pregnancy of the unhappy nymph is revealed to Diana by a group of her handmaidens.[3] The choice of subject was undoubtedly dictated by the popular comparison of the Virgin Queen with Diana, the Virgin Huntress. In this composition Elizabeth, in the

[1] John Nichols, *The Progresses . . . of Queen Elizabeth . . .*, vol. i (London, 1823), p. 50.

[2] Engraved by P. Miricenys, see *Cat. of Prints and Drawings in the British Museum*, Division I, Satires, vol. i (1870), No. 12.

[3] There are several versions of this painting, among them one in Vienna, and another in the Bridgewater Collection. There exists also an engraving after the painting. For the underlying text, see Ovid, *Metam.* II. 451 sqq.

character of Diana, is surrounded by four maidens, identifiable as four of the seven Netherland provinces. In the presence of this group an unhappy man is being stripped, not by nymphs of Diana but by Time and Truth, to reveal his pregnancy. The pregnant male is no other than the Pope. Beneath him there is a pile of eggs, the fruits of his fertility, each labelled with the name of one of his misdeeds: the murder of the Prince of Orange, the Inquisition, the Paris massacre, and so on.

This engraving shows a new treatment of the old material: not Time revealing Truth, but Time (with hour-glass and scythe) uniting with Truth (labelled *Die nacte waerheijt*) to unmask the vicious Pope. A poem, in English and Dutch versions, warns the Queen against the fate of the Dutch nobleman: 'Ther fore think uppon the Prince of Orijnges deth in tijm', and implores her aid against the Spanish oppressors of the Low Countries. By reference to the events to which this engraving alludes, its publication may be dated securely between July 1584 and April 1585, the date of the death of Pope Gregory XIII Buoncompagni who is specifically indicated by one of the eggs (marked *P*[*apa*] and hatching out a dragon, the Buoncompagni emblem). In August 1585 Elizabeth (who had declined the Netherlands crown, offered to her after the death of William of Orange) entered into a Pact of Intervention with the States General, and Leicester was sent to the Low Countries. A year after his return war broke out with Philip of Spain; and once again events came to be looked on as manifestations of the forces of Time and Truth.

A seventeenth-century engraving to celebrate the English victory shows Elizabeth on horseback, in full panoply, with her army and navy drawn up in the background ready for battle.[1] Under the horse's hooves is shown a hydra, who attacks a woman, wrapped in flames, emerging from a cave. This woman holds the old familiar book with its inscription, 'Truth'; and she hands to Elizabeth the lance with which she is to slay the hydra, and, as if in the character of Time, to accomplish the release of Truth.[2]

[1] British Museum, engraved by Th. Cecil, see Hind, *List of Works of English and Foreign Line-engravers in England*, 1905, p. 8. This engraving has been reproduced often.

[2] We have a proof of the popularity which the composition enjoyed in England, as late as 1601: 'William Wood, bookseller, whose shop was at the sign of Time, St. Paul's Churchyard, had as his mark an almost exact copy of one employed by Conrad Bade . . . (who had apparently adopted his from that of Knoblouch of

Fig. 5. Rubens, Medici-Cycle: Triumph of Truth
Paris, Musée du Louvre

Fig. 6. Rubens, Triumph of the Eucharist *Madrid, Prado*

Fig. 7. Poussin, Ceiling Decoration for Richelieu *Paris, Musée du Louvre*

§5. *Maria de' Medici*

At the end of this martial period of English history, the centre of interest in European affairs shifted to France, which now assumes the full responsibility of making war against the Hapsburgs. The favourite painter of both sides, winners and losers, is Rubens. For Maria de' Medici, the patroness of Richelieu, and also for the Hapsburg Isabella, the Spanish king's Stadholder in the Netherlands, Rubens painted representations of Time and Truth. His painting for Maria was a rather hollow-spirited piece of elegant court decoration; while that for Isabella was an allegory of faith.

Rubens's allegory of politics in the Medici cycle (Fig. 5) shows old Father Time dragging his buxom daughter, Truth, upward. It takes both his arms and all his strength to lift her robust form into the skies, where she is to take part in a symbolic action, the reconciliation of Maria de' Medici with her son Louis XIII. We know that when Rubens was at work upon this cycle it took all his cunning as a diplomat to keep some truths from coming to light which were better left in the dark; so we need not wonder that this last painting in the series lacks the ease and truthfulness which usually distinguish Rubens's art.

We may deplore the conception, artistically considered; but politically it was a stroke of genius. The King, who had not crossed his mother's threshold for ten years, came and admired it. The Queen herself was *restata con tanta soddisfattione, che non si può dir più*; and even that exacting critic, her counsellor, Richelieu, though he had some political objections to the later paintings in the cycle (among which this belongs), could not praise it enough.

§6. *Princess Isabella of Hapsburg*

If the best qualities of Rubens's art are clouded over in Maria's Reconciliation, they shine the more brightly in his other painting (Fig. 6) which shows Time effecting the triumph of the Roman faith over the unbelief of heretics. In this Rubens exhibits his full mastery of the artistic achievements of the great Catholic production of the sixteenth and seventeenth centuries. Time tears Truth out of the clutches of her enemies with a

Strassburg . . .): it represents a winged figure of Time helping a naked woman out of what appears to be a cave, with the motto *Tempore patet occulta Veritas.*' See W. Roberts, *Printers' Marks* (London, 1893), p. 91.

magnificent gesture, reminiscent of the Rape of Proserpine by Pluto. The false prophets, Luther and Calvin, lie struggling at Truth's feet; the forces of the enemy take flight into the darkness; and Truth points upward towards an inscription, *Hoc est corpus meum.*

The sixteenth-century block-cutters who first interpreted the motto *Veritas filia Temporis* adapted pictorial types originally elaborated for the purposes of Christian art. Though they were humanists they fell involuntarily into the mother-tongue of Christian iconography, even when their subject was unrelated to the teaching of the Church. Rubens, however, shows an opposite tendency. He finds pagan terms for his conceptions, even when they are most specifically Christian in subject-matter. Given the fundamental tenet of Catholicism, *Hoc est corpus meum,* he still contrives to represent it by a classical, pagan model. He finds his parallel to the Truth of his Catholic text in Demeter's virgin daughter; and Time, establishing the triumph of the Church, takes the part of Pluto, seizing her violently and carrying her away. Rubens's mind is filled with pagan imagery; but heathen figures and ideas are only part of a universe which is subject universally to the Church. *Veritas filia Temporis* means to him what it meant to Mary Tudor before him. Isabella of Hapsburg, His Most Christian Majesty's Stadholder in the Netherland Provinces, who ordered this series of tapestries made after the designs of Rubens, intended them, in fact, to acclaim the power of Catholicism and the predestined connexion between the victory of Catholicism and the House of Hapsburg. The first panels, therefore, show the triumph of the Roman faith, and the last, its supporters—the apostolic fathers, and immediately after them the princes of the Hapsburg House. Rubens's composition is a true child of Richelieu's time; for it combines the glorification of the Church with the magnification of individual political power.

Nevertheless, when Richelieu himself commissioned the painting of the theme, *Veritas filia Temporis,* for his own palace, it was given a significance far removed from that of either of the Rubens treatments.

§7. *Cardinal Richelieu*

Richelieu ordered a painting of this subject from Nicolas Poussin about 1641, more than ten years after the *Journée des dupes*, that is, after he had finally broken down the power of Maria de' Medici, and almost twenty years after he had given his consent to Rubens's flamboyant celebration of her reconciliation with the King. Richelieu stood at the height of his political career. He was prepared to denounce as Falsehood matters which in his earlier character of favourite and counsellor to the Queen he had consented to see hailed as Truth revealed by Time.

In the following year, 1642, the Cardinal's detractors launched their last great organized attack upon him; but he forestalled them, and wiped them out. Envy and Calumny had been the constant followers of Richelieu's career. His fight against them had brought him repeatedly face to face with death. So when the time came for him to choose a theme for the decoration of his apartments he elected the Triumph of Truth, symbolic of his triumph over enemies at court, as princes in the Renaissance had painted on their ceilings the auspicious planets of their horoscopes.

The first intensely personal application of the motto, *Veritas filia Temporis*, originated in the circle of Aretino, the Scourge of Princes, despiser and, some say, slanderer of courts. Now Richelieu, the intimate of princes, the arbiter of courts, converts the same motto to his case. As he nears the end of his lifelong conflict with the forces of flattery and slander, he espouses with vigour the cause which Aretino battled for, Truth in the seats of government. He still harps on the shortcomings of his former patroness, Maria de' Medici, judges and condemns her harshly in the chapter of his *Political Testament* which bears the title, *Du mal que les flatteurs, médisants, et critiques causent d'ordinaire aux États, et combien il est important de les éloigner d'auprès des Rois et les bannir de leurs cours.*

The sympathy between Richelieu's views and those of Aretino on the subject of Truth is not paralleled in Poussin's painting (Fig. 7) by any corresponding reflection of Marcolino's graphic conception. Poussin's design looks back not to the Venetian woodcut but to a work in Rome, a ceiling painted about 1615 by Domenichino in the Palazzo Costaguti (Fig. 8).[1] Domeni-

[1] Through the generous help of Ecc^{za} Colasanti and of Professor Serra, Director of the Gabinetto fotografico della Direzione Generale delle Antichità e Belle Arti, Rome, I am able to reproduce the ceiling for the first time in its entirety. I am very much indebted to both.

chino's painting shows a fundamentally new conception of Truth, based immediately upon a platonic conception. According to Plato the sun is the offspring of goodness, its likeness in the visible world.[1] *Solem igitur vel Phoebum Musarum, id est intelligentiae, ducem, una cum Platonicis atque Dionysio imaginem Dei conspicuam conclude*, says Marsilio Ficino.[2] On the other hand it is this idea of goodness, personified by the sun, that gives truth to the objects of knowledge. It is the cause of knowledge and of truth as far as it is known. This platonic theory has been converted into allegorical form by Domenichino or some one of his circle.

In Domenichino's ceiling at the Costaguti Helios occupies the centre, and Truth soars upward towards him. The platonic conception is, however, extended by the introduction of a further element: as Time promotes the recognition of Truth, the venerable winged figure of Time in Domenichino's allegory helps Truth on her upward flight towards Helios, the Good. He does not, however, rise with her, but seems to stay behind, only using his forces to advance her progress.

In all the earlier compositions Truth has stood either for personal conviction or for religious faith. Her triumph has stood either for fame or for salvation (Catholic or Protestant as the case might be). Domenichino's is the first graphic interpretation we know of a conception of Truth apart from personal or religious conflict. In his painting a universal, impersonal idea is represented. It is intended to stimulate enthusiasm for the general qualities of Goodness and Truth, and is not concerned with their application to any special case or type of case. Domenichino's figures of Goodness, Truth, and Time are reinforced by the presence of *putti* with the attributes of (1) the Club of Heracles, for Virtue, (2) the Apple of Paris, for Beauty, (3) a musical instrument, for Harmony. These figures are endlessly remote from the dramatic associations with the dismal kinsmen of *Calumnia* into which their more worldly cousins have been drawn.

It is apparently from this design of Domenichino's that Poussin takes the underlying scheme of his ceiling in the Palais Richelieu. The group of Time and Truth, which is only a portion of Domenichino's work, forms the main theme of Poussin's, and is given a different function. In place of the allegories of

[1] *Republic*, vi, p. 508 b,c.

[2] *Opera* (Basileae, 1576), I. p. 971.

the abstract qualities of Harmony, Beauty, and Virtue, viewed apart from any application, Poussin's composition exhibits the reintroduction of the motive of conflict. The emphasis is placed not upon the Goodness towards which Truth, with the aid of Time, aspires, but upon the evils, Anger and Envy, from which Time rescues her. In the universe of Richelieu there is no room for the Sun of Plato. The sun is gone, and only light in the sky remains.

The composition recalls, probably by Poussin's intention, the Christian iconography of the Assumption. It is the Assumption of Truth. Truth, carried aloft by Time, flings her arms wide to embrace the light of Eternity, just as the Virgin Mary does when she is borne to Heaven by the angelic host, or as the Apostle Paul does in the course of his ascension.[1] Domenichino's composition becomes, as it were, christianized by Poussin to adapt it to the taste of Richelieu.

In spite of this surface colouring of Christian form Poussin's design, like the Venetians', gives a secular, humanistic, and primarily personal interpretation of the theme.[2] Richelieu, though he was a priest, perpetuated the religious schism from which Spain would have liberated Europe if she had been successful in opposing him. Richelieu conquered his own enemies and those of France at the same time. The triumph of the *raison d'état* is embodied in his person.

§8. *Bernini*

Poussin's painting for Richelieu cannot fail to distress the believer in the progress of mankind. It is disheartening to see a graphic formula devised for the representation of a platonic conception converted to the purposes of courtly eulogy and the praise of a painful political victory over wrath and jealousy. Poussin's composition was not lost sight of, but it did not inspire further developments. The treatment which fixed the canon for

[1] Indeed, Domenichino's treatment of the *Ascension of St. Paul* may have been as influential upon this work of Poussin's as his Costaguti ceiling.

[2] Poussin did, in fact, know either Marcolino's *impresa* or one of its derivatives, that is, one of those representations which draw upon the classical allegory of *Calumnia*. This is demonstrated by a painting of his which we know only from engravings. In this lost work Poussin seems to have dealt with the subject with a lighter touch than his Renaissance predecessor. He deals not with the conflict about Truth, but with the situation which developed after the intervention of Time. Truth is still in sad plight, but her enemies have withdrawn, and less violent activity is demanded of Saturn than of his prototype in Marcolino's woodcut.

Fig. 8. Domenichino (and Tassi), Ceiling Decoration

Rome, Palazzo Costaguti

the representation of Truth in the seventeenth and eighteenth centuries was evolved by Bernini, who turned again to showing Truth as an abstract conception (Fig. 9).

Our earliest design was Knoblouch's illustration of the psalm text, *Veritas de terra orta est*. The same verse forms the subject of a painting by Palma Giovine, intended for the Magistrato della Quarantia Criminale in the Doge's Palace, and now in the Accademia at Venice (Fig. 10). The purpose of this allegory of victorious Truth and Justice was to inspire those qualities in the Venetian magistrates. Palma's *Veritas* floats away from the earth very much like the figure of Truth in Marcolino's woodcut; but the naked figure of the earlier work, unprovided with accessories, is given a modest veil and abundant attributes in Palma's painting. In her left hand she holds a book and a palm. The book is open to the words *Veritas de terra orta est, et iustitia de celo prospexit*. Her left foot is planted on two other books, and at the left of those there stands an hour-glass, to bring the thought of Time. A large globe at her right seems to stand for the Earth from which, according to the text, she has just sprung. In her right hand she raises a mask of Helios, into whose face she gazes, and her figure is illumined by its effulgence.

We need not look to Platonism for explanation of this scene: it is well enough accounted for by the common metaphors of truth and the light of day. But the upraised glance of *Veritas* gives the whole composition its proper accent. *Veritas* gazes into the sun, the source of Truth and Justice, just as the Magdalene bends her eyes to Heaven. The sort of Truth which will prevail in some ultimate realm of perfect peace was the ideal to be set before the arbiters of Venetian jurisdiction.

In the gradual development of Bernini's artistic intention we may discern a fusion of his original idea—Truth being unveiled (which was not at first related to Palma's conception)—and the Biblical idea of Truth springing from the Earth.

That the unveiling was Bernini's starting-point appears from one of his finest drawings (Fig. 11). Truth lies cramped and diffident within her veil, poised on the globe from which the Psalmist says she comes; and Time, the familiar figure of Marcolino's woodcut, winged, and bearing in his left hand his scythe, flies to Truth's aid, and with his right hand draws aside the veil which hides her.

The unveiling of the Infant Christ was treated in a similar

FIG. 9. Bernini, Truth unveiled
Rome, Villa Borghese

FIG. 10. Palma Giovine, Justice and Truth
Originally in the Ducal Palace, now in the Academy, Venice

FIG. 11. Bernini, Drawing: Time reveals Truth *Ariccia, Pallazzo Ch*

manner in the sixteenth century. The Madonna delicately draws aside the veils that cover the Holy Child and discloses Him to all the world. In a painting attributed to Marco Venusti, in the Ashmolean Museum at Oxford, the Madonna thus uncovers the Child with her left hand, while in her right hand she holds an open book inscribed with the words of the Psalm, *Veritas de terra orta est, et iustitia de coelo prospexit.* The symbolic significance of this seemingly idyllic act of unveiling becomes clear: Truth has appeared on earth through the birth of Christ, and Truth is uncovered in the same gesture as the Child to all who recognize Him as the Saviour.

Bernini's reflection of this Christian motive in his earlier design demonstrates the religious character of its base. In his sculpture done later he keeps to the original plan, and makes the action of uncovering the main theme of his composition, but develops it in the direction indicated by the Biblical text. Truth is no longer the passive sufferer of the sixteenth-century illustrations. She surrenders herself deliberately and gladly to the superior power. This is an indication of the same optimistic spirit as that in which Palma interpreted the Psalm.[1] *Veritas* sets her foot upon the globe and turns her eyes towards the approaching figure of Time. Her unveiling and her active detachment from the earth are made to coincide.

To appreciate the significance of this transformation as a moral achievement we must take into account the circumstances of Bernini's life. When he was defeated in the competition for the façade of St. Peter's he retired from the world, intending to spend his bitterness and anger in carving a memorial to his own powers, for posterity. The legacy of Lucian descends to him from Aretino: the determination to reveal, without a veil, the Truth of his artistic intention. The drawing, in which Truth still appears as a tormented, suffering creature, tells the tale of Bernini's own self-pity. He saw the bitter effects of *Calumnia* and *Invidia* in the same symbolical forms as the Venetians of a hundred years before had done; but these provided only his primary impulse. No unschooled beholder would see a polemic motive in his final work.

The novelty of this image of Truth, however, lies less in its freedom from biographical and theological applications than

[1] Bernini may, of course, actually have seen and been inspired by some work of art of the type represented by Palma's painting.

in the striking animation of the figure itself. Poussin's *Veritas*, borne upward in the arms of Time, unfolds her arms towards the Eternal with languid elegance. Her face shows the cold, emotionless beauty of marble. Bernini's *Veritas*, in contrast, seems inspired by a passion to ascend. She longs for the moment of unveiling like a bride. There is a sensuality in the action which is intended to touch the spectator. He is to forget all petty strife and suffering, the struggle for success and fame, in contemplation of the miracle before his eyes, the revelation of Truth, the mystic union of *Veritas, filia Dei*, reminiscent of the mystic marriage of Santa Teresa with Christ.

Bernini's plastic conception of Truth comprises experience of human life and suffering, but does not reduce it to a special case. It keeps the quality of universality. His treatment of Time is not simply the hero-deliverer of the Perseus type: he becomes the menacing wielder of the scythe as well. Time, in the character of mower-down of all things temporal, reveals Truth, who springs from the Earth and rises up towards Heaven.

§9. *Descartes and Newton*

Bernini's work, though often imitated, was never surpassed. Eighteenth-century art follows a different course; but a by-path finally leads us to the subjects to which this volume is dedicated —Philosophy and History.

Readers trained in philosophy will have recalled long since that *Veritas filia Temporis* has been an element in theories of historical understanding at least since the days of Giordano Bruno and Bacon.[1] Truth cannot be ascertained once for all. Perception of truth may be steadily amplified in the course of time. But (let me say, in defence of this contribution to *Philosophy and History*) philosophers' discussions of a theme like this reveal their bearing upon actual life more clearly when they are weighed in conjunction with the manifestations of the theme in humanistic, religious, and political connexions. It is significant that the philosophers' interpretation of the phrase found no appropriate expression in the arts as long as significant artists were themselves engaged upon it. Abstract theories are the last to be illustrated.

[1] See Giovanni Gentile, 'Veritas filia temporis', in *Giordano Bruno e il pensiero del Rinascimento* (Florence, 1925), pp. 225–48.

Poussin's painting for Richelieu was engraved by a certain Bernard Picart. This same Picart engraved a frontispiece for a *Thèse de philosophie soutenue par M. Brillon de Jouy, le 25 juillet, 1707*. In this engraving (Fig. 12) Truth is represented as the object of pursuit not by mankind at large but by a chosen few, the philosophers. Time, who dispels the clouds which veil Truth's figure, does not disclose her all at once or equally to all her followers. Her effulgence lights up brightly the leader of the group of philosophers, Descartes. The Ancients, Plato, Aristotle, Zeno, Socrates, and the seven sages of Greece who accompany him are only dimly irradiated by the light of Truth. They stand in the background; and at their sides and overhead allegorical figures are shown. *Philosophie* singles out Descartes, and taking him by the hand sets his feet in the straight path to Truth.

To this engraving is appended a text from *In multitudine separavit eos, et immutavit vias eorum*. This is not prophetic, like the Psalmist's *Veritas de terra orta est*, or like St. Matthew's *Nihil est tectum* illustrated in the *Goodlye Prymer* of 1535. Picart's text does not presuppose a single and indivisible Truth, by which mankind shall measure all knowledge and belief. It merely implies that the paths of men, even of those in quest for Truth, are manifold.

This print displays a wealth of detail. In addition to the allegories of Time and Truth, and Truth's opponent, *la Prévention*, Minerva appears, expelling Ignorance. A building in the background represents a classical school. The foreground is occupied by a Copernican *planetarium* and a still-life of modern physical instruments. Of the philosophers only Descartes and Socrates are portrayed in detail; but the rest are characterized by attributes reminiscent of their teachings. Diogenes has his cask; Epicurus is reflecting upon atoms; Pythagoras is busy with his figures; and Descartes, head of this modern 'School of Athens', holds a scroll upon which his theory of *tourbillons* is so distinctly indicated that, as the text says, *on ne serait pas excusable de s'y méprendre*.

The very profusion of these details warns us that we are drawing near the end. This is not the representation of an idea but the illustration of a theory. Most of the designs on this theme, *Veritas filia Temporis*, which have been mentioned here possess some quality of fire, emotion, or appeal, because they have come into being in response to the demands of some specific, genuine human situation. Picart's engraving has no such quality because it has no comparable origin. It is too wise, too impartial, too abstract, remote, and knowing, to carry any conviction, or to strike any spark.

Descartes's sceptical attitude towards historical experience and his postulate of a new starting-point for perception had become axiomatic. The scientific achievements of the new era were too impressive for any modern to deny successfully that the Ancients possessed a smaller store of knowledge than Copernicus or Galileo. This was agreed; the zest of the championship of modern times against antiquity had worn off, and the idea of progress had become established. Once the relative validity of intellectual perceptions (relative to their own time) was acknowledged, there was no flavour left in the *Querelle des Anciens et des Modernes.* Indeed, after the death of Perrault in 1703, Tourreil had definitely settled this controversy in his speech before the Académie.[1]

'La noble jalousie, dit un poète grec, est utile aux mortels. Celle-là, loin de souffler la discorde, et d'allumer la haine entre les concurrents, les remplit de cette ardeur magnanime, qu'elle répandait dans les plus célèbres jeux de la Grèce, où les vaincus, contents d'avoir disputé le prix, dépouillaient à la fin tout sentiment de rivalité pour le vainqueur et s'empressaient à l'envie de le couronner.'

When Picart's print appeared in 1707 the centenary of Bacon's *Novum Organum* was at hand. The French inscription on this print, and the Latin *Conclusiones philosophiae* of the thesis which it illustrated, laid down that *multa scitu digna invenerunt maiores, plura retexit melior aetatis nostrae fortuna*; and this was no more than a paraphrase of what had been maintained by Bacon almost a hundred years before—*Recte enim Veritas filia Temporis dicitur, non Auctoritatis.*[2]

After so much complex iconography we may turn in closing to a page from the history of human folly, and find in it, perhaps, both entertainment and instruction. There is an English version of the Picart engraving,[3] all but identical, slavishly re-

[1] H. Rigault, *Histoire de la querelle des anciens et des modernes* (Paris, 1856), p. 272.

[2] Cf. Francis Bacon, *Works*, ed. Ellis and Spedding, vol. i (1857), p. 191.

[3] This English print (Fig. 13) has been brought to light by Otto Kurz; he and Erna Mandowsky have passed on to me much valuable material in connexion with the subject of this paper.

produced in all the minutest detail from the French original. The text is taken over into English with equal conscientiousness. In the passage relating to the main figure, for instance, the English follows the French exactly: 'And had not a special Care been taken to draw his Picture, yet this favourite Place, which is so lawfully his Due, would make him easily known.' The translator, however, incurred some difficulty in the following sentence: *D'ailleurs ses Tourbillons, qu'il tient à la main, le designent si précisément qu'il ne seroit pas excusable de s'y méprendre.* This unmistakable allusion to the theory of Descartes had to be changed by the English engraver; and we are astonished to discover that the philosopher in the print holds an empty scroll. The *tourbillons* are missing. The engraver evidently considered that these small expurgations were enough to fit the drawing to his purpose—which was to substitute Sir Isaac Newton for Descartes as the philosopher-hero of the piece.[1] Wherever Descartes's name appeared in Picart's text Newton's is substituted in the English; and that with no alterations whatever in composition, details, or description which Picart had conceived as fitting Descartes's case minutely and exclusively. These documents together raise up a monument to the inherent constancy of symbols which human genius and human folly are alike slow to modify.

The meaning which Bacon read into our dictum was never more graphically proved than in this English parody of Picart's print. The new generation, represented by Newton, receives the full light of Truth, and the old withdraws into the shadow. History set the stamp of its approval on the silly enterprise of the English copyist. He created unintentionally a symbol of Descartes's defeat through Newton, an illustration of what Voltaire expressed brilliantly at the beginning of his London letter *Sur Descartes et Newton*:[2] *Un Français qui arrive à Londres, trouve les choses bien changées en Philosophie, comme dans tout le reste. Il a laissé le Monde plein, il le trouve vide. A Paris on voit l'univers composé de Tourbillons, de Matière subtile; à Londres on ne voit rien de cela.* To close with the words which Voltaire makes Newton himself say in the following letter, *Histoire de l'Attraction*: *Ce sont les Tourbillons qu'on peut appeler une qualité occulte, puisqu'on n'a jamais*

[1] Newton's portrait has been substituted for that of Descartes, and also his coat has been slightly modernized.

[2] *Mélanges de Littérature et de Philosophie*, Chapitre xvi et Chapitre xvii.

prouvé leur existence; l'Attraction du contraire est une chose réelle, puisqu'on en démontre les effets, et qu'on en calcule les proportions. La cause de cette cause est dans le sein de Dieu.

Procedes huc, et non ibis amplius.

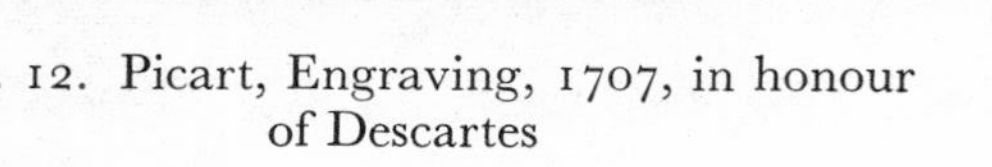

FIG. 12. Picart, Engraving, 1707, in honour of Descartes

FIG. 13. English copy after Picart's engraving, in honour of Newton

FIG. 1. Nicolas Poussin, 'Et in Arcadia ego' *Paris, Musée du Louvre*

ET IN ARCADIA EGO

ON THE CONCEPTION OF TRANSIENCE IN POUSSIN AND WATTEAU

By ERWIN PANOFSKY

IN Anglo-Saxon countries many people know and occasionally use the phrase, *Et tu in Arcadia vixisti* ('You, too, have lived in Arcadia'). In other European countries the more usual form is: 'I, too, have lived in Arcadia'; but both versions express the same idea, namely, the retrospective vision of an unsurpassable happiness, enjoyed in the past, unattainable ever after, yet enduringly alive in the memory. Eighteenth- and early nineteenth-century literature particularly abounds in passages in which this Arcadian happiness is conjured up, be it elegiacally lamented (as is most usual), or accusingly though unsuccessfully demanded (as occurs with the frustrated hero of a celebrated Schiller poem who has renounced Pleasure and Beauty in favour of Hope and Truth and now requests compensation, challenging: *Auch ich war in Arkadien geboren*), or almost triumphantly evoked, as is the case with Goethe, who uses the phrase *Auch ich in Arkadien* as a motto for the description of his blissful journey to Italy.

The original version of this celebrated phrase, however, is in Latin and its original place is a tomb. In the year 1769 Johann Georg Jacobi, a German writer, penned the following sentimental lines: 'Whenever, in a beautiful landscape, I encounter a tomb with the inscription: "I too was in Arcadia", I point it out to my friends, we stop a moment, press each other's hands, and proceed.'[1] And in the same year Sir Joshua Reynolds

[1] J. G. Jacobi, *Winterreise*. This is believed to be the earliest appearance of the celebrated phrase in German literature (according to Büchmann, *Geflügelte Worte*, 27th edition, p. 441 f., where many other instances, mostly from the *Empfindsamkeitsperiode*, may be found). In the nineteenth century the hedonistic conception of Arcadian happiness as championed by Goethe (cf., for instance, also *Faust*, ii, iii:

> Gelockt, auf sel'gem Grund zu wohnen,
> Du flüchtetest ins heiterste Geschick!
> Zur Laube wandeln sich die Thronen,
> Arcadisch frei sei unser Glück!)

was to degenerate into the trivial conception of 'having a good time', as is the case, for instance, in the well-known aria in Offenbach's 'Orpheus': *Als ich noch Prinz* painted a portrait of two particularly lovely ladies, Mrs. Bouverie and Mrs. Crewe, in which was also seen a tomb inscribed 'Et in Arcadia ego'.[1]

This now is the canonical formula as used in the best-known pictorial interpretation of the Arcadia theme: it is found in the famous Louvre painting by Nicolas Poussin probably executed around 1640–5 (Fig. 1). Three handsome shepherds are both fascinated and moved by an austerely simple tomb, one of them kneeling on the ground, so as to decipher the half-effaced inscription, *Et in Arcadia ego*, the second explaining its meaning to a lovely girl, who listens to him in a quiet, thoughtful attitude, the third trajected into a sympathetically brooding melancholy. It is as though the youthful people, all silent, were listening to or pondering over this imaginary message of a former fellow-being: 'I, too, lived in Arcadia, where you now live; I, too, enjoyed the pleasures which you now enjoy; and yet I am dead and buried.' We instantly perceive a strange ambiguous feeling which suggests both a mournful anticipation of man's inevitable destiny and an intense consciousness of the sweetness of life.

Thus the inner meaning of Poussin's picture[2]—an elegiac sentiment aroused by the contrast between friendship and love amid beautiful scenery and the tomb of one who has left these joys for ever—seems fairly clear. But when we come to think of it, we are puzzled by two problems, one bearing upon the Arcadia conception as a whole, the other—seemingly a mere philological one, but in reality connected with what I should like to call the 'History of Types'—bearing upon the wording of the inscription, which, as it stands, is not at all in harmony with the above analysis.

I

First of all: how is it that that particular region of central Greece, Arcadia, was destined to become the visionary realm of

war von Arkadien. It is, however, a significant fact that the original French text does not speak of 'Arcadie' but of 'Béotie'—the above development being the negative result of a specifically German *Bildungstradition*.

On the other hand, the term 'Arcadian' could become a synonym of 'Utopian', 'imaginary', or even 'unfeasible', as in Jean Paul's *Dr. Katzenbergers Badereise*, 24. Summula: *Doch sind das nicht ganz arkadische Träume*.

[1] Cf. below, p. 233f., n. 1. The picture is still preserved at Crewe Hall.

[2] Special literature about this picture: Henry Lemonnier, 'Les sources des "Bergers d'Arcadie" ', *Revue de l'art ancien et moderne*, xlvii, 1925, pp. 273 ff., and W. Weisbach, 'Et in Arcadia ego', *Die Antike*, vi, 1930, pp. 127 ff.

Love and Beauty, the dream incarnate of ineffable happiness, surrounded nevertheless with a halo of sweet melancholy resignation?[1] True, Arcadia was held to be the domain of Pan, the shepherds' god, who could be heard playing the syrinx among the pine trees of Mount Maenalus.[2] The Arcadians were renowned for their rustic virtue, their hospitality, and primordial simplicity, as well as for their complete ignorance of what was happening in the outer world, but at the same time also for their musical accomplishments; for theirs was the only land where 'music was considered an indispensable thing instead of a merely desirable one', to speak in the words of the historian Polybius, Arcadia's most famous son.[3] The interesting thing, however, is that Polybius describes his country as utterly devoid of such natural charms as might be expected from an ideal land of pastoral happiness. Arcadia, according to him, was a rough, poor, bare, and rocky country, which scarcely afforded the necessities of life for meagre goats and frugal shepherds. We can well understand, therefore, that the Greek poets refrained from selecting Arcadia as the scene of their bucolics. The pastorals of Theocritus were staged in Sicily, so richly endowed with all those qualities which Arcadia conspicuously lacked. Pan himself condescended to come down to Sicily when the dying Daphnis wished to return his shepherd's flute.

It was in Latin art and literature that the specific poetic significance that seems to be a matter of course to the modern mind was attached to Arcadia[4] (witness the well-known fresco

[1] Cf. A. Gercke, 'Auch ich war in Arkadien geboren', *Neue Jahrbücher für das Klassische Altertum*, xxiv, 1921, pp. 313 ff., and R. Helm in *Bursians Jahresbericht über die Fortschritte der klassischen Altertumswiss.*, 30, 1902, ii, p. 24. Furthermore, the commented editions of Theocritus' Idylls and Virgil's Bucolics, especially: *Virgils Gedichte, erklärt von Ladewig, Schaper und Deuticke*, i, *Bucolica und Georgica*, 9. Aufl., bearbeitet von Paul Jahn, 1915.

[2] Pausanias, *Periegesis*, viii. 36. 8: 'Mount Maenalus is particularly sacred to Pan, so that the people assert that Pan could be heard there playing the syrinx.'

[3] Polybius, *Historiae*, iv. 20.

The negative aspects of primordial simplicity were emphasized by such authors as Juvenal, who characterized a peculiarly boring orator as an 'Arcadian youth' (vii. 160) and Philostratus (*Vita Apollonii*, viii. 7), who calls the Arcadians 'acorn-eating swine'. Even their musical achievements were disparaged by Fulgentius, who by *Arcadici aures* meant 'ears not susceptible to real beauty' (p. 90, Helm).

[4] The existence of a pastoral poetry in Arcadia, as conjectured by R. Reitzenstein (*Epigramm und Skolion*, 1893, pp. 131 and 249), seems rather improbable, and even Helm's opinion that an unknown Alexandrian poet might have shifted the scenery of pastoral poetry from Sicily to Arcadia (Helm, l.c.) remains a mere hypothesis (cf. Jahn, l.c., p. xxv and p. 268, footnotes). To our present knowledge Virgil is

from Herculaneum),[1] and even within the Latin culture we can distinguish between two manners of approach: Ovid connects Arcadia with a mythical cosmogony which in turn is possibly one of the sources of later Hermetic doctrines,[2] while Virgil uses it for the ideal scene of his bucolics.

Ovid's conception of Arcadia foreshadows that of truly 'primitive life' as imagined by such Renaissance authors as Alberti or Filarete, and later on idealized by Jean Jacques Rousseau. According to Ovid, the Arcadians, ruled by Pan, existed before the birth of Jupiter and the creation of the moon, and lived the life of primitive savages. They knew nothing of agriculture, architecture, clothes, tools, and domestic animals: *Vita ferae similis, nullos agitata per usus—Artis adhuc expers et rude volgus erat.* It is a Golden Age in which no gold exists; innocently simple, but rough and decidedly unenjoyable.[3] Obviously Ovid drew to some extent from Polybius' description, but synthesized the Polybian traits with the cosmogonical ideas which were mentioned above; thus he emphasized the characteristics of a poor and primitive life while eliminating the characteristics of a specifically musical mentality, and he also shoved the whole conception back into a mythical past.

Virgil, however, interpreted and used Polybius in quite the opposite way.[4] For Virgil the emotional values of Arcadian life

the first author who selected Arcadia as the realm of pastoral happiness (cf. Cartault and Legrand, quoted by Jahn, l.c., p. 268).

[1] Cf. E. Löwy, *Festschrift für Julius Schlosser*, 1927, pp. 46 ff., Plate I.

[2] I feel indebted to Dr. Klibansky for reminding me of these connexions. Cf. Th. Zielinski, *Hermes und die Hermetik*, *Archiv für Religionswissenschaft*, ix. 1906, pp. 25 ff.

[3] Ovid, *Fast.* ii. 289 ff.

[4] Jahn argues that Virgil's Arcadian shepherds originally belonged to the ordinary Theocritean variety, and were but subsequently transformed into 'Arcades', when the poet had been informed (either through a learned footnote to Theocritus, i. 3 *μετὰ Πᾶνα τὸ δεύτερον ἆθλον ἀποισῇ* or i. 124 *ἀμφιπολεῖς Μαίναλον*, or through an Alexandrian poet) that Arcadia was the *eigentliches Hirtenland.* However, to become aware of the 'pastoral' significance of Arcadia, Virgil did not need such hypothetical sources, but could, and did, draw from sources open to Pausanias and from Polybius. To me this fact was pointed out by Prof. Ernst Kapp, to whom I feel much indebted in many other respects also. Thus the *soli cantare periti Arcades* in Ecl. X, v. 32 was obviously inspired by Polybius' fervent description of Arcadia's musical accomplishments (cf. p. 225, n. 3), which description also accounts for Ecl. IV, v. 58 ff., where 'Arcadia' is called upon as a judge in the imaginary contest between the poet and Pan. And the famous lines Ecl. VII. 4–5, *Arcades ambo / Et cantare pares et respondere parati* (especially famous by their somewhat cynical reinterpretation in Byron's *Don Juan*, iv, st. 93, 'Arcades ambo, id est blackguards both') are an almost literal translation of Polybius' *ἀνὰ μέρος ᾄδειν ἀλλήλοις προστάττοντες*. The important thing, however, is that Virgil realized

eclipsed its cultural shortcomings, and while Ovid had transferred the Arcadian primitiveness to an imaginary period, Virgil transferred the Arcadian purity and musical sensitiveness to a Utopian space. Thus it was Virgil who achieved the paradisaical conception which the modern mind automatically connects with the term 'Arcadia'.

Technically speaking, he did nothing but transplant the bucolics of Theocritus to what he decided to call 'Arcadia' (so that now Arethusa, the Naiad of Syracuse, must swim to Arcadia while in Theocritus Pan had had to desert Mount Maenalus for Sicily).[1] But by this rearrangement Virgil created a new visionary realm endowed with both the sweetness of the real Sicily as described by Theocritus and the emotional fascination of the real Arcadia as described by Polybius—a realm sufficiently remote from Roman everyday life to defy any realistic interpretation (the very names of the characters, as well as of the plants and animals, suggest an unreal far-off atmosphere when they occur in the context of Latin verse), yet sufficiently saturated with visual concreteness to appeal directly to the inner experience of the reader.

Thus, thanks to the imaginative power of a Roman poet, a somewhat bleak and chilly region of Greece became transfigured so as to survive in the memory of mankind as an ideal realm of perfect bliss. But behold! At the very moment when this new Arcadia was created, a dissonance made itself felt between its preternatural perfection and the fundamental limitations of human nature as such: even in Arcadia there existed the two

the immense increase of emotional values to be gained by a visionary synthesis between the real Sicily as described by Theocritus and the real Arcadia as described by Polybius (for in Ecl. VIII. 22 ff.

> Maenalus argutumque nemus pinosque loquentes
> Semper habet, semper pastorum ille audit amores
> Panaque, qui primus calamos non passus inertes

Virgil obviously not only transplants Theocritus' whispering pine trees to Arcadia but also utilizes the sources of the Pausanias passage quoted p. 225, n. 2). After the completion of this article there appeared a new discussion of the subject by Herta Wendel, *Arkadien im Umkreis bukolischer Dichtung in der Antike und in der französischen Literatur*, *Giessener Beiträge zur romanischen Philologie*, Heft 26, 1933. She adduces much new material but fails to realize the importance of Ovid as well as the connexion between Virgil and Polybius, and does not much contribute to the interpretation of Poussin's pictures and their inscription. However, she too confirms the fact that Virgil was *der Hauptfaktor für das Klassisch-Werden Arkadiens für die stereotype Verbindung von 'Arkadien' und 'Hirtengedicht'* (p. 30).

[1] Compare Virgil, Ecl. X, v. 1 ff. with Theocritus, Id. i (Daphnis), v. 123 ff.

fundamental tragedies of human life, inextricably connected with one another: frustrated love and death.

True enough, in the 'Thyrsis' of Theocritus Daphnis had also died, though he had died through love and not of love as we shall shortly see. But if we compare the episode of the death of Daphnis in Theocritus to corresponding episodes in Virgil we are struck by a fundamental difference. Virgil infuses into the subject a new sentimental and melancholy feeling aroused by the consciousness of a discrepancy between human suffering and ideal environment. He uses the Daphnis story in two Eclogues. One (the fifth) is almost an imitation of the poem of Theocritus. In Theocritus, however, we actually witness the last moments of Daphnis and listen to his dying words foretelling that after his death everything in nature will be reversed, so that pears will grow on pine trees and the deer will pursue the hound. In Virgil's fifth Eclogue, on the other hand, Daphnis is already dead, and we listen to the elegiac complaints of the survivors who are preparing a memorial ceremony and a tombstone inscribed with a sentimental distich (here, then, is the first appearance of the Tomb in Arcadia, so indispensable a feature in later 'Arcadian' art and poetry).[1] Nature is described as disfigured, not that her laws are merely reversed as in the Theocritean instances of the pears on the pine trees, &c., but health and beauty have turned to poison and ugliness, barley has been supplanted by darnel, violets and narcissi by prickly thistles. In Virgil's second and more original poem inspired by the Daphnis episode, the tenth Eclogue, the dying Daphnis is boldly transferred into a real person, namely Virgil's friend Gallus, who is described as suffering in agony and foretelling his death, while sympathizing shepherds and divinities surround him. But while the Daphnis of Theocritus is really fated to die, Virgil's Gallus merely yearns and languishes; while Daphnis is put to death by Eros because he has refused to love, Gallus suffers because his Lycoris has left him for a rival. Thus mythical veracity gives way to subjective

[1] Spargite humum foliis, inducite fontibus umbras,
pastores (mandat fieri sibi talia Daphnis)
et *tumulum facite et tumulo superaddite carmen :*
'*Daphnis ego in silvis, hinc* usque ad sidera notus,
formosi pecoris custos, formosior ipse'.

Obviously this Eclogue is the main inspiration of the frequent descriptions of tombs and funeral ceremonies in Sannazzaro's *Arcadia,* the very parent-poem of modern Arcadian art and poetry.

sentiment revelling in the contrast between the Utopian beauty of Arcadia and the sadness of unreciprocated love: Lycoris dwells in the dreary north—Arcadia abounds with flowery meadows, shadowy groves, and crystalline springs—how beautiful it could be if she were present![1]

This elegiac interpretation of Arcadia, which in Virgil was still limited to a few episodes and might be called a literary phenomenon rather than a psychological one, was destined to sink into oblivion for many centuries. During the Middle Ages, when the aims of human nostalgia had been shifted to the Beyond, pastoral poetry assumed a rather worldly, realistic character. Some learned poet of the twelfth century would celebrate his small country estate in the manner of Horace rather than of Virgil.[2] Petrarch sings of his hermitage of Vaucluse, near Avignon. In pastoral poetry in the technical sense of the term the characters are called 'Robin' and 'Jeannette' instead of 'Daphnis' and 'Chloe'. The scene of Boccaccio's 'Ameto', where the name of 'Arcadia' reappears for the first time, is laid near Cortona in Tuscany (although the landscape already teems with satyrs, dryads, and hamadryads), and Boccaccio's 'Alcesto di Arcadia' competing with a shepherd from Sicily, 'Achaten di Achademia', contrasts the Polybian conception of rough healthy laboriousness with the Sicilian ideal of wealth and comfort which leads to an idle and materialistic attitude towards life.[3]

In the Renaissance, however, Virgil's Arcadia emerged from the past like an enchanting vision. Only, for the modern mind, Arcadia was not only something distant and ideal, but it also

[1] Even the motive that the frustrated lover foresees the glorification of his fate in future poetry is drawn from Theocritus (Aïtes). But while, in Theocritus, the lover wishes that his and his friend's mutual love might become a shining specimen of perfect happiness, Virgil's Gallus feels comforted by the idea that his sufferings will be the subject of an Arcadian song. Here, too, we are struck by the beautiful sentimentality of Virgil's reinterpretation.

[2] Marbod of Rennes, quoted by W. Ganzenmüller, *Geschichte des Naturgefühls im Mittelalter*, Leipzig, 1914, pp. 224 ff.; see Migne, *Patrologia latina*, vol. clxxi, cols. 1665–7. Marbod's attitude is rather unusual and almost surprising in a period practically estranged from the classic conception of *Otium*, meaning the blissful state of a mind entirely belonging to and satisfied with itself. In general the reinstatement of this feeling was a Renaissance phenomenon, while to the medieval mind, unfamiliar as it was with the conception of human mental self-sufficiency, a leisurely time neither devoted to work nor to the communion with God meant a dangerous or even sinful thing (*Acedia*).

[3] Boccaccio, *Ameto*, Canzone v (Florent. edition of 1529, p. 23 verso ff.).

belonged to what was now conceived as the *Sacrosancta Vetustas* and considered as a 'Consummation devoutly to be wished'. The imaginary realm of Arcadia, which for the Roman writers had no common denominator with actual life, was to become the object of a very real nostalgia, a psychological factor instead of a literary fiction: it developed into a haven not only from a faulty reality but also from a questionable present.[1]

At the height of the Quattrocento an attempt was made to conquer the visionary kingdom of Arcadia by means of a metaphorical identification with real scenery, so as to smooth away the chasm between the present and the past. As was proved by Saxl, the Medici villa at Fiesole was celebrated as 'Arcadia' by such poets as Angelo Poliziano and even Lorenzo the Magnificent, while the various members of the Medicean circle appeared as Arcadia's inhabitants.[2] This alluring fiction lies also at the bottom of Signorelli's marvellous Berlin picture, which shows a sweetly melancholy Pan surrounded by musical shepherds and beautiful nymphs (one of them, depicted asleep, refers to the 'sacred hour of Pan':

> Die Nymphe darf nicht munter sein,
> Und wo sie stand, da schläft sie ein,[3]

to speak in the terms of Goethe).

Soon, however, the realm of Arcadia was established as a sovereign domain. While in Boccaccio's 'Ameto' Arcadia had only figured as a distant home of rustic purity, and while again the Medicean poets had praised the villa at Fiesole using the conception of Arcadia as a mere classical disguise or drapery, a monumental poem by Jacopo Sannazzaro entitled 'Arcadia' (1502) glorified Arcadia for Arcadia's sake,[4] and this glorifica-

[1] Cf. E. Panofsky and F. Saxl, *Classical Mythology in Mediaeval Art*, Metropolitan Museum Studies, iv, 1933, pp. 228 ff., conclusion.

[2] Cf. F. Saxl, 'Antike Götter in der Spätrenaissance', *Studien der Bibliothek Warburg*, viii, 1927, pp. 22 ff.

[3] Goethe, *Faust II*, ii. 1.

[4] *Jacobo Sannazzaro, Arcadia*, ed. M. Scherillo (with illuminating introduction), 1888. Sannazzaro's poem is based on both Italian and classical sources (Petrarch and Boccaccio on the one hand, Virgil, Polybius, Catullus, Longus, Nemesius, &c., on the other), thereby resuscitating the Virgilian conception of Arcadia within the limits of a modern, more subjective *Weltanschauung*.

Sannazzaro's is the first pastoral poem actually staged *in* Arcadia, and it is a significant fact that the few allusions to the real life of contemporary Naples were added, or at least made explicit, only in the second edition of 1504. The author primarily aims at reviving the imaginary realm of Arcadia as an emotional ex-tion gave rise to innumerable poems of the same nature, as well as to the founding of literary societies of a highly cultured character. Arcadia, according to Sannazzaro, is intrinsically a Utopian realm, but for this very reason it is wrapped in a subtle veil of melancholy—for the more completely the vision of ideal happiness took shape the more sharply those two inevitable tragedies, Love and Death, inevitable even in Arcadia, came to be felt: *La musa vera del Sannazzaro è la Malinconia*, as an Italian scholar puts it.[1] And in truth Sannazzaro's poem abounds in funeral hymns and ceremonies, yearning love-songs and melancholy memories.[2] Thus the elegiac feeling, foreshadowed, though not yet fully developed in Virgil's Eclogues, impresses us as the essential quality of the Arcadian atmosphere, not in spite but because of Arcadia's unattainable perfection.[3]

A further step is taken in Tasso's 'Aminta'. In it the unbroken sweetness and innocent freedom of Arcadian life is explicitly contrasted with the constrained and conscience-stricken spirit of modern civilization, particularly torn and oppressed at this moment by the intrinsic tensions of the Counter-Reformation. The famous chorus at the end of the first act 'O bella età

perience *sui generis*, and only incidentally connects it with the facts of real life, while the earlier Renaissance poets indulged in a literary glorification of their and their patrons' actual surroundings.

[1] A. Sainati, *La lirica latina del Rinascimento*, i, 1919, p. 184 (already adduced by Saxl, l.c.).

[2] I should like to adduce some passages particularly centring around the idea of the *Tomb in Arcadia*: p. 70, lines 49 ff. (according to Scherillo's edition); p. 145, lines 246 ff. (a literal translation of Virgil, Ecl. X, v. 31 ff.); and pp. 296 ff.

In the great Trio on the death of Phyllis the situation visualized in Poussin's Louvre picture is almost foreshadowed in the song of Barcinio:

> . . . farò tra questi rustici
> La sepoltura tua famosa et celebre.
> Et da' monti Thoscani et da' Ligustici
> Verran pastori ad venerar quest' angulo,
> Sol per cagion che alcuna volta fustici,
> *Et leggeran nel bel sasso quadrangulo*
> *Il titol che ad tutt' hore il cor m'infrigida*,
> Per cui tanto dolor nel petto strangulo:
> 'Quella che ad Meliseo si altera et rigida
> Si mostrò sempre, hor mansueta et humile
> Si sta sepolta in questa pietra frigida' . . .

[3] Cf. Jean Paul, *Brief an Emanuel*, 11 July 1795 (*Die Briefe Jean Pauls*, ed. Berend, 1922, vol. ii, p. 94): 'Es ist sonderbar, dass der Mensch gerade in der Freude — in der Jugend — in der schönsten Gegend — in der schönsten Jahreszeit mehr zur Schwärmerei der Sehnsucht, zum Blicke jenseits der Welt, zum Gemälde des Todes fähig ist als im entgegengesezten Fall, in der Noth, im Alter, in Grönland, im Winter.'

de l'oro . . .' is not solely an enthusiastic eulogy of the Arcadian past, but even more an invective against the poet's own period, in which, owing to social conventions, the very spring of pleasure is polluted—flowing hair and nude bodies are bound and concealed in nets and clothing, behaviour and carriage have grown sophisticated, and the very gift of Love is perverted into theft. Here is the outburst of a man who feels himself excluded from Arcadia[1] (as though an actor would appear before the footlights to contrast his private misery with the splendour of his role). It is a tragic accusation in which civilization, even a special form of civilization, is made responsible for the fateful tragedy of human life as such.

This brings us back to Poussin's picture in the Louvre. In it the sombre pathos of Tasso and the lingering melancholy of Sannazzaro have given way to an earnest though uncomplaining pensiveness, and this calm attitude is much in harmony both with the spirit of the new era that had overcome the struggles of the Counter-Reformation, and with the new style that had replaced the constraints and entanglements of Mannerism either with baroque richness and freedom or with classicistic dignity and equilibrium.

But now, what is the exact meaning of the inscription: *Et in Arcadia ego*? In recent literature these words are unanimously attributed to the dead person buried in the tomb, as is, after all, the case with most epitaphs worded after the fashion of Virgil's *Daphnis ego in silvis* . . . and the like. Thus it was quite logical to translate *Et in Arcadia ego* into 'I, too, was in Arcadia'. But this translation is based on two assumptions: first, that the missing verb should stand in the past tense; secondly, that the *Et* refers to *Ego*. Now the first assumption is an arbitrary one, and the second is downright wrong. According to the rules of Latin grammar the *Et* cannot but relate to *Arcadia*. Consequently the correct translation of the Latin formula *Et in Arcadia ego* is 'Even in Arcadia, there (am) I', and this, as a matter of fact, is its original and genuine meaning; for the subject of the sentence is not the man buried in the tomb, but the tomb itself—and the tomb in its turn is nothing but a substitute for death in person.

This interpretation is confirmed by a painting in which the

[1] Cf., among others, W. Stechow, *Kritische Berichte zur kunstgeschichtlichen Literatur 1928/29*, pp. 181 ff. (Review of Illa Budde, *Die Idylle im holländischen Barock*).

FIG. 2. Nicolas Poussin, 'Et in Arcadia ego'

Chatsworth, Duke of Devonshire

After an original photograph by Franz Hanfstaengl, Munich

FIG. 3. Guercino, 'Et in Arcadia ego' *Rome, Galleria Corsini*

FIG. 4. Gerard Honthorst, Vanitas *Rome, Galleria Corsini*

canonical—though certainly non-classical—formula *Et in Arcadia ego* seems to appear for the first time: an early Guercino in the Corsini Gallery in Rome, certainly executed not later than 1623, when the young painter left Rome for his native town of Cento (Fig. 3). In it the Arcadian shepherds are not absorbed in lasting contemplation, but are interrupted in their walk by the sudden sight of a death's-head gnawed by a mouse (a time-honoured and very well-known symbol for all-devouring time). The skull lies on a mouldering piece of masonry inscribed *Et in Arcadia ego*, and the shepherds almost stumble over this sinister *memento mori*.[1] So it is Death himself who stops the shepherds and

[1] The relationship between the two pictures was already pointed out by Lemonnier, l.c., though he speaks only of *un tableau italien dans la galerie Sciarra Colonna, aujourd'hui Corsini*, and strongly emphasized by Weisbach, l.c. (with illustration of the Guercino painting). Both authors, however, failed to realize the interior significance of this relationship, especially the role of Poussin's Devonshire picture, let alone the linguistic problem of the famous inscription. The Corsini picture, formerly attributed to Bartolommeo Schidone, and adduced as such by Büchmann, l.c., was recognized as an early Guercino by H. Voss, *Repertorium für Kunstwissenschaft*, xxxiv, 1911, p. 121. It seems, however, that the correct attribution was already known in the eighteenth century and had only sunk into oblivion in the second half of the nineteenth. For in their discussion of Reynolds's portrait of Mrs. Bouverie and Mrs. Crewe, brought to my attention by Dr. Edgar Wind, his biographers state that 'the thought (viz. of the tomb with the inscription *Et in Arcadia ego*) is borrowed from Guercino, where the gay frolickers stumble over a death's-head with a scroll proceeding from his mouth inscribed *Et in Arcadia ego*' (C. R. Leslie and Tom Taylor, *Life and Times of Sir Joshua Reynolds*, 1865, i, p. 325); and when they mention this portrait for the first time in connexion with the Arcadia picture by Angelica Kauffmann referred to in p. 237–8, n. 3, Tom Taylor explicitly adds: 'I find a sketch of Guercino's picture in Reynolds's Roman note-book' (l.c. i, p. 260). It was obviously from this sketch, probably bearing the usual explanatory note, that Tom Taylor learned about the Corsini picture and its author, and so surprising was this knowledge that a later biographer of Reynolds, ignorant as he was of the Guercino painting, ventured to state that Reynolds had been inspired by Poussin (W. Armstrong, *Joshua Reynolds*, übersetzt von E. von Kraatz, s.a., p. 89). The 'scroll' allegedly proceeding from the mouth of the skull is obviously due to a misinterpretation of the mouse's tail. Only, as I don't know the Reynolds sketch (unfortunately the 'Roman Sketchbook', formerly belonging to R. Gwatkin, cf. Leslie-Taylor, i, p. 51, could not be spotted in spite of the generous help of Messrs. K. T. Parker, Campbell Dodgson, Laurence Binyon, and G. W. Constable), I cannot tell whether Reynolds misinterpreted the picture or Tom Taylor misinterpreted the sketch. In any case this very misinterpretation shows that even at a comparatively recent period an unbiased observer of the Guercino composition naturally assumed that the words *Et in Arcadia ego* were voiced by the skull.

The significance of the mouse as a symbol of all-devouring time is already pointed out in Horapollon's *Hieroglyphica* (cf. K. Giehlow, *Jahrbuch d. Kunstslgn. d. Allerhöchsten Kaiserhauses*, xxxii, 1915, cod. Vind. 3255, fol. 60 r.) and remained a well-known thing throughout the centuries (cf. the medieval allegory of human life known as 'The tree of Barlaam'; according to Condivi, *Vita di Michelangelo*, cap.

sets them thinking with the awful warning: 'I hold sway, even in Arcadia.' For in this case it cannot be doubted that the words are meant to be voiced by the death's-head, all the more so because the conception of a speaking death's-head was quite a usual thing in those days. It was a common feature in art and literature, and is even alluded to in a dialogue between Falstaff and Doll Tearsheet (*2 Henry IV*, II. iv) when he answers her well-intentioned warnings as to his conduct: 'Peace, good Doll, do not speak to me like a death's head, do not bid me remember mine end.'[1]

xlv, even Michelangelo had planned to include a mouse in the iconography of the Medici Chapel).

Viewed through the medium of 'Romantic irony' the motive of the Guercino picture looks as follows: 'Ein gar herrliches "Memento mori" ist . . . ein hübscher gebleichter *Menschenschädel* auf der Toilette. So ein leerer Hirnkasten . . . müsste Wunder tun, wenn die Macht der Gewohnheit nicht noch stärker wäre. . . . Man würde zuletzt das Dasein des Totenschädels ganz vergessen, wenn nicht schon zu Zeiten *eine Maus* ihn wieder lebendig gemacht . . . hätte' (C. J. Weber, *Demokritos oder hinterlassene Papiere eines lachenden Philosophen*, s.a., xii. 20, pp. 253 ff.: I owe my acquaintance with this chapter, referred to also on p. 238, n. 1, to Prof. F. Schalk, Rostock).

[1] As to the significance of skulls and skeletons in connexion with the general conception of life and destiny, cf. R. Zahn, *81. Berliner Winckelmanns-Programm*, 1923; T. Creizenach, 'Gaudeamus igitur', *Verhandlungen der 28. Versammlung Deutscher Philologen und Schulmänner*, Leipzig, 1872; C. H. Becker, 'Ubi sunt qui ante nos in mundo fuere?', *Aufsätze zur Kultur- und Sprachgeschichte, vornehmlich des Islam*, Ernst Kuhn zum 70. Geburtstage gewidmet, 1916, pp. 87 ff. It appears that the original significance of those morbid symbols primarily occurring on goblets and table decorations instead of on sepulchral monuments was a purely hedonistic one, viz. an invitation to enjoy the pleasures of life as long as it lasts, and only subsequently was turned into a moralistic sermon of resignation and penitence. This development took place in ancient Egypt as well as in the civilizations deriving from classical antiquity, both occidental and oriental. In them, the inversion of the original idea was chiefly due to patristic writings which in turn made ample use of Greek rhetoric. In point of fact, the *Vita brevis* idea is characterized by an intrinsic ambivalence implying both the Horatian *Carpe diem* and the Christian *surge, surge, vigila, semper esto paratus* (refrain of a song of 1267). From the later phase of the Middle Ages the 'speaking' skulls and skeletons became so common a symbol of the *memento mori* idea (in the Camaldulensian sense of this formula) that these motives invaded almost every sphere of everyday life. Innumerable instances are not only to be found in sepulchral art (mostly with such inscriptions as *Vixi ut vivis, morieris ut sum mortuus* or *Tales vos eritis, fueram quandoque quod estis*), but also in portraits, on clocks, on medals, and, most especially, on finger rings (many instances adduced in the London Shakespeare edition of 1785 with reference to the above dialogue between Falstaff and Doll Tearsheet). On the other hand, the menace of a 'speaking skull' could also be interpreted as a hopeful prospect for after-life, as is the case in a short stanza by the German seventeenth-century poet D. C. von Lohenstein, in which the *Redender Todtenkopff des Herrn Matthäus Machners* says: *Ja|wenn der Höchste wird vom Kirch-Hof erndten ein|So werd ich Todten-Kopff ein Englisch Antlitz seyn* (quoted in W. Benjamin, *Ursprung des deutschen Trauerspiels*, 1928, p. 215). The skull 'speaks' of course mostly in the name of the person to

Thus while Poussin's picture shows an elegiac absorption in the idea of mortality, Guercino's painting shows a dramatic meeting with Death which dumbfounds the shepherds by its very unexpectedness. Iconographically speaking, Guercino's composition is a synthesis between two widespread types of moralistic representations: First, the so-called 'Vanitas-pictures' so fashionable in late Renaissance and early Baroque art: a human being, preferably an attractive young lady such as the Magdalen or a girl personifying the *Contemplazione della Morte*,[1] is shown brooding over or warningly pointing at a death's-head while symbols of futile earthly pleasures and no less futile human endeavours in art and science are scattered around (Fig. 4; it is easy to see why Domenico Feti and other artists such as Nicolas Chaperon used Dürer's Melencolia as a model for this type of composition). Secondly, such visualizations of a dramatic encounter between death and frolicsome youth as 'Death and the Maiden', 'Death and the Lovers', or (and this was the earliest and most important type) the 'Legend of the Three Living and the Three Dead', where three young dandies setting out for a hunt come upon three corpses which rise from their tombs to warn them against their thoughtless indulgence in the pleasures of life. The best-known pictorial version of this legend is one of the frescoes in the Campo Santo in Pisa (Fig. 5).[2] Here the three riders actually stumble over the three coffins as later on Guercino's shepherds were to stumble over the death's-head. In both cases Death catches the young men by the throat, so to speak, right in the middle of a cheerful ramble; Guercino, however, sharpens this effect by shifting the scene to Arcadia in order to impress a favourite conception of Christian moral

whom it once belonged; in other instances, however, in the name of Death himself, which appears also from the fact that in the more ancient English texts it is always called a 'Death's head' (*caput mortis*), and not a 'dead man's head' (*caput mortui*).

[1] C. Ripa, *Iconologia* (1st ed., 1593), s.v. 'Meditatione della Morte'. On Ripa cf. E. Mâle, *Revue des deux mondes*, 1927, pp. 106 ff. and 375 ff., and E. Mandowsky, *Untersuchungen zur Iconologie des Cesare Ripa*, Dissertation, Hamburg, 1934 (private print). On the 'Vanitas' pictures and their interrelationship with the type of 'Melancholy' cf. Panofsky and Saxl, *Dürer's Melencolia*, I, 2nd edition (in preparation). Our Fig. 4 shows a picture by G. Honthorst which happens to be in the same collection as Guercino's *Et in Arcadia ego*, and curiously appeals to the beholder by the weird motive of an empty mirror which, were it real, would show his own reflection.

[2] Cf. K. Künstle, *Die Legende der drei Lebenden und der drei Toten*, 1908, p. 53; cf. also Millard Meiss in his excellent article on *Francesco Traini* (*The Art Bulletin*, xv, 1933, pp. 169 ff.).

theology upon a public which he knows to be enthusiastic abou the ideal milieu of classical pastoral poetry. This picture, now was to be the foundation of Poussin's painting in the Louvre.

The relationship can be proved by the fact that an earlie painting by Poussin, executed around 1626–8 and now in th collection of the Duke of Devonshire,[1] shows an intermediar stage between the Louvre version and the picture by Guercin (Fig. 2). Poussin has already added the female figure as well a the Arcadian river-god Alpheus, and has already ventured t transform the mouldering masonry into a sarcophagus inscribe with the usual phrase; but he still keeps to the idea that th shepherds are suddenly arrested by the sight of the monumen which they approach with a certain impetuousness instead o gathering around it in thoughtful attitudes (as in the Louvr version). Poussin also retains the motive of the death's-head though its importance is so much diminished that we hesitate t regard it as a subject of the ominous sentence 'Even in Arcadia there am I'. In the ultimate version, Poussin not only transform the rather picturesque sarcophagus into a tomb of severel classic cast and substitutes thoughtful contemplation fo frightened surprise, but he also eliminates the death's-hea altogether. This elimination is consistent with the essentia principles of classicistic art-theories which rejected *les objet bizarres*[2] and especially broken, gruesome, or tattered objects but this very elimination was to pose a startling problem t posterity.

As stated before, the death's-head, impersonating Death him self, had originally been the most important factor in the whol conception as a proclaimer of the sentence 'Even in Arcadia there am I'. Things became more complicated when the sen tence had to be voiced by a tomb, for a speaking tomb is les easy to imagine than a speaking death's-head. Yet Giovann Pietro Bellori, the first biographer of Poussin and a persona friend of the painter, gave an exact and correct interpretatio of the inscription when he wrote: '"Et in Arcadia ego"—cioè ch *il sepolcro* si trova *ancora* in Arcadia e che la Morte a luogo i

[1] Cf. P. Jamot, *Gazette des beaux-arts*, 1925, ii, p. 84 f. In the seventeenth centur the Devonshire picture apparently belonged for some time to Henri de Loméni Comte de Brienne, who describes the subject quite nicely as a 'sujet champêt et moral' (*Discours sur les ouvrages des plus excellents peintres*, published by L. Hourtic De Poussin à Watteau, 1921, p. 199).

[2] Cf. H. Jouin, *Conférences de l'Académie Royale de Peinture et de Sculpture*, 1883, p. 9

Fig. 5. Francesco Traini, The Legend of the Three Living and the Three Dead

Detail from a fresco in the Camposanto, Pisa

FIG. 6. J. H. Fragonard, Cupids embracing in a sarcophagus
Drawing. Vienna, Albertina

mezzo le felicità' ('"Et in Arcadia ego" means that the *grave* is to be found *even* in Arcadia and that death holds sway in the very midst of delight').[1]

But only a few years later Poussin's second biographer, André Félibien—though faithfully keeping to Bellori's text in every other particular—shrank already from the idea of a speaking tomb and substituted for it a buried person. 'Par cette inscription', he says, 'on a voulu marquer que *celui qui est dans cette sépulture a vécu* en Arcadie' ('This inscription emphasizes the fact that the person buried in this tomb has lived in Arcadia');[2] and this interpretation was destined to be accepted throughout the world[3] and to give rise to all those paraphrases in art and

[1] G. P. Bellori, *Le Vite de' pittori, scultori et architetti moderni*, Rome, 1672 (in the Pisa edition of 1821, vol. ii, p. 193; the complete description is reprinted in the Appendix. It is quite remarkable that King George III of England, when shown the Reynolds portrait of Mrs. Bouverie and Mrs. Crewe (cf. p. 224), instantly hit upon the grammatically correct interpretation of the inscription which Dr. Johnson utterly failed to understand: 'On a tomb in this year's picture of the two beautiful friends was written *Et in Arcadia ego*. When the Exhibition was arranging, the members and their friends went and looked the works over. "What can this mean?" said Dr. Johnson; "it seems very nonsensical—I am in Arcadia." "Well, what of that? The King could have told you", replied the painter. "He saw it yesterday, and said at once: 'Oh, there is a tombstone in the background. Ay, ay, *Death is even in Arcadia!*' ".' (Leslie-Taylor, l.c., i, p. 325.)

[2] A. Félibien, *Entretiens sur les vies et les ouvrages des peintres*, 1666 ff. (the fourth volume, containing the biography of Poussin, published in 1685): 'L'Arcadie est une contrée dont les poètes ont parlé comme d'un pais délicieux: mais par cette inscription on a voulu marquer que celui qui est dans ce tombeau a vécu en Arcadie, et que la Mort se rencontre parmi les plus grandes félicitez' (in the edition of 1705, vol. iv, p. 71; cf. also the inscription of Picart's engraving after the Louvre picture as quoted by Andresen, 'Nicolaus Poussin', *Verzeichnis der nach seinen Gemälden gefertigten Kupferstiche*, &c., Nr. 417).

[3] It is quite instructive to observe the gradual development of Félibien's mistranslation. While he had still omitted the *Et* (rendered by *ancora / anche* in Bellori's Italian translation), the Abbé du Bos completed the sentence by a *cependant* and, in addition, enhanced the sentimental value of the composition by the assumption that the group of shepherds includes two males and two females (instead of three males and one female), and that the tombstone shows the reclining figure of a girl in the prime of life: 'Le tableau dont je parle représente le paysage d'une contrée riante. Au milieu l'on voit le monument d'une jeune fille morte à la fleur de son âge: c'est ce qu'on connoît par la statue de cette fille couchée sur le tombeau, à la manière des anciens. L'inscription sépulcrale n'est que de quatre mots latins: "*Je vivois cependant en Arcadie*, Et in Arcadia ego". Mais cette inscription si courte fait faire les plus sérieuses réflexions à deux jeunes garçons et à deux jeunes filles parées de guirlandes de fleurs, et qui paroissent avoir rencontré ce monument si triste en des lieux où l'on devine bien qu'ils ne cherchoient pas un objet affligeant' (Abbé du Bos, *Réflexions critiques sur la poésie et sur la peinture*, i, section vi, Dresden edition of 1760, pp. 48 ff.). This passage was brought to my attention by Prof. Ernst Cassirer.

The 'final touch', it seems, was put by Diderot, who seems to be responsible for

literature which therefore can be considered as based on a grammatical error.

Nevertheless—and this is the truly illuminating fact—Félibien's interpretation, however erroneous as a translation of the Latin phrase, is more than justifiable as an exposition of the inner meaning of the picture; and this accounts for the fact that not only has his translation never been questioned, but has even been retranslated into Latin by the phrase, *Et tu in Arcadia vixisti.*[1]

Poussin, though still retaining Guercino's Latin sentence in the Louvre picture, has so outgrown Guercino's artistic conception that the inscription, if literally translated, practically no longer conforms to the psychological content of his representation. Not only is it difficult to imagine a speaking tomb instead

the insertion of the *aussi* at the wrong place: 'Il y a un paysage de Poussin où l'on voit de jeunes bergères qui dansent au son du chalumeau (!); et à l'écart, un tombeau avec cette inscription "*Je vivais aussi dans la délicieuse Arcadie*". Le prestige de style dont il s'agit, tient quelquefois à un mot qui détourne ma vue du sujet principal, et qui me montre de côté, comme dans le paysage du Poussin, l'espace, le temps, la vie, la mort ou quelque autre idée grande et mélancolique jetée toute au travers des images de la gaieté' ('De la poésie dramatique', *Œuvres*, ed. Assézat, vol. vii, p. 353; cf. also another reference to the Poussin picture in Diderot's 'Salon de 1767', ibid., vol. xi, p. 161: later on the misplaced *aussi* became as much a matter of course in French literature as the misplaced *Auch* in Germany, cf., for instance, Delille, *Les Jardins*, quoted by Büchmann, l.c.: *Et moi aussi, je fus pasteur dans l'Arcadie*). The picture described by Diderot seemed to bear out his well-known theory of the *contrastes dramatiques*, because he imagined that it showed the shepherds dancing to the sound of a flute. This error is either due to a confusion with other pictures by Poussin, such, for example, as the Bacchanal in the London National Gallery or the Feast of Pan in the Cook Collection, or to the impression of some later picture dealing with the same subject. Angelica Kauffmann, for instance, in 1766 exhibited a picture described as follows: 'a shepherd and shepherdess of Arcadia moralizing at the side of a sepulchre, while others are dancing at a distance' (cf. Lady Victoria Manners and Dr. W. C. Williamson, *Angelica Kauffmann*, London, 1924, p. 239; also Leslie-Taylor, *Life and Times of Sir Joshua Reynolds*, 1865, i, p. 260). As a significant contrast to this version of the subject I should like to adduce a strangely attractive etching by Carl Wilhelm Kolbe (1757–1835) transforming the Arcadian scenery into a phantasmagorically wild jungle, mostly composed of what in reality is a grotesque enlargement of grass, hops, and worm-eaten cabbage (Fig. 7).

[1] While this is a deliberate retranslation of the wrong meaning into correct Latin, there are other writers who, thanks to their intuitive feeling for Latin grammar, involuntarily shifted the words of the original phrase so as to conform them to the new interpretation. Thus C. J. Weber in his essay referred to in pp. 233–4, n. 1, quotes the famous formula as *Et ego in Arcadia* instead of *Et in Arcadia ego* ('Gräber und Urnen in englischen Gärten verbreiten die nämliche sanfte Wehmut wie ein Gottesacker oder ein "*Et ego in Arcadia*" in einer Landschaft von Poussin'), and the same erroneous reading, now fairly well explained, occurs in the earlier editions of Büchmann's *Geflügelte Worte* (in the 16th edition, for instance, on p. 582).

of a speaking death's-head, but the quiet pensive attitudes of the figures make it inconceivable that they should be meant to express the awful surprise caused by the sudden confrontation with a grim *memento mori*. While the intermediary Devonshire version, directly derived as it was from the Guercino picture, was still, to some extent, compatible with the original *memento mori* meaning of the canonical formula, though the emphasis no longer centred upon this thought,[1] the quiet contemplative atmosphere of the Louvre picture is virtually inconsistent with the direct menace conveyed by the sentence 'Even here, I, Death, hold sway'.

Therefore Félibien's interpretation, despite its linguistic incorrectness, reinstates the harmony between the text and the image. Only when attributed to a human being buried in the tomb does the Latin phrase, thereby transposed from the present to the past (the unexpressed verb becoming *vixi* instead of *sum*) actually conform with such an atmosphere of elegiac calm.

While the sentence 'Even in Arcadia, there am I' (namely Death) is a mere threat referring solely to the personal destiny of those addressed, the sentence 'I, too' (namely the person buried in the tomb) 'lived in Arcadia' is more than that: it not only warns the readers of the merciless future, but also opens a vision of the beautiful past in that it evokes the thought of a former fellow being who enjoyed the pleasure of life in the same place and under similar conditions. According to Félibien, the inscription means not only 'You, who are now happy, are doomed to die' but also 'I, who am now dead, was happy in my day', and thereby conveys a consolation as well as a warning; and this train of thought thoroughly agrees with the expression of the figures absorbed in both gloomy meditation and sweet remembrance.

It is now quite clear that the conception of Arcadia, as remodelled by Poussin's Louvre picture, could lead to considerations of almost opposite nature, depressing and melancholy on

[1] It is therefore very logical, and at the same time confirms our previous statements, that an Italian eighteenth-century painter called Cipriani (mostly active in England), who executed a 'variation' on the Devonshire picture by Poussin, exaggerating, however, the frightened expression of the surprised Arcadians and adding several gloomy figures, as well as various animals echoing the different emotions of the humans, not only renewed the prominence of the death's-head motive, but also adopted Bellori's translation for the inscription of the tomb; it reads: '*Ancora in Arcadia* More' (Fig. 8); 'More' is obviously a 'typographical error' for either *Morte* or *si muore*; the picture was brought to my attention by Dr. R. Wittkower.

the one hand, comforting and assuaging on the other. The very idea of death could fade from the memory of later generations (as occurred, for example, in Goethe's use of the expression *Auch ich in Arkadien*, which merely meant to him 'I, too, was happy'), and an artist of the eighteenth century like Fragonard could venture to reverse the original notion by depicting two Cupids—perhaps the spirits of deceased human lovers—clasped in an embrace within a broken sarcophagus, while a friendly genius suffuses the scene with the magic light of a nuptial torch —a visual refutation of Andrew Marvell's famous lines:

The Grave 's a fine and private place
But none I think do there embrace,

which could well be inscribed *Et hic Arcadia*, meaning: 'Even in the jaws of death, there may be Arcadian happiness' (Fig. 6).

II

The evolution which led from Guercino's Corsini picture to Poussin's Louvre painting gives us an insight into the mental processes of a great genius who, like Shakespeare in his Shylock, subconsciously conceives an entirely new idea while consciously keeping to a traditional formula; moreover, it throws light upon Poussin's attitude towards the fundamental problems of life and destiny.

The transformation of a mere *memento mori* into the revelation of a metaphysical principle which connects the present and the future with the past and overthrows the limits of individuality, means that 'Life' is conceived as transitory yet blessed with indestructible beauty and felicity; on the other hand, 'Death' is seen as a preserver as well as a destroyer. From this emerges the magnificent conception of a cyclical succession which subordinates the existence of individuals to the inexorable laws of cosmic principles, both natural and moral, endowing every stage of this existence, however transitory, with a substantial value of its own. Incidentally, I should like to mention that this attitude towards life is entirely in harmony with the formal qualities of Poussin's style; for if we study his pictures, we discover that he always endeavours to connect the single groups and figures by a rhythmic concatenation and manages to reconcile the perfect clarity of sheer classical design with the rich vitality of Venetian colorism by a kind of transparent, crystalline luminousness which at

Fig. 7. C. W. Kolbe, 'Et in Arcadia ego' *Etching*

Fig. 8. G. B. Cipriani, 'Et in Arcadia ego'
Engraving after an unidentified painting

FIG. 9. Nicolas Poussin, 'Ballo della Vita Humana'

London, Wallace Collection

FIG. 10. Nicolas Poussin, Phaeton before Helios

Berlin, Kaiser-Friedrich-Museum

the same time avoids statuesque isolation and pictorial fusion, stationary compactness and dissolved illusionism.

A fine illustration of these principles which happens to apply both to the composition and to the narrative is to be found in Poussin's so-called *Ballo della Vita humana* ('Dance of human Life') in the Wallace Collection (Fig. 9). Human life is conceived as an uninterrupted dance of four personifications: *Povertà* (Poverty), *Fatica* (Labour), *Ricchezza* (Wealth or Plenty), *Lusso* (Luxury), and *Povertà* again. An infant holds an hour-glass and another blows soap-bubbles (both these motives symbolize transience),[1] while Time plays the lyre and the whole scene is governed by the imperturbable movement of the Sun driving his chariot through the Zodiac.

Most of the symbolic figures and accessories are borrowed from the great iconographical handbook of the period, Cesare Ripa's *Iconologia*,[2] and the main idea can be ultimately traced to the well-known 'Wheel of Fortune', a favourite conception in medieval art, which represented Man's destiny as a sequence of rising, falling, and rising again ('I rule, I have ruled, I am deprived of my kingdom, I shall rule', as the usual inscription puts it); in French and English Renaissance poetry this idea had already been transformed in such a way as practically to antici-

[1] The motif of the soap-bubble as a symbol of perishableness was possibly suggested by the *Hypnerotomachia Polyphili*. In it we find the description of a 'Dance of Time' with fourteen figures, and the πομφόλυξ is mentioned as a symbol of worldly fame (pp. 15 and 72 of the French ed.). According to Winckelmann's *Versuch einer Allegorie*, 1766, p. 138, Raphael Mengs also used the soap-bubble motif to symbolize 'die Nichtigkeit und den Unbestand menschlicher Dinge'.

[2] C. Ripa, l.c. According to him, '*Povertà*' should be 'una Donna distesa sopra rami d'alberi secchi', '*Fatica estiva*' 'una Giovane robusta, vestita d'habito succinto e leggiero, con le braccie nude, che con la destra mano tenghi una falce de mietere il grano et con la sinistra uno scorreggiato strumento da batter il frumento, et appresso vi sia un bue', '*Ricchezza*' 'una Donna in habito regale riccamato con diverse gioie di gran stima, che nella destra mano tenga una corona imperiale et nella sinistra uno scettro, et un vaso d'oro a piedi'. For the personification of 'Luxury' Poussin used Ripa's 'Superbia', which is consistent with the fact that in the literary sources to be adduced in the following note 'Luxury' is either replaced or accompanied by 'Pride'. The hour-glass is a common symbol of Time and Death, but was much emphasized by Ripa under the heading of 'Vita breve':

> E come sia la vita nostra *un hora*,
> E noi *polvere* ed ombra, e sotto il Polo
> Ogni human speranza un fragil *vetro*.

The Lyre finally is mentioned by Ripa as a symbol of the 'Vita Humana' because its seven strings symbolize the hebdomadic principle by which human life is 'continuamente agitato'. As to further Ripa motives borrowed by Poussin, cf. Mâle, l.c., Mandowsky, l.c., and p. 253.

pate Poussin's conception: 'Peace' makes 'Plenty', 'Plenty' brings 'Envy', 'Envy' brings 'War', 'War' brings 'Poverty', and 'Poverty' brings 'Peace', and in some versions the Christian virtue of 'Patience' or 'Humility' is inserted as an intermediary between 'Poverty' and 'Peace'.[1] There are, however, startling differences between these prototypes and Poussin's representation: Ripa's images were amusingly encumbered with attributes: 'Fatica', for example, was shown as a vigorous maiden, her dress tucked up, her arms bare to the shoulders, she held a sickle and a flail and was escorted by a bull; 'Poverty' sat on withered branches, and so forth. Poussin manages to transform these images in such a way that the attributes neither prevent the figures from joining hands nor hamper their fluent movements ('Poverty', for instance, wears her withered branches as a becoming wreath). While in the medieval 'Wheels of Fortune', and even in such late poems as the Elizabethan *Histriomastix*, the revolving of Fate was caused by a superhuman or at least preterhuman force, whether blind Fortune or an immanent evolutionary principle—Poussin imagines the cycle as a dance performed by handsome female figures who, though subject to the implacable laws of cosmic time, nevertheless within these limits can move freely and connect rhythmically with one another, thereby impressing us as self-sufficient organisms;[2] and while before no active human effort had participated in what Clément Marot had called 'the endless chain of our deeds' (for 'Humility' is but a passive willingness to accept the decrees of God), Poussin inserts *Fatica*, the autonomous and active human endeavour, as a means of turning Poverty into Wealth. Thus Poussin's conception of life as a condition free though fatebound, dignified though pathetic, imperishable though variable, transpires even in a composition which seems to be nothing but the offshoot of a rather conventional allegorical tradition, while its subject was

[1] Marston's play *Histriomastix* (1599; reprinted in Richard Simpson, *The School of Shakespeare*, ii, 1878, pp. 17 ff.) was brought to my knowledge by Prof. E. Wolff, Hamburg. As to the sources of this play, Simpson (l.c., pp. 87 ff.) adduces among other instances Minfant's comedy *Fatal Destiny*, as quoted by Clément Marot in a letter to Marguérite of Navarre, dated October 1521, where 'Humility' appears as an intermediary between 'Poverty' and 'Peace', and Jehan de Mehun, where the same role is played by 'Patience'.

[2] In point of fact, the postures of the figures are inspired by the Dancing Maenads seen in a beautiful frieze formerly preserved in the Villa Borghese (now Louvre; illustrated in Pierre Gusman, *L'Art décoratif de Rome de la fin de la République au IVe siècle*, 1908 ss., vol. ii, pl. 113).

suggested, it seems, by an 'outsider', the learned and poetical Prelate Rospigliosi, later on Pope Clement IX.[1]

A similar attitude can be observed in Poussin's admirable picture of Phaethon in the Kaiser Friedrich Museum in Berlin (Fig. 10). While Michelangelo chose the Fall of Phaethon as an emphatically personal symbol of his tragic love for Tommaso Cavalieri (as can be inferred from a beautiful sonnet written by a poet who moved in Michelangelo's circle),[2] Poussin visualized the preliminary scene exhaustively described by Ovid[3] and developed it into another allegory of human destiny in general. Phaethon kneels before his father Helios, again encircled by the Zodiac, to ask his permission to drive his chariot, which is shown in the background, while in the foreground and middle planes can be seen the embodiments of Time, namely the four Seasons and old Chronos who stands for such special personifications as the Day, the Month, the Year, and the Century, all enumerated by Ovid. But while Ovid conceives the whole scene as a formal reception at court, with Helios enthroned in the hall of his palace and his acolytes standing on the right and left like a crowd of courtiers, Poussin shifts the scene to an unreal sphere above the clouds, lends intense emotional feeling to every figure, and arranges the whole composition in such a way that the personifications of Time, though not actually moving, form a rhythmical circle comparable to the *Ballo della Vita humana*, and in the centre of the circle he places Phaethon, the only mortal in the picture. Thus the figure of Phaethon seems to be invested with a more than individual significance, surrounded as he is by the powers of Fate from whom he implores a gift which will spell both his supreme happiness and his destruction

> ('Statque super, manibusque datas contingere habenas
> Gaudet . . .').

There is, in point of fact, a close relationship between Ovid's idea of Metamorphosis and Poussin's conception of human existence as a succession of stages which are both doomed to pass away and endowed with an imperishable fund of bliss and

[1] See Appendix, pp. 252 ff.

[2] Cf. E. Panofsky, *Jahrbuch für Kunstgeschichte*, i, 1921, Buchbesprechungen, pp. 1 ff.

[3] Ovid, *Metam.* ii. 19 ff. It is interesting to compare Poussin's interpretation of this passage with that by *Eustache Le Sueur* (Louvre), who transforms the scene into a gay and almost spectacular piece of decoration.

beauty, so that, to him, the very transitoriness of life means a guarantee of immortality.

No other painter would have invented a composition like the Dresden 'Realm of Flora' (Fig. 11), which in reality is an overwhelming visualization of the pure idea of Metamorphosis, an outright symbol of Poussin's metaphysical creed. In this picture, too, Helios encircled by the Zodiac drives his chariot through the sky symbolizing the inexorable cosmic laws, while the sphere below is ruled by Flora gracefully dancing, accompanied by Cupids, a light-hearted dispenser of beauty. Around her, however, the tragic origin of all this beauty is revealed in many groups and figures which show that the birth of a beautiful flower signifies the death of a beautiful human being. Ajax stabs himself with a sword to bring to life the red carnation. Hyacinthus dies by the disk of Apollo to revive as the purple-blue flower named after him. Narcissus becomes a victim of his own beauty, hypnotized as he is by his reflection in the vase proferred by the frustrated Echo. Clytia perishes of love for Helios to become transformed into the heliotrope. Smilax fades away in the lap of Crocus to be reborn as a convolvulus or morning glory. I say reborn, for we must bear in mind that the extinction of one beauty means the genesis of another, and that unending love is at the bottom of all these tragic deaths, which therefore do not signify annihilation but metamorphosis.

The principle of metamorphosis, based on an insight into what I should like to call a cosmic rhythm, and leading to what I should like to call a serene resignation, may be regarded as the very quintessence of Poussin's art. It even determines Poussin's attitude towards antiquity. Poussin is generally labelled as a '*classicist*', but in his pictures the classical figures, too, are 'metamorphosed' so as to preserve what strikes us as their 'innermost style', while the tangible motives are thoroughly changed. Thus, curiously enough, less direct 'borrowings' from the antique are to be found in the work of this so-called classicist than in the work of Rubens;[1] Rubens often paints seemingly

[1] It is a significant fact that literal 'borrowings' from the antique occur in Poussin's early works rather than in his mature and late ones, and that he draws, even then, from Roman paintings rather than from classical statuary. An instructive specimen is the figure Bacchus in one of Poussin's earliest pictures (Bacchus and Erygone, ill. in O. Grautoff, *Nicolas Poussin*, 1914, vol. ii, nr. I). It is obviously copied from a figure in a mural painting rediscovered in 1909 beneath the church of Ss. Giovanni e Paolo (F. Wirth, *Römische Wandmalerei vom Untergang Pompejis bis*

FIG. 11. Nicolas Poussin, The Realm of Flora *Dresden, Gemäldegalerie*

FIG. 12. Paul Bril, Roman Landscape *Dresden, Gemäldegalerie*

FIG. 13. Nicolas Poussin, Nativity *Dresden, Gemäldegalerie*

realistic figures which, upon analysis, prove faithfully classical in pose, while Poussin paints apparently classical figures which, in reality, are free inventions, or rather reincarnations of a classical entity.

In Poussin's painting even the ruins, so characteristic of a period's or an artist's conception of life and destiny, convey a unique feeling intrinsically in harmony with what we have termed 'serene resignation'. A work of human art such as an ancient structure cannot 'metamorphose', but is subject to nothing but material decay. Thus the Roman ruins inspired the medieval mind with a mingled feeling of admiration for the lofty magnificence of the original buildings, demoniacal fear because these structures were the work of unbelievers, and pious triumph because their decay betokened the defeat of paganism. During the Renaissance, which was deeply interested in and sympathetic with classical antiquity, this feeling gave way either to a cool archaeological interest or to a nearly romantic sentiment. For while the Middle Ages had exulted over the destruction of classical monuments because they were pagan, the Renaissance deplored the destruction of these very monuments because they were beautiful and powerful. Thus ruins came to be used as a symbol of the irresistibility of natural forces as compared to the transitoriness of human endeavour. They were usually placed amid luxuriant vegetation and grazing herds to emphasize the unbroken continuity of humble natural life in the very spot where proud human structures were crumbling away (Fig. 12).[1]

Poussin, however, indulged in no such romanticism. In accordance with medieval tradition he used the ruins not as a contrast with the continuity of vegetable and animal life, but as monuments of the pagan era in contrast with the Christian (Berlin, St. Matthew; Chicago, St. John; Dresden, 'Adoration of the Magi', Fig. 13). Only to him the pagan era meant of course not so much a domain of religious error as a domain of

zum Ende des 3. Jahrhunderts, 1934, Tafel 13; similar figures occur also in Pompeian murals, for instance in the famous 'Perseus rescuing Andromeda' from the *Casa dei Dioscuri*), and the same mural seems also to have influenced Poussin's 'Narcissus and Echo' in Dresden, likewise an early work. The 'Bacchus and Erygone' picture is, therefore, to be dated in Poussin's early Roman period, not in his pre-Italian days.

[1] As to 'Ruins in art', cf. W. Waetzoldt, *Das klassische Land*, 1927, *passim*; L. Ozzola, *Arte*, xvi, 1913, pp. 1 ff.

classical and above all indestructible beauty. Consequently he visualized the ruins so as to show not only the marks of material decay but also the pure design of immaterial forms. The remains of a classical temple, the very fragments of a fluted column are chosen, rendered, and arranged in such a way that the underlying formal principle is neither obscured by too conspicuous injuries or too advanced corrosion, nor disfigured by arbitrary foreshortenings. The classical ruins, however fragmentary, are never 'picturesque': they are placed frontally or at right angles to the frontal plane, and are made to display their flawless geometrical shapes. Thus in Poussin's paintings the very ruins illustrate no less the indestructibility of ideal forms than the perishableness of matter,[1] thereby affording an analogy to what was expressed by his interpretation of the phrase *Et in Arcadia*

[1] I am grateful to Dr. M. Schapiro for calling my attention to the fact that the development of this peculiar attitude towards ruins (an attitude that can be sensed even in a school-piece like 'Artists sketching amongst Ruins' in the Victoria and Albert Museum, there attributed to Poussin himself) can also be traced in French literature. Hildebert of Lavardin's famous 'Par tibi, Roma, nihil, cum sis prope tota ruina | Quam magna fueris integra, fracta doces', splendidly rejuvenated—and secularized—by such Renaissance poets as Joachim Du Bellay (*Antiquités de Rome*) assumes a more metaphysical character in such poems as Étienne Jodelle's *Chanson pour le Seigneur de Brunel*, and in Théophile Gautier the same train of thought leads to a conception almost coessential with Poussin's 'Platonism':

Tout passe—l'art robuste
Seul a l'éternité:
Le buste
Survit à la cité,
Et la médaille austère
Que trouve un laboureur
Sous terre
Révèle un empereur.

Les dieux eux-mêmes meurent,
Mais les vers souverains
Demeurent
Plus forts que les airains.

Sculpte, lime, cisèle;
Que ton rêve flottant
Se scelle
Dans le bloc résistant!

The opposite feeling, as expressed in the 'romanticizing' representation of ruins, is formulated by an English seventeenth-century writer: through 'perlustration of such famous Cities, Castles, Amphitheatres and Palaces, some glorious and new, some mouldred away and eaten by the Iron-teeth of Time, he came to discerne the best of earthly things to bee but frayle and transitory' (James Howell, *Epistolae Ho-elianae*, ed. Jos. Jacobs, 1890, i, pp. 85–6, as paraphrased by S. A. Larrabee, *Ideas of Greek Sculpture in English Poetry*, Diss. Princeton, 1934).

ego, as well as by his principle of metamorphosis—'Beauty that must die', and yet persists, whether as a deathless remembrance, or as a new being, or as an immaterial idea of pure form. It is not by accident that Poussin as a theorist is far more sincere a Platonist than any of his contemporaries. The usual academic theory as championed by Bellori and innumerable others tried to reconcile Platonic idealism with the claims of Renaissance naturalism. Poussin confesses the genuine Neoplatonic creed, which is also consistent with what I have termed his principle of 'transparent luminousness': 'The idea of beauty is altogether detached from matter which cannot approach it unless it (matter) has been made ready by means of incorporeal preparation with regard to its order, mode, and shape.'[1]

III

Antoine Watteau avoided ruins in the technical sense of the term; nevertheless there is a certain relationship between his *Fêtes Champêtres*[2] and such romanticizing representations of Roman remains as we have already discussed. He, too, likes to combine exuberant vegetation and flourishing life with the marks of decay. But to him this combination means a fusion rather than a contrast. He does not paint ruined classical temples or ancient torsos, but modern garden-statues mouldering away and covered with ivy, so that not only the past but the very present bears the marks of decay; he does not contrast rustic scenery with the work of human artists, but represents geometrical parks similar to those of Le Nôtre going to seed, yet full of people clad in fantastic mixtures of stage costumes, fancy dress, and up-to-date garments. Thus nature herself seems to be both the motivator and the object of form-destructive change, while the human beings appear as the inhabitants of a visionary realm beyond both imagination and reality.

Watteau's *Fêtes Champêtres*, too, may be called allegories of transience; however, they neither visualize the annihilation of the past, nor the persistence of ideal forms outlasting the destruction of matter. They depict the fading away of reality as such. Existence itself seems to be subject to transience; past,

[1] Cf. E. Panofsky, 'Idea', *Studien der Bibl. Warburg*, v. 1924, p. 117 f.

[2] Cf. (also in regard of bibliography) the very interesting book by M. Eisenstadt, *Watteaus Fêtes Galantes*, 1930 (rev. *Burlington Magazine*, vol. lviii, 1931, p. 54, and *Apollo*, vol. xii, 1930, p. 448).

present, and future fuse into a phantasmagoric realm in which the border-line between illusion and reality, dream and wakefulness, nature and art, mirth and melancholy, love and loneliness, life and the continuous process of dying, are thoroughly obliterated.

Watteau is perhaps the only artist who conceives transience as an abolition of the boundaries, normally sensed to be insurmountable, between the various spheres of thought and feeling. To him the universe means nothing but a fluctuation, permanent though not eternal, defying limitation though not infinite, and which therefore makes us divine an identity between existence and non-existence. Thus the conceptions of Watteau, serenely gay and playful though they seem to be, reveal a profoundly tragic attitude. There is, in many respects, an intrinsic congeniality between Watteau and Mozart (another genius of kindred quality is Keats). Watteau and Mozart were both doomed to die in the prime of life, so that their whole existence was somehow detached from ordinary life and overshadowed by the gloom of death (whether they realized it consciously, as was the case with Watteau, or were subject to a vague though unmistakable presentiment, as was the case with Mozart): they both avoided the traditional formulas of serious and tragic expression, already worn out and almost discredited in the eighteenth century. The mournful attitudes in the manner of Feti's 'Melancholia', or the impassioned outbursts in the style of Bernini, were by now as questionable as the wailing melodies in minor which Mozart mostly used when he wanted to convey a deliberate parody of dejection, as in the 'suicidal' arias of Osmin and Papageno, or in Barbarina's aria in the last act of *Le Nozze di Figaro*. In contrast to such conventionalized expressions of melancholy and passion these two geniuses conjured up an enchanted world beyond the standard of human psychology—a world in which tragedy can assume the appearance of supreme sweetness and serenity, because death turns out to be inextricably 'fused' with life.

In late Louis XIV painting, the discrepancy between the conventional ideal of baroque grandeur and a new 'realistic' treatment had led to what strikes the modern beholder as a theatrical attitude devoid of sincerity. Antoine Coypel's or Charles de la Fosse's representations of biblical and historical scenes scarcely differ from theatrical performances, and such mythological or pastoral portraits as Largillière's Élisabeth Charlotte, Madame de France, *en Naïade* (Chantilly), or Rigaud's Président Gueidan *en berger musicien* (Aix) can hardly be distinguished from portraits of actors or actresses on the stage.

It was the only real forerunner of Watteau, Claude Gillot, who discovered a rather paradoxical method of reinstating sincerity. He escaped from a domain of sham seriousness into a domain of genuine playfulness by plunging into the actual world of the theatre and the masquerades. Where his *grand goût* contemporaries involuntarily made histories and portraits look like scenes and characters on the stage, Gillot deliberately chose the scenes and characters of the stage as his subjects, so as to achieve a new form of genuineness and objectivity by faithfully rendering what was fictitious or fantastic in itself and by purposely overstyling the costumes, attitudes, and feelings of his figures. In doing this he obviously reverted to Callot, to whom he owes not only the subject-matter as such itself but also the taste for the stiff, pointed gracefulness of thin, puppet-like figures either rigidly erect or spiderily moving with mock pathos.

Watteau was deeply influenced by these innovations of Gillot's, as can be proved by many instances.[1] But while Gillot limited himself to a witty and faithful representation of the fictitious world of stage and masquerade, Watteau proceeded to a new interpretation of life in general. Aside from what he assimilated from Gillot, he took on some of the realism of Flemish genre-painting, as can be observed particularly during his earlier period, when not only his paintings but also his drawings remind us of such masters as Egbert van Heemskerck or Teniers,[2] sometimes *vu à travers le tempérament de Gillot*, so to speak, as is the case for instance in the *militaires* or in the delightful *Vraie Gaieté* in the Tenant Gallery. On the other hand, however, he reverted to the great Italian masters of the sixteenth century and of the Baroque, including both the Venetian colourists,

[1] Cf. especially E. Dacier, *Revue de l'art ancien et moderne*, xlv–viii, 1924–5, *passim*; de Fourcaud, *ibidem*, ix–x, 1901, and xvi, 1904, *passim*. Also P. Jamot, *Burlington Magazine*, vol. xliii, 1923, pp. 133 ff.

[2] A very good comparison are 'The Toper' and 'Autumn' by Teniers in the London National Gallery (Nos. 859 and 953), as compared to Watteau's 'Petit Marmotier' in Leningrad. As to Watteau's drawings, cf. the excellent publication by K. T. Parker, *The Drawings of Antoine Watteau*, 1931.

particularly Titian and Paolo Veronese, and such representatives of the Roman classical style as Annibale Caracci and even Raphael.[1]

But above all these Watteau was fascinated by Rubens,[2] and not only by his pictorial technique but by the very spirit of his art. The lordly and sensuous vitality which seems to throb in the mythological and allegorical pictures, and the glorified exaltation of social life which pervades the glamorous 'Garden of Love' in the Prado, appealed immensely to Watteau.

However, Rubens, despite his magnificent impetuousness and his unstinting use of mythological accessories, always preserves an extraordinary reality and compactness. Watteau, on the other hand, in his 'Fêtes Champêtres' operates a kind of transfiguration: the picturesque elusiveness of the theatre and the masquerades, the realistic qualities of Flemish genre-painting, the distinction of Italian classic art, the colouristic richness of the Venetians, the passionate *brio* of Rubens's festivals, fuse into one visionary whole.

In Watteau the difference between a natural and a supernatural creature can be abolished, but also the difference between a natural being and a work of art. His Cupids hardly differ from real children, and the same figure may occur as a living person and a garden statue. The 'Antiope' of the celebrated picture in the Louvre occurs later on as a statue in the first version of the 'Champs Élysées' in the Wallace Collection, thus bearing out what was said about the obliteration of the border-line between the various categories of ordinary life (Fig. 14).

Watteau's conception of the world as subject to an everlasting

[1] Cf. V. Miller, *Burlington Magazine*, vol. li, 1927, pp. 37 ff.

[2] Cf. P. Hendy, *Burlington Magazine*, vol. xlix, 1926, pp. 137 ff. I should like to add a few further instances particularly suitable to illustrate the principles of transformation applying to Watteau's borrowings from Rubens:

(*a*) The attitude of the Lady sitting by the counter in the Gersaint Sign-Board is derived from that of Marie de Médicis in Rubens's 'Birth of Louis XIII' (*Klassiker der Kunst*, ed. Oldenbourg, p. 259).

(*b*) The attitude of the couple of lovers in the left lower corner of Watteau's 'Surprise' (London, Buckingham Palace) strikingly resembles the interlaced group in the foreground of Rubens's 'Peasants' Dance' in the Prado (*Kl. d. K.*, p. 407).

(*c*) Watteau's 'Amour à la Campagne' (formerly in the collection of the German Emperor) is strongly influenced by Rubens's 'Landscape with the Rainbow' in Leningrad (*Kl. d. K.*, p. 356), both with respect to such single motives as the reclining couple in the foreground, the two figures standing at the left, and the shepherd with his flock of sheep, and to the general arrangement of the composition.

FIG. 14. Antoine Watteau, 'Les Champs Élysées' *London, Wallace Collection*

FIG. 15. Antoine Watteau, Gilles *Paris, Musée du Louvre*

Photograph, Musées Nationaux

and universal 'fluctuation' accounts even for his peculiar working methods. The eighteenth-century connoisseurs were already struck by the fact that Watteau, so fertile and painstaking a draftsman, avoided on the whole making *disegni storiati*,[1] that is, preliminary studies of entire compositions. He 'extemporized' his pictures on the basis of sketches of single groups or isolated figures, executed without any premeditated purpose and put together on the very canvas. On the other hand, it is a well-known fact that these pictorial improvisations were unusually often repeated, or rather, revised in several replicas. This means, of course, that in Watteau's art even the border-line between a preparatory and a final stage of execution is abolished. The creative process does not lead to a stage of finality, but continues throughout, so that the very paintings are still subject to the principle of fluctuation.

In the 'Champs Élysées' we can also observe a characteristic motive which is almost a symbol of Watteau's attitude towards life: an isolated person, absorbed though not participating in the transient happiness of the lovers and amorous groups around him. This excluded figure that is to be found in many other Watteau compositions can be considered an embodiment of that shy, wakeful aloofness with which his innermost feeling reacted upon the fluctuating transience of the world as he imagined it —an aloofness that meant melancholy loneliness and, at the same time, the only refuge left.

It is not by accident that in the most monumental painting ever executed by Watteau, the famous 'Gilles' in the Louvre (Fig. 15), the central figure is developed from what had been the most unhappy and lonely character of popular comedies. In the comedies 'Gilles' was an unfortunate frightened creature who would start at every noise. He tried by awkward jokes to ingratiate himself with the others, but found himself constantly teased and shunned. This was the character that Watteau thought most suitable to invest with the very quintessence of his own attitude towards life. Here is his Gilles: a lonely figure emerging from the emotions and fluctuations of common life which he denies and leaves behind, facing the only non-transient reality that he can accept, namely the void. I cannot help

[1] Cf. the passages quoted in K. T. Parker, *The Drawings of Antoine Watteau*, 1931, p. 8 ff.

feeling that the very face of Gilles shows a strange similarity to Watteau's own features as interpreted by himself in an earlier drawing (Fig. 16);[1] but even if 'Gilles' need not be called a self-portrait, he is certainly a self-revelation.

APPENDIX

POUSSIN AND THE PRELATE ROSPIGLIOSI, LATER POPE CLEMENT IX

Bellori continues his description of the *Ballo della Vita Humana* (l.c., vol. i, p. 448; he also points out that the motive of Helios driving his chariot through the Zodiac was borrowed from Raphael, meaning, of course, Marcantonio's engraving B. 245, the Judgement of Paris) with the following passage:

'*Il soggetto di questa morale poesia fu dato al Pittore da Papa Clemente IX in tempo che egli era Prelato*. Prevalse Niccolò nel concetto di si nobile e peregrina invenzione, et ancorchè le figure siano appena due palmi, *potè corrispondere in esse felicemente alla sublimità dell'Autore che aggiunse le due seguenti invenzioni:*

La Verità scoperta del Tempo.

Librasi il Tempo su l'ali, alzandosi da terra; con una mano prende il braccio della Verità e la solleva oppressa e giacente; con l'altra discaccia l'Invidia, che nel partire si morde il braccio, scuotendo le serpentine chiome, mentre *la Maledicenza* sua compagna, sedendo dietro la Verità, tutta accesa *scuote e vibbra due faci.*

La Felicità soggetta a la Morte.

La terza moral Poesia è la memoria della Morte nelle prosperità umane. Finse un Pastore della felice Arcadia, il quale, piegato un ginocchio a terra, addita e legge l'inscrizzione di un sepolcro scolpito in questi caratteri ET IN ARCADIA EGO; cioè che il sepolcro *si trova ancora in Arcadia*, e che la Morte hà luogo in mezzo le felicità. Evvi dietro un giovine inghirlandato, che s'appoggia a quel sepolcro, e guarda intento e pensieroso, et un altro incontro s'inclina, et addita le parole ad una leggiadra Ninfa vagamente adorna, la quale tiene la mano sù la spalla di esso, e nel riguardarvi sospende il riso e dà luogo al pensiero della morte. In altro simile soggetto figuro il fiume Alfeo. . . .'

If there is not a typographical error in the first paragraph of this passage (for example, the omission of a *si* between *in esse* and *felicemente*), *the sentence 'che aggiunse le due seguenti invenzioni' would be an adjectival clause relating to 'Autore', that is to say Clement IX. Thus*

[1] Frontispiece of Parker's publication. Reproduced here by kind permission of Mrs. Otto Gutekunst, London.

Fig. 16. Antoine Watteau, Self-Portrait

Drawing. Private Collection, London

it would appear that the latter not only suggested the subject of the '*Ballo della Vita Humana*' (which he apparently purchased for himself, as can be inferred from the inscription 'In Aedibus Rospigliosis' on the engraving Andresen 400), *but also the subjects* '*Truth rescued by Time*'*—and* '*Et in Arcadio Ego*'.

As far as the Truth-and-Time theme is concerned (cf. F. Saxl's exhaustive iconographical analysis in this very volume, pp. 197 ff.), this statement of Bellori, apparently disregarded by the Poussin specialists, seemingly contradicts the fact that the well-known Louvre version of the Truth-and-Time subject, mentioned by Bellori, l.c., p. 170, was painted for the Cardinal Richelieu. Yet Bellori may be absolutely right. For while the Richelieu picture, now preserved in the Louvre (engravings Andresen 403–6), characterizes the adversaries of *Veritas* as *Invidia* and *Ira*, the latter provided with a torch and a dagger—both figures are borrowed from Ripa, as was rightly pointed out by Mâle and Mandowsky, l.c.—another composition, transmitted only through the engravings Andresen 407 and 408, is actually consistent with Bellori's description of the alleged Rospigliosi picture, in that it shows a *Maledicenza* brandishing two torches, and not the *Ira* with one torch plus a dagger. In addition the engraving Andresen 408, executed by J. Dughet, is dedicated to Pope Clement IX (cf. W. Friedländer, *Nicolas Poussin*, 1914, p. 117; incidentally, it should be mentioned that Poussin's *Maledicenza*, reappearing in the somewhat doubtful Chantilly drawing published by O. Grautoff, *Nicolas Poussin*, 1914, i, p. 207, and discussed by H. Brauer and R. Wittkower, *Die Zeichnungen des G. L. Bernini*, 1931, p. 45, is again borrowed from Cesare Ripa). These facts seem to bear out Bellori's statement as to the Truth-and-Time subject (he only committed the error of calling the *Ira* in the Richelieu picture, too, *Maledicenza*, but this is pardonable, as he had never seen the Louvre painting). It is not only possible but even probable that the lost composition known through the engravings Andresen 407 and 408 was in fact suggested by and executed for the prelate Rospigliosi and, some seven or eight years later, repeated for the Cardinal Richelieu, whereby a personification of *Ira* was substituted for the personification of *Maledicenza*. This substitution can even be accounted for by the difference of patrons and purposes. For while the conception of Truth rescued from *Maledicenza* is a general and rather commonplace idea which can be traced back to Apelles's 'Calumny' and even farther, the conception of Truth rescued from an armed *Ira* clearly alludes to the defeat of internal enemies, especially in the field of religion.

As far as the Arcadia subject is concerned, Bellori's statement seems much less convincing and is in fact fraught with considerable difficulties, for we know that the theme of Poussin's pictures was taken over from the Guercino painting in the Corsini Gallery, and that the Devonshire version was probably executed not later than about 1630. Thus it is rather improbable that the subject was suggested to Poussin by the prelate Rospigliosi, whom he could hardly have met before 1632, when the latter returned to Rome after having held a professorship at the University of Pisa since 1623.

On the other hand Bellori's statements as to Poussin, with whom he lived in fairly close personal contact during the latter's later years, are quite reliable as a rule. Thus what he tells about the prelate's connexion with Poussin's Arcadia pictures might not be altogether groundless either, though slightly incorrect owing to a slip of memory, whether the painter's or the biographer's. What actually might have happened is this: the prelate Rospigliosi might have ordered the Louvre picture from Poussin, and on this occasion might have mentioned the fact that he, the prelate, could boast the original invention of the subject which, in this case, he would have suggested not to Poussin but to Guercino. Him he could easily have met at any time between 1621 and 1623, when the young nobleman studied at Rome with the Jesuits, while the young painter worked at his famous 'Aurora Ludovisi'—all the more easily as the 'Aurora Ludovisi' is known to be a transformation or rather a practical criticism, so to speak, of a mural painting which was the pride of the later Pope's own family: Guido Reni's 'Aurora' in the Casino Rospigliosi.

If this were true it would be no less illustrious a person than Pope Clement IX who had transplanted to the soil of Arcadia the medieval conception as expressed in the legend of the Three Living and the Three Dead (in a similar way as he had transformed the content of *Histriomastix*, &c., into the scene represented in Poussin's *Ballo della Vita Humana*), and had coined the phrase *Et in Arcadia ego* which, in point of fact, cannot be traced back beyond its appearance in Guercino's Corsini picture.

I give this conjecture only for what it is worth, but it would be in comparative harmony with the statement of Bellori and in entire harmony with the somewhat moralizing, yet highly humanistic, spirit of Rospigliosi's literary and poetical works (cf. G. Beani, *Clemente IX*, 1893; G. Canevazzi, *Papa Clemente IX, Poeta*, Modena, 1900; D. Alaleona, *Bulletino della Società Filologica Romana*, 1904, pp. 71 ff.).

SOME POINTS OF CONTACT BETWEEN HISTORY AND NATURAL SCIENCE

By EDGAR WIND

I SHALL be concerned here with some, but by no means with all, of the points of contact between history and the natural sciences. It is not my intention, for instance, to dwell on well-known facts which have not ceased to be facts for being ignored or forgotten by professional philosophers. In spite of Fichte—and some minor autonomists of the mind—history (taken in the customary sense of the term, as history of human fate and achievement) began only at a certain stage of the development of nature. The earth had to separate from the sun and acquire such motion, shape, and temperature that living beings could develop on it before History was (to adopt Kant's phraseology) 'made possible'.

When we, therefore, speak of 'points of contact' between nature and history, we may begin by recalling the trivial fact that between the two there is a contact in time and hence a transition. Once the form of this transition is being inquired into, the most dreaded questions begin to make their appearance. What is the relation between inorganic matter and organic life? How did we evolve from a state of nature to one of conscious control? How did 'primitive' man, magically subjecting himself to nature's powers and apparently living in an almost a-historical form, produce his 'civilized' descendant who, in the moulding of his surroundings, creates and experiences historic changes?—I shall not discuss any of these questions. My problem is far more modest. Instead of inquiring into cosmic or cultural events which may illustrate the temporal intersection of the worlds of nature and history, I shall confine myself to indicating some formal points of correspondence between these two worlds—or, to be more precise, between the scientific methods which render each of them an object of human knowledge and experience.

The mere assertion that there are such correspondences may appear heretical to many.[1] German scholars have taught for decades that, apart from adherence to the most general rules of

[1] The following refers in particular to the schools of Dilthey, Windelband, and Rickert.

logic, the study of history and the natural sciences are to each other as pole and antipole, and that it is the first duty of any historian to forswear all sympathy with the ideals of men who would like to reduce the whole world to a mathematical formula. This revolt was no doubt an act of liberation in its time. To-day it is pointless. The very concept of nature in opposition to which Dilthey proclaimed his *Geisteswissenschaft* has long been abandoned by the scientists themselves, and the notion of a description of nature which indiscriminately subjects men and their fates like rocks and stones to its 'unalterable laws' survives only as a nightmare of certain historians.

Thus it need not be symptomatic of a sinful relapse into the method of thought so generously abused as 'positivistic', if in what follows some examples are chosen to illustrate how the very questions that historians like to look upon as their own are also raised in natural science. The all too sedentary inhabitants of the 'Globus intellectualis' may, it is true, think it incredible that their antipodes do not stand on their heads.

I. *Document and Instrument*

In defiance of the rules of traditional logic, circular arguments are the normal method of producing documentary evidence.

An historian who consults his documents in order to interpret some political event can judge the value of these documents only if he knows their place within the very same course of events about which he consults them.

In the same way, an art-historian who from a given work draws an inference concerning the development of its author turns into an art-connoisseur who examines the reasons for attributing this work to this particular master: and for this purpose he must presuppose the knowledge of that master's development which was just what he wanted to infer.

This change of focus from the object to the means of inquiry, and the concomitant inversion of object and means, is peculiar to most historical studies, and the instances given may be multiplied *ad lib*. An inquiry concerning the Baroque, which uses Bernini's theoretical utterances as a source for explaining the style of his works, turns into a study of the role of theory in the creative process of Bernini. An inquiry concerning Caesar's monarchy and the principate of Pompey, making use of

Cicero's writings as its main source, becomes a study of the part played by Cicero in the conflict between the Senate and the usurpers.

Generally speaking this might be termed the dialectic of the historical document: that the information which one tries to gain with the help of the document ought to be presupposed for its adequate understanding.

The scientist is subject to the very same paradox. The physicist seeks to infer general laws of nature by instruments themselves subject to these laws. For measuring heat, a fluid like quicksilver is chosen as a standard, and it is claimed that it expands evenly with increasing warmth. Yet how can such an assertion be made without knowledge of the laws of thermodynamics? And again, how can these laws be known except by measurements in which a fluid, e.g. quicksilver, is used as a standard?

Classical mechanics employs measuring rods and clocks that are transferred from one place to another; the assumption being that this alteration of place leaves untouched their constancy as measuring instruments. This assumption, however, expresses a mechanical law (viz. that the results of measurement are independent of the state of motion) the validity of which must be tested by instruments which, in their turn, are reliable only if the law assumed is valid.

The circle thus proves in science as inescapable as in history. Every instrument and every document *participates* in the structure which it is meant to reveal.[1]

II. *The Intrusion of the Observer*

It is curious that Dilthey should have considered this *participation* as one of the traits which distinguish the study of history from the natural sciences. In his *Einleitung in die Geisteswissenschaften* he admits that the study of 'social bodies' is less precise than that of 'natural bodies'. 'And yet', he adds, 'all this is more than counterbalanced by the fact that I who experience and know myself inwardly, am part of this social body. . . . The individual is, on the one hand, an element in the interactions

[1] For a more detailed analysis of this fact and an exposition of some of its wider implications, cp. *Das Experiment und die Metaphysik*, Tübingen, 1934, and 'Can the Antinomies be restated?' *Psyche*, vol. xiv, 1934.

of society, . . . reacting to its effects in conscious will-direction and action, and is at the same time the intelligence contemplating and investigating all this' (p. 46 sq.).

That human agents, who form the substance of what Dilthey calls 'the socio-historical reality', experience and know themselves 'inwardly' is a bold assertion. It transforms one of the most troublesome moral precepts ('Know thyself!') into a plain and ordinary matter of fact, which is contradicted by both ancient and modern experience. Whatever objections may be made to the current psychology of the unconscious, it is undeniable that men do not know themselves by immediate intuition and that they live and express themselves on several levels. Hence, the interpretation of historical documents requires a far more complex psychology than Dilthey's doctrine of immediate experience with its direct appeal to a state of feeling. Peirce wrote in a draft of a psychology of the development of ideas: 'it is the belief men *betray*, and not that which they *parade*, which has to be studied.'[1]

Once the direct appeal to inner experience is abandoned, Dilthey's remark ceases to contain anything that a physicist might not apply to himself: 'I myself, who am handling apparatuses and instruments, am a part of this physical world; the individual (i.e. the physical technician and observer) is, on the one hand, an element in the interactions of nature, . . . and he is at the same time the intelligence calculating and investigating all this.'

Let it not be objected that by this 'physical travesty' the meaning of Dilthey's statement is completely destroyed. True, the profundity has disappeared, and what remains seems to be rather trivial. But what the statement now conveys is not only simple, but also true: *The investigator intrudes into the process that he is investigating*. This is what the supreme rule of methodology demands. In order to study physics, one must be physically affected; pure mind does not study physics. A body is needed —however much the mind may 'interpret'—which transmits the signals that are to be interpreted. Otherwise, there would be no contact with the surrounding world that is to be investigated. Nor does pure mind study history. For that purpose, one must

[1] 'Issues of Pragmaticism', in *The Monist*, xv, 1903, p. 485. Reprinted in *Collected Papers of Charles Sanders Peirce*, v, p. 297, Harvard University Press, 1934 (ed. by Charles Hartshorne and Paul Weiss).

be historically affected; caught by the mass of past experience that intrudes into the present in the shape of 'tradition': demanding, compelling, often only narrating, reporting, pointing to other past experience which has not as yet been unfolded. Again, the investigator is in the first instance a receiver of signals to which he attends and which he pursues, but on whose transmission he has only a very limited influence. The registering and digesting of these signs, the functioning of this whole 'receiving apparatus', cannot be reduced to the vague formula of traditional antitheses ('body and soul', 'inward and outward'). The only antithesis that does apply is that between 'part' and 'whole'. By his intrusion into the process that is to be studied, the student himself, like every one of his tools, becomes part-object of investigation; 'part-object' to be taken in a twofold sense: he is, like any other organ of investigation, but a *part* of the whole object that is being investigated. But equally it is only a *part* of himself that, thus externalized into an instrument, enters into the object-world of his studies.

A limiting case might certainly be imagined where this part of his person becomes equal to the whole: where the historian ceases to be anything but a product of the history he imagines himself writing; where the student of documents is himself at best only another document of the historical contagion to which he is a prey. Nor will it be denied that this limiting case is occasionally *almost* reached; just as there are said to be physicists whose working process comes alarmingly near to that of the machines with which they are conversant. But if any one were to look upon this as the normal condition, and to proclaim the 'inescapability of such material ties'—without a sense of the steps and grades that hold good here—he would commit the mistake opposite to that which dissolves all material connexions into mere associations of ideas. However true it remains that pure mind cannot pursue either history or physics, because these things do not affect it materially, it is also true that the material contact does not suffice to supply these sciences with a conscious agent. If the physicist were nothing but a physical apparatus, there would be no physics; nor would history exist, if the historian were merely an historical document. (The very formulation of these sentences contains a contradiction, for the words 'apparatus' and 'document' cannot be defined at all without relation to some one who uses them for some purpose.)

It follows that we must admit a major or minor feat of intelligence in every act of measurement or textual criticism, but that we ought to define this feat of intelligence as a mode of behaviour, that is, as a type of event. The critical interpretation of a document by an historian, considered as an act in time, is in the first instance an *event*, no less than, say, the anger or joy caused by this document, as a biased contemporary may have felt it. In the historian, too, if he is enthusiastic about his subject, something of this anger or joy will reverberate. However, by the application of the critical method the raw excitement is refined to a more thoughtful mode of behaviour. He does not simply follow his spontaneous emotion, instead he appeals (more or less accurately and successfully) to a system of grammatical and critical rules, on which he bases his interpretation and which, in their turn, are tested by being applied.

Corresponding to these grammatical and critical axioms, the experimental physicist has his axioms of measurement. He presupposes them and appeals to their rules, in order to show that his method is correct. But what is the basis of his confidence that these rules will be a safe guide in the investigation of his subject? A 'pre-established harmony', in the sense of Leibniz, is unacceptable to-day. So is Spinoza's doctrine of a necessary identity in the order and connexion of 'things' and 'ideas'.[1] Kant had tried to eliminate the problem by the 'Copernican emotion' in his *Critique of Pure Reason*, which made the order of things dependent upon the order of ideas, i.e. the forms of judgement. Yet, in the *Critique of Judgement*, the problem of the 'harmony of nature with our understanding' (*die Zusammenstimmung der Natur zu unserem Erkenntnisvermögen*) is again raised; only to be solved once more by that *a priori* and generalizing method of reasoning which is called 'transcendental deduction'. Here we have the crux of all such theories:—the problem is neither capable, nor in need, of a *universal* solution. What is actually an experimental hypothesis has been taken for a metaphysical or epistemological principle; which explains why all these doctrines, without exception, provide a theory of truth, but not of error.[2] Error

[1] *Ethica*, pars ii, prop. vii: 'Ordo et connexio idearum idem est ac ordo et connexio rerum.'

[2] Cf. Spinoza's 'privative' explanation of error (*Ethica*, pars ii, prop. xxxv) based on the proposition: 'Nihil in ideis positivum est, propter quod falsae dicuntur' (prop. xxxiii).

can only be accounted for if the methodical rules of investigation are considered as *part of the experimental hypothesis.* The investigator who constructs and manipulates his instruments believing that his method conforms with the general laws of nature, may be compared with the driver of a vehicle who, in a country whose language and habits he knows but imperfectly, assumes that he is conforming with traffic regulations. An epoch-making event in a laboratory is often not so very different from an ordinary road accident. However, it is peculiar to the physicist that—within controllable limits—he does not shun but seeks these collisions, because by them he learns something of the structure of the occurrences he wants to investigate, and of the rules of the game which he hypothetically presupposes. 'The physicist about to abandon one of his hypotheses ought to rejoice, for he finds an unexpected opportunity for a discovery' (Poincaré, *Science et Hypothèse*, iv, p. 9). It is for the sake of these discoveries that he inserts himself into the process, and the rules according to which he does so are proved by the outcome of the experiment to be either true or false, or doubtful.

This intrusion, of which every investigator must be guilty if he wishes to make any sort of contact with his material and to test the rules of his procedure, is a thoroughly real event. A set of instruments is being inserted, and the given constellation is thereby disturbed. The physicist disturbs the atoms whose composition he wants to study. The historian disturbs the sleep of the document that he drags forth from a dusty archive. This word 'disturbance' is not to be taken as a metaphor, but is meant literally. Even the astronomical physicist acts disturbingly on nature when he splits up a beam of light that has come from the stars, in order to infer the direction and speed of their motion. True, he does not disturb the star, but the nexus of nature in which the star is only a member. To the historian it might, indeed, sound like a metaphor if he is told that the document is disturbed by him. For involuntarily he pictures it as a material piece of paper, which does not mind whether it is lying in a cupboard or on a table. However, if we look upon it as an historical object, and consider its present status—viz. how it has been discarded and forgotten—as part of the historic process itself, then this process is indeed 'disturbed' by him who brings the forgotten words back to memory; often a very unpleasant disturbance—as when a traditional hero-worship is endangered by a disclosure of the hero's weakness. If the term 'disturbance' is taken in a sufficiently wide sense, so that it embraces every amplification, confirmation, or intensification, that is to say, every qualitative as well as every factual alteration of our belief, no historical inquiry is ever undertaken without the intention of creating such a disturbance.

It will be noticed that I am now speaking of disturbances that concern ourselves, our own belief and our own behaviour, rather than the objective order of historical events, which is the subject of our studies. But between the objective order of historical events and our own belief that is directed to and determined by it, no sharp boundary can be drawn. If I speak of a traditional hero-worship as being disturbed by a documentary discovery, this can be expressed in two forms, the one having the objective order of events, the other our own belief, for its subject:

1. The effect (*Nachwirkung*) of this man is modified by this discovery.
2. Our present opinion of this man, owing to this discovery, differs from that previously held.

Both sentences are *perfectly equivalent*, and I would strongly protest were any one to say that the first sentence is metaphorical, and only the second can be taken literally. Viewed as an historical event, the 'effect' of which the first sentence speaks is no less real than, let us say, the transmission of light from a star, taken as a physical process. It can be traced in historical space and time with the same precision as the migration of light in the space-time-continuum of physics. It is true that in the former case the way is not paved with Gaussian co-ordinates that expand in four interchangeable dimensions, but is marked by symbols of historical origin; yet they speak a language at least as insistent and significant as any mathematical equation. In fact, in a competition between science and history, the historians would be sure to score *one* point: in dealing with their symbols, they have long realized what the physicists, dazzled by the polished appearance of their equations, have only recently noticed; namely, that every discovery regarding the objects of their inquiry reacts on the construction of their implements; just as every alteration of the implements makes possible new discovery. The 'Hermeneutics' of Schleiermacher and Boeckh, who in the field of philology gave this rule its classic expression, might have carried as a motto the words that Eddington put at the end of his book on the modern theory of gravitation: 'We have found a strange foot-print on the shores of the unknown. We have devised profound theories, one after another, to account for its origin. At last, we have succeeded in reconstructing the creature that made the foot-print. And lo! it is our own.'[1]

III. *The Self-Transformation of Man*

I may be pardoned for returning to the natural sciences with this anthropomorphic phrase. For it would almost seem as if we had not yet carried anthropomorphism far enough in this field. With the historical approach it has proved impossible to separate man from his historical antecedents. Every change of our ideas about our ancestors entails a change of our ideas about ourselves and will indirectly affect our behaviour. In precisely the same way, it ought to be recognized that those successful disturbances by which we intrude into the natural world which surrounds us amount in the last resort to disturbances, that is modifications, of our personal equipment. The dividing line between man and his surroundings can no more be fixed in this case than the line of division between man and his antecedents could be fixed in the other.

It is an old puzzle where to draw the line between man and the objects of his environment. His head, we dare say, quite certainly belongs to him; without it, he would lose his 'identity'. But how about his hair? And if we let him have that, how about his hat? If his hat is taken away, or its shape is altered, is not the entire form of the man altered as well? A man accustomed to walking with a stick becomes another man if this stick is taken from him. His gait changes, his gestures, possibly his whole constitution.[2] There is much in the magic doctrines of sympathy which, after rational sifting and re-interpreting, might help to illuminate this problem. But there is no need to descend to such gloomy depths to bring this wisdom to light. Did not Plato dread even art and banish it from the state, because it transmutes ('charms' is his word) the man who exposes himself to

[1] *Space, Time and Gravitation*, Cambridge, 1929, p. 201.

[2] These observations do not refer to the problem of external and internal relations. The question I am discussing is that of bio-physical, not of logical, transformation.

it? Right up to the most recent times the poets, often without being aware of it, have agreed with him, and gloried in their power to transform.[1]

Scholars have as a rule been more cautious. Their claim is based on even juster foundations, but its exercise would entail a far greater risk, as the evidence in their case is more striking. Students of history are still surprised, though this fact has long been known, that any alteration of our knowledge of past events may also alter our present behaviour. The corresponding claim in natural science is more generally recognized. Any discovery within the domain of what is usually called 'the external world of physics' may lead to technical innovations which change our personal behaviour. These technical innovations may at first have a limited scope. Perhaps it is only a new way of handling some instrument in the laboratory. Soon, however, the effect infringes on the pragmatism of daily life, where it evokes wonder or horror. 'There is no great invention, from fire to flying, which has not been hailed as an insult to some god. But if every physical and chemical invention is a blasphemy, every biological invention is a perversion.'[2]

Until recently, the study of Nature and History was considered a 'contemplative occupation', confined to men who locked themselves up in their libraries and laboratories, where they escaped from the turmoil of the world into the quiet and seclusion of their thoughts. To-day, intentionally or not, they threaten the world by their 'discoveries'.

In an age when not only reformers but despots as well often base their prestige less on 'God' than on a limited knowledge of nature and history, experimental and documentary evidence mould the destiny which controls our lives for better or for worse. But even those scholars who desire, now as before, to safeguard their work from the tumults of the moment, cannot ignore the fact that apparently independent lines of study converge to-day in one point: this point is the self-transformation of man who has become lord and victim of his own cognitions.

In the study of this self-transformation, scientific and historical research have worked too long independently. It is time that they should be combined.

Translated from the German.

[1] See the synopsis in 'Θεῖος Φόβος, Untersuchungen über die Platonische Kunstphilosophie', *Zeitschrift für Aesthetik u. allgem. Kunstwissenschaft*, vol. xxvi, 1932, pp. 349–73.

[2] J. B. S. Haldane, *Daedalus*, London, 1924, p. 24.

THE PHILOSOPHICAL SIGNIFICANCE OF COMPARATIVE SEMANTICS

By HENDRIK J. POS

EVEN to the inexperienced immature mind speech is an object of wonder. In so far as this attitude produces an intellectual content, it leads to a conception of the relation of speech to that which is expressed by it, namely objects. Word and meaning, which in the unreflective activity of speech are always bound together, are by intellectual analysis brought face to face, and thus there arises a relation which is at the same time a comparison. Wonder, in breaking up the identity, brings to light a distinction in virtue of which the process of speech is analysed into sound and thing. The suppressed identity tries to re-establish itself by means of the question: How can the word represent the object, how can it stand for the object? The answer to this question does not lead back to the original identity, but does lead in the direction of it. From this arises the attempt to trace the sound back in some way to the object, to show the sound as proceeding from the object already in existence. Here we have the copy theory of speech as an answer to the question. This theory attempts to understand the relation between word and object on the basis of similarity. It takes its stand on those instances which seem to be examples of such similarity, where sound signifies sound. It seeks to grasp the original elements of speech in the imitation of sound shown in actual speech. The relatively few instances in which a sound signifies a sound seem to place the origin of the rise of speech clearly before us. Sound, before it became the symbol of the object, was identical with the object: it was the object before it came to mean it.

The conception of an original similarity of sound and meaning holds only within narrow limits, for most words are not like their objects. The copy theory must take a new form here, if it is to maintain itself. Where there can be no similarity between word and object, such a correspondence must nevertheless have been present originally. This way out, however, is only a partial help. A similarity of sound and object is only possible with objects which, if not themselves sounds, are at least like sounds. Now most of the objects signified by words do not conform to this condition. Thus, the similarity which is said to exist between objects and the words which signify them cannot be an immediate but only a mediated similarity. It has to be mediated because of the irreducible difference between sound and object, in virtue of which the sound, while as a rule unlike the object, may yet correspond to it. Not only sounds but also gestures are related to objects to which they cannot have, and do not try to have, any similarity. Even here, however, a strict rule regulates the relation of sound to object. The object may differ in many respects from the speech which represents it; through speech the mind obtains command of the object in a manner appropriate to the nature of the mind itself. The correspondence of sound to object is the mediator between mind and object.

To have seen that speech does not copy the world of objects, but corresponds to it, is to have taken the essential step towards a symbolic conception of speech. The comparison of sound and object which tries to find them related as copy to thing copied shows itself inadequate to the task of grasping in its fullness the relationship between the world of speech and the world of objects. Where the concept of similarity shows itself unable to make clear the relationship of speech to world, it becomes evident that the idea of correspondence not only makes clear that relationship which would otherwise be unintelligible, but also embraces the instances in which similarity is actually found. These instances provide us with the idea of an extreme at which the difference between speech and world is almost concealed, in so far as here there is, as it were, no opportunity for mind and objects to bring out the contrast between them in their structural form. Thus onomatopoeia, while apparently the clearest, is in reality the least appropriate example from which the essential relationship between the world of speech and that of objects may be illustrated.

The copy theory leaves the mind passive in its relation to objects. According to it, the world seems to tell man how it is to be reproduced in speech. Sound serves as the pattern of this relationship, since the reproduction of sound in speech cannot prove unlike its original. In extreme contrast to this interpretation of speech we find the conception of the world adjusting itself to speech, and not speech to the world, the conception of speech telling the world how it is or ought to be. This is the interpretation which makes of speech a wonder worker, the exact antithesis of the conception of the process of speech as receptive. In the end, a world which corresponds to speech and a speech which is to mirror the world as it is exhibit only two forms of a relationship understood in one and the same sense; the result is in both cases the harmony of speech and the world.

The fact that our observations start from the recollection of these primitive interpretations of speech is due to the effort to exhibit the changes through which the conception of speech passes, as it transforms its fundamental ideas in accordance with its widening circle of experience. When we begin in this way, elements which originally seemed constant are seen to be relative, and new rules are set up. This process by which philosophical knowledge corrects itself seems to be related, as far as direction and result are concerned, to the process by which the natural sciences correct themselves.

The realistic or magic conception of the relation between speech and the world rests on the assumption that there is such a thing as a world given to us in perception and existing independently of speech, a world which offers to speech the pattern on which it is to be constructed. The characteristic of this interpretation is that it itself makes that which it thinks it finds, on the one hand a world of speech and on the other a world of objects, two worlds which are to be bound together in a pre-established correspondence. Although it is only in exceptional cases that it can succeed in pointing to the presence of this correspondence, it nevertheless holds that in principle the separation of word from object has sprung from an original correspondence. It is bound by its point of view to produce the contrast between speech and object which it uses to compare them, a contrast which, however, remains fixed and abstract, and leads to insoluble problems as to the original correspondence between object and sound. This method of comparison, which opposes speech to objects without being able to unite them again, precedes the real science of comparative philology, which emerges at the point where it becomes clear that the word which stands for an object does not remain one and the same, as the object does, but can differ at different times and in different places. The fact of differences of language, a fact which the conception of speech must take into account, brings about a fundamental change in that conception, for we are no longer concerned to exhibit the original correspondence which was supposed to exist between word and object. It is not the apparent dissimilarity of the two which prevents us from exhibiting their correspondence, but the actually experienced variety of expressions for one and the same thing. How are we to think of a word in one language, rather than of the corresponding word in another language, as the proper expression for an object?

In its beginnings, comparative philology will follow a tendency opposed to that followed by the primitive interpretation of speech. It will refuse to answer the question which we first ask in naïve surprise, the question as to the original relation between sound and object. With the discovery of the variety of languages this question is set aside. It was relevant only as long as there seemed to be only one single expression for one object. But in refusing to answer this question, comparative philology is all the more concerned to fix the object itself in its identity, precisely as the object of different linguistic symbols. From now on, the question is not about the relation of each word to its object, but about the possibility of establishing a relation between such an object and the given multiplicity of expressions for it; we are not trying to show that there is something which directly corresponds to each word, but that there are identical objects to which the many words of many languages can all be referred.

The naïve interpretation of speech took its start from the original identity of word and object. It derived the word from the object. Comparative philology does much the same in so far as it seeks to trace back the variety of languages to a single world as their common basis. At this stage, however, the required correspondence is no longer evident to perception. It is the bearer of significance by virtue of which every word of every language receives a meaning by being set in a context of meanings. The study of speech, being concerned with the variety of languages, presupposes this objective significance which is to set the standard for the meaning of words. Here, also, we must distinguish those cases in which the common objective significance makes itself evident in the process of comparison from those in which it is only postulated. Wherever individual words correspond to one another, there the common object is given. The correspondence is, then, especially striking when the object can easily be separated from the meanings, so that it can be shown to be the meeting-point of all of them. This happens mostly with objects of sense perception.

Semantic comparative philology takes account, as we have seen, of a number of linguistic correspondences between two languages which indicate quite openly and obviously the presence of a common object. An outward sign of this is that the word in question can always be rendered by an equivalent word of the other language. This correspondence between two languages gives us conformity at its closest. But, as we know, these instances of conformity make us believe in complete conformity, much as the imitation of sound makes us believe that each word copies its object. The practice of translation, which is nothing but a concrete application of comparative philology, shows how limited the unequivocal correspondence of word to word is, and how often conformity to the object is best reached if we allow ourselves to translate the same word, now by one word, now by another, according to the context. A word which, as an isolated element of speech apart from any context, can be identified with an isolated element of another language may have to be translated in a particular context by a different word, precisely for the sake of accuracy and the sense. A language as a whole, a significant collection of words, cannot as a rule be put into another language through the conformity of the structural parts of each. A whole can be translated only by a corresponding whole, and that only if we give up the idea of a harmony of parts involving a word-for-word correspondence between the two languages. In this context it is not essential to distinguish between syntactic and semasiological unities. Even if to one word of a certain language there correspond two words of another, only the context can determine which of these two, in one case or in another, the translation requires, and the fact that there are two signifies only that now the one word now the other is to be chosen.

From this point of view the science of comparative philology may be built up as a system of diversities and conformities. In so far as it aims at philosophical totality, it will not restrict itself to the sciences of phonetics and morphology, but will also take within its scope syntax and semantics, and will, moreover, take into consideration the most concrete product of linguistic creation, the literatures of the world and the problems which arise in translating them. In general we find that the external conformity lessens according as the structures to be translated are more comprehensive. The spirit of a language can manifest itself in the elements of the language only in so far as a particular word of one language can be substituted for a particular word of another, and this often makes it look as if the second word could stand for the first in every instance. But we find that it is not in the elements, but in the more comprehensive linguistic structures, that the spirit of a language can manifest itself in its unity, and that in these it becomes more and more difficult to establish a correspondence with another language. If we compare the spirit of one language with that of another, the resulting impression we gain is one of difference, as Wilhelm von Humboldt has made clear with his comprehensive knowledge of languages and subtle insight into the individual elements of each.

Communication by means of speech is not limited to the sphere of objects of sense perception. These objects can be taken as the patterns of such communication, in the same way as the imitation of sounds illustrates the giving of names. The relation to sense perception is, however, not necessary. Within one's own language most words are not related to objects of sense. In using them as a means of communication, we see that they are not meaningless although they cannot be referred to sense perception. Their objects are meanings which, measured by the standard of sense perception, are subjective in character, expressions created by language, but, measured by the use which the community agrees to make of them, they are objective in character, objects possessing significance.

If, in this way, language can have an objective character without being based on sense perception, this objectivity, established by the community and finding its justification in its intelligibility and not in the world of mere perception, is once more put to the proof when, as a closed system of speech and thought, it is confronted by another such system with similar claims. The idea that we have here an objectivity similar to that of sense perception can arise only if the two confronting systems can be equated in detail. If, to the supersensible element in one language, there corresponds a supersensible element in the other, then, and only then, can it look as if the common objects, which constitute the correspondence between the two languages, were given in advance in a way not indeed the same as, but analogous to, the way in which the material of sense perception is given. The comparison of languages leads, however, as we have already seen, to the opposite result, and deprives the realistic view of its provisional justification. For this comparison finds points of correspondence which indeed constitute a common world, but this world is like a common level above which the peaks of the different languages rise separately.

As long as comparison restricts itself to the external, it can only point out what it finds to be equivalent, or to be more, less, or not at all capable of translation among the different worlds of speech. In contrast to this, however, there arises the question as to an internal law which will make intelligible the different degrees of conformity. This law can be set forth only when the semasiological homogeneity of the translatable and untranslatable meanings has in some way been more closely determined. Now, according to this law, the meanings which can be translated belong to the world of pragmatic objects, while, as a rule, those which cannot be translated represent the world of the mind. The less translatable expressions of a language present the categories by which the mind imposes form on experience. These few technical terms govern the far greater number of objects mutually interchangeable and belonging to the world of experience, and govern them as the mind governs individual things. The spirit of the language remains in the background as long as speech is concerned only to indicate things of the world of space and time, using these as the common medium of human communication. But as soon as we have passed beyond this stage of stringing together individual things and are seeking by some means to reach a whole, there appear in our representation of things differences which were concealed in the detailed conformity.

Every comprehensive representation of a manifold is an interpretation, which introduces elements belonging to another dimension than that of perceived objects. Even the comprehension of purely given details is already an interpretation, a reaction of the mind to experience, which, arising out of a synthesis, sets a limit to a purely differentiating and objectifying activity. In the development of the mind this tendency is quite natural and necessary. The activity of detailed enumeration cannot do other than transform itself into an activity of unification. The comprehension of a universe of things is always something qualitatively different from the mere designation of detached things. In the whole all the parts are preserved but at the same time interpreted. Only an act of comprehension which would remain purely formal would add nothing to the content. It would only assert that the empirical manifold also formed a unity.

The comprehension of things in a unity does not express only that unity which would add nothing to the content, but expresses it as a determinate unity of such and such a nature. The whole is a new object into which the parts have entered, but which may be looked at from different sides. Each constituent part, also, is capable of determination from different aspects, the essential limit of such determination being that each thing is determined in its distinctness from co-ordinate things. The whole cannot be intuitively determined in such a way as to allow the limits of the comprehensive view of it to be defined. If it is an object of intuition, bearing some analogy in this to empirical objects, it is the object of an intellectual intuition, in which the empirical can be made use of only as a symbol.

Thus it comes about that the intuition of wholes turns out so differently in different languages. Even where there exists an external conformity as with the words *κόσμος*, *mundus*, *Welt*, *monde*, or *λόγος*, *ratio*, *Vernunft*, *raison*, the internal difference is essential. It is not that these terms cannot on occasion be substituted for one another, but that closer observation discloses differences even in external usage. Here the science of semantics cannot be exact and concrete as long as it only encounters in an external fashion corresponding words in different languages, since what is necessary here is that we should be intuitively aware of and attentive to the different ways in which, from time to time, things apparently identical come to be spoken of. In particular, the rhythm and frequency of the recurrence to the use of certain words are decisive for the discovery of a category of interpretation. In a certain sense the categories of a language are constituted by those words to which we always come back in every situation. These present the basic form which, from time to time, gives order to the endless variety of changing experiences; and this order differs according to the spirit of a language, and within a language according to the nature of the individual who speaks. The contents of experience, taken in a certain sense from the neutral world of things, or at all events reducible to that world, arrange themselves in the way that the spirit of the language points out to them.

Thus, the thinking which seeks a unity is a thinking which is qualitative, synthetic, subjective, and of a kind that changes the object of intuition. This holds good in a higher degree of those reactions in which the mind manifests itself concretely as the unity of thought, feeling, and action. Here we are in the sphere of values and the appreciation of values. In values, still more than in the philosophical or theoretical search for unity, does the transition from the formation of a common world to the task of individual interpretation make itself evident. Unifying expressions such as world, life, being, mind, indicate what only appear to be objects in the usual sense. As matters of subjective intuition their use is always limited and individual, although the individual parts are included in the intuition. If we search in its vocabulary for the sense of values deposited in a language, the preponderance of diversities over conformities makes itself evident. Such words, for example, as the Greek *καλόν*, the Latin *honestum*, and the French *honnête*, cannot be adequately translated. Their meaning cannot be reduced to purely objective elements. Their application follows an inner law not to be elicited from the practice of translation, which knows no fixity and is never more than approximate. The inconstancy, as we may call it, of translation is always an expression of the fact that a certain meaning, a certain point of view, does not exist in the language into which we are attempting to translate. The translatable reduces itself to what can be an object of common intuition, and the sharper our powers of observation are the more limited does this sphere of common intuition show itself to be.

In the untranslatable there is, nevertheless, no insuperable obstacle for the understanding mind. We pass from an external and superficial impression of conformity to an appreciation of the variety of mental categories, and this appreciation includes within it a knowledge of the individual character of the alien categories. It is not as if we were altogether ignorant of the meaning of these categories, for we know just this—that they cannot be translated by the categories of our own language. We become aware of this when we attempt to translate. Since our knowledge establishes the failure of translation, there must be at work in our minds an intuition which understands the alien category without being able to think in it. The alien category may then appear so essential that the lack of it will be felt as a deficiency in our own language, and we shall accordingly adopt it. If then the adopted category changes its meaning in its new context, this will be a further proof of the individuality of each system of categories.

The investigation of remote and primitive cultures has shown that in these the world of sensible objects is built up and ordered in a way that is quite different from that of the culture which possesses our type of language; for in the former concrete distinctions, such as can be perceived, preponderate over abstract synthesis. Yet a certain correspondence with European languages can be produced by means of transliteration. When primitive speech indicates the different aspects and conditions of a thing by means of single terms, this indeed points to a type of intuition different from ours, but still the identity of the object can easily be established. This, however, is not possible with the interpretative categories, with such concepts, for example, as world, life, happiness, fate. There seems to be no object separable from and corresponding to the meanings which arise on the level of interpretation in the different languages. In these meanings the very essence of the interpretation of experience seems to be concentrated; they present in their individuality the view of the universe, whatever it may be, that is contained in the language to which they belong.

From these considerations we can reach some points of view of fundamental importance for the investigation of the history of civilization through comparative semantics. This inquiry should be specially directed to the unique, fundamental concepts of interpretation belonging to each sphere of life. It should strive not to be content with a mere external rendering of particular terms, but, with a deeply rooted suspicion of such a task, it should renounce it, and should try to understand the meanings in question, as they are found actually at work in the concrete context of the world to which they belong. In doing so we should find that the meanings which are fully expressed in the common world of perception are not only secondary, but also rather conceal an actual difference than indicate its absence.

The principle of the identity of indiscernibles holds of the world common to the different languages. The principle that there are fundamental differences between different languages proves its usefulness, not only when we consider remote cultures where the principle is plainly to be seen, but also when we consider the interpenetration of different types of insight as seen in European civilization. Even the external appropriation of Greek categories by the spirit of the Latin language was not accomplished without difficulty, as we can see in Cicero and Seneca, who worked for that end with a highly cultivated sense for language. But it is not even certain that, in those cases in which an external equivalent was successfully found, this was not accompanied by an unconscious inner change. If we take as an example the way in which the medieval controversy about realism took over a problem from ancient philosophy, it may be doubted whether the Greek thinkers ever understood the term 'Reality' in the sense in which it has been understood since the Middle Ages, and in which it has in modern times developed into a fundamental category of thought. Above all, when we compare modern and ancient philosophy we find the most striking discrepancies in the meaning of terms, even where the moderns have based their terminology on that of the ancients. Kant, for example, took his terms 'Stoff' and 'Form' from Aristotle, but in the long process of change they have taken on an entirely different meaning from that which Aristotle gave to them.

Having emphasized, for the sake of objectivity and accuracy, the differences between different languages and intellectual worlds with developed systems of categories, let us consider finally the fundamental opposition between two philosophical ideas which appear to govern the science of comparative semantics. One of these ideas is that of the universality of the mind, and of a corresponding objective system of all meanings. According to this idea, the systems of categories which express the various intellectual worlds occurring in the course of history are only parts cut out, as it were, from a comprehensive whole, much as all the bodies in a part of space are determined by that space and contained in it. The meanings which actually emerged had to be seen to be realizations of possibilities already indicated in the universal system. For this view which, in Husserl's sense, revives the *mathesis universalis* of Leibniz, the historical activity of choice is something secondary, as compared with the timeless, objective system of meanings. Moreover, the different intellectual worlds which we find in actuality do not in principle exclude one another, since they are all derived from the universal system of possible meanings. This theory, which we have expounded, may well be the foundation of any attempt to give systematic order to meanings, but from the historical point of view it is seen to be inadequate, in so far as we are not in a position to determine the concrete forms of the categories in advance of experience. Now we find even in the author of the concept of the *mathesis universalis* the complementary idea of the monads as spiritual individualities which cannot be reduced to a universal of which they would be instances or parts, resembling their original. The different intellectual forms which we find in experience are not, however, interchangeable, and the system of possible meanings from which these forms are said to be derived has not so far been drawn up. When we consider the categories as they are historically given, we come very near to thinking of them, this theory maintains, as nothing but realizations of timeless possibilities.

But although the theory is incapable of bringing out the individuality of the intellectual activity of giving meaning, it never lacks understanding of the alien intellectual world which confronts it. This alien world can always be related in some way to the point of view which is assigned to the investigator by the concrete world of meanings in which he lives. Philosophical knowledge is never deductive in the sense in which a process of mathematical reasoning is; it remains relative, being in itself the product of the interpenetration, within certain actual limits, of alien categories and those proper to itself. This relativity is the condition of an objectivity which regards none of the intellectual worlds as derivable from another higher than itself, but sees each as a starting-point from which we may reach a complete understanding of all the others. If this is so, then the idea of universality is unsatisfactory as a theoretical starting-point, and yet it proves as an historical fact its own value as a continuous advance towards understanding. And this universalism does not need to presuppose any mere empty possibility; it is concrete in the effort to penetrate the monad-like worlds of speech and of the mind, and to be penetrated by them without losing itself.

Wilhelm von Humboldt has given us insight into the variety of these worlds, and so has laid the foundation for a systematic study of human experience and civilization (*Geistes-* and *Kulturwissenschaft*). Ernst Cassirer's *Philosopy of Symbolic Forms* has formulated this insight in general philosophic terms, and it is especially thanks to his work that the philosophical study of the history of the mind and the fruitful co-operation of the comparative study of languages and the history of philosophy have become possible.

Translated by Sheila A. Kerr, University of Glasgow.

HISTORIOGRAPHY

Introduction to an unpublished work:
German Historians from Herder to Burckhardt

By FRIEDRICH GUNDOLF

HISTORIOGRAPHY is an integral part of general literature. In recent German text-books or courses on literature it does not receive its full measure of attention, because it is usually treated (especially in Germany) in conjunction with the history of science. The estimation of its exponents is determined almost exclusively by their contributions to historical research, by their discovery of new documents (so-called sources), by their method of obtaining these, or even merely by the accidental causes which have gained them a reputation for astuteness and industrious investigation. Novelty of material or of method was the usual criterion in judging historical literature. This criterion is, to be sure, in no sense to be discarded or depreciated. But historians should receive more attention than hitherto from students of German literature with regard to their gift of creating an image. This gift is determined in the first instance by the intuitive power of their combined human faculties, of which the scientific observation, the collecting and arranging of data, is but a particular function; and, further, upon their gift of expressing in language what they behold and perceive. The fame of the great historians of antiquity rests on their power of presentation, their qualities as writers, their spirit as orators—in short, precisely upon their peculiar gift as historians. The title of 'Father of History' is given to Herodotus—to that wayfarer and explorer of lands and peoples, who dedicated his work to the Muses, and created a new species of human discourse, by using words to bring clearly before the inward eye knowledge which he had conscientiously acquired by investigation. Herodotus, being a Greek, could not yet easily dissociate 'sense', the logical cohesion of experience, from the 'senses', from visual perception. Where sight and sense are still conceived together, language gives both the image and its meaning simultaneously, that is to say, it is 'mythical'. In the days before Herodotus the epic, and especially the Homeric epic, had performed both functions by means of which the tales of past events and occurrences, deeds and sufferings had assailed the minds of men perceptive of Time and Space. With the expansion, enlightenment, and wider dispersion of humanity, with its unification and civilization in Hellenism and the Roman Empire, with the growing independence of individuals, whether active or contemplative, the *genres* of history multiplied and detached themselves from their mythical origins. The opposite extremes of ancient historiography are represented by the memoirs and the universal histories, Caesar and Diodorus. What began with the awakening of the historical sense in Herodotus attained completion in Saint Augustine's philosophy of history, which put history to sleep, as it were, by resolving it into the workings of Providence. I am bound to speak of this, because the ancient *genres* of historical writing have continued to exercise their influence on historians even up to the present day, either as clarifying prototypes, or as models for imitation, or as superseded patterns, or—and this is true of all important authors of the period I shall deal with—as exemplars and masters of style, or at least as personalities which insidiously caught the imagination of enthusiasts. All the influential German historians of the eighteenth and nineteenth centuries, especially Herder, Johannes von Müller, and Ranke, desired not merely to unearth unknown facts or to establish new valuations, but to master the German language as historians and stylists, thus following in the footsteps of classical writers, upon whom they modelled themselves more or less closely. Herder, the most fertile and profound of all historical thinkers of Christianity, is of such teeming exuberance, restlessness, insatiability of mind, that the pains which he bestowed upon matters of style frequently escape notice. Nevertheless, style was vital even to him. The true prophet and founder of the doctrine of Genius, with its belief in organic growth and originality, he did not insist on patterns and rules, as did the rationalists of the classical school, whose reign he overthrew once and for all. But his lieutenant in the sphere of history proper, the founder of historical writing both scientific and artistic, Ranke's nearest and greatest predecessor, and (a fact which has been insufficiently appreciated) the master whom Ranke at first imitated almost slavishly—Johannes von Müller—was positively obsessed and bewitched by the classical models of historical writing: Caesar, Thucydides, Tacitus. Although he tended to become estranged from his ideals by his subject, medieval Swiss history, by the intellectual and emotional atmosphere of his day, and by his own totally different character, all of which drove him into a style quite peculiar to himself, yet the path he opened out remained under the jurisdiction of the stylists of antiquity.

I begin with the age when the writing of history in Germany first became part and parcel of German culture as a whole, and was not merely a subsidiary branch of theological training or political activity or else mere data laboriously collected by the erudite. In the days of Luther we have two historians of genius: one the last and greatest of the medieval chroniclers and withal the first true historical scholar, Johannes Aventinus; the other the first theosophist historian of the Reformation, Sebastian Franck. Both currents flow from the Middle Ages through the centuries of the Reformation and of the Baroque period into the age of German humanism. They represent two dominant factors of all historiography, namely, (1) the desire to preserve what actually was, 'as it actually was' (according to Ranke's formula), for sheer delight both in the telling and the matter told; and (2) to interpret earthly events in the light of the will of God or of Providence or of universal laws. These are, indeed, fundamental human impulses, which in the beginning of thought, speech, and writing still operate, complementing and yet repelling each other, contrasting and yet concentric, a fact which is fundamental to the poetic myths of this early period. As soon as a state of civilization is reached, the desire simply to see and tell on the one hand, or to view in perspective and interpret, on the other, diverge more and more and even enter into conflict with one another. In the nineteenth century the war waged by exact historical science under the leadership of Niebuhr and Ranke, or even before them by Johannes von Müller, against Schelling's and most especially Hegel's philosophical construction of history is only a manifestation of the same contrast embodied at the beginning of post-medieval German historiography in the persons of Aventinus and Sebastian Franck. Often enough, and most readily in times agitated by philosophical thinking, as in post-Leibnizian and still more in post-Kantian Germany, the zest for collecting data and the yearning for true vision will struggle for supremacy in one and the same soul, as, for instance, in Johannes von Müller and Schiller. Those sciences whose business it was to fit the world into universal laws according to the desire or the delusion of those who practised them, that is, theology, mathematics, and that transcendental philosophy which was first the servant then the master of the other two—and the sciences whose business it was to determine accurately the working of phenomena in time and space, have been engaged in more or less violent, more or less open warfare with one another, at least since the days of Hegel. Not until our own age of perfected historical sense have historians awakened to the legitimate tenets of philosophy, and philosophers refrained from offending the autonomy of the experimental sciences (as Hegel did with naïve arrogance), no longer dispensing with the signs, which nature and history, more accurately and thoroughly explored, display before them and force upon their notice; nor could they still do so with as good a conscience as the despotic thinkers of times when the results of experimental science had not reached such impressive proportions. Moreover, it was not the ignorance but the dictatorial attitude of philosophers which broke their tyranny; Leibniz, Kant, Schelling, Hegel, Schopenhauer possessed encyclopedic knowledge of the first order, but they derived it not from their book-learning, like the polyhistorians of the seventeenth, eighteenth, and nineteenth centuries, but from thought, genius, vision. And these powers are only the modern manifestations of what was formerly called inspiration, the grace of God, revelation, illumination; that is, they represent once again the contrasting and complementary views of life, which tower at the gateway of European philosophy in the persons of Plato and Aristotle. Aristotle, who with such clear insight and such pride freed science, as an instrument of knowledge, from myth, which Plato still fervently desired and glorified by using it as a poetic parable, though without literal faith (origin of allegory)—even Aristotle, with a disdainful side-glance, declared poetry, i.e. myth, to be more philosophical, i.e. richer in knowledge, than history. This means that he, the thinker of antiquity who most delighted in empirical knowledge, was already aware of the antinomy between the single phenomenon on the one hand, and the universal law, the concept of the eternal idea, the immortal myth, on the other. Schopenhauer, the professed contemner of history among the great German philosophers, delighted in quoting these words of Aristotle.

The very history of historiography reflects the border feuds and struggles for supremacy between its affinities with philosophy on the one hand and empirical science on the other. German historical writings of the nineteenth century often bear the mark of this. The names with which I intend to begin and to end, Herder and Burckhardt, are symbolic of this polarity. Herder, a philosopher for whom the history of the world is the most eloquent parable of divine infinity, as revealed in its evolution to him before all others; and Jakob Burckhardt, an historian who, in contemplating the field he had so extensively explored, sought release from life's heaviness, from world horror, even from awe of the Godhead—a man akin to Schopenhauer in mood, though not in creed, and not a disciple of his doctrine. German historical science is the immediate offspring of Herder's doctrine. Without him Ranke is even less thinkable than without Niebuhr. Müller is his disciple. Jakob Burckhardt, perhaps not the most powerful historian of the nineteenth century—this title is due to Mommsen—but surely the mellowest, the most imaginative and most limpid mind, the sage among historians, at the end of his life plunges his image-laden eyes into Nirvana, where all history is blotted out; and he does so with the philosophical equanimity of a mind which has discovered what is discoverable and serenely bears it with him into the unfathomable Beyond. And as the historians Johannes von Müller and Ranke, than whom we know none more genuinely historical, follow upon Herder, the philosopher, so upon Burckhardt there follows Friedrich Nietzsche, the true prophet of history and growth, the man whose yea or nay, whether heeded or contested, heard or unheard, side by side with or in opposition to Karl Marx, has most powerfully affected the historical thought of our time, through media as manifold and as contrasting as were Hegel's in his time. Just as Lenin derives from Karl Marx, so Mussolini from Nietzsche. Nietzsche inherited many of his own historical views, notably his ideas of the Renaissance and of the Greeks, his notion of the superman (*Herrenmensch*), of Dionysiac ecstasy and the dream-state, from the gentle and remote hermit of Basle. No doubt, like every inheritor of genius, he wrestled with this inheritance and absorbed it, transmuting it into his own possession, before it could go forth and shake the world. I mention this only in order to suggest how historiography and the conscientious toil of self-denying investigators, sometimes perceptibly, sometimes imperceptibly, make history in their turn.

The contemplative mind can enflame passions which will convulse the nations, while conversely migrations of peoples and world-wars can be condensed into enduring creations of wisdom and hallowed beauty. Every being presupposes and contains within himself the whole history of the world, a warning, surely, against any pretence to 'final explanations', 'exhaustive expositions', or 'conclusive results'. A warning of this kind is particularly necessary in the case of any treatise on historiography. What we know concerning ourselves is not even a millionth part of what happens to us and what we are. That is pre-eminently true of the inner cohesion of history. No one grasped this more intimately than that most universal of all historical thinkers, Herder. This certainly does not release us from the obligation of securing, testing, and sifting whatever we can make clear to ourselves, whatever we can establish, if only because this selecting and collecting can alone produce true and full representations, honestly acquired knowledge, and sober insight. Those who start out relying on sudden illumination will not be vouchsafed it, and the true seers of the world have always been those who were most thoroughly informed.

Translated by W. E. Delp, University of London.

HISTORY AS A SYSTEM

By JOSÉ ORTEGA Y GASSET

I

HUMAN life is a strange reality concerning which the first thing to be said is that it is the basic reality, in the sense that to it we must refer all others, since all others, effective or presumptive, must in one way or another appear within it.

The most trivial and at the same time the most important note in human life is that man has no choice but to be always doing something to keep himself in existence. Life is given to us; we do not give it to ourselves, rather we find ourselves in it, suddenly and without knowing how. But the life which is given us is not given us ready-made; we must make it for ourselves, each one his own. Life is a task. And the weightiest aspect of these tasks in which life consists is not the necessity of performing them but, in a sense, the opposite: I mean, that we find ourselves always under compulsion to do something but never, strictly speaking, under compulsion to do something in particular, that there is not imposed on us this or that task as there is imposed on the star its course or on the stone its gravitation. Each individual before doing anything must decide for himself and at his own risk what he is going to do. But this decision is impossible unless one possesses certain convictions concerning the nature of things around one, the nature of other men, of oneself. Only in the light of such convictions can one prefer one act to another, can one, in short, live.

It follows that man must ever be grounded on some belief, and that the structure of his life will depend primordially on the beliefs on which he is grounded; and further that the most decisive changes in humanity are changes of belief, the intensifying or weakening of beliefs. The diagnosis of any human existence, whether of an individual, a people or an age, must begin by establishing the repertory of its convictions. For always in living one sets out from certain convictions. They are the ground beneath our feet, and it is for this reason we say that man is grounded on them. It is man's beliefs that truly constitute his state. I have spoken of them as a repertory to indicate that the plurality of beliefs on which an individual, a people or an age is grounded never possesses a completely logical articulation, that is to say, does not form a system of ideas such as, for example, a philosophy constitutes or aims at constituting. The beliefs that coexist in any human life, sustaining, impelling, and directing it, are on occasion incongruous, contradictory, at the least confused. Be it noted that all these qualifications attach to beliefs in so far as they partake of ideas. But it is erroneous to define belief as an idea. Once an idea has been thought it has exhausted its role and its consistency. The individual, moreover, may think whatever the whim suggests to him, and even many things against his whim. Thoughts arise in the mind spontaneously, without will or deliberation on our part and without producing any effect whatever on our behaviour. A belief is not merely an idea that is thought, it is an idea in which one also believes. And believing is not an operation of the intellectual mechanism, but a function of the living being as such, the function of guiding his conduct, his performance of his task.

This observation once made, I can now withdraw my previous expression and say that beliefs, a mere incoherent repertory in so far as they are merely ideas, always constitute a system in so far as they are effective beliefs; in other words, that while lacking articulation from the logical or strictly intellectual point of view, they do none the less possess a vital articulation, they *function* as beliefs resting one on another, combining with one another to form a whole: in short, that they always present themselves as members of an organism, of a structure. This causes them among other things always to possess their own architecture and to function as a hierarchy. In every human life there are beliefs that are basic, fundamental, radical, and there are others derived from these, upheld by them and secondary to them. If this observation is supremely trivial, the fault is not mine that with all its triviality it remains of the greatest importance. For should the beliefs by which one lives lack structure, since their number in each individual life is legion there must result a mere pullulation hostile to all idea of order and incomprehensible in consequence.

The fact that we should see them, on the contrary, as endowed with a structure and a hierarchy allows us to penetrate their hidden order and consequently to understand our own life and the life of others, that of to-day and that of other days.

Thus we may now say that the diagnosing of any human existence, whether of an individual, a people, or an age, must begin by an ordered inventory of its system of convictions, and to this end it must establish before all else which belief is fundamental, decisive, sustaining and breathing life into all the others.

Now in order to determine the state of one's beliefs at a given moment the only method we possess is that of comparing this moment with one or more other moments. The more numerous the terms of comparison the more exact will be the result—another banal observation whose far-reaching consequences will emerge suddenly at the end of this meditation.

II

A comparison of the state of beliefs in which the European finds himself to-day with that obtaining a mere thirty years ago makes it clear that this has changed profoundly, because the fundamental conviction has changed.

The generation that flourished about the year 1900 was the last of a very long cycle, a cycle which began towards the end of the sixteenth century and was characterized by the fact that men lived on their faith in reason. In what does this faith consist?

If we open the *Discours de la Méthode*, the classical programme of the new age, we find that it culminates in the following sentences:

'Ces longues chaînes de raisons, toutes simples et faciles, dont les géomètres ont coutume de se servir pour parvenir à leurs plus difficiles démonstrations, m'avaient donné occasion de m'imaginer que toutes les choses qui peuvent tomber sous la connaissance des hommes s'entresuivent en même façon, et que, pourvu seulement qu'on s'abstienne d'en recevoir aucune pour vraie qui ne le soit, et qu'on garde toujours l'ordre qu'il faut pour les déduire les unes des autres, *il n'y en peut avoir de si éloignées auxquelles enfin on ne parvienne, ni de si cachées qu'on ne découvre.*'[1]

These words are the cockcrow of rationalism, the moving reveille that ushers in a whole new age, our so-called modern age, that modern age whose death agony, whose swan-song, as it seems to many, we are to-day witnessing.

There is at least no denying that between the Cartesian

[1] *Œuvres*, ed. Adam et Tannery, vi, p. 19.

attitude of mind and our own no slight difference exists. What joy, what a tone of vigorous challenge to the universe, what an early-morning presumptuousness these magnificent words of Descartes reveal! The reader has observed: apart from the divine mysteries which his courtesy bids him leave on one side, to this man there is no problem that cannot be solved. He assures us that in the universe there are no arcana, no unconquerable secrets before which humanity must halt in defenceless terror. The world that surrounds man all about, existence within which constitutes his life, is to become transparent, even to its farthest recesses, to the human mind. At last man is to know the truth about everything. It suffices that he should not lose heart at the complexity of the problems, and that he should allow no passion to cloud his mind. If with serene self-mastery he uses the apparatus of his intellect, if in particular he uses it in orderly fashion, he will find that his faculty of thought is *ratio*, reason, and that in reason he possesses the almost magic power of reducing everything to clarity, of turning what is most opaque to crystal, penetrating it by analysis until it is become self-evident. According to this the world of reality and the world of thought are each a cosmos corresponding one to the other, each compact and continuous, wherein nothing is abrupt, isolated, or inaccessible, but rather such that from any point in it we may without intermission and without leaping pass to all other points and contemplate the whole. Man with his reason may thus plunge tranquilly into the abysmal depths of the universe, certain of extracting from the remotest problem, from the closest enigma, the essence of its truth, even as the Coromandel diver plunges into the deeps of ocean to reappear straightway bearing between his teeth the pearl of great price.

In the closing years of the sixteenth century and these early years of the seventeenth in which Descartes is meditating western man believes, then, that the world possesses a rational structure, that is to say, that reality possesses an organization coincident with the organization of the human intellect, taking this, of course, in its purest form, that of mathematical reason. Here accordingly is a marvellous key giving man a power over things around him that is theoretically illimitable. Such a discovery was a pretty stroke of fortune. For suppose that Europe had not then come by this belief. In the fifteenth century it had lost its faith in God, in revelation, either because man had completely lost that faith or because it had ceased to be in him a living faith. Theologians make a very shrewd distinction, one capable of throwing light on not a few things of to-day, between a live and a sluggish faith. Generalizing this, I should formulate it thus: we believe in something with a live faith when that belief is sufficient for us to live by, and we believe in something with a dead, a sluggish faith when, without having abandoned it, being still grounded on it, it no longer acts efficaciously on our lives. It is become a drag, a dead-weight; still part of us, yet useless as lumber in the attic of the soul. We no longer rest our existence on that something believed in; the stimuli, the pointers we live by no longer spring spontaneously from that faith. The proof is that we are constantly forgetting we still believe in it, whereas a living faith is the constant and most active presence of the entity we believe in. (Hence the perfectly natural phenomenon that the mystic calls 'the presence of God'. For a living love is likewise distinguished from a lifeless, dragging love in this, that the object loved is present to us without need of trance or fear of eclipse. We do not need to go in search of it with our attention; on the contrary we have difficulty in removing it from before our inner eye. And this is not to say that we are always nor even frequently *thinking* about it, but simply that we constantly 'count on it'.) An illustration of this difference in the present situation of the European I shall shortly adduce.[1]

Throughout the Middle Ages the European had lived on revelation. Lacking it, limited to his own naked strength, he would have felt incapable of dealing with the mysterious surroundings that made up his world, with the misfortunes and trials of existence. But he believed with a living faith that an all-powerful, all-knowing being would unfold to him gratuitously all that was essential to his life. We may follow the vicissitudes of this faith and witness, almost generation by generation, its progressive decay. It is a melancholy story. Gradually the living faith ceases to take nutriment, loses its colour, becomes paralysed, until, from whatever motives—these lie outside my present inquiry—towards the middle of the fifteenth century that living faith is clearly seen to have changed to a tired, ineffective faith, if indeed the individual soul has not uprooted it entirely. The man of that age begins to perceive

[1] In his book *On Liberty*, chap. ii, Stuart Mill makes very opportune use of this same distinction, expressed in the same terms of 'living faith' and 'dead, inert faith'.

that revelation does not suffice to illumine his relations to the world; once more he is conscious of being lost in the trackless forest of the universe, face to face with which he lacks alike a guide and a mediator. The fifteenth and the sixteenth centuries are, therefore, two centuries of tremendous restlessness, of fierce disquiet, two centuries, as we should say to-day, of crisis. From this crisis western man is saved by a new faith, a new belief: faith in reason, in the *nuove scienze*. Man, having again fallen, is born again. The Renaissance is the parturient disquiet of a new confidence based on physico-mathematical science, the new mediator between man and the world.

III

Beliefs constitute the basic stratum, that which lies deepest, in the architecture of our life. By them we live, and by the same token we rarely think of them. Whatever is still to us more or less in debate, that we think of. Hence we say that we *hold* such and such ideas, whereas rather than holding our beliefs we are them.

One may symbolize the individual life as a bank of issue. The bank lives on the credit of a gold reserve which is rarely seen, which lies at the bottom of metal coffers hidden in the vaults of the building. The most elementary caution will suggest that from time to time the effective condition of these guarantees—of these *credences*, one might say, that are the basis of *credit*—be passed in review.

To-day it is become urgent that we should do the same with the faith in reason by which the European, obedient to tradition—a tradition of close on three centuries—has been living. It may be said that until twenty years ago the state of this belief had not suffered modification in its general outline, but that in the last few years it has changed most profoundly. So much is demonstrated by innumerable facts, facts that are only too well known and that it would be depressing to enunciate once more.

It will be superfluous to point out that in speaking of the traditional faith in reason and of its present-day modification I am not referring to what happens in this or that individual as such. Apart from what individuals as individuals, that is to say, each for himself and on his own account, may believe, there exists always a collective state of belief. This social faith may or may not coincide with that felt by such and such an individual. The decisive factor in the matter is that whatever may be the private belief of each one of us we are confronted with a state of faith collectively constituted and established, a faith, in short, that is socially operative.

The faith in science to which I refer was not merely and firstly an individual opinion. It was on the contrary a collective opinion, and when something is a collective or social opinion it is a reality independent of individuals, outside them as stones are outside the landscape, a reality with which individuals must reckon willy-nilly. Our personal opinion may run counter to social opinion, but this will not invalidate one iota the reality of the latter. What constitutes and gives a specific character to collective opinion is the fact that its existence does not depend on its acceptance or rejection by any given individual. From the view-point of each individual life public belief has, as it were, the appearance of a physical object. The tangible reality, so to speak, of collective belief does not consist in its acceptance by you or by me; instead it is it which, whether we acquiesce or not, imposes on us its reality and forces us to reckon with it. To this characteristic of social faith I apply the term 'operative'. A law is said to be operative when, far from its effectiveness hingeing on my recognition of it, it acts and functions independently of my adhesion. And in like manner collective belief has no need of my belief in it as a particular individual in order to exist and weigh upon me and even, perchance, crush me. If now it be agreed, for our better understanding, to apply the term 'social dogma' to the content of a collective belief, we are in a position to continue our meditation.

When, equipped with these instrumental concepts, we compare the situation in which the European found himself about the year 1910 with that of to-day, the perception of the change, the mutation, that has occurred ought to cause in us a salutary terror. A mere twenty years, that is to say only a portion of a man's life, in itself so short, have sufficed to invert the order of things to the point that, whereas then one might in any part of Europe have invoked faith in science and the rights of science as the maximum human value, and this urge functioned automatically, the social body accepting in all docility its imperative and reacting thereto with efficacy, energy, and promptitude, to-day there are already nations where such an invocation would provoke only smiles—nations that some years ago were considered precisely as being in the van of science—and I do not believe there is any, at the time of writing, in which it would call forth even a throb from the social body.

IV

Science is in danger. In saying this I do not think I exaggerate. For this is not to say that Europe collectively has made a radical end of its belief in science, but only that its faith, once living, is in our day become sluggish. This is sufficient to cause science to be in danger and to make it impossible for the scientist to go on living as he has lived till now, sleep-walking at his work, believing that the society around him still supports, sustains, and venerates him. What has happened to bring about such a situation? Science to-day knows with incredible precision much of what is happening on remote stars and galaxies. Science is rightly proud of the fact, and because of it, although with less right, it spreads its peacock feathers at academic gatherings. But meanwhile it has come about that this same science, once a living social faith, is now almost looked down upon by society in general. And although this has not happened on Sirius but only on our own planet, it is not, I conceive, bereft of importance. Science cannot be merely science about Sirius; it claims also to be science about man. What then has science, reason, got to say to-day, with reasonable precision, concerning this so urgent fact that so intimately concerns it? Just nothing. Science has no clear knowledge on the matter. One perceives the enormity of the position, the shame of it. The upshot is that, where great human changes are concerned, science, strictly so called, has got nothing exact to say. The thing is so enormous that it straightway reveals to us the reason. For it causes us to note that the science, the reason, in which modern man placed his social faith is, speaking strictly, merely physico-mathematical science together with biological science, the latter based directly on the former and benefiting, in its weakness, from the other's prestige—in short, summing both up together, what is called natural science or reason.

The present position of physical science or reason is in consequence somewhat paradoxical. If there is anything in the repertory of human activities and pursuits that has not proved a failure, it is precisely this science, when one considers it circumscribed within its genuine territory, nature. Within this order and ambit, far from having failed, it has transcended all our hopes. For the first time in history the powers of realization, of achievement, have outstripped those of mere fantasy. Science has achieved things that irresponsible imaginings had never so much as dreamed of. This is so unquestionable that one has difficulty in understanding straightway why man is not to-day on his knees before science as before some magic power. The fact remains that he is not on his knees; on the contrary he is beginning to turn his back. He does not deny, he is not unaware of, its marvellous power, its triumph over nature, but he realizes at the same time that nature is only one dimension of human life and that a resounding success with regard to nature does not preclude failure with regard to the totality of our existence. Life at any instant is an inexorable balance, in which 'physical reason' (*la razón física*) for all its partial splendour does not rule out the possibility of a heavy deficit. Even more, the lack of equilibrium between the perfection of its partial efficiency and its failure from the comprehensive point of view, which is final, is such in my opinion that it has contributed to the aggravation of our universal disquiet.

Man thus finds himself, when confronted with physical reason, in a state of mind comparable to that of Cristina of Sweden, as described by Leibniz, when, after her abdication, she caused a coin to be struck bearing the effigy of a crown and had these words inscribed in the exergue: *Non mi bisogna e non mi basta.*

In the upshot the paradox resolves itself into a supremely simple observation. What has not collapsed in physics is physics. What has collapsed in it is the rhetoric, the trimmings of childish presumption, of irrational and arbitrary additions it gave rise to, what, many years ago, I styled 'the terrorism of the laboratory'. This is why ever since I began to write I have combated what I called scientific *Utopianism.* Open, for example, *El tema de nuestro tiempo* at the chapter entitled 'The historic sense of Einstein's theory', written about 1921. There the following passage will be found:

'It is incomprehensible that science, whose only pleasure lies in attaining to a true image of things, should nourish itself on illusions. I recall a detail whose influence on my thought was decisive. Many years ago I was reading a lecture of the physiologist Loeb on tropism. The tropism is a concept which has been invoked to describe and throw light on the law governing the elemental movements of the Infusoria. The concept serves, indifferently well and with corrections and additions, to help us understand some of these phenomena. But at the close of this lecture Loeb adds: "The day will come when what we now call moral acts in man will be explained simply as tropisms." Such temerity perturbed me exceedingly, for it opened my eyes to many other judgements of modern science that are guilty, if less ostentatiously, of the same error. So then, I thought, a concept like the tropism, which is scarce capable of plumbing the secret of phenomena so simple as the antics of the Infusoria, may at some vague future date suffice to explain phenomena as mysterious and complex as man's ethical acts! What sense is there here? Science has to solve its problems in the present, not transport us to the Greek kalends. If its present methods are insufficient to master now the enigmas of the universe, discretion would suggest that they be replaced by other and more effective ones. But the science *à la mode* is full of problems which are left intact because they are incompatible with its methods. As if it was the former that were under obligation to subordinate themselves to the latter, and not the other way round! Science is full of achronisms, of Greek kalends.

When we emerge from a science so devoutly simple, bowing in idolatrous worship before pre-established methods, and approach the thought of Einstein there comes upon us as it were a fresh morning breeze. Einstein's attitude is radically different from that of tradition. With the dash of a young athlete we see him make straight for his problems and take them by the horns, using the method that lies nearest to his hand. Out of the apparent defects and limitations of science he draws virtue and tactical efficiency.'

From this idea of the Greek kalends all my philosophic thought has emanated. There in germ is my whole conception of life as the basic reality and of knowledge as an internal—and not an independent or Utopian—function of life. Just as Einstein was then telling us that in physics it is necessary to elaborate concepts such as will make perpetual motion impossible (perpetual motion is immeasurable and before what cannot be measured physics is impotent), I considered it essential to elaborate a philosophy that should take its point of departure, its formal principle, from the exclusion of the Greek kalends. Because life is the opposite of these kalends. Life is haste and has urgent need to know what it is up against, and it is out of this urgency that truth must derive its method. The idea of progress, placing truth in a vague to-morrow, has proved a dulling opiate to humanity. Truth is what is true now and not what remains to be discovered in an undetermined future. Herr Loeb—and his whole generation is with him—gives up his claim to a present truth of morality on the strength of the future attaining to a physics of morality: a curious way of existing at the expense of posterity while leaving one's own life shorn of foundations, of roots, of any profound implications in the scheme of things. The viciousness of this attitude is so radical that it appears already in the 'provisional morality' of Descartes. And so it happens that the first blow directed against the superficial framework of our civilization, our economics, our morals, our politics, finds man possessed of no truths of his own, of no clear, firm position on anything of importance.

The only thing he believed in was physical science, and when this received the urgent call to propound its truth on the most human problems, it did not know what to say. And suddenly western man has received the impression of losing his footing, of finding himself without support, and has known a panic terror and believed himself to be sinking, making shipwreck in the void.

And yet, a measure of serenity is all that is needed for our feet once more to experience the delicious sensation of touching hard, solid mother earth, an element capable of sustaining man. As always, it is essential—and sufficient—instead of giving way to panic and losing one's head, to convert into a source of support the very factor that had engendered the impression of an abyss. Physical science can throw no clear light on the human element. Very well. This means simply that we must shake ourselves free, radically free, from the physical, the natural, approach to the human element. Let us instead accept this in all its spontaneity, just as we see it and come upon it. In other words, the collapse of physical reason leaves the way clear for vital, historical reason.[1]

V

Nature is a thing, a great thing, that is composed of many lesser things. Now, whatever be the differences between things, they all have one basic feature in common, which consists simply in the fact that things *are*, they have their being. And this

[1] The form I first gave to this thought, in my youth, may be found in *El tema de nuestro tiempo*, 1923 (English translation by James Cleugh, 1932).

signifies not only that they exist, that there they are, in front of us, but also that they possess a given, fixed structure or consistency. Given a stone, there exists forthwith, for all to see, what a stone is. Its every change and mutation, world without end, will be in specific combinations of its fundamental consistency. The stone can never be something new and different. This consistency, given and fixed once and for all, is what we customarily understand when we speak of the being of a thing. An alternative expression is the word 'nature'. And the task of natural science is to penetrate beneath changing appearances to that permanent nature or texture.

When naturalist reason studies man it seeks, in consistence with itself, to reveal his nature. It observes that man has a body, which is a thing, and hastens to submit it to physics; and since this body is also an organism, it hands it over to biology. It observes further that in man as in animals there functions a certain mechanism incorporeally, confusedly attached to the body, the psychic mechanism, which is also a thing, and entrusts its study to psychology, a natural science. But the fact is that this has been going on for three hundred years and that all the naturalist studies on man's body and soul put together have not been of the slightest use in throwing light on any of our most strictly human feelings, on what each individual calls his own life, that life which, intermingling with others, forms societies, that in their turn, persisting, make up human destiny. The prodigious achievement of natural science in the direction of the knowledge of things contrasts brutally with the collapse of this same natural science when faced with the strictly human element. The human element escapes physico-mathematical reason as water runs from a sieve.

And here we have the explanation why our faith in reason has entered upon a phase of lamentable decadence. Man cannot wait any longer. He demands that science illumine for him the problems of humanity. At bottom he is somewhat tired by now of stars and nervous reactions and atoms. The earliest generations of rationalists believed that with their physical science they could throw light on human destiny. Descartes himself wrote a treatise *De homine*. To-day we know that all the marvels of the natural sciences, inexhaustible though they be in principle, must always come to a full stop before the strange reality of human life. Why? If all things have given up a large part of their secret to physical science, why does this alone hold out so stoutly? The explanation must go deep, down to the roots. Perchance it is no less than this: that man is not a thing, that it is false to talk of human nature, that man has no nature. I conceive that a physicist, on hearing this, may well feel his hair stand on end, since it signifies, in other words, an assertion that physics is radically incompetent to speak of man. But it is useless to shelter behind illusions: whether our consciousness of this be clear or not so clear, whether we suspect or not the existence of another mode of knowledge, another reason capable of speaking of man, the conviction of this incompetence is to-day a fact of the first magnitude on the European horizon. Physicists in the presence of it may feel irritated or pained—although both attitudes may here seem somewhat puerile—but this conviction is the historical precipitate of three centuries of failure.

Human life, it would appear then, is not a thing, has not a nature, and in consequence we must make up our minds to think of it in terms of categories and concepts that will be *radically* different from such as shed light on the phenomena of matter. The enterprise is no easy one, since for the last three centuries 'physicism' has accustomed us to leaving behind us, as an entity having neither importance nor reality, precisely this strange reality of human life. And so, while the naturalists devoted themselves with pious absorption to their professional tasks, the whim has taken this strange reality to veer to another point of the compass, and on enthusiasm for science there have followed lukewarmness and aversion. To-morrow, who knows, it may be frank hostility.

VI

It will be said that the more patent became the resistance of the human phenomenon to physical science, the more prominent became another form of science opposed to this: against the natural sciences, in effect, there arose and developed the so-called sciences of the spirit, the moral or cultural sciences. To this I reply, to begin with, that these sciences of the spirit, *Geisteswissenschaften*, have not so far been successful in moving the European to belief in the way that the natural sciences were.

And this is easily understood. The representatives of the spiritual sciences were combating the avowed intent of the others to investigate the human element by means of naturalistic ideas; but it happens that the spiritual sciences have in fact represented so far no more than a disguised attempt to do the same. Let me explain.

Geist? Wer ist der Bursche? asked Schopenhauer, with an ill-humoured insolence that was not lacking in common sense. This great Utopian concept of the spirit sought to oppose itself to nature. One felt intuitively that nature was not the only reality, and above all, that it was not the primary or fundamental one. The more one got to grips with it, the more it appeared to depend on the human element. German idealism, like the positivism of Comte, signifies the attempt to place man before nature. It was the former that gave man, in so far as he is not nature, the name *Geist*, spirit.

But it happened that in the effort to comprehend the human element as a spiritual reality things did not go any better: human phenomena showed the same resistance, the same stubborn reluctance to let themselves be hemmed in by concepts. Further, it was a privilege reserved to the thought of that age to indulge in the most scandalous and irresponsible Utopias. One readily appreciates Schopenhauer's ill-humour and insolence. Hegel's *Philosophy of History* and Comte's 'law of the three estates' are, beyond a doubt, two works of genius. In affixing to them this qualification of genius, however, all we are clearly doing is to applaud a man's magnificent dexterity as such, to applaud him for his agility, for what he has of the juggler or the athlete. If we study these works, chiefly Hegel's, from the decisive point of view, that of intellectual responsibility, and consider them as symptomatic of a moral climate, we soon perceive that they would have been impossible, *ceteris paribus*, in any normal epoch of thought, in any age of restraint, proportion, and sensitive respect for the function of the intellect.

I am bold to say this solely as an extrinsic indication of the fact that the interpretation of man as a spiritual reality could not but be violent, arbitrary, and a failure. Because in this context it is not permissible to continue using the word 'spirit' vaguely; it must needs be referred to the cycle of exact meanings it has borne in the philosophy of the past two centuries.

If now we ask why the concept of spirit has shown itself insufficient to explain the human element we are led to the following fundamental consideration.

When the knights-errant of the spirit sallied forth to wage war on naturalism, determined to give a scrupulous representation of human phenomena in their genuine essence and putting far from them the concepts and categories that nature imposes on our thinking, they did not take heed that, as they set out, they had already left the enemy behind. In nature they saw only certain peculiar attributes, spatiality, force, their sensorial manifestation, and the like, and they believed it sufficient to replace these by other antagonistic attributes, *cogitatio*, consciousness, apperception, and the like, in order to place themselves outside nature. In short, they were guilty of the same mistake Descartes made when he held it enough, in order to define the self, to oppose it as a *res cogitans* to the *res extensa*. But can the fundamental difference between that strange reality, man, the *ego*, and that other reality, things, consist in the fact that the *ego* thinks while things have extent? What difficulty would there be in the *res* that thinks having extent and the *res* that has extent thinking? Descartes is wont to add, astutely, that the *res* that thinks has no extent and the *res* that has extent does not think. But this denial, coming as an afterthought, is wholly arbitrary, and Spinoza, who was not easily imposed upon, calmly draws the inference that one and the same *res*—*Natura sive Deus*—thinks and has extent. To compose the issue it would be necessary to do what Descartes did not do, to wit, to ask oneself what is this *res* business, what is its structure, before proceeding to classify it as thinking or as having extent. For if the attributes of *cogitatio* and *extensio* are in such wise antagonistic that they cannot coexist in the same *res*, the suspicion arises that each of them must react on the very structure of the *res* as *res*. Or, which comes to the same thing, that the term *res* is equivocal in both expressions.

Now, the concept *res* had already been established by traditional ontology. The error made by Descartes and by the knights-errant of the spirit lay in not carrying down to bedrock their reform of philosophy, in applying unthinkingly to the new reality they aspired to establish—*pensée*, *Geist*—the old doctrine of being. Can an entity that consists in thinking have *being* in the same sense as one that consists in having extent has *being*? Apart from the difference implied in the fact that one thinks while the other has extent, are they not differentiated also in their very being, as entities *sensu stricto*?

In traditional ontology the term *res* is always linked with the term *natura*, whether as a synonym or in the sense that *natura* is the real *res*, the beginning of *res*. The concept of nature we know to be of pure Greek descent: it is first stabilized in Aristotle, then, modified by the Stoics, it comes into the Renaissance, and through that mighty portal inundates the modern age. In Robert Boyle it finds the expression that still holds: '*natura* is the rule or system of rules according to which phenomena behave—in short, their law.'[1]

To go back over the history of the concept of nature is not possible here, and any summary of it must be futile. For the sake of brevity I shall content myself with a single allusion: is it not surprising that the term 'nature' should have come, with unbroken continuity, from meaning what it meant to Aristotle to mean the law of phenomena? Is not the distance between the two meanings enormous? That distance, be it noted, implies nothing less than the whole change in our way of thinking of the universe from ancient to modern man. What then, down this long evolution, has remained constant in the concept of nature?

There are few themes in which one may see so clearly as here the extent to which European man is heir to the Greek. Inheritance, however, is not only treasure; it is, at the same time, a charge and a bond. Concealed in the concept of nature we have received the bonds that make us the slaves of Hellenic destiny.

Greek thought is formulated in Parmenides. Parmenides represents beyond question the pure essence of Hellenism, for it is a fact that Eleaticism has always held sway in Hellenic minds. What was not Eleaticism, simple or compound, was merely opposition. This Greek destiny continues to weigh on us, and in spite of some notable rebellions we are still prisoners within the magic circle described by Eleatic ontology.

Ever since Parmenides, the orthodox thinker in search of an object's being holds that he is searching for a fixed, static consistency,[2] hence something that the entity *already* is, which already composes or constitutes it. The prototype of this mode of being, possessed of the characteristics of fixity, stability, and actuality (a being *already* what it is), was the being of mathe-

[1] Cassirer, *Das Erkenntnisproblem in der Philosophie und Wissenschaft der neueren Zeit*, ii. 433.

[2] Alongside the term *existence* I use that of *consistency*. The entity that *exists* has a consistency, that is to say, it *consists of* something or other.

matical concepts and objects, an invariable being, a being-always-the-same. Since observation showed that the things in the world around were changeable, were 'movement', he begins by denying their reality. Aristotle, more prudent, renounces such absolutism and adopts a solution of the *juste milieu.* In the changeable object he seeks that which in the midst of change does not vary, that which in its movement remains motionless. This accordingly is what he called the 'nature' of things, that which in the real object *appears* to shrink from having a being similar to the being of mathematical concepts and objects. The φύσις was the invariable principle of variations. In this way it became possible to retain the fundamental Eleatism of being and yet to conceive as realities those objects which in the eyes of absolute Eleaticism lacked authentic reality, οὐσία. The idea of time, interposing itself between the invariable οὐσία and the diverse states of the object served as bridge between the latent unity of being and its apparent multiplicity. The *res* was thus conceived of as something possessing at heart—in its ἀρχή—the same ontological condition as the concept and the triangle: identity, radical invariability, stability—the profound tranquillity that the term *being* signified to the Greek.

The process that causes the *natura* of Aristotelianism to evolve into Boyle's stable rule or law of unstable phenomena, far from being a degeneration, is a purification of the original concept and as it were a sincere confession of it. Thus in Comte and Stuart Mill everything hangs as from a nail on 'the invariability of the laws of nature'. The nature of positivism is already pure and declared 'invariability', a being fixed, static . . . Eleatic.[1]

Now, in laying down as a condition of reality, before admitting it as such, that it should consist in an element of identity, Parmenides and the orthodox Greeks in general revealed their colossal arbitrariness. Into the origin of what I call sublime 'arbitrariness' I do not propose here to inquire, although the theme is one of infinite attractiveness. The word is an express concept, and the concept is a reality that is peculiar among realities in consisting of identity, one might say in being made of identity. When we speak of reality—*onto-logy*—we are under obligation to be faithful at once to the conditions of the

[1] I do not enter here into the question whether this is compatible with the relativism of Comte. This is a theme which I hope to develop in a forthcoming study on *The Unknown Comte.*

reality of which we are thinking and to the conditions of the thought with which we 'manipulate' the reality.

One can readily understand that philosophy, in its first phase, should have lacked the agility necessary to distinguish, in thinking of reality, between that element in the resulting thought that belonged to the intellect and that which belonged properly to the object. Until Kant, strictly speaking, no one had even begun to see clearly that thought is not a copy and mirror of reality but a transitive operation performed on it, a surgical intervention. Hence philosophy since Kant has embarked on what Plato would call its *δεύτερος πλοῦς*, its second voyage, its second apprenticeship. This rests on the observation that if there be possible a knowledge of authentic reality, *αὐτὸ τὸ ὄν* (and only philosophic knowledge claims to be such), it must consist in a duplicate thinking, a going and coming—that is to say, in a thinking that, having once thought something concerning reality, turns back on the thought and strips it of what is mere intellectual form, leaving only the intuition of reality in all its nakedness. This is fearsome, and paradoxical, but there is no other way out. In the formidable crusade for the liberation of man that constitutes the mission of the intellect there has come a moment when man needs to deliver himself from his most intimate slavery, to wit, from himself. It follows from this that, precisely because Kant has taught us that thought has its own forms and projects these on to the real, the end of the process initiated by him consists in uprooting from reality all those forms that are at once inevitable and foreign to it, and in learning to think with a mind ever on the alert, in an unceasing *modus ponendo tollens*. In short, we must learn to dis-intellectualize the real if we are to be faithful to it.

Eleatism was the radical intellectualization of being. It is this that constitutes the magic circle already referred to, that we so urgently need to rise above. In naturalism what prevents our conceiving of human phenomena, what veils them to our minds, is not the secondary attributes of things, *res*, but the very idea of *res* founded on identical being and, since identical, fixed, static, predetermined. Wherever this subtle attribute persists, there naturalism, invariable being, is still to be found. Naturalism is, at bottom, intellectualism, i.e. the projection on to the real of the mode of being peculiar to concepts. Let us renounce valiantly, joyously, this convenient presumption that the real is logical and recognize that thought alone is logical.[1] Even the mathematical object presents chasms of illogicality as tremendous as the 'labyrinth of the difficulties of continuity' and all the problems that inspired Brouwer's attempt to overthrow the *principium tertii exclusi*. To-day physics too has sprung a dramatic surprise on us with its states of indeterminateness of the atomic elements.

This article, I need not point out, is not a treatise, quite the contrary; it is a series of theses that are submitted without defence to the meditative fair play of the reader. I believe none the less that some meaning will now attach to my previous enigmatic assertion according to which the concept of spirit is a disguised naturalism and in consequence inoperative when faced with naturalistic conceptions, its presumed enemies.

Spirit, if it is anything in this world, is identity, and hence *res*, a thing—though as subtle and ethereal as you please. Spirit possesses a static consistency: it is already, to begin with, what it is going to be. The revolt of the human element against any conception of it as static was so obvious that soon, with Leibniz, there came the attempt to rise above the static by making spirit consist in dynamic activity.[2] A vain attempt, for that activity, like all activity, is always one and the same, fixed, prescribed, ontologically motionless! Hegel's movement of the spirit is a pure fiction, since it is a movement within the spirit, whose consistency lies in its fixed, static, pre-established truth. Now the entity whose being consists in identical being evidently possesses already, to begin with, all it needs in order to be. For this reason identical being is substantive being, substance, a being that suffices to itself, sufficient being. This is the *thing*. Spirit is no other than a thing. It appears indeed that other things are things in virtue of their materiality, their spatiality, their force. But all this would serve them in no stead if they were not also and previously identical, *that is to say, concepts*. The *proto*-thing, the *Urding*, is the intellect. It identi-fies, thing-ifies—*ver-dinglicht*—all the rest.

[1] Vide '"La Filosofía de la Historia" de Hegel y la historiología', *Revista de Occidente*, February, 1928.

[2] Only Fichte constitutes a case apart. One is aware that he touches the true being of life, but his intellectualism does not allow him to see what it is he is touching, and he is compelled forcibly to think Eleatically. Whence the pathetic resemblance to a blind traveller we see in Fichte as he journeys across the mountain ranges of metaphysics.

The knights-errant of the spirit have no right to the revulsion, that amusing Plotinian revulsion, they feel where nature is concerned. Because the profound error of naturalism is the reverse of what is supposed: it does not consist in our treating ideas as though they were corporeal realities, but on the contrary in our treating realities—corporeal or no—as if they were ideas, concepts, in short, identities.

When Heine, assuredly after reading Hegel, asked his coachman, 'What are ideas?' the answer he got was: 'Ideas? . . . Ideas are the things they put into your head.' But the fact is that we can say, more formally, that things are the ideas that come out of our heads and are taken by us as realities.

The need to rise above, to transcend the idea of nature comes precisely from this, that this idea can have no validity as an authentic reality: it is something relative to the human intellect, which in its turn has no detached, independent reality—herein lies the error of all idealism or 'spiritualism'—but is only real when functioning in a human life, by whose constitutive urgencies it is moved. Nature is a transitory interpretation that man has given to what he finds around him in life. To this then, as to a radical reality, including and preforming all others, we are referred.

Faced with this, what we are indeed now conscious of is a liberation from naturalism, because we have learnt to immunize ourselves from intellectualism and its Greek kalends. Here is the 'fact' previous to all facts, that which holds all others in solution and from which all flow: human life as it is lived by each one of us. *Hic Rhodus, hic salta.* Our need is to think on it with urgency, just as we behold it in all its primary nakedness, by the aid of concepts bent only on describing it and which admit no imperative whatever from traditional ontology.

That undertaking, needless to say, is not one that can be pursued within the bounds of the present article. My purpose here is limited to the suggestion of so much as is indispensable if my title—'History as a System'—is to have an exact meaning.

VII

Physico-mathematical reason, whether in its crude form of naturalism or in its beatific form of spiritualism, was in no state to confront human problems. By its very constitution it could do no other than search for man's nature. And, naturally, it did not find it. For man has no nature. Man is not his body, which is a thing, nor his soul, psyche, conscience, or spirit, which is also a thing. Man is no thing, but a drama—his life, a pure and universal happening which happens to each one of us and in which each one in his turn is nothing but happening. All things, be they what they may, are now mere interpretations which he exercises himself in giving to whatever he comes upon. Things he does not come upon: he poses or supposes them. What he comes upon are pure difficulties and pure facilities for existing. Existence itself is not presented to him ready-made, as it is to the stone; rather, shall we say, looping the loop begun in the opening words of this article, on coming up against the fact of his existence, on existence happening to him, all he comes up against, all that happens to him is the realization that he has no choice but to do something in order not to cease existing. This shows that the mode of being of life, even as simple existing, is not a *being already*, since the only thing that is given us and that *is* when there is human life is the having to make it, each one for himself.[1] Life is a gerundive, not a participle: a *faciendum*, not a *factum*. Life is a task. Life, in fact, sets us plenty of tasks. When the doctor, surprised at Fontenelle's having reached the age of a hundred in full health, asked him what he felt, the centenarian replied: *Rien, rien du tout . . . seulement une certaine difficulté d'être*. We ought to generalize and say that life always, and not only at a hundred, consists in *difficulté d'être*. Its mode of being is formally a being difficult, a being which consists in problematic toil. Compared with the sufficient being of the substance or thing, life is an indigent being, an entity which possesses, properly speaking, only needs, *Bedürfnisse*. The star, on the other hand, continues ever on the line of its orbit, asleep like a child in the cradle.

At every moment of my life there open before me divers possibilities: I can do this or that. If I do this, I shall be A the moment after; if I do that, I shall be B. At the present moment the reader may stop reading me or may go on. And, however

[1] Bergson, the least Eleatic of thinkers, whom we must allow to-day to have been right on so many points, constantly uses the expression *l'être en se faisant*. But a comparison of his sense with that which I here give to the same words shows a radical difference. In Bergson the term *se faisant* is merely a synonym of *devenir*. In my text *making oneself* is not merely *becoming* but in addition the way in which human reality *becomes*, which is the effective and literal *making oneself*, a *fabricating oneself*, we might say.

slight the importance of this article, according as he does the one or the other the reader will be A or will be B, will have made of himself an A or a B. Man is the entity that makes itself, an entity which traditional ontology only stumbled upon precisely as its course was drawing to a close, and which it in consequence gave up the attempt to understand: the *causa sui*. With this difference, that the *causa sui* had only to 'exert itself' in being the *cause* of itself and not in determining what *self* it was going to cause. It had, to begin with, a *self* previously determined and invariable, consistent, for example, to infinity.

But man must not only make himself: the weightiest thing he has to do is to determine *what* he is going to be. He is *causa sui* to the second power. By a coincidence that is not casual, the doctrine of the living being, when it seeks in tradition for concepts that are still more or less valid, finds only those which the doctrine of the divine being tried to formulate. If the reader has resolved now to go on reading into the next moment, it will be, in the last instance, because doing this is what is most in accordance with the general programme he has mapped out for his life, and hence with the man of determination he has resolved to be. This vital programme is the *ego* of each individual, his choice out of divers possibilities of being which at every instant open before him.[1]

Concerning these possibilities of being the following remarks fall to be made:

1. That they likewise are not presented to me. I must find them for myself, either on my own or through the medium of those of my fellows with whom my life brings me in contact. I invent projects of being and of doing in the light of circumstance. This alone I come upon, this alone is given me: circumstance.[2] It is too often forgotten that man is impossible without imagination, without the capacity to invent for himself a conception of life, to 'ideate' the character he is going to be. Whether he be original or a plagiarist, man is the novelist of himself.[3]

2. That among these possibilities I must choose. Hence, I am free. But, be it well understood, I am free *by compulsion*, whether

[1] Vide my *Goethe desde dentro*, 1932.

[2] Vide *Meditaciones del Quijote*, 1914. In this early book of mine it is already suggested that *I* am no more than one ingredient in that radical reality 'my life', whose other ingredient is circumstance.

[3] Be it recalled that the Stoics spoke of an 'imagining of oneself', φαντασία ἑαυτοῦ.

I wish to be or not. Freedom is not an activity pursued by an entity that, apart from and previous to such pursuit, is already possessed of a fixed being. To be free means to be lacking in constitutive identity, not to have subscribed to a determined being, to be able to be other than what one was, to be unable to instal oneself once and for all in any given being. The only attribute of the fixed, stable being in the free being is this constitutive instability.

In order to speak, then, of man's being we must first elaborate a non-Eleatic concept of being, as others have elaborated a non-Euclidean geometry. The time has come for the seed sown by Heraclitus to bring forth its mighty harvest.

Man is an infinitely plastic entity of which one may make what one will, precisely because of itself it is nothing save only the mere potentiality to be 'as you like'. Let the reader pass in review for a moment all the things that man has been—that is to say, that he has made of himself—and has then ceased to be—that is to say, has cast off from himself—from the palaeolithic 'savage' to the young *surréaliste* of Paris. I do not say that at any moment he may make of himself anything whatever. At each moment there open before him limited possibilities—what these limits are we shall see straightway. But if instead of one moment we take all moments, it is impossible to see what frontiers can be set to human plasticity. From the palaeolithic female there have issued Madame Pompadour and Lucile de Chateaubriand, from the indigene of Brazil, unable to count above five, have come Newton and Henri Poincaré. Lessening the distance in time, be it remembered that in 1873 the liberal Stuart Mill, in 1903 the most liberal Herbert Spencer, were still alive, and that already in 1921 Stalin and Mussolini are in power.

Meanwhile man's body and psyche, his *nature*, have experienced no change of importance to which these effective mutations may be clearly ascribed. What has taken place, on the contrary, is the 'substantial' change in the reality 'human life' implied by man's passing from the belief that he must exist in a world composed only of arbitrary wills to the belief that he must exist in a world where there are 'nature', invariable consistencies, identity, &c. Human life is thus not an entity that changes accidentally, rather the reverse: in it the 'substance' is precisely change, which means that it cannot be thought of

Eleatically as substance. Life being a 'drama' that happens, and the 'subject' to whom it happens being, not a thing apart from and previous to his drama, but a function of it, it follows that the 'substance' of the drama would be its argument. And if this varies, it means that the variation is 'substantial'.

Since the being of whatever is alive is a being always distinct from itself—in the terms of the schools, a being that is metaphysically and not only physically mobile—it must be thought of in concepts that annul their own inevitable identity. This is not so terrifying as it may appear at first sight, though it is a question that I cannot even touch the fringe of here. I would only recall to the reader, that I may not leave his mind adrift on an uncharted sea, that thought has a much greater capacity for avoiding itself than is commonly supposed. Thought is constitutively generous, it is the great altruist. It is capable of thinking what lies at the opposite extreme to thought. One example will suffice. There are concepts called by some 'occasional'; e.g. the concept 'here', the concept 'I', the concept 'this'. Such concepts or significations have a formal identity that serves precisely to guarantee the constitutive non-identity of the matter signified or thought of through them. All concepts that seek to think of the authentic reality, life, must be 'occasional' in this sense. There is nothing strange in this, since life is pure occasion. It is for this reason Cardinal Nicholas of Cusa calls man a *Deus occasionatus*, for, according to him, man once he is free is a creator like God inasmuch as he is a being creating its own entity. Unlike God, however, his creation is not absolute but is limited by the occasion. Whence, literally, what I am bold to affirm: that man makes himself in the light of circumstance, that he is a God as occasion offers, a 'second-hand God' (*un Dios de ocasión*).

Every concept, in Husserl's phrase, is a universal meaning (*allgemeine Bedeutung*). But whereas in other concepts the universality consists in the fact that when applying them to one singular case we must always think the *same* as when applying them to another singular case, in the occasional concept it functions precisely by inviting us never to think the *same* when we apply it. The supreme example is this very concept 'life' in the sense of human life. Its signification *qua* signification is, of course, identical, but what it signifies is something not merely singular, but unique. Life is the life of each one of us.

And here, for the sake of brevity, I may be allowed to interrupt these considerations and to refrain from dealing with the most obvious difficulties they give rise to.[1]

VIII

Yesterday I made the acquaintance of Hermione. She is a fascinating woman. Towards me she was deferential, insinuating. I think of making love to her, and of attempting to win her love in return. But can my authentic being, what I call *I*, consist in 'being Hermione's lover'? Scarcely have I conjured up my love for Hermione in the mind's eye with a measure of precision when I emphatically turn down such a project of being. Why? I can find no objection to raise against Hermione, only the fact is . . . that I am fifty, and at fifty, although the body may have retained all the elasticity of thirty and the psychic impulses have lost none of their vigour, I cannot now 'be Hermione's lover'. But why? The point is this, that being a man of years I have already had time to be the lover of Cidalisa and the lover of Arsinoe and the lover of Glykeia, and I know now what 'being a lover' is. I know its excellences, I know also its limitations. In short, I have experienced to the full that form of life that is called 'loving a woman', and, frankly, I have had enough. And so it happens that the 'cause' of my not being a lover to-morrow is precisely the fact that I have been one. If I had not been a lover, if I had not already experienced love to the full, I should be Hermione's lover.

Here, then, is a new dimension in this strange reality of life. Before us lie the diverse possibilities of being, but behind us lies what we have been. And what we have been acts negatively on what we can be. When I was a child I was a Christian; now I am one no longer. Does this mean, strictly speaking, that I do not go on being a Christian? The Christian I was, is he dead, annihilated? Of course not; of course I am still a Christian, but in the form of having been a Christian. Had I

[1] For example, whether two lives whose attributes were the same and, in consequence, indistinguishable, would not be the *same* life. The idea of life obliges us, in fact, to invert the Leibnizian principle and to speak of 'the discernibility of identities'. Or again, how, if life is unique, it is at the same time multiple, since we can speak of the lives of others, &c., &c. All these difficulties are engendered in the old intellectualist habits. The most interesting and fruitful of them consists in asking how it is that we 'define' life by means of general characteristics, saying that in all its possible cases it is this and this and this.

not known the experience of being a Christian, did I not have it behind me and go on being a Christian in this form of having been one, it is possible that, faced with the difficulties of life to-day, I might now resolve to be a Christian. And what has happened to me in this matter is happening to many Europeans, who *were* Christians either on their own account or vicariously, from the recollection of their forefathers. Who knows, if one got to the bottom of things, whether it might not be said that it is happening to everybody, including those who believe in all good faith that they still are Christians? That it is possible to be a Christian to-day, just like that, in the fullness of the term and without reservations, is not so very certain. And the same might be said about being 'a democrat', being 'a liberal', being '*ancien régime*', being 'feudal'.

If I do not make love to Hermione, if I do not turn Christian, accordingly, if the reality of my life at the moment is what it is, what it is going to be depends on what is commonly called 'experience of life'. This is a knowledge of what we have been that memory has preserved for us and that lies always to hand, accumulated in our to-day, in our actuality or reality. And it happens that this knowledge determines my life negatively in its 'real' aspect, in its being. And from this it follows that constitutively my life is experience of life. My fifty years signify an absolute reality, not because the body may be growing weak or the psyche losing its grip, things that do not always happen, but because at that age one has accumulated a longer living past, one has been more things and one 'has more experience'. The conclusion to be drawn from which is that man's being is irreversible, he is compelled ontologically always to advance on himself, and this not because a given instant of time cannot recur: on the contrary, time does not recur because man cannot go back to being what he has been.

But experience of life is not made up solely of my past, of the experiences that I personally have had. It is built up also of the past of my forbears, handed down to me by the society I live in. Society consists primarily in a repertory of usages, intellectual, moral, political, technical, of play and pleasure. Now, in order that a form of life—an opinion, a line of conduct—may become a usage, a thing of social validity, it is necessary, first, that time should elapse, and second, that the form in question should cease to be a spontaneous form of personal life. Usage is tardy in taking shape. Every usage is old. Expressed differently, society is, primarily, the past and, relatively to man, tardigrade. For the rest, the establishing of a new usage —a new 'public opinion' or 'collective belief', a new morality, a new form of government,—the determination of *what* at each moment society *is going to be*, depends on what it has been, just as in the individual life. Western societies are finding in the present political crisis that they cannot, without more ado, be 'liberal', 'democratic',' monarchical', 'feudal' or . . . 'Pharaonic', precisely because they have already been these things, either in themselves or from experience of how others have been them. In the 'political public opinion' of to-day, in the usage at present in force, an enormous amount of the past continues active; that opinion, that usage, is accordingly this past in the form of having been it.[1]

Let the reader simply take note of what happens to him when, faced with the great political problems of the day, he desires to take up an attitude. First there arises in his mind a certain form of government, let us say, authoritarianism. In it he sees, rightly, a means of surmounting some of the difficulties of the public situation. But if this solution is the first or one of the first to occur to him it is not by chance. It thrusts itself upon him precisely because it already lay there to his hand, because he did not need to invent it for himself. And it lay to his hand not merely as a project but as an experiment already made. The reader knows, from personal experience or from reference, that there have been absolute monarchies, Caesarisms, unipersonal or collective dictatorships. And he knows further that all these forms of authoritarianism, if they solve some difficulties, leave others unsolved and in fact bring new ones of their own. The reader is thus led to reject this solution

[1] I have already shown excessive temerity, and incurred excessive risk, in thus attacking at the gallop, like the Median warriors of old, the most fearsome themes of general ontology. Now that I have come to a point where, if I were to be moderately clear, it would be necessary to establish carefully the difference between so-called 'collective or social life' and personal life, I would ask permission to renounce emphatically any intention of so doing. Should the reader be moved to curiosity concerning my ideas on the matter or, in general, concerning the development of all that has preceded, he will find both set forth, as adequately as may be, in two books shortly to be published. In the first, under the title *El hombre y la gente*, I have tried faithfully to expound a sociology which does not, as in the past, avoid the truly basic problems. The second, *Sobre la razón viviente*, is an attempt at a *prima philosophia*.

and to essay another in his mind which will avoid the drawbacks of authoritarianism. But here the same thing happens over again, and so it goes on until he has exhausted all the obvious forms of government, those that lay already to his hand, those he knew about because they had already been tried. At the end of this intellectual journey through forms of government he finds that, if he is to be sincere and act with full conviction, there is only one he could accept: to wit, a new one, one different from any that has been before, one invented by himself. He must either invent a new being of the State himself—even though it be only a *new* authoritarianism or a *new* liberalism—or search around for some one who has invented such or who is capable of inventing it. Here, then, may be seen how in our present political attitude, in our political being, there persists all the past of mankind that is known to us. That past is past not because it happened to others but because it forms part of our present, of what we are in the form of having been, because, in short, it is *our* past. Life as a reality is absolute presence: we cannot say that *there is* anything unless it be present, of this moment. If, then, *there is* a past, it must be as something present, something active in us *now*. And, in effect, if we analyse what we are now, if we take the consistency of our present and hold it up against the light in order to reduce it to its component elements as the chemist or the physicist may an object, we find to our surprise that this life of ours that is always this, the life of this present, actual moment, is *composed* of what, personally or collectively, we have been. And if we speak of *being* in the traditional sense as a *being already* what one is, as a fixed, static, invariable and given being, we shall have to say that the only element of being, of 'nature', in man is what he has been. The past is man's moment of identity, his only element of the thing: nothing besides is inexorable and fatal. But, for the same reason, if man's only Eleatic being is what he has been, this means that his authentic being, what in effect he is—and not merely 'has been'—is distinct from the past, and consists precisely and formally in 'being what one has not been', in non-Eleatic being. And since we cannot hope ever to rid the term 'being' of its traditional static signification, we should be well advised to dispense with it. Man *is* not, he 'goes on being' this and that. The concept 'to go on being' is, however, absurd: under promise of something logical it turns out in the end to be completely irrational. The term we can apply, without absurdity, to 'going on being' is 'living'. Let us say, then, not that man *is*, but that he *lives*.

On the other hand, it is advisable to take due note of the strange mode of knowledge, of comprehension, represented by this analysis of what, concretely, our life, that of the present, is. In order to understand my conduct with regard to Hermione and to Christianity, or the reader's with regard to public problems, in order to discover the reason of our being or, what comes to the same thing, *why* we are as we are, what have we done? What was it that made us understand, *conceive*, our being? Simply the telling, the narrating that *formerly* I was the lover of this and that woman, that *formerly* I was a Christian, that the reader in himself or through others he has heard of was an absolutist, a Caesarist, a democrat, &c. In short, the reasoning, the *reason*, that throws light here consists in a narration. Alongside pure physico-mathematical reason there is, then, a narrative reason. To comprehend anything human, be it personal or collective, one must tell its history. This man, this nation does such a thing and is in such a manner, *because* formerly he or it did that other thing and was in such another manner. Life only takes on a measure of transparency in the light of *historical reason*.

The most disparate forms of being *happen* to man. To the despair of the intellectualist, *being* is in man mere *happening*, *happening to him*: it 'happens to him to be' a Stoic, a Christian, a rationalist, a vitalist. It happens to him to be the palaeolithic female and the Marquise de Pompadour, Jenghiz Khan and Stefan George, Pericles and Charles Chaplin. Man does not actively subscribe to any of these forms: he passes through them—he lives them—like Zeno's arrow, moving, in spite of Zeno, during the whole of its flight.

Man invents for himself a programme of life, a static form of being, that gives a satisfactory answer to the difficulties posed for him by circumstance. He essays this form of life, attempts to realize this imaginary character he has resolved to be. He embarks on the essay full of illusions and prosecutes the experiment with thoroughness. This means that he comes to *believe* deeply that this character is his real being. But meanwhile the experience has made apparent the shortcomings and limitations of the said programme of life. It does not solve all the difficulties, and it creates new ones of its own. When first seen it was full face, with the light shining upon it: hence the illusions, the enthusiasm, the delights believed in store. With the back view its inadequacy is straightway revealed. Man thinks out another programme of life. But this second programme is drawn up in the light, not only of circumstance, but also of the first. One aims at avoiding in the new project the drawbacks of the old. In the second, therefore, the first is still active; it is preserved in order to be avoided. Inexorably man shrinks from being what he was. On the second project of being, the second thorough experiment, there follows a third, forged in the light of the second and the first, and so on. Man 'goes on being' and 'unbeing'—living. He goes on accumulating being—the past; he goes on making for himself a being through his dialectical series of experiments. This is a dialectic not of logical but precisely of historical reason—the *Realdialektik* dreamt of somewhere in his papers by Dilthey, the writer to whom we owe more than to any one else concerning the idea of life, and who is, to my mind, the most important thinker of the second half of the nineteenth century.

In what does this dialectic that will not tolerate the facile anticipations of logical dialectic consist? This is what we have to find out on the basis of facts. We must know what is this series, what are its stages, and of what nature is the link between one and the next. Such a discovery is what would be called history were history to make this its objective, were it, that is to say, to convert itself into historical reason.

Here, then, awaiting our study, lies man's authentic 'being'—stretching the whole length of his past. Man is what has happened to him, what he has done. Other things might have happened to him or have been done by him, but what did in fact happen to him and was done by him, this constitutes a relentless trajectory of experiences that he carries on his back as the vagabond his bundle of all he possesses. Man is a substantial emigrant on a pilgrimage of being, and it is accordingly meaningless to set limits to what he is capable of being. In this initial illimitableness of possibilities that characterizes one who has no nature there stands out only one fixed, pre-established, and given line by which he may chart his course, only one limit: the past. The experiments already made with life narrow man's future. If we do not know what he is going to be, we know what he is not going to be. Man lives in view of the past.

Man, in a word, has no nature; what he has is . . . history. Expressed differently: what nature is to things, history, *res gestae*, is to man. Once again we become aware of the possible application of theological concepts to human reality. *Deus, cui hoc est natura quod fecerit* . . ., says St. Augustine.[1] Man, likewise, finds that he has no nature other than what he has himself done.

It is comic in the extreme that 'historicism' should be condemned because it produces or corroborates in us the consciousness that the human factor is changeable in its every direction, that in it there is nothing concrete that is stable. As if the stable being—the stone, for instance—were preferable to the unstable! 'Substantial' mutation is the condition on which an entity as such can be progressive, the condition on which its being may consist in progress. Now concerning man it must be said, not only that his being is variable, but also that his being grows and, in this sense, that it progresses. The error of the old doctrine of progress lay in affirming *a priori* that man progresses towards the better. That is something that can only be determined *a posteriori* by concrete historical reason: it is precisely the great discovery we await from this, since to it we look for the clarifying of human reality and, along with this, for light on the nature of the good, the bad, the better and the worse. But that our life does possess a simply progressive character, this we can affirm *a priori* with full evidence and with a surety very different from that which has led to the supposition of the improgressivity of nature, that is to say, the 'invariability of its laws'.[2] The same knowledge that discovers to us man's variation makes patent his progressive consistency. The European of to-day is not only different from what he was fifty years ago, his being now includes that of fifty years ago. The European of to-day finds himself without a living faith in science precisely *because* fifty years ago he did believe wholeheartedly in it. That faith that held sway half a century ago may now be defined with reasonable precision; were this done it would be seen that it was such *because* about 1800 the same faith in science wore a different profile, and so successively until we come to the year 1700 or thereabouts, at which date faith in reason is constituted as a 'collective belief', as something socially operative. (Earlier than 1700 faith in reason is an individual belief or the

[1] *De Genesi ad litteram*, vi, 13. 24 (*Patrologia Latina*, vol. xxxiv).

[2] I refer the reader to the last words of the note on p. 307.

belief of particular small groups that live submerged in societies where faith in God, if already more or less inert, yet continues operative.) In our present 'crisis', in our present doubt concerning reason, we find then included the whole of that earlier life. We are, that is to say, all those forms of faith in reason, and we are in addition the doubt engendered by that faith. We are other than the man of 1700, and we are more.

There is no cause, therefore, for weeping overmuch concerning the mutability of everything human. This is precisely our ontological privilege. Progress is only possible to one who is not linked to-day to what he was yesterday, who is not caught for ever in that being which is already, but can migrate from it into another. But this is not enough: it is not sufficient that man should be able to free himself from what he is already and take on a new form, as the serpent sloughs its skin and is left with another. Progress demands that this new form should rise above the old and to this end should preserve it and turn it to account, that it should take off from the old, climbing on its shoulders as a high temperature mounts on lower ones. To progress is to accumulate being, to store up reality. This increase of being, it is true, when referred only to the individual, might be interpreted naturalistically as the mere development or *enodatio* of an initial disposition. With the evolutionary thesis still unproved, whatever its probability, it can be said that the tiger of to-day is neither more nor less a tiger than was that of a thousand years ago: it is being a tiger for the first time, it is always a first tiger. But the human individual is not putting on humanity for the first time. To begin with, he finds around him, in his 'circumstance', other men and the society they give rise to. Hence his humanity, that which begins to develop in him, takes its point of departure from another, already developed, that has reached its culmination: in short, to his humanity he adds other humanities. He finds at birth a form of humanity, a mode of being a man, already forged, that he need not invent but may simply take over and set out from for his individual development. This does not begin for him—as for the tiger, which must always start again—at zero but at a positive quantity to which he adds his own growth. Man is not a first man, an eternal Adam: he is formally a second man, a third man, &c.

Mutable condition has thus its ontological virtue and grace, and invites one to recall Galileo's words: *I detrattori della corruttibilità meriterebber d'esser cangiati in statue.*

Let the reader reflect closely on his life, studying it against the light as one looks at a glass of water to study its Infusoria. If he asks himself why his life is thus and not otherwise, it will appear to him that not a few details had their origin in inscrutable chance. But he will find the broad lines of its reality perfectly comprehensible once he sees that he is thus because, in the last resort, the society—'collective man'—in which he lives is thus. And in its turn the mode of being of society will stand revealed, once there is discovered within it what that society was—what it believed, felt, preferred—at an earlier stage. That is to say that in his individual and fleeting to-day man will see, foreshortened, the whole of man's past still active and alive. For we can only throw light on yesterday by invoking the day before yesterday; and so with all yesterdays. History is a system, the system of human experiences linked in a single, inexorable chain. Hence nothing can be truly clear in history until everything is clear. We cannot properly understand what this 'rationalist' European is unless we know exactly what it was to be a Christian, nor what it was to be a Christian unless we know what it was to be a Stoic: and so the process goes on. And this systematism of *res gestae* becomes re-operative and potent in history as *cognitio rerum gestarum.* Every historic term whatsoever, to have exactness, must be determined as a function of all history, neither more nor less than each concept in Hegel's *Logic* has value only in respect of the niche left for it by the others.[1]

[1] A simple example will make clearer what I have sought, with extreme concision, to convey in these last few lines. In an excellent book recently published by Paul Hazard, *La Crise de la conscience européenne, 1680–1715*, the third chapter begins thus: '*L'Europe semblait être achevée. Chacun de ses peuples avait des caractères si bien connus, et si décidément marqués, qu'il suffisait de prononcer son nom pour que surgît une série d'adjectifs qui lui appartenaient en propre, comme on dit que la neige est blanche et le soleil brûlant.*'

This means that about the year 1700 one of the active ingredients of human life here in the West was the conviction felt by European peoples that they knew one another. Let us admit the facts, referred to by the author, whose collective enunciation forms this proposition. Is this enough to make the proposition true? For it happens that exactly the same proposition might be valid for the life of Europe to-day. Who can doubt, none the less, that the knowledge of one another that European peoples believe they possess to-day is something very different from that of two centuries ago? And different, be it clearly understood, not solely nor chiefly by its content, but in the certainty, the fullness, the daily presence and general sense it has for us. This means, however, that as an active factor in our

History is the systematic science of that radical reality, my life. It is therefore a science of the present in the most rigorous and actual sense of the word. Were it not a science of the present, where should we find that past that is commonly assigned to it as theme? The opposite—and customary—interpretation is equivalent to making of the past an abstract, unreal something lying lifeless just where it happened in time, whereas the past is in truth the live, active force that sustains our to-day. There is no *actio in distans.* The past is not yonder, at the date when it happened, but here, in me. The past is I—by which I mean, my life.

IX

Man stands in need of a new revelation. And whenever man feels himself in contact with a reality distinct from himself, there is always revelation. It does not matter what the reality be, provided it appear to us absolute reality and not a mere idea, presumption, or imagination of our own concerning a reality.

Physical reason was, in its day, a revelation. Astronomy previous to Kepler and Galileo was a mere play of ideas, and when one *believed* in any of the various systems then current or in such and such a modification of those systems, it was always a pseudo-

lives its reality is in consequence very different from the reality of two centuries ago. Hence Hazard's proposition and the concept its terms express are inadequate, since they are equivocal. If they are valid for to-day, they are invalid for 1700. And if they are valid for both, they will be equally valid for 1500, for it is beyond question that then too the nations of Europe believed they knew one another. Now, in the measure in which a concept has validity for different epochs of humanity, it is an abstraction. Yet the conception that Hazard is trying to express is of an essentially concrete order, and it escapes through the abstract meshes of his proposition. Had this been thought in terms of the reality of 1500 and of that of 1900, for example, it is evident that it would have thrown much more light on what was in fact happening in 1700. In history there come in—and once it has resolutely constituted itself historical reason, there must come in still more—abstract concepts that are valid for whole ages and even for the whole of man's past. But this is a question of concepts whose object is also an abstract moment of reality, of the same degree of abstraction as themselves. In the measure of their abstractness they are clearly formal: they do not, in themselves, think anything real but demand to be made concrete. When therefore we say that they are valid for different ages, their validity is to be understood as one of forms requiring a content, as an instrumental validity; they do not describe 'historic forces'. An approximate analogy may be seen in geometrical concepts, which are valid for, but do not explain, physical phenomena, because they do not represent forces.

The need to think systematically in history has many corollaries, one of which is this, that it will have to increase substantially the number of its terms and concepts. Naturalists will not take this amiss if they reflect that they possess to-day some millions of concepts and terms to describe the vegetable and animal species.

belief that was at issue. One believed in this theory or in that as a theory. Its content was not reality but simply a 'saving of appearances'. Now the adhesion that a certain reasoning or combination of ideas commands in us does not go beyond these. Called forth by ideas as such, with them it ends. One believes that *within the sphere and play of ideas* these ideas are those best worked out, the strongest, the most subtle, but one does not on that account experience the devastating impression that in these ideas reality itself is breaking through, hence that they are not merely 'ideas' but pores opening in us through which there penetrates into our consciousness something ultramental, something transcendent throbbing fearfully directly beneath our touch.

Ideas represent, then, two very distinct roles in human life. At times they are *mere ideas*. Man is aware that, in spite of the subtlety and even the exactitude and logical rigour of his thoughts, these are no more than inventions of his own, in the last instance an intrahuman, subjective, and non-transcendent activity. The idea in this case is the opposition of a revelation—it is an invention. But at other times the idea *qua* idea disappears, converted into a pure mode of sensitive presence elected by an absolute reality. The idea now appears to us neither as an idea nor as our own. The transcendent reveals itself to us on its own account, invades and inundates us—and this is the revelation.[1]

For over a century now we have been using the word 'reason', giving to it a meaning that has become more and more degraded until to-day it signifies in effect the mere play of ideas. That is why faith appears as opposed to reason. We forget that at its birth in Greece, as at its rebirth in the sixteenth century, reason was not the play of ideas but a radical and tremendous conviction that in astronomic thought man was in indubitable contact with an absolute order of the cosmos, that through the medium of physical reason cosmic nature loosed within man its formidable and transcendent secret. Reason was, therefore, a faith. On this account, and on this account only—not in virtue of its other peculiar attributes and graces—it was able to wage war with the religious faith that till then had held the field. Vice versa, it has not been realized that religious faith is also reason, because of the narrow and fortuitous conception

[1] Vide the series of articles, 'Ideas y creencias', published in *La Nación*, Buenos Aires, for October and November, 1935.

one held of reason. It was claimed that reason did not pass beyond what took place in laboratories or the cabalism of the mathematicians. The claim as we see it to-day is ridiculous enough—one form, it might be called, out of a thousand intellectual provincialisms. The truth is that the specific characteristic of religious faith rests on a structure every bit as conceptual as dialectics or physics. It is a matter of profound surprise to me that there should not yet exist—that I am aware of—any exposition of Christianity as a pure system of ideas, expounded as one may expound Platonism, Kantianism, or positivism. Did such exist—and it would not be a difficult task—its relationship to all other theories as such would become evident, and religion would no longer seem so abruptly separated from ideology.

All the definitions of reason that made its essence consist in certain particular modes of setting the intellect in operation have not only been narrow, they have sterilized reason by amputating or devitalizing its decisive dimension. To me reason, in the true and rigorous sense of the word, is every such act of the intellect as brings us into contact with reality, every act by means of which we come upon the transcendent. The rest is nothing but . . . intellect, a mere homely exercise leading nowhere, that first amuses, then depraves, and finally causes man to despair and to despise himself.[1]

[1] To Descartes, it must not be forgotten, truth is that specific characteristic of thought in virtue of which this transcends itself and reveals to us a being, brings us into contact with something that is not itself. The criterion by which we may distinguish when, in effect, thought does transcend is immanent in thought itself, this being the only means we possess of arriving at being. But the immanence of the criterion is not to be confused with that of the characteristic, 'truth': the latter is not immanent, it is transcendence itself. '*La vérité étant une même chose avec l'être . . .*'

Contemporary subjectivism is idealism. It maintains that there is no reality transcending thought, that the only reality or being is thought itself. A thing 'has being' when we think of it as being—and hence that being is immanent in thought since it is very thinking. The consequence of this is to take away from the concept of reality as transcendence its primary, ingenuous, and sincere meaning. All reality is but thought reality, nothing more. On the other hand, it gives to everything thought a certain value as reality, as being, that it had not before. Before, the observation that something was only a thought implied that it had no reality whatever: it was *ens rationis*, the pseudo-entity. Thus: the mathematician to-day holds a theorem true when he believes he has succeeded in demonstrating that the ideas composing it, as ideas and solely to the extent that they are ideas, fulfil certain requirements. That is to say, he considers his mathematics to be effective knowledge although it may have no validity—and he himself may have no interest in whether or not it has such validity—for any extra-ideal reality. He holds, that is, as truth a thought directed to an imaginary or intra-ideal being. Now the

Hence the necessity in the present state of humanity to leave behind, as archaic fauna, the so-called 'intellectuals' and to set our course anew towards the man of reason, of revelation.

Man has need of a new revelation. He loses himself in the infinite arbitrariness of his inner cabalism when he cannot assay this and discipline it in the impact with something that smacks of authentic, relentless reality. Reality is man's only true pedagogue and ruler. Without its inexorable and sensitive presence culture, seriously speaking, does not exist, the State does not exist, even—and this is the most terrible of all—reality in his own personal life does not exist. When man is left, or believes himself left, alone with no reality other than his ideas to impose its stern limits on him, he loses the sensation of his own reality, he becomes to himself an imaginary, spectral, phantasmagoric entity. It is only under the formidable pressure of something transcendent that our person becomes compact and solid and we are enabled to discriminate between what, in effect, we are and what we merely imagine ourselves to be.

Now, physical reason by its very evolution, by its changes and vicissitudes, is come to a point where it recognizes itself as being mere intellect, if indeed as the highest form of this. To-day we are beginning to see that physics is a mental combination and nothing more. Physicists themselves have discovered the merely symbolic, that is to say, domestic, immanent,

Greeks, the thinkers of the Middle Ages, and Descartes himself would call such mathematics poetry—since poetry is a thinking imaginary entities. They would not call it 'knowledge'.

At the beginning of the century it was fashionable to forget this and to interpret Descartes arbitrarily, making of him an idealist. Descartes, it is true, prepares the way for idealism, but he is not yet an idealist himself. What gave rise to this erroneous interpretation is the fact that, purely because Descartes is not an idealist, purely because he does not suspect the idealist attitude, it never occurs to him to take precautions against such a failure to understand him. Be it recorded, then, that whenever Descartes speaks of 'truth' and of 'knowledge', he understands a thinking with the power to transcend itself, a thinking, that is to say, that poses a reality beyond thought, a reality outside itself. By mathematics he understands a science of realities, not of *entia rationis*, and by logic the same.

It is for this reason that Descartes, like Leibniz, who is already frankly half an idealist, cannot hold it sufficient to set out from a formal reality, that is, from one placed among ideas as such, but needs urgently a first truth in which formal truth, the truth set among ideas, shall be at the same time a real truth, valid for things, a truth, in a word, which will guarantee the transcendence of thought. Bordas-Demoulin was never more Cartesian than when he pointed out that the divine freedom, in creating truths and placing these in our spirit, appears to give to our knowledge the character of revelation. (Vide Hamelin, *Le Système de Descartes*, p. 233.)

intrahuman, character of their knowledge. In natural science these or those mutations may come about, Einstein's physics may give way to another, the quantum theory be followed by other theories, the electron conception of the structure of matter by other conceptions: no one looks for these modifications and advances ever to leap beyond their symbolic horizon. Physics brings us into contact with no transcendence. So-called nature, at least what the physicist examines under this name, turns out to be an apparatus of his own manufacture that he interposes between authentic reality and himself. And, correlatively, the physical world appears not as a reality but as a great machine ready to man's hand for him to manage and exploit. The faith that still attaches to physics to-day comes down to faith in the uses to which it can be put. What is real in it—and not mere idea—is only its utility.[1] That is why we have lost our fear of physics, and with fear our respect, and with respect our enthusiasm.

But whence, then, can there come to us this new revelation that man stands in need of?

Every disillusionment consequent on depriving man of faith in some reality on which he had set store brings into the foreground and permits the discovery of the reality of what remains to him, a reality that had previously escaped his attention. So the loss of faith in God leaves man alone with his nature, with what he has. Of this nature the intellect forms a part, and man, obliged to have recourse to it, forges for himself his faith in physico-mathematical reason. Now, having lost his faith—in the manner here described—in that reason also, man finds himself compelled to take his stand on the only thing still left to him, his disillusioned life. And here we see the reason why in our day we are beginning to discover the great reality of life as such, in which the intellect is no more than a simple function, and which possesses in consequence a more radical character of reality than all the worlds constructed by the intellect. We find ourselves, then, in a disposition that might be styled 'Cartesianism of life' and not of *cogitatio*.

Man asks himself, What is this solitary thing that remains to me—my life, my disillusioned life? How has it come to being

[1] It is not extravagant to see a resemblance between what physics means to man to-day and what the 'divinatio artificiosa' that Posidonius speaks of (vide Cicero, *De divinatione*, i) meant to the ancients.

nothing but this? And the answer is the discovery of man's trajectory, of the dialectical series of his experiences, which, I repeat, though it might have been different, has been what it has been, and which must be known because it is . . . *the* transcendent reality. Man set outside himself is brought up against himself as reality, as history. And, for the first time, he sees himself forced to a concern with his past, not from curiosity nor in the search for examples which may serve as norms, but because it is all he *has*. Things are never done seriously until the lack of them has been seriously felt. For this reason the present hour is the appointed time for history to re-establish itself as historical reason.

Until now history has been the contrary of reason. In Greece the two terms reason and history were opposed. And it is in fact the case that scarcely any one up till now has set himself to seek in history for its rational substance. At most, attempts have been made to impose on it a reason not its own, as when Hegel injected into history the formalism of his logic or Buckle his physiological and physical reason. My purpose is the exact reverse: to discover in history itself its original, autochthonous reason. Hence the expression 'historical reason' must be understood in all the rigour of the term: not an extra-historical reason which appears to be fulfilled in history but, literally, *a substantive reason constituted by what has happened to man*, the revelation of a reality transcending man's theories and which is himself, the self underlying his theories.

Until now what we have had of reason has not been historical and what we have had of history has not been rational.

Historical reason is, then, *ratio*, *logos*, a rigorous concept. It is desirable that there should not arise the slightest doubt about this. In opposing it to physico-mathematical reason there is no question of granting a licence to irrationalism. On the contrary, historical reason is still more rational than physical reason, more rigorous, more exigent. Physical reason does not claim to understand what it is that it is talking about. It goes farther, and makes of this ascetic renunciation its formal method, the result being that the term 'understanding' takes on a paradoxical sense against which Socrates already protested in the *Phaedo* when describing to us his intellectual education. The protest has been repeated by every subsequent philosopher down to the establishment of empirical rationalism at the end of the seventeenth century. We can understand in physics the analytical operation it performs in reducing complex facts to a repertory of simpler facts. But these elemental, basic facts of physics are unintelligible. Impact conveys exactly nothing to intellection. And this is inevitable since it is a fact. Historical reason, on the contrary, accepts nothing as a mere fact: it makes every fact fluid in the *fieri* whence it comes, it *sees* how the fact takes place. It does not believe it is throwing light on human phenomena by reducing them to a repertory of instincts and 'faculties'—which would, in effect, be crude facts comparable to impact and attraction. Instead it shows what man does with these instincts and faculties and even expounds to us how these facts—the instincts and faculties—have come about: they are, of course, nothing more than ideas—interpretations—that man has manufactured at a given juncture of his life.

In 1844 Auguste Comte wrote: 'On peut assurer aujourd'hui que la doctrine qui aura suffisamment expliqué l'ensemble du passé obtiendra inévitablement, par suite de cette seule épreuve, la présidence mentale de l'avenir.' (*Discours sur l'esprit positif*, ed. Schleicher, p. 63.)

Translated by Professor William C. Atkinson, University of Glasgow.

THE PHILOSOPHIC CHARACTER OF HISTORY

By RAYMOND KLIBANSKY

I

THE increasing predominance of the dividing forces of Understanding over the unifying forces of Faith brought about a loosening of the strict hierarchy of all provinces of thought, valuation, and life which characterizes the intellectual world of the Middle Ages. Uniformly with this process the single forms under which men seek to understand the world began to break away from the framework of their comprehensive organization and to develop towards autonomy. The magnificent efflorescence of the individual branches of knowledge which, in dependence upon this evolution, starts at the commencement of the modern era is bought with the sacrifice of the unitary orientation of the whole of knowledge. Whereas previously in the gradation of the intellectual cosmos the reference to theology had given to every individual discipline its unambiguous position, its sharply defined place, and thereby its fixed limits, now the victory of the autonomous tendencies, along with the sudden rise of the particular sciences, brought about the decay of the philosophy (*Weltsicht*) which had embraced them all in a single totality. With the possible exception of Cusanus, the men who embody the new ideal of knowledge characteristic of the Renaissance—men of universal genius in the eyes of our own time—when measured against the great masters of the Middle Ages, against Averroes, Maimonides, Albertus, and Thomas, appear as superb specialists or talented virtuosi.

It is Descartes who first among the moderns clearly realizes the state of aggregation or unrelated juxtaposition into which the emancipated sciences had got after the break-up of their solid frame, and who undertakes the attempt to find a new law of their interrelation. With the impressiveness of a programme, at the age of twenty-two, he indicates in his diary the task: to free the single sciences from the masks isolating them, and to reveal the law of their connexion in the *catena scientiarum.*[1] Just

[1] Descartes, *Cogitationes privatae*, 1 January 1619 (*Œuvres inédites*, Première partie, p. 4, Paris 1859): 'Larvatae nunc scientiae sunt, quae larvis sublatis pulcherrimae

as the light of the sun suffers no essential change from the variety of the things which it illuminates, so the multiplicity of sciences is nothing but the expression of the *one* human wisdom which remains the same however diverse the objects upon which it is directed. To grasp that single fundamental power of the mind, in order to gain insight into the essential connexion of the disparate domains of knowledge, is a task the execution of which shows the greatness as well as the limitations of the Cartesian programme.

The principle that now joins the single links of knowledge in a chain, the organizing work of pure understanding, proves, indeed, capable of indicating the strict rule which connects in the law of their structure disciplines as different as arithmetic and geometry, music and astronomy, statics and mechanics. Yet the flood of illumination shed by Descartes's sun of knowledge on the structure of those sciences that are defined as *exact* only deepens the darkness that is spread over all those modes of cognition whose peculiar nature is irreducible to the formula of counting and measurement. In the system of the new science of the *mathesis universalis* the *historical* form of thought has no place. In its endeavour to find in *science* the firm support which it had formerly derived from the bond uniting it to a divine being the speculative mind was led to look upon this kind of knowledge, wherein mere opinion, mere arbitrary subjectivity, seemed to take up so much room and where the results proved so unstable and changeable, as an inferior, confused form of knowledge.

This philosophical foundation of the new type of cognition gave rise to the distinction of knowledge into *Sciences* and *Belles-Lettres*, into strictly obligatory thinking and aesthetic contemplation. This forms the *one* fundamental presupposition of that rigid separation of the sciences from the arts which dominates the theory of knowledge from the beginning of the nineteenth century onwards. No doubt there has been a fundamental change in the *valuation* of history since Vico's prophetic work, since Montesquieu and Rousseau, above all since Herder and Winckelmann. No doubt history, from being a chronicle of

apparerent: catenam scientiarum pervidenti non difficilius videbitur eas animo retinere quam seriem numerorum.' Descartes's diary was copied by Leibniz during his stay in Paris, 1 June 1676, and published by Comte Foucher de Careil from Leibniz's copy in the Hanover Library.

manners and customs, a collection of examples, a compendium of useful precepts, an embellishment of life, an ornament of culture, has become a force stirring the foundations of life itself. Nevertheless, the strict division of the two domains subsists unchanged. History, indeed, under Herder's influence, is no longer looked upon by post-Kantian philosophy as an inferior degree of knowledge. It now runs the opposite risk of being seized on by speculative metaphysics and lifted to the height of *a priori* construction, or—after the overthrow of the metaphysical systems—of being monopolized by the so-called exact sciences in the sphere of positivism. It is the achievement of the German historical school and of certain historians in England and France to have adhered, as against all these encroachments—against dialectical subtilization and naturalistic schematization—to historical investigation in its own right, to the love of the individual phenomenon, of individuality for its own sake and that of its concrete significance. This defensive warfare, waged with the certainty of instinct rather than with methodical consciousness, received its logical foundation and philosophic legitimation through the works of Windelband and Rickert, who, towards the end of last century, tried to settle the boundaries of scientific conceptions, and thereby to secure the domain of history against inadmissible trespass. As a consequence of their subtle distinctions and the resulting methodological feuds, it is easily forgotten that, long before, Nietzsche formulated, more concisely and more profoundly, history's right to independence from generalizing interference.[1]

If we now try to determine the place due to history to-day in the structure of the intellectual world, the first question concerns the justification of that cleavage of the structure of knowledge into sciences and arts. Looking at the historical genesis of this separation we see that, apart from the rationalistic division above mentioned into sciences and *belles-lettres*, the determining factor has been a metaphysical assumption—a dogma of post-Kantian idealism—which opposes in radical antithesis the world of nature to the world of the mind, as to something totally different. Upon the far-reaching consequences of

[1] Nietzsche, *Thoughts out of Season, Part II. The Use and Abuse of History*, transl. by A. Collins, Edinburgh and London 1909, p. 84: '. . . should we call the effects of leaden folly, imitation, love and hunger—laws? We may admit it: but we are sure of this too—that so far as there are laws in history, the laws are of no value and the history of no value either.'

this perpetuation of the fatal idealist rift between mind and nature we need not enter here. A realization of the peculiar historical circumstances which conditioned this division may shake our confidence in its absolute value. But we must systematically reflect that we have here a logically incomplete disjunction, and that, e.g.—quite apart from the often embarrassing borderline cases—the 'purest' of sciences, mathematics, has no place in it. This reflection alone will justify us in looking upon it as a merely provisional and much compromised means of orientation, and even in rejecting it if it makes dogmatic claims; and will necessitate the attempt to create a new systematic order.

II

While it must be accepted as a fundamental characteristic common to all dogmatic theories of knowledge that they consider the object of cognition as something fixed and given, and while for them the task of science consists in an ever more perfect and adequate reflection of a world of things existent in absolute and unambiguous definiteness, for the Critical philosopher the object which had so far been taken to be the one unshakable certainty becomes a subject of inquiry and search. Provided he takes Kant's transcendental postulate seriously, he will, wherever there is a form of intellectual law out of which a definite structure of reality arises, feel debarred from starting with an absolute object from which knowledge is to receive its credentials. He will rather be convinced that wherever there is a creative activity of the mind producing a form of being (whatever its kind may be), the starting-point of philosophical reflection is constituted not by the being which is formed but by the very mode of giving it form, by the ἐνέργεια of the formative activity; not by the visible object but by the manner of the visualization, on which the object depends for its peculiar form.

As a consequence, according to this fundamental intuition of Critical thought, the separation into sciences of nature (*Naturwissenschaften*) and sciences of the mind (*Geisteswissenschaften*), which is determined by the assumption of a fixed existence of their objects, will not be admissible. In fact, what is needed is a classification of the forms of scientific activity according to the way in which the knowing consciousness views whatever happens to be its object.

Starting, therefore, from the modes of formative activity we have two fundamental aspects of our understanding of the world confronting one another. We shall designate them, to begin with, that of number and that of image, that of *quantum* and that of *quale*. Thus we obtain a series of those sciences, beginning with mathematics (wherein we see number in its abstract purity), which strive to reduce their specific world of objects to the element of mere quantity. These sciences find their task—like modern physics—in translating everything that is given and qualitatively determined into the form of a pure numerical manifold. Inseparably bound up with this *quantifying* thinking is the tendency towards the functional connexion of the single qualitative spheres that are transposed into exactly definable quantities. The direction in which this kind of thinking points is, as has been shown by Ernst Cassirer,[1] towards the transformation of all substance into function, of all essence into relation.

Fundamentally different from this mode of interpreting the world, and in no way reducible to it, is the other kind of view, which we may call here, shortly, the *qualifying*. Whereas the sciences grouped under the aspect of number tend to raise all sensuous qualities to the rank of exactly definable quantities, here inversely the pure *quale*—in scholastic language pure *quiditas*—has come to be an ultimate, to the understanding of which all quantitative determinations are made subservient. The signature of development in the quantifying sciences is—to quote an eminent physicist[2]—the progressive emancipation from anthropomorphic elements. In the qualifying sciences, on the other hand, the goal is precisely the ever purer apprehension and representation of the specifically human element. And finally, whereas the numerical aspect leads to a dissolution of everything substantial into a relation of the functional, here all relation has significance only as a means towards understanding the essence; every general *How much?* has significance only as a means towards knowledge of the peculiar *How?* and the particular *What?*

This mode of scientific contemplation under the aspect of image is that of history. If history is taken as knowledge, under-

[1] E. Cassirer, '*Substanzbegriff und Funktionsbegriff. Untersuchungen über die Grundfragen der Erkenntniskritik*', 2nd ed., Berlin, 1923; English transl. by W. C. and M. C. Swabey, Chicago and London, 1923.

[2] M. Planck, *Das Weltbild der neuen Physik*, Leipzig, 1930, p. 15.

standing, and interpretation of a past charged with meaning, and of the enduring manifestations of past mind, obviously all quantitative elements, all fixations of their content at a definite point in the time-continuum regarded as homogeneous, are in themselves of quite subordinate significance, and serve only to form the frame setting off the historical picture. A fact derives historical dignity, not from them—any more than from causal explanation as such—but only from orientation towards a significant image.

III

That reorganization of the structure of the sciences which seeks to base itself on the totality of the knowing mind must admit the insufficiency of the *one* principle of the abstractly measuring, causally connecting, reason for the purpose of joining the links of the chain into a unity; it must call to its aid a *second* faculty of the mind, which is the constitutive condition of all knowledge that is not quantitatively determined—imagination. It is that faculty which for Kant represents 'an *a priori* condition of the possibility of all combination of the manifold in *one* cognition', which 'brings the multiplicity of intuition into an image'. It is at bottom the *φαντασία* of the Stoics, the *imaginatio* of Boethius and Scholasticism, which enables us to represent an object that is not actually present to the senses.[1]

The cause of the ill repute, and even oblivion, into which this power of the mind has fallen in modern philosophy, after having been looked upon as quite legitimate in former times, is easily understood. We have only to remember that it was *ratio* which fought the decisive battles in which the modern scientific consciousness freed itself from loyalty to the old images, and which ever since has claimed as the spoils of war the right to cite before its tribunal whatever laid claim to the name of science. This claim, that all scientific activity must vindicate its legitimacy at the bar of *ratio*, nobody will contest. If, however, blind

[1] In the history of philosophy we find two quite distinct attitudes towards this faculty. On the one hand, it is considered as a *debilitata sensio* (Hobbes); on the other, imagination, or at least its 'nobler part', is regarded as an active, creative power. This view, originating with Posidonius and certain Neoplatonists of later Antiquity (e.g. Iamblichus, quoted by Priscianus, *Metaphrasis in Theophrasti De sensu et de phantasia* [pp. 262–3, ed. Wimmer, Lips. 1862], translated by Marsilius Ficinus [published at Venice, 1516]), is taken up by Paracelsus, Campanella (*Universalis Philosophia* V 1, art. 3 ff., pp. 344 ff., Paris, 1638), and Boehme, through whom it is handed down to Baader.

to other forces that may happen to be operative, it poses as monarch in the realm of science, it is guilty of overstepping its judicial competence.

> 'Intuitive observers are themselves productive, and knowledge, in the process of its own advancement, unconsciously requires, and passes over into, intuition; and though men of science may cross themselves devoutly in the presence of fantasy, before they know where they are, they have to call to their aid *productive imagination*.'

This observation of Goethe's (in the *Preliminary Studies for a Physiology of Plants*) applies in a very special measure to historical thinking.

The most important prerequisite, therefore, of a *critique of historical reason*, which remains to be written and which is foreshadowed by Dilthey, is a critique of imagination, 'whereby and in accordance with which alone [as Kant says] images become possible'.

Trying briefly to characterize its constitutive categories or, rather, its 'schemata' we find *time* the most essential. The peculiarity of imaginative time, which determines the character of history, becomes apparent by contrast with the time-concept of theoretic, rational science. In the recent evolution of mathematico-physical thought, time has been divested of all its specific particularity; in a universal world-metric, defining the world as a four-dimensional (i.e. $3+1$) metrical manifold, each particular point is fixed by its time-space co-ordinates x_1, x_2, x_3, x_4, the temporal determination having become a purely numerical positional value, freely exchangeable with the other co-ordinates.

As against this, every civilization and every epoch of civilization, and even every form of historical contemplation, is characterized by the fact that its time-aspect in each case has its specifically conditioned qualitative tone, and points in each case in a clearly defined direction. Though all qualitative time needs the support of a quantitative time-sequence—no concrete *quale* being imaginable without a *quantum*—yet the primacy of quality is so great that (to give one instance only) not even the most inveterate pedant has seriously entertained the idea of correcting our chronology, which is determined relatively to the year of the birth of Christ, on the ground of our knowledge that in reality Jesus was born four years before the beginning of this era. The consciousness of the qualitative particularity which makes this event appear as the beginning of a new age so greatly predominates that the quantitative fixation is in comparison regarded as quite indifferent, and a mistake in all our chronological statements is put up with as a matter of course, which it is very far from being.

In contrast with the mere time-in-which-things-are-ordered (*Ordnungszeit*) and the mere time-in-which-things-happen (*Geschehenszeit*), the specific stamp of this time-form of history may be more particularly characterized by calling it the time of destiny (*Schicksalszeit*). Long before the awakening of a really scientific contemplation, and later on along with it, this time-form becomes the stimulating problem at all those turning-points of historical evolution at which a hitherto unquestioned view of time becomes questionable, a hitherto authoritative time-direction loses its validity, and a new time-consciousness calls for a hearing. We see this first in Ephesus and Elea, when the philosophic thought of the Greeks began to rid itself of mythical bonds and overthrew the old gods; when in the colonial cities of Asia Minor and lower Italy Heraclitus daringly calls Aion, the all-embracing world-time, a sporting, draught-playing boy; when in the solemnly measured march of Parmenides' archaic rhythms there sounds the triumph of Logos, who by his word of command banishes afar the daemonic powers of time, declaring them non-existent. We see it in the religious consciousness of the prophet who at the fall of the Kingdom of Israel makes his God speak the words: *Remember ye not the former things, neither consider the things of old. Behold I will do a new thing*. We see it again in the founders of the New Covenant, then in the crisis of mediaeval piety, in Joachim de Floris's *Evangelium aeternum* of the Third Empire, in the dawn of the Renaissance, and in the Reformation. Finally, with the decline of the creed of a materialistic epoch, Bergson was the first to protest, in brilliant language and with impressive arguments, against the fragmentary and, as it were, atrophied character of a purely mechanistic notion of time, and sought to establish the primacy of the pure intuition of time over every dogmatically fixed reality, every settled concept of existence. Since then the tension resulting from the disturbed relation between the domains of being and of time has never been relieved. It stimulated the French novel in Proust and German poetry in Hofmannsthal and Rilke, '*Und in kleinen Schritten gehn die Uhren neben unserm eigentlichen Tag*'. At last, in an atmosphere of complete mental collapse and *Daseinssorge*, the problem took possession of the post-revolutionary phase of the phenomenological school.

But most important from our point of view is that determination of the nature of time which emerges when, for the first time in the history of European thought, the problem of its dialectic peculiarity becomes, in all its gravity and in its full extent, the subject of philosophic reflection; when in the epoch of the declining empire St. Augustine in his *Confessions* expresses, in the most concise way, the problematic nature of the time-concept: 'What then is time? If no one asks of me, I know; if I wish to explain to him who asks, I know not.' St. Augustine's analysis shows that logical thought, unless it is to be involved in inescapable contradictions, must not view time—as when naïvely represented as an infinite straight line—as something absolute which is divided into three no less absolute parts. The division into present, past, and future ceases to be one of substance; it concerns exclusively our *knowledge* of the given reality. To understand time, therefore, does not mean to compose it of three separate entities. Rather, it is a question of understanding how three distinct intentions of homogeneous consciousness—upon the Now, upon the Before, and upon the After—here combine into the unity of a single meaning. We must no longer speak as if three times existed. On the contrary, there is only the one present, which is, however, the present of the past, the present of the present, the present of the future. Thus time is stripped of its character as a thing and recognized as a function of bringing things into the present, which includes a threefold orientation; the present of the past is determined as memory, the present of the present as intuition, the present of the future as expectation. From this it is clear that in the one fundamental power of the mind, in the pure consciousness of the *Now*, memory and expectation are in the most intimate way connected with each other.

The fundamental significance of this conclusion from the Augustinian analysis becomes surprisingly evident when we see how both modern psychology since James and Ernst Cassirer's phenomenology of cognition, in their inquiries into the nature of memory, demonstrate not only the close relationship between the essential functions of memory and the orientation towards the future, but also the positive dependence of recollection on the particular expectation.

IV

Let us apply this knowledge to history. History deals with a world that has sunk into the past, and even though lasting documents concerning this world are preserved for it, the mind that produced them is extinguished. Therefore the mode of being of its object is a past summoned to the present, a recollected past,[1] the being—in recollection—of the *Has-been.* Every recollection, however, being in the last resort determined by expectation, by the will towards the future, the backward look into the past is most intimately bound up with the forward look into the future.

From these reflections upon qualitative time it follows that every history, even the scientific history of our days, is, by dint of this constitutive category, undeniably working under a condition which ties it to the individual time-view; and it would be easy, starting from this point, to show how our given forms of history are conditioned by the specific time-aspect of their civilization, and even how in differentiated periods the particular time-illusion of the individual historian makes itself felt.

Seeing that history itself, even scientific history, is thus subject to the change of time, we must ask whether an unambiguous, generally valid knowledge of the past is at all possible. Nowhere is this possibility defended with greater insistence than in the sphere of classical scholarship.[2] Eminent representatives of this branch of learning claim for themselves an adequate knowledge of their subject, which seems to indicate the triumph of a highly developed method over all the subjective and temporal limitations attaching to the scientific study of the world. A critical examination of this claim reveals, indeed, that there is in those disciplines an element that is binding and which must be judged obligatory for every thinking creature of every time. Yet on closer inspection of the compass and function of this element we soon perceive that its binding force is restricted to the purely quantitative in its widest sense, especially to the dating and localization of an event, to functional association of moments of process, that is to say, to those quantitative elements *without which* scientific historical knowledge is not possible, but *which*

[1] *erinnerte Vergangenheit.* [2] *klassische Philologie.*

by themselves alone could never cross the threshold of history. If we go beyond this to claim adequate knowledge of the historical picture in its fullness of reality, it can only be from the standpoint of a theory of knowledge according to which the soul of the knower seems a *tabula rasa* on which all the impressions of things observed are ingenuously supposed to register themselves faithfully. Since in the course of philosophical evolution the insufficiency of this doctrine has become more and more obvious, a critique of historical reason will have to demonstrate within its own province the inadmissibility of the claim which emanates from that realistic way of thinking.

We name here briefly the most important parts of such a critique. There must be a doctrine of *understanding*, which is the monad's endeavour to transcend its isolated existence, an endeavour the result of which can never have more than a hypothetical character. Further, there must be an examination of the categories of *representation* and *crystallization*, i.e. condensation of events into historical facts. Finally, there must be a determination of that perspective under the directing influence of which that condensation takes place.

The subjective conditions which even at this stage of our inquiry prove unavoidable for any theory of history show their necessity still more clearly when we reflect on the nature of universal history. In every examination of the whole of history it becomes manifest that—unless there is to be a sort of *encheiresis historiae*—the intellectual bond keeping the parts together appears in the form of the *meaning* in accordance with which the evolution is viewed, and of the driving forces which guide it. That this meaning is a given one can only be asserted from the standpoint of a definite dogma. And we actually see the pretensions of the dogmatists of all persuasions to a knowledge of that meaning, and the rise of that form of the philosophy of history which claims to have gained insight, by dint of thought, into the plan of the world, which is supposed to be operative above and in the phenomena. We observe that in this way tremendous world-structures originate, which—given adequate genius on the part of their author—may be attended by extraordinary effects in the way of illuminating history, if we look upon them as comprehensive hypotheses and penetrating world-views. At the same time, however, we see that every pretence that this meaning is unquestionable, not breathed into, but apparently revealed by, the phenomena, leads to those dialectical subreptions of metaphysical thought which do violence to the phenomena themselves, and whose presence is felt wherever the rule of a general principle is canonized, be it Hegelian reason, Marxian forces of production, or the *Existenznot* of modern phenomenologists.

Now, *Critical philosophy*, if understood as respect for the boundaries of knowledge, will forbid all talk of the givenness of a meaning in events or in history; and will emphasize that, wherever there is an attempt to determine the guiding forces of historical evolution, totally alogical assumptions are necessarily implied.

At the same time, however, critical philosophy will be aware of the fact that it is precisely the element of significance (*Sinnerfüllung*) which distinguishes history from a mere collection of facts, from the encyclopaedic inventories of the past which, from Varro's *Antiquitates*, from Isidore, Rabanus, and Vincentius, down to the source-books of the present, have been the subject of learned interest. Hence it will realize that the principle by which the individual features are moulded into the whole of the picture is always something posited by the mind observing it and only ostensibly abstracted from the facts. 'One phenomenon after the other [this is how Schiller describes this characteristic process] begins to withdraw itself from blind chance and lawless liberty, and to subordinate itself, as a fitting member, to a harmonious whole, even though it exists only in the historian's idea.'

V

Thus, every finding of a meaning implies the imparting of a meaning. Hence eighteenth-century Pyrrhonism would seem to be right in treating history as, at best, a *fable convenue*. Hence, too, the door seems to be flung wide open to subjectivity—though not indeed to that vicious subjectivity which assumes importance with arbitrary and obtrusive judgements of value, for that has been suitably discredited by the logical distinction between theoretical value-relation and practical valuation. It is now no longer a question of the overt intentions, the recognizable interests; it is a question of the hidden ideal, the secret, imperceptible fantasy that guides the historian's retrospect.

And beyond this tie which cannot be ignored there still remains the logical fact that the historical judgement is not related to 'value' in general, but always to a concrete and specific form of value, varying according to the general conceptions of the epoch and the particular cultural background of the historian.

Thus the realization that the logical structure of the historical judgement contains of necessity subjective elements of various kinds will limit the claims of dogmatism. But history now seems to be at the mercy of a more dangerous foe, the destructive forces of the modern *sociology of knowledge*, which calls in question every claim to objectivity and therewithal the scientific character of history. No doubt a glance at the tacit ontological presuppositions on which those forces depend shows that sociology itself, the 'destroyer of knowledge', stands on very frail foundations. This insight into the weakness of the adversary, however, cannot exempt us from the inquiry as to how far history as a science is possible. If it has proved necessary to recognize the relativity of all historical knowledge, this appears to furnish a serious argument against its scientific character. Science, defined as an organized body of theoretic knowledge arranged according to principles, leaves no room for a mode of knowledge wherein subjective elements play a necessary part.

Fundamentally, this concept of science, which is prevalent in the philosophical theory of our days, goes back to Kant's precept 'only that can properly be termed science, the certainty of which is apodictic'. We are faced here with the curious circumstance that Critical philosophy, charged with transforming dynamically everything given into something imposed as a task, has stopped short of the concept of science itself.

We shall understand this peculiar phenomenon if we regard Kant's achievement in its connexion with a millennial evolution of European thought. Since the clash between the oriental mystery religions and Greek *logos* the basic theme of philosophy within the cultural sphere of Europe and Asia Minor has been the attempt to solve the conflict between knowledge and faith. Towards the end of the ninth century, by a surprising coincidence, the problem received its conceptual formula in Basra and Bagdad, in Sura and Paris, in Arabian, Jewish, and Christian philosophy. Following the Latin Averroism and the Nominalism of the later Middle Ages there develops an ever clearer distinction between the two provinces; the Spinozistic postulate, *Fidem a philosophia separare*, becomes more and more urgent; until at last Kant's words 'I had to abolish knowledge in order to make room for faith' seemed to bring about their final separation.

Thus faith was freed from knowledge, but now knowledge held itself free of all relation with faith, and imagined itself standing altogether on its own ground. Yet the consideration of the axioms underlying the single sciences and also philosophy, and of the presuppositions which can never be verified, but only justified, by the judgements developing from them, shows that the irrational elements of faith have found here, on the very soil of the realm of *ratio*, a habitation from which *ratio* can never drive them away. However, it is the nature of *ratio* never to cease illuminating these hidden foundations, and, by objectifying them, constantly to encroach on those powers on which it rests. As this means that the frontier between the domains is not rigid but is always demarcated anew, it follows that the concept of science can no longer be thought of as static and fixed.

On the contrary, the element of motion which is imparted to science by the ever renewed delimitation of its domain must be incorporated into its definition, and the old formulation be supplemented by a new one which takes science as *intentio*, as *idea*—idea, that is, in a threefold signification: in the Stoic sense of a germ of reason, a force stirring consciousness; in the Kantian sense of a regulative principle ordering phenomena; in the Platonic sense of the normative pattern towards which the empirical form of human knowledge is directed.

If history is taken as science in this sense, the objections raised against it on account of its subjective elements will lose their force, for the notion of *objectivity* has now changed its nature. From a *fixum* confronting the thinking consciousness it has become a pure intention of thought itself, a tendency of consciousness towards gaining as far as possible objective knowledge of phenomena.

Though the objectivity of history only grows from a subjective basis, this cannot imperil its value as a form of knowledge. To say that the attempt to reach an absolute *Always* must for ever start from a relative *Now* and *Here*, can betoken a depreciation only in the eyes of one who fancies himself standing, like a dogmatist of the old learning, in a space without time; or to an intelligence suspended *in vacuo* which considers itself to be bound by neither space nor time.

We notice in all creations of the human mind, in the most primitive stages of language, in magic and religious myth as well as in all branches of art, the spontaneous tendency to force into stable shapes the flux of things that come and go. In the same way, we recognize this transcending of time and of death as being also the essential intention of all philosophy and all science. In the sciences of number and the modern development of mathematical physics, according to Minkowski's well-known formula, 'Space by itself and Time by itself become mere shadows, and the independence of both is preserved only by a sort of union.' Here, therefore, a transcending of time is taking place which consists in the elimination of its separate being. On the other hand, the transcending of time which we observe in history amounts to an ever deeper immersion in the time of past destiny, and to an ever new condensation of its changing appearances into lasting pictures.

Translated by D. R. Cousin, University of Glasgow.

BIBLIOGRAPHY OF ERNST CASSIRER'S WRITINGS

by RAYMOND KLIBANSKY *and* WALTER SOLMITZ

In the first edition of *Philosophy and History* we included a bibliography of the writings of Ernst Cassirer, listing in systematic order those publications which had appeared before 1936. This formed subsequently the basis of an enlarged list, chronologically arranged, *viz.* "Bibliography of the Writings of Ernst Cassirer, to 1946," compiled by C. H. Hamburg and W. M. Solmitz (contained in *The Philosophy of Ernst Cassirer,* edited by P. A. Schilpp, The Library of Living Philosophers, Vol. VI, Evanston, Ill., 1949). For the present volume, the bibliography has been thoroughly revised and brought up to date, preserving the systematic arrangement adopted by us in the original edition.

In the years following Ernst Cassirer's death on 13 April 1945, and especially in the last decade, many new editions of his writings have been published, and numerous translations have appeared, in various languages. Some, at least, of his major works are now available in English.

In tracing these posthumous publications, we were able to make use of the records kept during her lifetime by Cassirer's widow, Mrs. Toni Cassirer, and kindly put at our disposal by their daughter, Mrs. Anne Appelbaum.

We are indebted to the Wissenschaftliche Verlagsgesellschaft, Darmstadt, to La Nuova Italia Editrice, Florence, to Bruno Cassirer, Ltd., Oxford, and to other European publishing houses for answering our enquiries. Lastly, we wish to express our thanks to Miss Barbara Gerike and to Miss Désirée Park, M.A., for their help in preparing the manuscript and in carrying out bibliographical research.

A. SYSTEMATIC PHILOSOPHY

I. EPISTEMOLOGY AND LOGIC

1. *Der kritische Idealismus und die Philosophie des 'gesunden Menschenverstandes'.* Giessen: Töpelmann. viii, 35 pp. (*Philosophische Arbeiten,* hrsg. v. Cohen und Natorp. Vol. I, No. 1.) 1906.
2. "Zur Frage nach der Methode der Erkenntniskritik. Eine Entgegnung." (*Vierteljahrsschrift für wissenschaftliche Philosophie und Soziologie.* Vol. XXXI, pp. 441–465, Leipzig.) 1907.

   Das Erkenntnisproblem in der Philosophie und Wissenschaft der neueren Zeit. 1906–57. Vide No. 52.
3. *Substanzbegriff und Funktionsbegriff. Untersuchungen über die Grundfragen der Erkenntniskritik.* Berlin, 1910: Bruno Cassirer. xv, 459 pp. 2nd ed. 1923.
   Russian translation, 1912.
   English translation, in: *Substance and Function, and Einstein's Theory of Relativity.* Transl. by W. C. Swabey and M. C. Swabey. Chicago and London, 1923: The Open Court Publ. Co. Reprint: New York, 1953: Dover Publications.
4. Review of R. Hönigswald, *Beiträge zur Erkenntnistheorie und Methodenlehre.* (*Kant-Studien.* Vol. XIV, No. I, pp. 91–98.) 1909.
5. Review of J. Cohn, *Voraussetzungen und Ziele des Erkennens* (*Deutsche Literaturzeitung.* Vol. XXXI, No. 39.) 1910.
6. "Erkenntnistheorie nebst den Grenzfragen der Logik." (*Jahrbücher der Philosophie.* Vol. I, pp. 1–59. Berlin: E. S. Mittler.) 1913.
7. "Erkenntnistheorie nebst den Grenzfragen der Logik und Denkpsychologie." (*Jahrbücher der Philosophie.* Vol. III, pp. 31–92. Berlin: E. S. Mittler.) 1927.
8. "Zur Theorie des Begriffs. Bemerkungen zu dem Aufsatz von G. Heymans." (*Kant-Studien.* Vol. XXXIII, pp. 129–36. Berlin: Reuther u. Reichard.) 1928.
9. "Inhalt und Umfang des Begriffs. Bemerkungen zu Konrad Marc-Wogau's gleichnamiger Schrift." (*Theoria.* Vol. II, pp. 207–232. Göteborg.) 1936.

   "Die Begriffsform im mythischen Denken." Vide No. 38.
10. "Rationalism." (*Encyclopaedia Britannica,* 14th edition. Vol. XVIII, pp. 991–993. London and New York.) 1929.
11. "Substance." (*Encyclopaedia Britannica,* 14th edition. Vol. XXI, pp. 500–502. London and New York.) 1929.
12. "Transcendentalism." (*Encyclopaedia Britannica,* 14th edition. Vol. XXII, pp. 405–406. London and New York.) 1929.
13. "Truth." (*Encyclopaedia Britannica,* 14th edition. Vol. XXII, pp. 522–524. London and New York.) 1929.
14. "Formen und Formwandlungen des philosophischen Wahrheitsbegriffs." (*Hamburgische Universität. Reden, geh. bei der Feier des Rektorwechsels am 7. Nov. 1929,* pp. 17–36. Hamburg: Boysen.) 1929.
    Japanese translation, by Dr. T. Yura, 1930.
15. "Was ist 'Subjektivismus'?" (*Theoria.* Vol. V, pp. 111–140. Göteborg.) 1939.

    "The Concept of Group and the Theory of Perception." Vide No. 31.

II. THE PHILOSOPHY OF MATHEMATICS AND NATURAL SCIENCE

Kant und die moderne Mathematik. 1907. vide No. 91.

16. "Das Problem des Unendlichen und Renouviers 'Gesetz der Zahl'." (In *Philosophische Abhandlungen, Hermann Cohen zum 70. Geburtstag dargebracht,* pp. 85–98. Berlin: Bruno Cassirer.) 1912.

17. "Philosophische Probleme der Relativitätstheorie." (*Die Neue Rundschau.* Vol. XXI, No. 12, pp. 1337–1357. Berlin: S. Fischer.) 1920.

18. *Zur Einsteinschen Relativitätstheorie. Erkenntnistheoretische Betrachtungen.* Berlin: Bruno Cassirer, 1921, 134 pp.; 2nd ed. 1925. Reprinted in *Zur modernen Physik,* 1957. Vide No. 21.
    Russian translation, 1922.
    Japanese translation, 1923.
    English translation, Chicago and London, 1923. Vide No. 3. Reprint: New York, 1953.
    "Einstein's Theory of Relativity from the Epistemological Point of View." *The Monist,* July 1922, pp. 412–418. (English translation of selected parts.)

19. *Determinismus und Indeterminismus in der modernen Physik. Historische und systematische Studien zum Kausalproblem. Göteborgs Högskolas Årsskrift,* XLII, 1936: 3. Göteborg: Elanders Boktryckeri. ix, 265 pp. 1937. Reprinted in *Zur modernen Physik,* 1957. Vide No. 21.
    English translation: *Determinism and Indeterminism in Modern Physics: Historical and systematic studies of the problem of causality.* Transl. by O. T. Benfey, with a Preface by H. Margenau. New Haven: Yale University Press, 1956. xxiv, 227 pp.

20. Review of A. C. Benjamin, *An Introduction to the Philosophy of Science.* (New York, 1937.) *Lychnos.* Annual of the Swedish History of Science Society. Uppsala and Stockholm: Almqvist & Wiksells Boktr., 1938, pp. 456–461.

21. *Zur modernen Physik.* Darmstadt: Wissenschaftliche Buchgesellschaft, 1957. Oxford: Bruno Cassirer, 1957. [Reprints of *Zur Einsteinschen Relativitätstheorie* (No. 18) and *Determinismus und Indeterminismus in der modernen Physik* (No. 19).] 397 pp.

"The Influence of Language upon the Development of Scientific Thought." Vide No. 43.

"Mathematische Mystik und mathematische Naturwissenschaft." Vide No. 53.

"Mythischer, ästhetischer und theoretischer Raum." Vide No. 45.

III. MORAL AND POLITICAL PHILOSOPHY

22. *Die Idee der Republikanischen Verfassung: Rede zur Verfassungsfeier am 11. August 1928.* Hamburg: Friederichsen. Berlin: de Gruyter. 1929. 33 pp.

23. "Deutschland und Westeuropa im Spiegel der Geistesgeschichte." (Inter Nationes. Zeitschrift f. d. kulturellen Beziehungen Deutschlands zum Ausland. Vol. I, No. 3 and 4. Berlin: de Gruyter.) 1931.

24. "Vom Wesen und Werden des Naturrechts." (*Zeitschrift f. Rechtsphilosophie.* Vol. VI, No. 1. Leipzig: Meiner.) 1932.

25. "Force and Freedom: Remarks on the English edition of Jacob Burckhardt's *Reflections on History.*" (*The American Scholar,* Vol. XIII, pp. 407–417. New York.) 1944.

26. "Judaism and the Modern Political Myths." (*Contemporary Jewish Record,* Vol. VII, pp. 115–126. New York.) 1944.
Swedish translation: "Judendomen och de Moderna Politiska Myterna." *Judisk Tidskrift,* No. 9, pp. 266–274, Sept. 1946.

27. "The Myth of the State." (*Fortune,* Vol. XXIX, No. 6, pp. 164–167, 198, 201, 202, 204, 206. Chicago.) June 1944.

28. *The Myth of the State.* New Haven: Yale University Press. London: Oxford University Press. 1946. xii, 303 pp. Foreword by Charles W. Hendel. Reprint: New York, Doubleday, 1955.
German translation: *Vom Mythos des Staates.* Transl. by F. Stoessl. Zürich: Artemis-Verlag, 1949.
German translation (Ch. XVIII only): "Der Mythos als politische Waffe," in *Die Amerikanische Rundschau,* Munich, 1946, No. 11, pp. 30–41.
Italian translation: Torino: Longanesi, 1950.
Japanese translation: Tokyo: Riso-Sha, Ltd., 1957.
Korean translation, by Myang-Kwan Choe: Seoul.
Portuguese translation: Lisboa: Publicacões Europa.
Spanish translation: Mexico: Fondo de cultura Economica, 1947.
Swedish translation: Stockholm: Natur och Kultur, 1948.

"Albert Schweitzer as Critic of Nineteenth-Century Ethics." Vide No. 107.

IV. PSYCHOLOGY

29. "Étude sur la pathologie de la conscience symbolique." Traduit par A. Koyré. (*Journal de Psychologie normale et pathologique.* Vol. XXVI, No. 5–8, pp. 289–336; 523–566. Paris: Alcan.) 1929.

30. "Die Sprache und der Aufbau der Gegenstandswelt." (*Bericht üb. d. XII. Kongress d. deutschen Gesellschaft f. Psychologie, Hamburg, 1931.*) Jena: G. Fischer, 1932.
French translation: "Le langage et la construction du monde des objets." Traduit par P. Guillaume. (*Journal de Psychologie normale et pathologique.* Vol. XXX, No. 1–4, pp. 18–44. Paris: Alcan.) 1933. Reprint in: *Psychologie du langage,* par H. Delacroix, E. Cassirer, etc., pp. 18–44. (Bibliothèque de Philosophie contemporaine. Paris: Alcan.) 1933.

31. "Le concept de groupe et la théorie de la perception." (*Journal de Psychologie* norm. et path. Vol. XXXV, pp. 368–414. Paris: Alcan.) 1938.
English translation: "The Concept of Group and the Theory of Perception." *Philosophy and Phenomenological Research,* Vol. V, 1944, pp. 1–35.

32. "William Stern: Zur Wiederkehr seines Todestages." (*Acta Psychologica,* Vol. V, pp. 1–15.) 1940. Reprinted in: William Stern, *Allgemeine Psychologie auf personalistischer Grundlage.* 2nd ed., mit Beiträgen von G. Stern-Anders, E. Cassirer u. einer ergänz. Bibliogr. Haag: M. Nijhoff, 1950, pp. xxxiii–xlvii.

V. PHILOSOPHY OF SYMBOLIC FORMS

('Philosophie der symbolischen Formen')

(a) General

33. "Der Begriff der symbolischen Form im Aufbau der Geisteswissenschaften." (*Vorträge d. Bibliothek Warburg.* Vol. I, 1921–2, pp. 11–39.) Leipzig and Berlin: Teubner, 1923. Reprinted in: *Wesen und Wirkung des Symbolbegriffs.* Darmstadt, 1956. Vide No. 37.

34. *Philosophie der symbolischen Formen.* Berlin: Bruno Cassirer. Vol. I: *Die Sprache,* 1923. xii, 293 pp. Vol. II: *Das mythische Denken,* 1925. xvi, 320 pp. Vol. III: *Phänomenologie der Erkenntnis,* 1929. xii, 559 pp. *Index,* bearb. von H. Noack, 1931. 92 pp.
Second edition: Darmstadt: Wissenschaftliche Buchgemeinschaft, 1953; and Oxford: B. Cassirer, 1954. *Index,* 1954. Vol. I reprinted 1956.
English translation: *Philosophy of Symbolic Forms.* Transl. by R. Manheim. New Haven: Yale University Press. Vol. I: *Language.* Preface and Introduction by C. W. Hendel, 1953. Vol. II: *Mythical Thought,* 1955. Vol. III: *Phenomenology of Knowledge,* 1957.
Italian translation: *Filosofia delle forme simboliche.* Vol. I, transl. by E. Arnaud. Firenze: La Nuova Italia, 1961. Vol. II in preparation.

35. "Das Symbolproblem und seine Stellung im System der Philosophie." (*Zeitschrift f. Aesthetik u. allgem. Kunstwissenschaft.* Vol. XXI, pp. 295–312.) 1927.

36. "Zur Logik des Symbolbegriffs." (*Theoria,* Vol. IV, pp. 145–175.) 1938. Reprinted in: *Wesen und Wirkung des Symbolbegriffs.* Vide No. 37.

37. *Wesen und Wirkung des Symbolbegriffs.* Darmstadt: Wissenschaftliche Buchgesellschaft, 1956. Oxford: B. Cassirer, 1956. [Reprints of "Die Begriffsform im mythischen Denken" (No. 38); "Sprache und Mythos" (No. 40); "Der Begriff der symbolischen Form . . ." (No. 33); "Zur Logik des Symbolbegriffs" (No. 36)]. 230 pp.

(b) Language, Myth, Arts

38. *Die Begriffsform im mythischen Denken.* (Studien d. Bibliothek Warburg, Vol. I.) Leipzig and Berlin: Teubner, 1922. v, 62 pp. Reprinted in *Wesen und Wirkung des Symbolbegriffs.* Darmstadt: Wissenschaftliche Buchgesellschaft, 1956.

39. "Zur 'Philosophie der Mythologie'." (*Festschrift für P. Natorp zum 70. Geburtstage.* pp. 23–54. Berlin: de Gruyter.) 1924. (Vide also No. 34, Vol. II, Introduction.)

40. *Sprache und Mythos. Ein Beitrag zum Problem der Götternamen.* (Studien d. Bibliothek Warburg, Vol. VI.) Leipzig and Berlin: Teubner, 1925. 87 pp.
Reprinted in: *Wesen und Wirkung des Symbolbegriffs.* Vide No. 40.
English translation: *Language and Myth,* transl. by Susanne K. Langer. New York: Harper & Brothers, 1946. x, 103 pp. Reprinted: New York: Dover Publications, 1953.
Spanish translation: Buenos Aires: Nueva Vision, 1959.

"Die Kantischen Elemente in Wilh. von Humboldts Sprachphilosophie." Vide No. 98.

41. "Die Bedeutung des Sprachproblems für die Entstehung der neueren Philosophie." (*Festschrift für Carl Meinhof.* pp. 507–514. Hamburg.) 1927.

42. "Structuralism in Modern Linguistics." (*Word.* Journal of the Linguistic Circle of New York, Vol. I, No. 11, pp. 99–120.) August 1946.

43. "The Influence of Language upon the Development of Scientific Thought." (*The Journal of Philosophy,* Vol. XXXIX, No. 12, pp. 309–327. New York.) June 4, 1942.
French translation in *Journal de Psychologie normale et pathologique,* Vol. XXXIX, 1946, pp. 129–152.

44. "Form und Technik." (*Kunst und Technik.* Aufsätze hrsg. von Leo Kestenberg, pp. 15–61. Berlin: Volksverband der Bücherfreunde, Wegweiser-Verlag.) 1930.

45. "Mythischer, ästhetischer und theoretischer Raum." (*Vierter Kongress für Aesthetik und allgem. Kunstwissenschaft.* Bericht hrsg. von H. Noack. Stuttgart, 1931. pp. 21–36.) 1931.
"Die Sprache und der Aufbau der Gegenstandswelt." 1932. Vide No. 30.

VI. 'KULTURPHILOSOPHIE'

46. "Naturalistische und humanistische Begründung der Kulturphilosophie." (*Göteborgs Kungl. Vetenskaps- och Vitterhets-Samhälles Handlingar.* 5[e] följden, Ser. A, Vol. 7, No. 3. Göteborg: Elanders Boktr.; Wettergren & Kerber, 28 pp.) 1939. Reprinted in *Der Bogen,* Vol. II, No. 4. Wiesbaden: Scholz-Verlag, 1947.

47. *Zur Logik der Kulturwissenschaften. Fünf Studien. Göteborgs Högskolas Årsskrift.* Vol. XLVIII: 1. Göteborg: Wettergren & Kerber. 1942. 139 pp. Reprinted: Darmstadt: Wissenschaftl. Buchgesellschaft. 1961.
English translation: *The Logic of the Humanities.* Transl. by C. Smith Howe. New Haven: Yale University Press, 1961. 217 pp.
Spanish translation (abbreviated version): Mexico: Fondo de Cultura Economica, 1952.

48. *An Essay on Man: An Introduction to a Philosophy of Human Culture.* New Haven: Yale University Press; London: Oxford University Press, 1944. ix, 237 pp. Reprint: New York: Doubleday, 1951.
Hebrew translation: Tel-Aviv: Oved Ltd., 1955.
Italian translation: Torino: Longanesi, 1948.
Japanese translation: Iwanami Gendai Sosho, 1951.
Korean translation, by M. K. Choe, Seoul, 1959.
Spanish translation: *Antropologia filosofica: Introducción a una filosofia de la cultura.* Transl. by E. Imaz. Mexico: Fondo de Cultura Economica, 1945. ix, 419 pp.

B. HISTORY OF PHILOSOPHY

I. GENERAL

(a) Ancient Philosophy

49. *Die Philosophie der Griechen von den Anfängen bis Platon.* (*Lehrbuch*

der Philosophie, hrsg. v. M. Dessoir. Vol. I: *Die Geschichte der Philosophie.*) Berlin: Ullstein, 1925. 139 pp.

50. "Die Antike und die Entstehung der exakten Wissenschaft." *Die Antike.* Vol. VIII, pp. 276–300. Berlin: de Gruyter, 1932.

51. "Logos, Dike, Kosmos in der Entwicklung der griechischen Philosophie." (*Göteborgs Högskolas Årsskrift,* Vol. XLVII: 6. Göteborg: Elanders Boktr. 31 pp.) 1941.

(b) Modern Philosophy

52. *Das Erkenntnisproblem in der Philosophie und Wissenschaft der neueren Zeit.* Berlin: Bruno Cassirer. Vol. I, 1906 (2nd revised ed. 1911; 3rd ed. 1922), XVIII, 608 pp. Vol. II, 1907 (2nd ed. 1911; 3rd ed. 1922), XV, 832 pp. Vol. III, *Die Nachkantischen Systeme,* 1920 (2nd ed. 1923), VIII, 483 pp. Vol. IV: *Von Hegels Tod bis zur Gegenwart (1832–1932)* (Stuttgart: W. Kohlhammer), 1957, 331 pp.

   English translation of Vol. IV: *The Problem of Knowledge: Philosophy, Science, and History since Hegel.* Transl. by W. H. Woglom and C. W. Hendel. With a Preface by C. W. Hendel. New Haven: Yale University Press; London: Oxford University Press, 1950. XVIII, 334 pp.

   Italian translation: Vol. I, 1952; Vol. II, 1953; Vol. III, 1955; Vol. IV, 1958. Biblioteca di cultura filosofica. Torino: Einaudi.

   Spanish translation: Vol. I, 1953; Vol. II, 1956; Vol. III, 1957; Vol. IV, 1948. Mexico: Fondo de Cultura Economica.

53. "Mathematische Mystik und mathematische Naturwissenschaft. Betrachtungen zur Entstehungsgeschichte der exakten Wissenschaft." (*Lychnos.* Annual of the Swedish History of Science Society. Uppsala and Stockholm: Almqvist & Wiksells Boktr. pp. 248–265.) 1940.

54. *Individuum und Kosmos in der Philosophie der Renaissance.* With appendices: "Nicolai Cusani liber de mente," ed. J. Ritter, transl. H. Cassirer (pp. 203–297; 434–452); and "Caroli Bovilli liber de sapiente," ed. R. Klibansky (pp. 299–412; 453–458). Leipzig and Berlin: Teubner. (*Studien der Bibliothek Warburg,* Vol. X), 1927. ix, 458 pp. Reprint: Darmstadt: Wissensch. Buchgesellschaft, 1963.

   English translation: *The Individual and the Cosmos in Renaissance Philosophy.* Transl. with an Introduction by Mario Domandi. New York: Harper Torchbooks, 1964.

   Italian translation: *Individuo e cosmo nella filosofia del Rinascimento.* Transl. by F. Federici. Firenze: La Nuova Italia, 1935. Reprinted 1950.

   Spanish translation: Buenos Aires: Emece Editores, 1951.

55. "Some Remarks on the Question of the Originality of the Renaissance." (*The Journal of the History of Ideas,* Vol. IV, pp. 49–56.) 1943.

56. "The Place of Vesalius in the Culture of the Renaissance." (*The Yale Journal of Biology and Medicine,* Vol. XVI, No. 2, pp. 109–119.) December 1942.

57. *Die Platonische Renaissance in England und die Schule von Cambridge.* Leipzig and Berlin: Teubner. (*Studien der Bibliothek Warburg,* Vol. XXIV), 1932. viii, 143 pp.

   English translation: *The Platonic Renaissance in England.* Transl.

by J. P. Pettegrove. Austin: University of Texas Press; Edinburgh: Nelson, 1953. [1954]. vii, 207 pp.
Italian translation: *La Rinascenza Platonica in Inghilterra e la Scuola di Cambridge.* Transl. by R. Salvini. La Nuova Italia, 1947.

58. *Die Philosophie im 17. und 18. Jahrhundert.* (Published in *Chronique Annuelle,* publ. par l'Institut International de Collaboration Philosophique.) Paris: Hermann & Cie, 1939, 94 pp.
59. "Enlightenment." (*Encyclopaedia of the Social Sciences,* Vol. V, pp. 547–552. New York.) 1931. Reissued 1937.
60. *Die Philosophie der Aufklärung.* Tübingen: Mohr, 1932. xvii, 491 pp.
English translation: *The Philosophy of the Enlightenment.* Transl. by F. C. A. Koelln and J. P. Pettegrove. Princeton: Princeton University Press, 1951. xiii, 366 pp. Reprint: Boston: Beacon Press, 1955; London: Mayflower Publ., 1960.
Italian translation: *La Filosofia dell' Illuminismo.* Transl. by E. Pocar. Firenze: La Nuova Italia, 1935. (Reprinted in 1945 and 1952).
Spanish translation: *Filosofía de la Ilustración.* Transl. by E. Imaz. Mexico: Fondo de Cultura Economica, 1943.
61. "Neo-Kantianism." (*Encyclopaedia Britannica,* Vol. XVI, pp. 214–215, 14th edition. London and New York.) 1929.
62. " 'Geist' und 'Leben' in der Philosophie der Gegenwart." (*Die Neue Rundschau,* Vol. XLI, pp. 244–264.) Berlin: S. Fischer, 1930.
English translation: " 'Spirit' and 'Life' in Contemporary Philosophy." Transl. by R. W. Bretall and P. A. Schilpp. In *The Philosophy of Ernst Cassirer,* ed. by P. A. Schilpp. The Library of Living Philosophers, Vol. VI, pp. 855–880. Evanston, Illinois. 1949.

II. STUDIES OF PARTICULAR PHILOSOPHERS

1. Plato

63. "Eidos und Eidolon: Das Problem des Schönen und der Kunst in Platons Dialogen." *Vorträge der Bibliothek Warburg,* Vol. II, 1st part, 1922–23, pp. 1–27. Leipzig and Berlin: Teubner, 1924.
64. "Goethe und Platon." Vortrag in der Goethe-Gesellschaft Berlin. (*Sokrates.* 48th year of issue, No. 1. Berlin: Weidmann.) 1922.
Reprinted in *Goethe und die geschichtliche Welt;* vide No. 112.

"Aristoteles und Kant." Vide No. 92.

2. Marsilio Ficino and Giovanni Pico

65. "Ficino's Place in Intellectual History." (Review of P. O. Kristeller, *The Philosophy of Marsilio Ficino* in *The Journal of the History of Ideas,* Vol. VI, No. 4, pp. 483–501.) 1945.
66. "Giovanni Pico della Mirandola: A Study in the History of Renaissance Ideas." (*The Journal of the History of Ideas,* Vol. III, No. 2, pp. 123–144 and 319–346.) 1942.
German translation in: *Agora.* Darmstadt: Wissenschaftl. Buchgesellsch., 1959.

3. Galileo and Kepler

67. "Wahrheitsbegriff und Wahrheitsproblem bei Galilei." (*Scientia.* Vol. LXII, pp. 121–130; 185–193. Bologna) Sept.–Oct. 1937.

68. "Galileo: A New Science and a New Spirit." (*The American Scholar,* Vol. XII, pp. 5–19.) 1943.

69. "Galileo's Platonism." In *Studies and Essays in the History of Science.* Offered in homage to George Sarton. Edited by M. F. Ashley Montagu. New York: H. Schumann, 1946, pp. 276–297.

70. "Keplers Stellung in der europäischen Geistesgeschichte." *Verhandlungen d. naturwissenschaftl. Vereins zu Hamburg.* Series 4, Vol. IV, pp. 135–147. Hamburg, 1930.

4. Descartes

71. *Descartes' Kritik der mathematischen und naturwissenschaftlichen Erkenntnis.* Inaugural-Dissertation. Marburg, 1899. Reprinted in: *Leibniz' System in seinen wissenschaftlichen Grundlagen,* pp. 3–102; vide No. 79.

72. "Descartes et l'idée de l'unité de la science." (*Revue de Synthèse.* Vol. XIV, No. 1, pp. 7–28. Paris.) 1937. Vide also No. 76, Part I.

73. "Descartes' Wahrheitsbegriff." (*Theoria.* Vol. III, pp. 161–187. Göteborg.) 1937. Vide also No. 76, Part I.

74. "Über Bedeutung und Abfassungszeit von Descartes' 'Recherche de la Vérité par la lumière naturelle.' Eine kritische Betrachtung." (*Theoria.* Vol. IV, pp. 193–234. Göteborg.) 1938.

75. "Descartes' Dialog 'Recherche de la vérité par la lumière naturelle' und seine Stellung im Ganzen der Cartesischen Philosophie. Ein Interpretations-Versuch." (*Lychnos.* Annual of the Swedish History of Science Society. Uppsala and Stockholm: Almqvist & Wiksells Boktr., pp. 139–179.) 1938. Reprinted in: *Descartes.* Vide No. 76, Part II, Ch. 2.
French translation: "La place de la 'Recherche de la vérité par la lumière naturelle' dans l'oeuvre de Descartes." *Revue Philosophique,* 1939, pp. 261–300.

76. *Descartes. Lehre—Persönlichkeit—Wirkung.* Stockholm: Bermann-Fischer Verlag, 1939. 308 pp.
French translation (selections): *Descartes, Corneille, Christine de Suède.* Transl. by Madeleine Francès and Paul Schrecker. Paris: Vrin, 1942.
Swedish translation (Ch. III only): *Drottning Christina och Descartes.* Stockholm: Bonniers, 1940. 140 pp.

5. Spinoza

77. "Spinozas Stellung in der allgemeinen Geistesgeschichte." (*Der Morgen.* Vol. VIII, No. 5, pp. 325–348. Berlin: Philo-Verlag.) 1932.

6. Malebranche

78. Review of *Oeuvres complètes de Malebranche,* publ. par D. Roustan et Paul Schrecker. (Vol. I, 1938). (*Theoria,* Vol. IV, pp. 297–300. Göteborg.) 1938.

7. Leibniz and Newton

Edition of Leibniz' *Works;* vide No. 120.

79. *Leibniz' System in seinen wissenschaftlichen Grundlagen.* Marburg: Elwert. xiv, 548 pp. 1902. Reprinted: Darmstadt: Wissenschaftl. Buchgesellschaft, 1962.

80. "Leibniz und Jungius." *Beiträge zur Jungiusforschung. Festschrift der Hamburgischen Universität.* pp. 21–26. Hamburg, 1929.
81. "Leibniz." (*Encyclopaedia of the Social Sciences.* Vol. IX, pp. 400–402. New York: Macmillan.) 1933. Reissued, 1937.
82. "Newton and Leibniz." (*Philosophical Review.* Vol. LII, pp. 366–391.) 1943.

8. Shaftesbury

83. "Shaftesbury und die Renaissance des Platonismus in England." (*Vorträge der Bibliothek Warburg.* Vol. IX, 1930–1931, pp. 136–155.) Leipzig and Berlin: Teubner, 1932.
"Schiller und Shaftesbury." 1935. Vide No. 116.

9. Lessing and Mendelssohn

84. "Die Idee der Religion bei Lessing und Mendelssohn." *Festgabe zum 10jährigen Bestehen der Akademie für die Wissenschaft des Judentums,* pp. 22–41. Berlin: Akademie-Verlag, 1929.
85. "Die Philosophie Moses Mendelssohns." In *Moses Mendelssohn. Zur 200jährigen Wiederkehr seines Geburtstages.* Published by the Encyclopaedia Judaica, pp. 40–60. Berlin: Schneider, 1929.

10. Rousseau

86. "Das Problem Jean Jacques Rousseau". *Archiv für Geschichte d. Philosophie.* Vol. XLI, pp. 177–213; 479–513, 1932.
English translation: *The Question of Jean-Jacques Rousseau.* Transl. and ed. with an Introd. and addit. notes by Peter Gay. New York: Columbia University Press, 1954. vii, 129 pp.
Italian translation: *Il problema Gian Giacomo Rousseau.* Transl. by M. Albanese. In *Civiltà Moderna,* Firenze, 1933–1934. Reprinted separately: Firenze: La Nuova Italia, 1938 (Again in 1948 and 1956).
87. "L'unité dans l'oeuvre de J.-J. Rousseau." X. Léon, E. Cassirer, etc. (In: *Bulletin de la Société Française de Philosophie.* 32e Année, pp. 45–85.) 1933.
88. *Rousseau, Kant, and Goethe: Two Essays.* Translated from the German by J. Gutmann, P. O. Kristeller, and J. H. Randall, Jr. Princeton: Princeton University Press, 1945. ix, 98 pp. (Contains "Kant and Rousseau," and "Goethe and the Kantian Philosophy"). Reprinted: Hamden, Conn.: Shoe String Press, 1945. Archon Books, 1961. New York: Harper Torchbooks, 1963, with Introduction by Peter Gay.

11. Thorild and Herder

89. *Thorilds Stellung in der Geistesgeschichte des achtzehnten Jahrhunderts. Kungl. Vitterhets Historie och Antikvitets Akademiens, Handlingar.* Vol. 51: 1. Stockholm: Wahlström & Widstrand, 1941, 125 pp.
90. "Thorild und Herder." (*Theoria.* Vol. VII, pp. 75–92. Göteborg.) 1941.

12. Kant

Edition of Kant's Collected Works. Vide No. 74.
91. "Kant und die moderne Mathematik. Mit Beziehung auf Bertrand

Russells und Louis Couturats Werke über die Principien der Mathematik." (*Kant-Studien,* Vol. XII, pp. 1–40.) 1907.

92. "Aristoteles und Kant. Zu Görlands Buch: Aristoteles und Kant." (*Kant-Studien*. Vol. XVI, pp. 431–447.) 1911.

93. "Die Grundprobleme der Kantischen Methodik und ihr Verhältnis zur nachkantischen Spekulation." (*Die Geisteswissenschaften*. Vol. I, pp. 784–787; 812–815. Leipzig: Veit.) 1914.

94. *Kants Leben und Lehre*. Immanuel Kants Werke. In Gemeinschaft mit Hermann Cohen u. a. hrsg. v. Ernst Cassirer. Vol. XI (Ergänzungsband). viii, 449 pp. Berlin: Bruno Cassirer, 1918. (2nd ed. 1921)
Spanish translation, by W. Roces: Mexico, Fondo de Cultura Economica, 1948.

95. "Kant und das Problem der Metaphysik. Bemerkungen zu Martin Heideggers Kantinterpretation." (*Kant-Studien*. Vol. XXXVI, pp. 1–26.) 1931.

96. "Kant." (*Encyclopaedia of the Social Sciences,* Vol. VIII, pp. 538–542. New York: Macmillan.) 1932. Reissued 1937.

97. "Neuere Kant-Literatur." (*Theoria*. Vol. VI, pp. 87–100. Göteborg.) 1940.

Rousseau, Kant, and Goethe. Vide No. 88.

13. Wilhelm von Humboldt

98. "Die Kantischen Elemente in Wilhelm von Humboldts Sprachphilosophie." In *Festschrift für Paul Hensel,* pp. 105–127. Greiz i. V.: Ohag, 1923.

14. Recent Thinkers

99. "Hermann Cohen und die Erneuerung der Kantischen Philosophie." (*Kant-Studien*. Vol. XVII, pp. 252–273.) 1912.

100. "Hermann Cohen. Worte gesprochen an seinem Grabe." (*Neue Jüdische Monatshefte*. No. 15–16.) 1918.

101. "Hermann Cohen." Vortrag. *Korrespondenzblatt d. Vereins zur Gründung und Erhaltung einer Akademie d. Judentums*. Vol. I. Frankfurt: Kauffmann, 1920.

102. "Hermann Cohen, 1842–1918." (*Social Research*. Vol. X, No. 2, pp. 219–232. New York.) 1943.

103. "Paul Natorp." (*Kant-Studien*. Vol. XXX, pp. 273–298.) 1925.

104. "Worte zur Beisetzung von Professor Dr. Aby M. Warburg." (In *Aby M. Warburg zum Gedächtnis*. Printed for private circulation. Hamburg.) 1929.
Reprinted in: *Hamburgische Universität. Reden, gehalten bei der Feier des Rektorwechsels am 7. Nov. 1929,* pp. 48–56. Hamburg: Boysen, 1929.

105. "Henri Bergsons Ethik und Religionsphilosophie." (*Der Morgen*. Vol. IX, No. 1. Berlin: Philo-Verlag.) 1933.
Swedish translation: Judisk Tidskrift. Vol. XIV, pp. 13–18, 1941.

106. *Axel Hägerström. Eine Studie zur schwedischen Philosophie der Gegenwart*. Göteborgs Högskolas Årsskrift, XLV. Göteborg: Elanders Boktr.; Wettergren & Kerber, 1939, 120 pp.

107. "Albert Schweitzer as Critic of Nineteenth-Century Ethics." In *The Albert Schweitzer Jubilee Book*. Edited by A. A. Roback. Cam-

bridge, Mass.: Sci-Art Publishers, 1946, pp. 239–258.
William Stern; vide No. 32.

C. PHILOSOPHY AND GERMAN LITERATURE

1. General

108. *Freiheit und Form. Studien zur deutschen Geistesgeschichte.* Berlin: Bruno Cassirer, 1916. xix, 575 pp. 2nd ed., 1918; 3rd ed., 1922. Reprint of 3rd edition: Darmstadt: Wissenschaftl. Buchgesellschaft. 1961.

109. *Idee und Gestalt. Fünf Aufsätze.* Contains: "Goethes Pandora," vide No. 110; "Goethe und die mathematische Physik;" "Die Methodik des Idealismus in Schillers Philosophischen Schriften;" "Hölderlin und der deutsche Idealismus," vide No. 118; "Heinrich von Kleist und die Kantische Philosophie," vide No. 117. Berlin: Bruno Cassirer, 1921. vi, 200 pp. 2nd ed., 1924.

2. Lessing

"Die Idee der Religion bei Lessing und Mendelssohn," 1929. Vide No. 84.

3. Goethe

110. "Goethes Pandora." *Zeitschrift für Aesthetik u. allgem. Kunstwissenschaft.* Vol. XIII, pp. 113–134, 1918. Reprinted in *Idee und Gestalt;* vide No. 109.

"Goethe und Platon." Vide No. 64; reprinted in No. 112.

111. "Goethe und das achtzehnte Jahrhundert." (*Zeitschrift f. Aesthetik u. allgem. Kunstwissenschaft.* Vol. XXVI, pp. 113–148.) 1932. Reprinted in No. 112.

112. *Goethe und die geschichtliche Welt. Drei Aufsätze.* Contains: "Goethe und die geschichtliche Welt;" "Goethe und das 18. Jahrhundert," vide No. 111; "Goethe und Platon," vide No. 64. Berlin: Bruno Cassirer, 1932. 148 pp.

113. "Goethes Idee der Bildung und Erziehung." (*Pädagogisches Zentralblatt,* Vol. XII, pp. 340–358.) 1932.

114. "Der Naturforscher Goethe." (*Hamburger Fremdenblatt.*) March 19, 1932.

"Goethe und die mathematische Physik." 1921. Vide No. 109.

Rousseau, Kant, and Goethe. Vide No. 88.

115. "Thomas Manns Goethe-Bild. Eine Studie über 'Lotte in Weimar'." (*Germanic Review.* Vol. XX, No. 3, pp. 166–194. New York.) 1945.

4. Schiller—Kleist—Hölderlin

"Die Methodik des Idealismus in Schillers Philosophischen Schriften." 1921. Vide No. 109.

116. "Schiller und Shaftesbury." *The Publications of the English Goethe Society.* New Series, Vol. XI, pp. 37–59. Cambridge: The University Press, 1935.

117. "Heinrich von Kleist und die Kantische Philosophie." (*Philosophische Vorträge,* veröffentl. von der Kant-Gesellschaft., No. 22, 56 pp. Ber-

lin: Reuther u. Reichard.) 1919. Reprinted in *Idee und Gestalt,* vide No. 109.

118. "Hölderlin und der deutsche Idealismus." (*Logos,* Vol. VII, pp. 262–282; Vol. VIII, pp. 30–49. Tübingen.) 1917–1918. Reprinted in *Idee und Gestalt;* vide No. 109.

D. PHILOSOPHY AND THOUGHT IN SWEDEN

Vide No. 76, No. 89, No. 90, No. 106.

E. EDITIONS AND TRANSLATIONS

119. *The Renaissance Philosophy of Man.* Selections in translation, ed. by E. Cassirer, P. O. Kristeller, J. H. Randall, Jr. Chicago: The University of Chicago Press, 1948. vi, 405 pp. Reprinted: *Ibid.,* Phoenix paperback edition, 1955.

120. *G. W. Leibniz. Philosophische Werke.* Vol. I and II. *Hauptschriften zur Grundlagung der Philosophie.* Übersetzt v. A. Buchenau. Durchges. u. mit Einleitungen u. Erläuterungen hrsg. v. E. Cassirer. (*Philosoph. Bibliothek.* Vol. 107 and 108.) Vol. I, 1904; Vol. II, 1906 Leipzig: Duerr'sche Buchhandlung. Leipzig: F. Meiner, 2nd ed., 1924. Vol. III. *Neue Abhandlungen über den menschlichen Verstand.* In 3. Aufl. mit Benutzung der Schaarschmidt'schen Übertragung neu übersetzt, eingeleitet u. erläutert v. E. Cassirer. (*Philosoph. Bibliothek,* Vol. 69). Leipzig: F. Meiner, 1915. New edition, with indexes of authors and subjects, *Ibid.,* 1926.

121. *Immanuel Kants Werke.* In Gemeinschaft mit Hermann Cohen, Artur Buchenau, Otto Buck, Albert Görland, B. Kellermann, Otto Schöndörfer, hrsg. v. Ernst Cassirer. Edition of collected works in ten volumes and a supplementary volume. Volumes edited by Ernst Cassirer: Vol. IV, *Schriften von 1783–1788.* Hrsg. von A. Buchenau und Ernst Cassirer; Vol. VI, *Schriften von 1790–1796.* Hrsg. von Ernst Cassirer und Artur Buchenau; Vols. IX and X, *Briefe von und an Kant.* Hrsg. von Ernst Cassirer; Supplementary Volume; vide No. 94.

122. *Philosophische Vorträge.* Veröffentlicht von der Kantgesellschaft. Unter Mitwirkung von E. Cassirer u. M. Frischeisen-Köhler hrsg. von A. Liebert. Heft 1–12. Berlin: Reuther & Reichard, 1912–1916.

123. *Kant-Studien.* Unter Mitwirkung von E. Adickes, E. Cassirer, R. Eucken (et al.) hrsg. von P. Menzer u. A. Liebert. Vols. XXIX–XXXVII. Berlin: Pan-Verlag, 1924–32.

124. *Hermann Cohens Schriften zur Philosophie und Zeitgeschichte.* Hrsg. v. Albert Görland u. Ernst Cassirer. 2 Vols. *Veröffentlichungen d. Hermann Cohen-Stiftung b. d. Akademie f. d. Wissenschaft d. Judentums.* Berlin: Akademie-Verlag, 1928.

SOME ESTIMATES OF CASSIRER'S PHILOSOPHY

1. Hermann Bahr, "Über Ernst Cassirer." (*Die Neue Rundschau.* Vol. XXVIII, No. 11, pp. 1483–1515. Berlin: S. Fischer.) 1917.
2. Heinrich Levy, "La filosofia di Ernst Cassirer." (*Giornale critico della filosofia italiana,* Anno XV, Seconda Serie. Vol. II, fasc. IV–V, pp. 247–280. Firenze.) 1933.
3. P. A. Schilpp, editor, *The Philosophy of Ernst Cassirer* (*The Library of Living Philosophers,* Vol. VI). Evanston, Illinois: The Library of Living Philosophers, Inc., 1949. xviii, 936 pp.
4. Dimitry Gawronsky, "Ernst Cassirer: His Life and His Work. A Biography." In P. A. Schilpp, ed., *The Philosophy of Ernst Cassirer;* vide No. 3, pp. 1–37.
5. Toni Cassirer, *Aus meinem Leben mit Ernst Cassirer.* Privately issued. New York, 1950. iv, 332 pp.
6. Toni Cassirer, *Ernst Cassirer in America.* Italian translation of an extract from No. 5, pp. 257–312. Transl. by G. and R. Pedroli. Torino: Edizioni di "Filosofia," 1955. 40 pp.
7. Émile Meyerson, "L'Histoire du Problème de la Connaissance de M. E. Cassirer." (*Revue de Métaphysique et de Morale.* Vol. XIX, pp. 100–129. Paris.) 1911.
8. H. Lindau, "Beleuchtung des Problems Staat und Freiheit bei Cassirer." (*Europäische Staats- und Wirtschaftszeitung,* pp. 996–1000.) 1916.
9. A. Jospe, *Die Unterscheidung von Mythos und Religion bei Hermann Cohen und Ernst Cassirer in ihrer Bedeutung für die jüdische Religionsphilosophie.* Inaug.-Dissert. Breslau, 1932. Oppeln: F. Wiercimok, 1932. vi, 147 pp.
10. B. Karlgren, *Inbjudning till åhörande av de offentliga föreläsningar med vilka Professorn . . . A. M. Lindqvist och Professorn i Teoretisk Filosofi Ernst Cassirer komma att tillträda sina ämbeten vid Göteborgs Högskola* [*av Högskolans Rektor*]. Göteborg, 1935.
11. F. W. Kearney, "On Cassirer's Conception of Art and History." (*Laval théol. et philos.* Vol. I, No. 2, pp. 131–153. Québec.) 1945.
12. F. Leander, *Estetik och Kunskapsteori: Croce, Cassirer, Dewey.* Göteborg: Elanders Boktr., 1950. 253 pp.
13. C. W. Hendel, "Introduction to the Philosophy of Symbolic Forms"; in No. 34 (English transl.), Vol. I, pp. 1–65. New Haven: Yale University Press; London: Oxford University Press, 1953.
14. W. Flitner, "Rede auf Ernst Cassirer, gehalten am 16. Dezember 1954 auf einer Gedenkfeier in der Universität anlässlich seines 80. Geburtstages am 24. Juli 1954." Hamburg: Selbstverlag der Universität (*Hamburger Universitätsreden,* 19), 1955, 12 pp.
15. C. H. Hamburg, *Symbol and Reality: Studies in the Philosophy of Ernst Cassirer.* The Hague: Martinus Nijhoff, 1956. ix, 172 pp.
16. R. Wells, "Philosophy of Language," in *Philosophy in the Mid-Century,* ed. by R. Klibansky. Vol. II, pp. 142–144. Firenze: La Nuova Italia, 1958; 2nd ed., 1962.

CHRONOLOGICAL LIST OF THE PRINCIPAL WORKS OF ERNST CASSIRER

1899 DESCARTES' KRITIK DER MATHEMATISCHEN UND NATURWISSENSCHAFTLICHEN ERKENNTNIS.

1902 LEIBNIZ' SYSTEM IN SEINEN WISSENSCHAFTLICHEN GRUNDLAGEN.

1904–1915 G. W. LEIBNIZ. PHILOSOPHISCHE WERKE. (Introductions and commentaries to the German translation).

1906 DAS ERKENNTNISPROBLEM IN DER PHILOSOPHIE UND WISSENSCHAFT DER NEUEREN ZEIT. Vol. I.

1907 DAS ERKENNTNISPROBLEM IN DER PHILOSOPHIE UND WISSENSCHAFT DER NEUEREN ZEIT. Vol. II.

1907 KANT UND DIE MODERNE MATHEMATIK.

1910 SUBSTANZBEGRIFF UND FUNKTIONSBEGRIFF. UNTERSUCHUNGEN UBER DIE GRUNDFRAGEN DER ERKENNTNISKRITIK. (English translation: SUBSTANCE AND FUNCTION, 1923.)

1912–1921 IMMANUEL KANTS WERKE. GESAMTAUSGABE. (Editor of complete works.)

1916 FREIHEIT UND FORM. STUDIEN ZUR DEUTSCHEN GEISTESGESCHICHTE.

1918 KANTS LEBEN UND LEHRE.

1920 DAS ERKENNTNISPROBLEM IN DER PHILOSOPHIE UND WISSENSCHAFT DER NEUEREN ZEIT. DIE NACHKANTISCHEN SYSTEME. Vol. III.

1921 IDEE UND GESTALT.

1921 ZUR EINSTEINSCHEN RELATIVITÆTSTHEORIE. (English translation: EINSTEIN'S THEORY OF RELATIVITY, 1923.)

1922 DIE BEGRIFFSFORM IM MYTHISCHEN DENKEN.

1923 PHILOSOPHIE DER SYMBOLISCHEN FORMEN. DIE SPRACHE. Vol. I. (English translation: PHILOSOPHY OF SYMBOLIC FORMS: LANGUAGE. Vol. I, 1953.)

1925 DIE PHILOSOPHIE DER GRIECHEN VON DEN ANFÆNGEN BIS PLATON.

1925 PHILOSOPHIE DER SYMBOLISCHEN FORMEN. DAS MYTHISCHE DENKEN. Vol. II. (English translation: PHILOSOPHY OF SYMBOLIC FORMS: MYTHICAL THOUGHT. Vol. II, 1955.)

1925 SPRACHE UND MYTHOS. (English translation: LANGUAGE AND MYTH, 1946.)

1927 INDIVIDUUM UND KOSMOS IN DER PHILOSOPHIE DER RENAISSANCE. (English translation: THE INDIVIDUAL AND THE COSMOS IN RENAISSANCE PHILOSOPHY, 1963.)

1929 PHILOSOPHIE DER SYMBOLISCHEN FORMEN: PHÆNOMENOLOGIE DER ERKENNTNIS. Vol. III. (English translation: PHILOSOPHY OF SYMBOLIC FORMS: PHENOMENOLOGY OF KNOWLEDGE. Vol. III, 1957.)

1932 DAS PROBLEM JEAN JACQUES ROUSSEAU. (English translation: THE QUESTION OF JEAN-JACQUES ROUSSEAU, 1954.)

1932 DIE PHILOSOPHIE DER AUFKLÆRUNG. (English translation:

THE PHILOSOPHY OF THE ENLIGHTENMENT, 1951.)

1932 DIE PLATONISCHE RENAISSANCE IN ENGLAND UND DIE SCHULE VON CAMBRIDGE. (English translation: THE PLATONIC RENAISSANCE IN ENGLAND, 1953.)

1932 GOETHE UND DIE GESCHICHTLICHE WELT.

1937 DETERMINISMUS UND INDETERMINISMUS IN DER MODERNEN PHYSIK. (English translation. DETERMINISM AND INDETERMINISM IN MODERN PHYSICS, 1956).

1939 AXEL HÆGERSTRŒM.

1939 DESCARTES. LEHRE–PERSŒNLICHKEIT–WIRKUNG.

1941 THORILDS STELLUNG IN DER GEISTESGESCHICHTE DES ACHTZEHNTEN JAHRHUNDERTS.

1942 ZUR LOGIK DER KULTURWISSENSCHAFTEN. (English translation: THE LOGIC OF THE HUMANITIES, 1961.)

1944 AN ESSAY ON MAN: AN INTRODUCTION TO A PHILOSOPHY OF HUMAN CULTURE.

1945 ROUSSEAU, KANT, AND GOETHE. (English translation from the German).

1946 THE MYTH OF THE STATE.

1950 THE PROBLEM OF KNOWLEDGE: PHILOSOPHY, SCIENCE AND HISTORY SINCE HEGEL. (Translation).
DAS ERKENNTNISPROBLEM IN DER PHILOSOPHIE UND WISSENSCHAFT DER NEUEREN ZEIT. VON HEGELS TOD BIS ZUR GEGENWART (1832–1932). Vol. IV, 1957. (Original text).

1956 WESEN UND WIRKUNG DES SYMBOLBEGRIFFS. (Reprint of earlier essays.)

INDEX

Revised Nov., 1963

harper torchbooks

HUMANITIES AND SOCIAL SCIENCES

American Studies

JOHN R. ALDEN: The American Revolution, 1775-1783. **Illus.* TB/3011

RAY A. BILLINGTON: The Far Western Frontier, 1830-1860. **Illus.* TB/3012

RANDOLPH S. BOURNE: The War and the Intellectuals: *A Collection of Essays, 1915-1919. Edited with an Introduction by Carl Resek* TB/3043

JOSEPH CHARLES: The Origins of the American Party System TB/1049

T. C. COCHRAN & WILLIAM MILLER: The Age of Enterprise: *A Social History of Industrial America* TB/1054

FOSTER RHEA DULLES: America's Rise to World Power, 1898-1954. **Illus.* TB/3021

W. A. DUNNING: Reconstruction, Political and Economic, 1865-1877 TB/1073

CLEMENT EATON: The Growth of Southern Civilization, 1790-1860. **Illus.* TB/3040

HAROLD U. FAULKNER: Politics, Reform and Expansion, 1890-1900. **Illus.* TB/3020

LOUIS FILLER: The Crusade against Slavery, 1830-1860. **Illus.* TB/3029

EDITORS OF FORTUNE: America in the Sixties: *the Economy and the Society. Two-color charts* TB/1015

LAWRENCE HENRY GIPSON: The Coming of the Revolution, 1763-1775. **Illus.* TB/3007

FRANCIS J. GRUND: Aristocracy in America: *Jacksonian Democracy* TB/1001

OSCAR HANDLIN, Editor: This Was America: *As Recorded by European Travelers to the Western Shore in the Eighteenth, Nineteenth, and Twentieth Centuries. Illus.* TB/1119

MARCUS LEE HANSEN: The Atlantic Migration: 1607-1860. *Edited by Arthur M. Schlesinger; Introduction by Oscar Handlin* TB/1052

MARCUS LEE HANSEN: The Immigrant in American History. *Edited with a Foreword by Arthur Schlesinger, Sr.* TB/1120

JOHN D. HICKS: Republican Ascendancy, 1921-1933.* *Illus.* TB/3041

JOHN HIGHAM, Ed.: The Reconstruction of American History TB/1068

ROBERT H. JACKSON: The Supreme Court in the American System of Government TB/1106

JOHN F. KENNEDY: A Nation of Immigrants. *Illus.* TB/1118

WILLIAM E. LEUCHTENBURG: Franklin D. Roosevelt and the New Deal, 1932-1940. **Illus.* TB/3025

LEONARD W. LEVY: Freedom of Speech and Press in Early American History: *Legacy of Suppression* TB/1109

ARTHUR S. LINK: Woodrow Wilson and the Progressive Era, 1910-1917. **Illus.* TB/3023

BERNARD MAYO: Myths and Men: *Patrick Henry, George Washington, Thomas Jefferson* TB/1108

JOHN C. MILLER: The Federalist Era, 1789-1801.**Illus.* TB/3027

PERRY MILLER & T. H. JOHNSON, Editors: The Puritans: *A Sourcebook of Their Writings*
Volume I TB/1093
Volume II TB/1094

GEORGE E. MOWRY: The Era of Theodore Roosevelt and the Birth of Modern America, 1900-1912.**Illus.* TB/3022

WALLACE NOTESTEIN: The English People on the Eve of Colonization, 1603-1630. **Illus.* TB/3006

RUSSEL BLAINE NYE: The Cultural Life of the New Nation, 1776-1801. **Illus.* TB/3026

GEORGE E. PROBST, Ed.: The Happy Republic: *A Reader in Tocqueville's America* TB/1060

FRANK THISTLETHWAITE: America and the Atlantic Community: *Anglo-American Aspects, 1790-1850* TB/1107

TWELVE SOUTHERNERS: I'll Take My Stand: *The South and the Agrarian Tradition. Introduction by Louis D. Rubin, Jr.; Biographical Essays by Virginia Rock* TB/1072

A. F. TYLER: Freedom's Ferment: *Phases of American Social History from the Revolution to the Outbreak of the Civil War. Illus.* TB/1074

GLYNDON G. VAN DEUSEN: The Jacksonian Era, 1828-1848. **Illus.* TB/3028

WALTER E. WEYL: The New Democracy: *An Essay on Certain Political and Economic Tendencies in the United States* TB/3042

LOUIS B. WRIGHT: The Cultural Life of the American Colonies, 1607-1763. **Illus.* TB/3005

LOUIS B. WRIGHT: Culture on the Moving Frontier TB/1053

Anthropology & Sociology

W. E. LE GROS CLARK: The Antecedents of Man: *An Introduction to the Evolution of the Primates. Illus.* TB/559

ST. CLAIR DRAKE & HORACE R. CAYTON: Black Metropolis: *A Study of Negro Life in a Northern City. Introduction by Everett C. Hughes. Tables, maps, charts and graphs*
Volume I TB/1086
Volume II TB/1087

CORA DU BOIS: The People of Alor. *New Preface by the author. Illus.*
Volume I TB/1042
Volume II TB/1043

L. S. B. LEAKEY: Adam's Ancestors: *The Evolution of Man and his Culture. Illus.* TB/1019

ROBERT H. LOWIE: Primitive Society. *Introduction by Fred Eggan* TB/1056

TALCOTT PARSONS & EDWARD A. SHILS, Editors: Toward a General Theory of Action: *Theoretical Foundations for the Social Sciences* TB/1083

SIR EDWARD TYLOR: The Origins of Culture. *Part I of "Primitive Culture." Introduction by Paul Radin* TB/33

SIR EDWARD TYLOR: Religion in Primitive Culture. *Part II of "Primitive Culture." Introduction by Paul Radin* TB/34

W. LLOYD WARNER: Social Class in America: *The Evaluation of Status* TB/1013

****The New American Nation Series*, edited by Henry Steele Commager and Richard B. Morris.**

Art and Art History

EMILE MÂLE: The Gothic Image: *Religious Art in France of the Thirteenth Century. 190 illus.* TB/44

ERWIN PANOFSKY: Studies in Iconology: *Humanistic Themes in the Art of the Renaissance. 180 illustrations* TB/1077

ALEXANDRE PIANKOFF: The Shrines of Tut-Ankh-Amon. *Edited by N. Rambova. 117 illus.* TB/2011

JEAN SEZNEC: The Survival of the Pagan Gods: *The Mythological Tradition and Its Place in Renaissance Humanism and Art. 108 illustrations* TB/2004

HEINRICH ZIMMER: Myths and Symbols in Indian Art and Civilization: *70 illustrations* TB/2005

Business, Economics & Economic History

REINHARD BENDIX: Work and Authority in Industry: *Ideologies of Management in the Course of Industrialization* TB/3035

THOMAS C. COCHRAN: The American Business System: *A Historical Perspective, 1900-1955* TB/1080

ROBERT DAHL & CHARLES E. LINDBLOM: Politics, Economics, and Welfare: *Planning and Politico-Economic Systems Resolved into Basic Social Processes* TB/3037

PETER F. DRUCKER: The New Society: *The Anatomy of Industrial Order* TB/1082

ROBERT L. HEILBRONER: The Great Ascent: *The Struggle for Economic Development* TB/3030

PAUL MANTOUX: The Industrial Revolution in the Eighteenth Century: *The Beginnings of the Modern Factory System in England* TB/1079

WILLIAM MILLER, Ed.: Men in Business: *Essays on the Historical Role of the Entrepreneur* TB/1081

PERRIN STRYKER: The Character of the Executive: *Eleven Studies in Managerial Qualities* TB/1041

PIERRE URI: Partnership for Progress. TB/3036

Contemporary Culture

JACQUES BARZUN: The House of Intellect TB/1051

JOHN U. NEF: Cultural Foundations of Industrial Civilization TB/1024

PAUL VALÉRY: The Outlook for Intelligence TB/2016

History: General

L. CARRINGTON GOODRICH: A Short History of the Chinese People. *Illus.* TB/3015

DAN N. JACOBS & HANS BAERWALD: Chinese Communism: *Selected Documents* TB/3031

BERNARD LEWIS: The Arabs in History TB/1029

SIR PERCY SYKES: A History of Exploration. *Introduction by John K. Wright* TB/1046

History: Ancient and Medieval

A. ANDREWES: The Greek Tyrants TB/1103

HELEN CAM: England before Elizabeth TB/1026

NORMAN COHN: The Pursuit of the Millennium: *Revolutionary Messianism in medieval and Reformation Europe and its bearing on modern totalitarian movements* TB/1037

G. G. COULTON: Medieval Village, Manor, and Monastery TB/1022

F. L. GANSHOF: Feudalism TB/1058

J. M. HUSSEY: The Byzantine World TB/1057

SAMUEL NOAH KRAMER: Sumerian Mythology TB/1055

FERDINAND LOT: The End of the Ancient World and the Beginnings of the Middle Ages. *Introduction by Glanville Downey* TB/1044

J. M. WALLACE-HADRILL: The Barbarian West: *The Early Middle Ages, A.D. 400-1000* TB/1061

History: Renaissance & Reformation

JACOB BURCKHARDT: The Civilization of the Renaissance in Italy. *Introduction by Benjamin Nelson and Charles Trinkaus. Illus.* Volume I TB/40
Volume II TB/41

ERNST CASSIRER: The Individual and the Cosmos in Renaissance Philosophy. *Translated with an Introduction by Mario Domandi* TB/1097

EDWARD P. CHEYNEY: The Dawn of a New Era, 1250-1453 †*Illus.* TB/3002

WALLACE K. FERGUSON, et al.: Facets of the Renaissance TB/1098

WALLACE K. FERGUSON, et al.: The Renaissance: *Six Essays. Illus.* TB/1084

MYRON P. GILMORE: The World of Humanism, 1453-1517. †*Illus.* TB/3003

JOHAN HUIZINGA: Erasmus and the Age of Reformation. *Illus.* TB/19

PAUL O. KRISTELLER: Renaissance Thought: *The Classic, Scholastic, and Humanist Strains* TB/1048

NICCOLÒ MACHIAVELLI: History of Florence and of the Affairs of Italy: *from the earliest times to the death of Lorenzo the Magnificent. Introduction by Felix Gilbert* TB/1027

ALFRED VON MARTIN: Sociology of the Renaissance. *Introduction by W. K. Ferguson* TB/1099

J. E. NEALE: The Age of Catherine de Medici TB/1085

ERWIN PANOFSKY: Studies in Iconology: *Humanistic Themes in the Art of the Renaissance. 180 illustrations* TB/1077

J. H. PARRY: The Establishment of the European Hegemony: 1415-1715: *Trade and Exploration in the Age of the Renaissance* TB/1045

HENRI PIRENNE: Early Democracies in the Low Countries: *Urban Society and Political Conflict in the Middle Ages and the Renaissance. Introduction by John H. Mundy* TB/1110

FERDINAND SCHEVILL: The Medici. *Illus.* TB/1010

FERDINAND SCHEVILL: Medieval and Renaissance Florence. *Illus.* Volume I: *Medieval Florence* TB/1090
Volume II: *The Coming of Humanism and the Age of the Medici* TB/1091

G. M. TREVELYAN: England in the Age of Wycliffe, 1368-1520 TB/1112

VESPASIANO: Renaissance Princes, Popes, and Prelates: *The Vespasiano Memoirs: Lives of Illustrious Men of the XVth Century. Introduction by Myron P. Gilmore. Illus.* TB/1111

History: Modern European

FREDERICK B. ARTZ: Reaction and Revolution, 1815-1832. †*Illus.* TB/3034

MAX BELOFF: The Age of Absolutism, 1660-1815 TB/1062

ROBERT C. BINKLEY: Realism and Nationalism, 1852-1871. †*Illus.* TB/3038

CRANE BRINTON: A Decade of Revolution, 1789-1799. †*Illus.* TB/3018

†***The Rise of Modern Europe Series*, edited by William L. Langer.**

J. BRONOWSKI & BRUCE MAZLISH: The Western Intellectual Tradition: *From Leonardo to Hegel* TB/3001

GEOFFREY BRUUN: Europe and the French Imperium, 1799-1814. †*Illus.* TB/3033

WALTER L. DORN: Competition for Empire, 1740-1763. †*Illus.* TB/3032

CARL J. FRIEDRICH: The Age of the Baroque, 1610-1660. †*Illus.* TB/3004

LEO GERSHOY: From Despotism to Revolution, 1763-1789. †*Illus.* TB/3017

ALBERT GOODWIN: The French Revolution TB/1064

CARLTON J. H. HAYES: A Generation of Materialism, 1871-1900. †*Illus.* TB/3039

J. H. HEXTER: Reappraisals in History: *New Views on History and Society in Early Modern Europe* TB/1100

A. R. HUMPHREYS: The Augustan World: *Society, Thought, and Letters in Eighteenth Century England* TB/1105

DAN N. JACOBS, Ed.: The New Communist Manifesto *and Related Documents* TB/1078

HANS KOHN, Ed.: The Mind of Modern Russia: *Historical and Political Thought of Russia's Great Age* TB/1065

SIR LEWIS NAMIER: Vanished Supremacies: *Essays on European History, 1812-1918* TB/1088

JOHN U. NEF: Western Civilization Since the Renaissance: *Peace, War, Industry, and the Arts* TB/1113

FREDERICK L. NUSSBAUM: The Triumph of Science and Reason, 1660-1685. †*Illus.* TB/3009

RAYMOND W. POSTGATE, Ed.: Revolution from 1789 to 1906: *Selected Documents* TB/1063

PENFIELD ROBERTS: The Quest for Security, 1715-1740. †*Illus.* TB/3016

PRISCILLA ROBERTSON: Revolutions of 1848: *A Social History* TB/1025

N. N. SUKHANOV: The Russian Revolution, 1917: *Eyewitness Account.* Edited by Joel Carmichael
Volume I TB/1066
Volume II TB/1067

JOHN B. WOLF: The Emergence of the Great Powers, 1685-1715. †*Illus.* TB/3010

JOHN B. WOLF: France: 1814-1919: *The Rise of a Liberal-Democratic Society* TB/3019

Intellectual History

HERSCHEL BAKER: The Image of Man: *A Study of the Idea of Human Dignity in Classical Antiquity, the Middle Ages, and the Renaissance* TB/1047

J. BRONOWSKI & BRUCE MAZLISH: The Western Intellectual Tradition: *From Leonardo to Hegel* TB/3001

NORMAN COHN: The Pursuit of the Millennium: *Revolutionary Messianism in medieval and Reformation Europe and its bearing on modern totalitarian movements* TB/1037

ARTHUR O. LOVEJOY: The Great Chain of Being: *A Study of the History of an Idea* TB/1009

ROBERT PAYNE: Hubris: *A Study of Pride. Foreword by Sir Herbert Read* TB/1031

BRUNO SNELL: The Discovery of the Mind: *The Greek Origins of European Thought* TB/1018

Literature, Poetry, The Novel & Criticism

JAMES BAIRD: Ishmael: *The Art of Melville in the Contexts of International Primitivism* TB/1023

JACQUES BARZUN: The House of Intellect TB/1051

W. J. BATE: From Classic to Romantic: *Premises of Taste in Eighteenth Century England* TB/1036

RACHEL BESPALOFF: On the Iliad TB/2006

R. P. BLACKMUR, et al.: Lectures in Criticism. *Introduction by Huntington Cairns* TB/2003

ABRAHAM CAHAN: The Rise of David Levinsky: *a novel. Introduction by John Higham* TB/1028

ERNST R. CURTIUS: European Literature and the Latin Middle Ages TB/2015

GEORGE ELIOT: Daniel Deronda: *a novel. Introduction by F. R. Leavis* TB/1039

ETIENNE GILSON: Dante and Philosophy TB/1089

ALFRED HARBAGE: As They Liked It: *A Study of Shakespeare's Moral Artistry* TB/1035

STANLEY R. HOPPER, Ed.: Spiritual Problems in Contemporary Literature TB/21

A. R. HUMPHREYS: The Augustan World: *Society, Thought, and Letters in Eighteenth Century England* TB/1105

ALDOUS HUXLEY: Antic Hay & The Gioconda Smile. TB/3503

ALDOUS HUXLEY: Brave New World & Brave New World Revisited. *Introduction by C. P. Snow* TB/3501

ALDOUS HUXLEY: Point Counter Point. *Introduction by C. P. Snow* TB/3502

HENRY JAMES: The Princess Casamassima: *a novel. Introduction by Clinton F. Oliver* TB/1005

HENRY JAMES: Roderick Hudson: *a novel. Introduction by Leon Edel* TB/1016

HENRY JAMES: The Tragic Muse: *a novel. Introduction by Leon Edel* TB/1017

ARNOLD KETTLE: An Introduction to the English Novel. Volume I: *Defoe to George Eliot* TB/101
Volume II: *Henry James to the Present* TB/1012

JOHN STUART MILL: On Bentham and Coleridge. *Introduction by F. R. Leavis* TB/1070

PERRY MILLER & T. H. JOHNSON, Editors: The Puritans: *A Sourcebook of Their Writings*
Volume I TB/1093
Volume II TB/1094

KENNETH B. MURDOCK: Literature and Theology in Colonial New England TB/99

SAMUEL PEPYS: The Diary of Samuel Pepys. *Edited by O. F. Morshead. Illustrations by Ernest Shepard* TB/1007

ST.-JOHN PERSE: Seamarks TB/2002

O. E. RÖLVAAG: Giants in the Earth. *Introduction by Einar Haugen* TB/3504

GEORGE SANTAYANA: Interpretations of Poetry and Religion TB/9

C. P. SNOW: Time of Hope: *a novel* TB/1040

DOROTHY VAN GHENT: The English Novel: *Form and Function* TB/1050

E. B. WHITE: One Man's Meat. *Introduction by Walter Blair* TB/3505

MORTON DAUWEN ZABEL, Editor: Literary Opinion in America
Volume I TB/3013
Volume II TB/3014

Myth, Symbol & Folklore

JOSEPH CAMPBELL, Editor: Pagan and Christian Mysteries TB/2013

MIRCEA ELIADE: Cosmos and History: *The Myth of the Eternal Return* TB/2050

C. G. JUNG & C. KERÉNYI: Essays on a Science of Mythology: *The Myths of the Divine Child and the Divine Maiden* TB/2014

ERWIN PANOFSKY: Studies in Iconology: *Humanistic Themes in the Art of the Renaissance. 180 illustrations* TB/1077

JEAN SEZNEC: The Survival of the Pagan Gods: *The Mythological Tradition and its Place in Renaissance Humanism and Art. 108 illustrations* TB/2004

HEINRICH ZIMMER: Myths and Symbols in Indian Art and Civilization. *70 illustrations* TB/2005

Philosophy

HENRI BERGSON: Time and Free Will: *An Essay on the Immediate Data of Consciousness* TB/1021

H. J. BLACKHAM: Six Existentialist Thinkers: *Kierkegaard, Nietzsche, Jaspers, Marcel, Heidegger, Sartre* TB/1002

ERNST CASSIRER: Rousseau, Kant and Goethe. *Introduction by Peter Gay* TB/1092

FREDERICK COPLESTON: Medieval Philosophy TB/76

F. M. CORNFORD: From Religion to Philosophy: *A Study in the Origins of Western Speculation* TB/20

WILFRID DESAN: The Tragic Finale: *An Essay on the Philosophy of Jean-Paul Sartre* TB/1030

PAUL FRIEDLANDER: Plato: *An Introduction* TB/2017

ETIENNE GILSON: Dante and Philosophy TB/1089

WILLIAM CHASE GREENE: Moira: *Fate, Good, and Evil in Greek Thought* TB/1104

W. K. C. GUTHRIE: The Greek Philosophers: *From Thales to Aristotle* TB/1008

F. H. HEINEMANN: Existentialism and the Modern Predicament TB/28

IMMANUEL KANT: The Doctrine of Virtue, *being Part II of The Metaphysic of Morals. Translated with Notes and Introduction by Mary J. Gregor. Foreword by H. J. Paton* TB/110

IMMANUEL KANT: Lectures on Ethics. *Introduction by Lewis W. Beck* TB/105

WILLARD VAN ORMAN QUINE: From a Logical Point of View: *Logico-Philosophical Essays* TB/566

BERTRAND RUSSELL et al.: The Philosophy of Bertrand Russell. *Edited by Paul Arthur Schilpp*
Volume I TB/1095
Volume II TB/1096

L. S. STEBBING: A Modern Introduction to Logic TB/538

ALFRED NORTH WHITEHEAD: Process and Reality: *An Essay in Cosmology* TB/1033

WILHELM WINDELBAND: A History of Philosophy I: *Greek, Roman, Medieval* TB/38

WILHELM WINDELBAND: A History of Philosophy II: *Renaissance, Enlightenment, Modern* TB/39

Philosophy of History

NICOLAS BERDYAEV: The Beginning and the End TB/14

NICOLAS BERDYAEV: The Destiny of Man TB/61

WILHELM DILTHEY: Pattern and Meaning in History: *Thoughts on History and Society. Edited with an Introduction by H. P. Rickman* TB/1075

JOSE ORTEGA Y GASSET: The Modern Theme. *Introduction by Jose Ferrater Mora* TB/1038

H. J. PATON & RAYMOND KLIBANSKY, Eds.: Philosophy and History TB/1115

W. H. WALSH: Philosophy of History: *An Introduction* TB/1020

Political Science & Government

JEREMY BENTHAM: The Handbook of Political Fallacies: *Introduction by Crane Brinton* TB/1069

KENNETH E. BOULDING: Conflict and Defense: *A General Theory* TB/3024

CRANE BRINTON: English Political Thought in the Nineteenth Century TB/1071

ROBERT DAHL & CHARLES E. LINDBLOM: Politics, Economics, and Welfare: *Planning and Politico-Economic Systems Resolved into Basic Social Processes* TB/3037

JOHN NEVILLE FIGGIS: Political Thought from Gerson to Grotius: 1414-1625: *Seven Studies. Introduction by Garrett Mattingly* TB/1032

F. L. GANSHOF: Feudalism TB/1058

G. P. GOOCH: English Democratic Ideas in the Seventeenth Century TB/1006

ROBERT H. JACKSON: The Supreme Court in the American System of Government TB/1106

KINGSLEY MARTIN: French Liberal Thought in the Eighteenth Century: *A Study of Political Ideas from Bayle to Condorcet* TB/1114

J. P. MAYER: Alexis de Tocqueville: *A Biographical Study in Political Science* TB/1014

JOHN STUART MILL: On Bentham and Coleridge. *Introduction by F. R. Leavis* TB/1070

JOHN B. MORRALL: Political Thought in Medieval Times TB/1076

KARL R. POPPER: The Open Society and Its Enemies
Volume I: *The Spell of Plato* TB/1101
Volume II: *The High Tide of Prophecy: Hegel, Marx, and the Aftermath* TB/1102

JOSEPH A. SCHUMPETER: Capitalism, Socialism and Democracy TB/3008

Psychology

ANTON T. BOISEN: The Exploration of the Inner World: *A Study of Mental Disorder and Religious Experience* TB/87

WALTER BROMBERG: The Mind of Man: *A History of Psychotherapy and Psychoanalysis* TB/1003

SIGMUND FREUD: On Creativity and the Unconscious: *Papers on the Psychology of Art, Literature, Love, Religion. Intro. by Benjamin Nelson* TB/45

C. JUDSON HERRICK: The Evolution of Human Nature TB/545

ALDOUS HUXLEY: The Devils of Loudun: *A Study in the Psychology of Power Politics and Mystical Religion in the France of Cardinal Richelieu* TB/60

WILLIAM JAMES: Psychology: *The Briefer Course. Edited with an Intro. by Gordon Allport* TB/1034

C. G. JUNG: Psychological Reflections. *Edited by Jolande Jacobi* TB/2001

C. G. JUNG: Symbols of Transformation: *An Analysis of the Prelude to a Case of Schizophrenia*
Volume I TB/2009
Volume II TB/2010

C. G. JUNG & C. KERÉNYI: Essays on a Science of Mythology: *The Myths of the Divine Child and the Divine Maiden* TB/2014

ERICH NEUMANN: Amor and Psyche: *The Psychic Development of the Feminine* TB/2012

ERICH NEUMANN: The Origins and History of Consciousness Volume I *Illus.* TB/2007
Volume II TB/2008

RELIGION

Ancient & Classical

J. H. BREASTED: Development of Religion and Thought in Ancient Egypt. *Introduction by John A. Wilson* TB/57

HENRI FRANKFORT: Ancient Egyption Religion: *An Interpretation* TB/77

G. RACHEL LEVY: Religious Conceptions of the Stone Age *and their Influence upon European Thought. Illus. Introduction by Henri Frankfort* TB/106

MARTIN P. NILSSON: Greek Folk Religion. *Foreword by Arthur Darby Nock* TB/78

ALEXANDRE PIANKOFF: The Shrines of Tut-Ankh-Amon. *Edited by N. Rambova. 117 illus.* TB/2011

H. J. ROSE: Religion in Greece and Rome TB/55

Biblical Thought & Literature

W. F. ALBRIGHT: The Biblical Period from Abraham to Ezra TB/102

C. K. BARRETT, Ed.: The New Testament Background: *Selected Documents* TB/86

C. H. DODD: The Authority of the Bible TB/43

M. S. ENSLIN: Christian Beginnings TB/5

M. S. ENSLIN: The Literature of the Christian Movement TB/6

H. E. FOSDICK: A Guide to Understanding the Bible TB/2

H. H. ROWLEY: The Growth of the Old Testament TB/107

D. WINTON THOMAS, Ed.: Documents from Old Testament Times TB/85

Christianity: Origins & Early Development

EDWARD GIBBON: The Triumph of Christendom in the Roman Empire *(Chaps. XV-XX of "Decline and Fall," J. B. Bury edition). Illus.* TB/46

MAURICE GOGUEL: Jesus and the Origins of Christianity. *Introduction by C. Leslie Mitton*
Volume I: *Prolegomena to the Life of Jesus* TB/65
Volume II: *The Life of Jesus* TB/66

EDGAR J. GOODSPEED: A Life of Jesus TB/1

ADOLF HARNACK: The Mission and Expansion of Christianity *in the First Three Centuries. Introduction by Jaroslav Pelikan* TB/92

R. K. HARRISON: The Dead Sea Scrolls: *An Introduction* TB/84

EDWIN HATCH: The Influence of Greek Ideas on Christianity. *Introduction and Bibliography by Frederick C. Grant* TB/18

ARTHUR DARBY NOCK: Early Gentile Christianity and Its Hellenistic Background TB/111

JOHANNES WEISS: Earliest Christianity: *A History of the Period A.D. 30-150. Introduction and Bibilography by Frederick C. Grant* Volume I TB/53
Volume II TB/54

Christianity: The Middle Ages and After

G. P. FEDOTOV: The Russian Religious Mind: *Kievan Christianity, the tenth to the thirteenth centuries* TB/70

ETIENNE GILSON: Dante and Philosophy TB/1089

WILLIAM HALLER: The Rise of Puritanism TB/22

JOHAN HUIZINGA: Erasmus and the Age of Reformation. *Illus.* TB/19

A. C. McGIFFERT: Protestant Thought Before Kant. *Preface by Jaroslav Pelikan* TB/93

KENNETH B. MURDOCK: Literature and Theology in Colonial New England TB/99

H. O. TAYLOR: The Emergence of Christian Culture in the West: *The Classical Heritage of the Middle Ages. Intro. and biblio. by Kenneth M. Setton* TB/48

Judaic Thought & Literature

MARTIN BUBER: Eclipse of God: *Studies in the Relation Between Religion and Philosophy* TB/12

MARTIN BUBER: Moses: *The Revelation and the Covenant* TB/27

MARTIN BUBER: Pointing the Way. *Introduction by Maurice S. Friedman* TB/103

MARTIN BUBER: The Prophetic Faith TB/73

MARTIN BUBER: Two Types of Faith: *the interpenetration of Judaism and Christianity* TB/75

MAURICE S. FRIEDMAN: Martin Buber: *The Life of Dialogue* TB/64

FLAVIUS JOSEPHUS: The Great Roman-Jewish War, *with* The Life of Josephus. *Introduction by William R. Farmer* TB/74

T. J. MEEK: Hebrew Origins TB/69

Oriental Religions: Far Eastern, Near Eastern

TOR ANDRAE: Mohammed: *The Man and His Faith* TB/62

EDWARD CONZE: Buddhism: *Its Essence and Development. Foreword by Arthur Waley* TB/58

EDWARD CONZE, et al., Editors: Buddhist Texts Through the Ages TB/113

H. G. CREEL: Confucius and the Chinese Way TB/63

Philosophy of Religion

RUDOLF BULTMANN: History and Eschatology: *The Presence of Eternity* TB/91

RUDOLF BULTMANN AND FIVE CRITICS: Kerygma and Myth: *A Theological Debate* TB/80

RUDOLF BULTMANN and KARL KUNDSIN: Form Criticism: *Two Essays on New Testament Research. Translated by Frederick C. Grant* TB/96

MIRCEA ELIADE: The Sacred and the Profane TB/81

LUDWIG FEUERBACH: The Essence of Christianity. *Introduction by Karl Barth. Foreword by H. Richard Niebuhr* TB/11

ADOLF HARNACK: What is Christianity? *Introduction by Rudolf Bultmann* TB/17

FRIEDRICH HEGEL: On Christianity: *Early Theological Writings. Edited by Richard Kroner and T. M. Knox* TB/79

KARL HEIM: Christian Faith and Natural Science TB/16

IMMANUEL KANT: Religion Within the Limits of Reason Alone. *Introduction by Theodore M. Greene and John Silber* TB/67

PIERRE TEILHARD DE CHARDIN: The Phenomenon of Man TB/83

Religion, Culture & Society

C. C. GILLISPIE: Genesis and Geology: *The Decades before Darwin* TB/51

H. RICHARD NIEBUHR: Christ and Culture TB/3

H. RICHARD NIEBUHR: The Kingdom of God in America TB/49

ERNST TROELTSCH: The Social Teaching of the Christian Churches. *Introduction by H. Richard Niebuhr* Volume I TB/71
Volume II TB/72

Religious Thinkers & Traditions

AUGUSTINE: An Augustine Synthesis. *Edited by Erich Przywara* TB/35
KARL BARTH: Church Dogmatics: *A Selection: Introduction by H. Gollwitzer; Edited by G. W. Bromiley* TB/95
KARL BARTH: Dogmatics in Outline TB/56
KARL BARTH: The Word of God and the Word of Man TB/13
THOMAS CORBISHLEY: Roman Catholicism TB/112
ADOLF DEISSMANN: Paul: *A Study in Social and Religious History* TB/15
JOHANNES ECKHART: Meister Eckhart: *A Modern Translation by R. B. Blakney* TB/8
WINTHROP HUDSON: The Great Tradition of the American Churches TB/98
SOREN KIERKEGAARD: Edifying Discourses. *Edited with an Introduction by Paul Holmer* TB/32
SOREN KIERKEGAARD: The Journals of Kierkegaard. *Edited with an Intro. by Alexander Dru* TB/52
SOREN KIERKEGAARD: The Point of View for My Work as an Author: *A Report to History. Preface by Benjamin Nelson* TB/88
SOREN KIERKEGAARD: The Present Age. *Translated and edited by Alexander Dru. Introduction by Walter Kaufmann* TB/94
SOREN KIERKEGAARD: Purity of Heart. *Translated by Douglas Steere* TB/4
WALTER LOWRIE: Kierkegaard: *A Life*
Volume I TB/89
Volume II TB/90
GABRIEL MARCEL: Homo Viator: *Introduction to a Metaphysic of Hope* TB/97
PERRY MILLER & T. H. JOHNSON, Editors: The Puritans: *A Sourcebook of Their Writings*
Volume I TB/1093
Volume II TB/1094
A. D. NOCK: St. Paul TB/104
PAUL PFUETZE: Self, Society, Existence: *Human Nature and Dialogue in the Thought of George Herbert Mead and Martin Buber* TB/1059
F. SCHLEIERMACHER: The Christian Faith. *Introduction by Richard R. Niebuhr* Volume I TB/108
Volume II TB/109
F. SCHLEIERMACHER: On Religion: *Speeches to Its Cultured Despisers. Intro. by Rudolf Otto* TB/36
PAUL TILLICH: Dynamics of Faith TB/42
EVELYN UNDERHILL: Worship TB/10
G. VAN DER LEEUW: Religion in Essence and Manifestation: *A Study in Phenomenology. Appendices by Hans H. Penner* Volume I TB/100
Volume II TB/101

NATURAL SCIENCES AND MATHEMATICS

Biological Sciences

CHARLOTTE AUERBACH: The Science of Genetics TB/568
A. BELLAIRS: Reptiles: *Life History, Evolution, and Structure. Illus.* TB/520
LUDWIG VON BERTALANFFY: Modern Theories of Development: *An Introduction to Theoretical Biology* TB/554
LUDWIG VON BERTALANFFY: Problems of Life: *An Evaluation of Modern Biological and Scientific Thought* TB/521
HAROLD F. BLUM: Time's Arrow and Evolution TB/555
A. J. CAIN: Animal Species and their Evolution. *Illus.* TB/519
WALTER B. CANNON: Bodily Changes in Pain, Hunger, Fear and Rage. *Illus.* TB/562
W. E. LE GROS CLARK: The Antecedents of Man: *An Introduction to the Evolution of the Primates. Illus.* TB/559
W. H. DOWDESWELL: Animal Ecology. *Illus.* TB/543
W. H. DOWDESWELL: The Mechanism of Evolution. *Illus.* TB/527
R. W. GERARD: Unresting Cells. *Illus.* TB/541
DAVID LACK: Darwin's Finches. *Illus.* TB/544
J. E. MORTON: Molluscs: *An Introduction to their Form and Functions. Illus.* TB/529
O. W. RICHARDS: The Social Insects. *Illus.* TB/542
P. M. SHEPPARD: Natural Selection and Heredity. *Illus.* TB/528
EDMUND W. SINNOTT: Cell and Psyche: *The Biology of Purpose* TB/546
C. H. WADDINGTON: How Animals Develop. *Illus.* TB/553

Chemistry

A. FINDLAY: Chemistry in the Service of Man. *Illus.* TB/524
J. R. PARTINGTON: A Short History of Chemistry. *Illus.* TB/522
J. READ: A Direct Entry to Organic Chemistry. *Illus.* TB/523
J. READ: Through Alchemy to Chemistry. *Illus.* TB/561

Geography

R. E. COKER: This Great and Wide Sea: *An Introduction to Oceanography and Marine Biology. Illus.* TB/551
F. K. HARE: The Restless Atmosphere TB/560

History of Science

W. DAMPIER, Ed.: Readings in the Literature of Science. *Illus.* TB/512
ALEXANDRE KOYRÉ: From the Closed World to the Infinite Universe: *Copernicus, Kepler, Galileo, Newton, etc.* TB/31
A. G. VAN MELSEN: From Atomos to Atom: *A History of the Concept* Atom TB/517
O. NEUGEBAUER: The Exact Sciences in Antiquity TB/552
H. T. PLEDGE: Science Since 1500: *A Short History of Mathematics, Physics, Chemistry and Biology. Illus.* TB/506
GEORGE SARTON: Ancient Science and Modern Civilization TB/501
HANS THIRRING: Energy for Man: *From Windmills to Nuclear Power* TB/556
WILLIAM LAW WHYTE: Essay on Atomism: *From Democritus to 1960* TB/565
A. WOLF: A History of Science, Technology and Philosophy in the 16th and 17th Centuries. *Illus.*
Volume I TB/508
Volume II TB/509
A. WOLF: A History of Science, Technology, and Philosophy in the Eighteenth Century. *Illus.*
Volume I TB/539
Volume II TB/540

Mathematics

H. DAVENPORT: The Higher Arithmetic: *An Introduction to the Theory of Numbers* TB/526

H. G. FORDER: Geometry: *An Introduction* TB/548

GOTTLOB FREGE: The Foundations of Arithmetic: *A Logico-Mathematical Enquiry into the Concept of Number* TB/534

S. KÖRNER: The Philosophy of Mathematics: *An Introduction* TB/547

D. E. LITTLEWOOD: Skeleton Key of Mathematics: *A Simple Account of Complex Algebraic Problems* TB/525

GEORGE E. OWEN: Fundamentals of Scientific Mathematics TB/569

WILLARD VAN ORMAN QUINE: Mathematical Logic TB/558

O. G. SUTTON: Mathematics in Action. *Foreword by James R. Newman. Illus.* TB/518

FREDERICK WAISMANN: Introduction to Mathematical Thinking. *Foreword by Karl Menger* TB/511

Philosophy of Science

R. B. BRAITHWAITE: Scientific Explanation TB/515

J. BRONOWSKI: Science and Human Values. *Illus.* TB/505

ALBERT EINSTEIN: Philosopher-Scientist. *Edited by Paul A. Schilpp* Volume I TB/502; Volume II TB/503

WERNER HEISENBERG: Physics and Philosophy: *The Revolution in Modern Science. Introduction by F. S. C. Northrop* TB/549

JOHN MAYNARD KEYNES: A Treatise on Probability. *Introduction by N. R. Hanson* TB/557

STEPHEN TOULMIN: Foresight and Understanding: *An Enquiry into the Aims of Science. Foreword by Jacques Barzun* TB/564

STEPHEN TOULMIN: The Philosophy of Science: *An Introduction* TB/513

W. H. WATSON: On Understanding Physics. *Introduction by Ernest Nagel* TB/507

G. J. WHITROW: The Natural Philosophy of Time TB/563

Physics and Cosmology

DAVID BOHM: Causality and Chance in Modern Physics. *Foreword by Louis de Broglie* TB/536

P. W. BRIDGMAN: The Nature of Thermodynamics TB/537

LOUIS DE BROGLIE: Physics and Microphysics. *Foreword by Albert Einstein* TB/514

T. G. COWLING: Molecules in Motion: *An Introduction to the Kinetic Theory of Gases. Illus.* TB/516

A. C. CROMBIE, Ed.: Turning Point in Physics TB/535

C. V. DURELL: Readable Relativity. *Foreword by Freeman J. Dyson* TB/530

ARTHUR EDDINGTON: Space, Time and Gravitation: *An outline of the General Relativity Theory* TB/510

GEORGE GAMOW: Biography of Physics TB/567

MAX JAMMER: Concepts of Force: *A Study in the Foundation of Dynamics* TB/550

MAX JAMMER: Concepts of Space: *The History of Theories of Space in Physics. Foreword by Albert Einstein* TB/533

EDMUND WHITTAKER: History of the Theories of Aether and Electricity
Volume I: *The Classical Theories* TB/531
Volume II: *The Modern Theories* TB/532

G. J. WHITROW: The Structure and Evolution of the Universe: *An Introduction to Cosmology. Illus.* TB/504

Code to Torchbook Libraries:

TB/1+	: The Cloister Library
TB/501+	: The Science Library
TB/1001+	: The Academy Library
TB/2001+	: The Bollingen Library
TB/3001+	: The University Library

A LETTER TO THE READER

Overseas, there is considerable belief that we are a country of extreme conservatism and that we cannot accommodate to social change.

Books about America in the hands of readers abroad can help change those ideas.

The U. S. Information Agency cannot, by itself, meet the vast need for books about the United States.

You can help.

Harper Torchbooks provides three packets of books on American history, economics, sociology, literature and politics to help meet the need.

To send a packet of Torchbooks [*] overseas, all you need do is send your check for $7 (which includes cost of shipping) to Harper & Row. The U. S. Information Agency will distribute the books to libraries, schools, and other centers all over the world.

I ask every American to support this program, part of a worldwide BOOKS USA campaign.

I ask you to share in the opportunity to help tell others about America.

EDWARD R. MURROW
Director,
U. S. Information Agency

[*retailing at $10.85 to $12.00]